Contemporary Capitalism and Its Crises

This volume analyses contemporary capitalism and its crises based on a theory of capitalist evolution known as social structure of accumulation (SSA) theory. It applies this theory to explain the severe financial and economic crisis that broke out in 2008 and why new institutions are required to resolve it. The editors and contributors make available new work within this school of thought on such issues as the rise and persistence of the "neoliberal," or "free-market," form of capitalism since 1980 and the growing globalization and financialization of the world economy. The collection includes analyses of the U.S. economy as well as that of several parts of the developing world.

Terrence McDonough is Professor of Economics in the School of Business and Economics at the National University of Ireland, Galway. He is the author, coauthor, or coeditor of *Was Ireland a Colony? Economics, Politics, Ideology and Culture in the Irish Nineteenth Century* (2005), *Mind Your Own Business: Economics at Work* (with David Jacobson and Keith Warnock, 2001), *Uninhabited Ireland: Tara, the M3, and Public Spaces in Galway* (with Lionel Pilkington and Aine Ni Leime, 2009), and *Social Structures of Accumulation: The Political Economy of Growth and Crisis* (with Michael Reich and David M. Kotz, Cambridge University Press, 1994). His current research interests include globalization, American and Irish economic history, and political economy.

Michael Reich is Professor of Economics and Director of the Institute for Research on Labor and Employment at the University of California Berkeley. He is the author, coauthor, editor, or coeditor of thirteen titles in labor, industrial relations, and economic studies, including *Racial Inequality: A Political-Economic Analysis* (1981), *Segmented Work, Divided Workers: The Historical Transformation of Labor in the United States* (1982), *The Capitalist System* (1986), the aforementioned *Social Structures of Accumulation* (1994), *Work and Pay in the United States and Japan* (1997), the two-volume *Labor Market Segmentation and Labor Mobility* (2008), and *Labor in the Era of Globalization* (Cambridge University Press, 2009).

David M. Kotz is Professor of Economics at the University of Massachusetts Amherst. His previous books include *Russia's Path from Gorbachev to Putin* (with Fred Weir, 2007), *Revolution from Above: The Demise of the Soviet System* (with Fred Weir, 1997), *Bank Control of Large Corporations in the United States* (1978), and the aforementioned *Social Structures of Accumulation* (1994). His research interests include economic growth and crisis, institutional change in capitalist and the economies of Russia and China.

Contemporary Capitalism and Its Crises

Social Structure of Accumulation Theory for the 21st Century

Edited by

TERRENCE MCDONOUGH
National University of Ireland, Galway

MICHAEL REICH
University of California Berkeley

DAVID M. KOTZ
University of Massachusetts Amherst

CAMBRIDGE
UNIVERSITY PRESS

CAMBRIDGE UNIVERSITY PRESS
Cambridge, New York, Melbourne, Madrid, Cape Town, Singapore
São Paulo, Delhi, Dubai, Tokyo

Cambridge University Press
32 Avenue of the Americas, New York, NY 10013-2473, USA

www.cambridge.org
Information on this title: www.cambridge.org/9780521735803

First published 2010

Printed in the United States of America

A catalog record for this publication is available from the British Library.

Library of Congress Cataloging in Publication data
Contemporary capitalism and its crises: social structure of accumulation theory
for the 21st century / edited by Terrence McDonough,
Michael Reich, David M. Kotz.
p. cm.
Includes bibliographical references and index.
ISBN 978-0-521-51516-0
1. Capitalism. 2. Saving and investment. 3. Global Financial Crisis, 2008–2009.
4. United States – Economic conditions – 2009– I. McDonough, Terrence.
II. Reich, Michael. III. Kotz, David M. (David Michael), 1943– IV. Title.
HB501.C7258 2009
330.12′2–dc22 2009041191

ISBN 978-0-521-51516-0 Hardback
ISBN 978-0-521-73580-3 Paperback

Contents

List of Tables   *page* vii

List of Figures   ix

List of Contributors   xi

Acknowledgments   xiii

Introduction: Social Structure of Accumulation Theory for
the 21st Century   1
Terrence McDonough, Michael Reich, and David M. Kotz

PART I. THE THEORY OF SOCIAL STRUCTURES OF ACCUMULATION

1 The State of the Art of Social Structure of
   Accumulation Theory   23
   Terrence McDonough

2 Social Structure of Accumulation Theory   45
   Victor D. Lippit

3 A Reconceptualization of Social Structure of
   Accumulation Theory   72
   Martin H. Wolfson and David M. Kotz

PART II. GLOBALIZATION AND THE CONTEMPORARY
          SOCIAL STRUCTURE OF ACCUMULATION

4 Global Neoliberalism and the Contemporary Social
   Structure of Accumulation   93
   David M. Kotz and Terrence McDonough

5 Globalization or Spatialization? The Worldwide Spatial
   Restructuring of the Labor Process   121
   Michael Wallace and David Brady

 6 Financialization in the Contemporary Social Structure of
    Accumulation   145
    William K. Tabb

 7 Global Neoliberalism and the Possibility of Transnational
    State Structures   168
    Emlyn Nardone and Terrence McDonough

        PART III. THE CONTEMPORARY SOCIAL STRUCTURE OF
                ACCUMULATION IN THE UNITED STATES

 8 Labor in the Contemporary Social Structure of Accumulation   195
    Samuel Rosenberg

 9 The Rise of CEO Pay and the Contemporary Social
    Structure of Accumulation in the United States   215
    Robert Boyer

10 Social Structures of Accumulation and the Criminal
    Justice System   239
    *Susan M. Carlson, Michael D. Gillespie, and
    Raymond J. Michalowski*

        PART IV. SOCIAL STRUCTURE OF ACCUMULATION THEORY AND
              TRANSFORMATIONS OF THE CAPITALIST PERIPHERY

11 The Social Structure of Accumulation in South Africa   267
    James Heintz

12 Social Structures of Accumulation and the Condition of
    the Working Class in Mexico   286
    Carlos Salas

13 Social Structure of Accumulation Theory for the Arab
    World: The Economies of Egypt, Jordan, and Kuwait in
    the Regional System   309
    Karen Pfeifer

    Index   355

Tables

4.1   Growth Rate of Real Hourly Wages of Manufacturing
Workers for Selected Countries   *page* 105

4.2   Average Unemployment Rate in Five Countries   107

4.3   Growth Rates of Real Gross Domestic Product for
Selected Countries   113

5.1   Historical Overview of Social Structures of Accumulation
and Dominant Control Systems   129

9.1   Two Evaluations of the Impact of Stock-Options on
Corporate Profits in the United States   226

9.2   Contrasting Evolution of Tax Rates for Middle Class and
Rich Families   230

9.3   The Declining Share of the Federal Tax Burden Paid by
Corporations and the Rising Share of Payroll Taxes   231

9.4   The Finance-Led SSA Is Typical of the U.S. Few
Chances of Diffusion to the Rest of the World, with
the Exception of the United Kingdom   235

10.1   Bivariate Correlations between the Logarithmic Rate of
Change in Fixed Capital Stock and the Logarithmic Rate of
Change in Criminal Justice Expenditures   255

12.1   Employment by Industry and Share of Men in Sectoral
Employment, 1895–2000   292

12.2   Average Monthly Income   300

12.3   Gini Coefficient for Monetary Income, 1996–2006   301

Figures

4.1 Rate of profit in the United States and in three European economies *page* 110

4.2 Net dividends as a percentage of after-tax profits for U.S. nonfinancial corporations 111

4.3 Net new stock issued as a percentage of cash flow for U.S. nonfinancial corporations 112

9.1 Disciplining the managers by shareholder value 218

9.2 S&P 100 American corporations: high financial profitability due to the leverage of debt 219

9.3 U.S. CEOs' pay versus the average wage, 1970–1999 220

9.4 The 1990s: the alliance of investors and managers 221

9.5 Why stock options do not sort out the contribution of managers to the performance of the corporation 224

9.6 The systematic overstatements of profits after 1997: a slow process of adjustment in the U.S. 225

9.7 The main episodes and factors in the financialization of executive remuneration 229

9.8 A new finance-led accumulation regime 232

9.9 The main macroeconomic relations of a finance-led accumulation regime 233

10.1 Change in criminal justice expenditures and change in fixed capital stock across post–World War II SSA phases, 1954–2004 254

11.1 Annual rate of net accumulation of fixed capital stock, South Africa, 1951–2006 269

11.2 Estimated profit rate, South Africa, 1960–2006 273

11.3 Total public investment (gross) as a percentage of GDP, South Africa, 1970–2006 280

11.4   Real prime lending rates, South Africa, 1994–2006   282
12.1   GDP rate of growth and trend, Mexico 1921–2007   289
12.2   Per capita GDP rate of growth and trend, Mexico 1921–2007   290
12.3   Profit rate and trend, Mexico 1939–2004   290
13.1   Growth of real GDP per capita: Egypt, Jordan, Kuwait,
        1975–2005   314
13.2   Central government expenditure as a percentage of
        GDP: Egypt, Jordan, Kuwait, 1970–2004   318
13.3   Gross fixed capital formation as a percentage of GDP:
        Egypt, Jordan, Kuwait, 1960–2007   319
13.4   Remittances, Egypt, Jordan, Kuwait, 1985–2005   325
13.5   Human development index, Egypt, Jordan, Kuwait,
        1975–2005   328
13.6   Foreign direct investment, Egypt, Jordan, Kuwait, 2007   343
13.7   Growth projection for real GDP, Egypt, Jordan,
        Kuwait, 2007   348

Contributors

Robert Boyer, CEPREMAP (Centre pour la Recherche Economique et ses Applications), France

David Brady, Department of Sociology, Duke University

Susan M. Carlson, Department of Sociology, Western Michigan University

Michael D. Gillespie, Department of Sociology, Western Michigan University

James Heintz, Political Economy Research Institute, University of Massachusetts Amherst

David M. Kotz, Department of Economics, University of Massachusetts Amherst

Victor D. Lippit, Department of Economics, University of California Riverside

Terrence McDonough, Department of Economics, National University of Ireland, Galway

Raymond J. Michalowski, Department of Criminology and Criminal Justice, Northern Arizona University

Emlyn Nardone, Department of Economics, National University of Ireland, Galway

Karen Pfeifer, Department of Economics, Smith College

struggle, and conflicts over the role of gold and the structure of finance, which led to a profit squeeze. This crisis was resolved through the creation of a new monopoly SSA, characterized by an oligopolistic market structure, weak unions, U.S. expansionism in Latin America and Asia, and the creation of the Federal Reserve System. This SSA then ended in the Great Depression, with the SSA literature citing such causes as inadequate demand due to wages rising more slowly than profits, the collapse of a speculative bubble in the stock market, and the exclusion of the United States from areas of further overseas expansion.

The Great Depression then led to a long period of institutional reform, including new regulations in finance and an expanded role of the state in the economy. The economy did not revive fully until the economic stimulus of war production in the 1940s. The new SSA was consolidated following the end of World War II, with the institution of the Keynesian welfare/warfare state, industrial unions strong enough to impose a limited "capital-labor accord," U.S. international dominance, and a new Cold War ideology. The Great Stagflation of the 1970s marked the beginning of the end of the boom period. The decline and disintegration of the postwar SSA was visible in a squeeze on profits, an end to the capital-labor accord, a price/wage spiral, rising international disorder due to increasing European and Japanese competition, the end of the Bretton Woods system of fixed exchange rates, and two episodes of very rapid increases in oil prices. Beginning in the 1980s a new SSA, which we call the contemporary SSA, was established. We discuss the contemporary SSA in detail below and throughout this volume.

SSA theory bears a strong family resemblance to two other influential attempts to come to terms with the political economy of our time. These are Regulation Theory, which developed in France, and the Varieties of Capitalism School, as systematized by Peter Hall and David Soskice.

Regulation Theory

Although the term regulation had earlier been borrowed from systems theory by French Marxist scholars, regulation theory effectively began with Michel Aglietta's *A Theory of Capitalist Regulation,* published in French in 1976, and was developed subsequently by other French scholars, including Robert Boyer. Aglietta defines part of his project as seeking to show "that the institutionalization of social relations under the effect of class struggles is the central process of their reproduction (Aglietta

1979: 29)." He applies this understanding to capitalist regulation and crises (Aglietta 1979: 19):

This theoretical position will enable us to conceive crises as ruptures in the continuous reproduction of social relations, to see why periods of crisis are periods of intense social creation, and to understand why the resolution of a crisis always involves an irreversible transformation of the mode of production.

Subsequently, Robert Boyer emerged as a leading figure of what was referred to as the Parisian school of regulation theory. In a concise introduction to this work, Boyer (1990) carefully defines a number of intermediate concepts. The first concept, the regime of accumulation, includes the organization of production, the distribution of the value produced, and a related composition of social demand that is consistent with production possibilities. The regime of accumulation is conditioned and reproduced by further intermediate institutional forms, collected under five headings: forms of monetary constraint, configurations of the wage relation, forms of competition, position within the international regime, and forms of the state. These institutional forms together constitute the mode of regulation. The combination of the regime of accumulation and the mode of regulation is the mode of development. The objective of the regulation school is "to explain the rise and subsequent crises of modes of development" (Boyer 1990: 48).

The commonalities between regulation theory and SSA theory, which were discussed by Gordon and by Reich in presentations to Boyer's Paris seminars in the 1980s, led to joint work by Samuel Bowles and Robert Boyer (1988, 1990a, 1990b). Kotz (1994) identifies the similarities between the two approaches. He argues that both theories set out to explain long-run patterns of capital accumulation by analyzing the relationship between that process and the sets of social institutions that condition or regulate it. The SSA is roughly analogous to some combination of the regulation theory terms "regime of accumulation" and "mode of regulation." Both schools view capitalism "as moving through a series of stages, each characterized by a specific form of the accumulation process embedded in a particular set of institutions" (p. 86). Stages end in a long-term structural crisis that involves a significant reduction in the rate of accumulation over a prolonged period of time. These structural crises result from a failure of the institutions to continue to successfully secure the conditions of accumulation. The crisis ends when a new, more successful set of institutions is put in place.

Kotz observed that regulation theory maintained a closer fidelity to the Marxian perspective through its emphasis on production relations and the class distribution of income rather than a more Keynesian concern with the determinants of the capitalist investment decision. Regulation theory located the origin of long-term crises within the regime of accumulation whereas SSA theory located the origin of the crisis in the breakdown of the institutions of the SSA (closer to the mode of regulation in regulation theory).

Regulation Theory: The State of the Art, edited by Boyer and Saillard (2002 [1995]), demonstrates the emergence of two distinct theoretical strands within the regulation school. Olivier Favereau (2002: 315) distinguishes between regulation theory 1, as "similar to the Marxist analysis of the capitalist mode of production," and regulation theory 2, as "separate from this analysis and based on dynamic aspects of institutional forms."

More recently, regulation theory has placed a greater emphasis on the role of institutions (found predominantly within the mode of regulation) both in constituting the period of successful regulation and in the emergence of crisis. Aglietta (1998: 56) summarizes these developments:

... the various mediation mechanisms are dovetailed to form the framework of a mode of regulation. This dovetailing does not happen automatically, because each of these organizations has its own rationale, the integrity of its own structures that makes it persevere in its perceived social role. That is why the coherence of a mode of regulation does not conform to any pre-established general law. It is a historically unique entity that may be called a growth regime. By contrast, the symptoms of exhaustion of a growth regime, heralding a period of uncertainty, crisis and change, must be sought in malfunctions of the interaction between mediation mechanisms.

This formulation shifts the dynamics of the formation of the "growth regime" into the realm of the dynamic interaction of the institutions. The "general laws" of accumulation no longer dominate, and each growth regime is historically unique, constituted by the coherence of the institutions that make it up. Similarly, the malfunctioning interaction of the institutions – or "mediation mechanisms" – inaugurates the crisis of the growth regime. The description of the constitution and decay of capitalist social structures and the resulting alternating periods of expansion and crisis thus converges with the contingent description developed within the SSA approach.

The Varieties of Capitalism School

The Varieties of Capitalism (VoC) school, which was formulated by Peter Hall and David Soskice in 2001, draws upon a longer tradition of comparative analyses of European, U.S., and Japanese capitalisms (see Crouch and Streeck 1997; Hollingsworth and Boyer 1997). One such approach contrasts bank-centered and patient capitalism in Germany and Japan, with relatively strong states to shareholder-centered and impatient capitalism in the Anglo-American world, with relatively weak states. Another approach contrasts countries with relatively centralized employer and union structures, in which strong corporatist labor-management agreements could be negotiated, and those with more decentralized structures that would not be characterized as corporatist. The similarity of the VoC approach to both regulation theory and social structure of accumulation theory is evident in the following (Hall and Soskice 2001: 3):

During the 1980s and 1990s, a new approach to comparative capitalism that we will term a social systems of production approach gained currency. Under this rubric, we group analyses of sectoral governance, national innovation systems, and flexible production regimes ... Influenced by the French regulation school, they emphasize the movement of firms away from mass production toward new production regimes that depend on collective institutions at the regional, sectoral, or national level.

In addition to the social system of production, Hall and Soskice also emphasize the character of the financial system and the role of the state in their analysis. As synthesized in their 2001 book (Hall and Soskice 2001), they identify two main extant variants of capitalism in the industrialized countries. The first, typified by the United States and the United Kingdom, and also including Australia, Canada, Ireland, and New Zealand, consists of a set of liberal market economies (LMEs). The second, typified by Germany, and also including Japan, Switzerland, Belgium, the Netherlands, Austria, and the Scandinavian countries, consists of a set of coordinated market economies (CMEs). Hall and Soskice (2001: 16) contend that "differences in the institutional framework of the political economy generate systematic differences in corporate strategies across LMEs and CMEs" and (p. 17) that the "presence of institutional complementarities reinforces the differences between liberal and coordinated market economies." Precisely, because of these complementarities, the VoC school contends that capitalist countries have not converged to a single Anglo-American model. Although a small amount of convergence toward the Anglo-American model occurred during the boom years that ended with the onset of the financial and economic crisis in 2007, the crisis has undermined the Anglo-American model itself. One type of capitalism has not yet proven to perform better or to dominate the other.

By including in its purview relationships within and between firms, the character of the state, and the nature of the financial system, the VoC approach appears similar to the institutional focus of the SSA approach. Both approaches also emphasize that complementarities among institutions must be present for a system to be successful. The VoC approach has stimulated considerable research on the institutional frameworks of different national capitalisms (see, for example, Streeck and Thelen 2005). However, it has not addressed adequately the links among them – especially important in an era of globalized finance – and it has only recently begun to discuss how institutions have evolved over time, which is central to the SSA theory (Hancke et al. 2007, Hall and Thelen 2008). Nonetheless, it provides important analyses of the institutional variations that remain important in understanding specific countries and their policies.[2] For this reason, it contributes to our understanding of models that the United States or the United Kingdom might seek to emulate in a period of economic crisis.

Recent Historical Developments

Since the publication of our 1994 volume on the SSA theory, five important historical developments have affected both SSA theory and our understanding of contemporary capitalism. First, a shift in institutions, policies, and ideas that began around 1980, often referred to as "neoliberalism," has proven to be a long-lasting albeit much-debated phenomenon.[3] Second, the balance of power between workers and employers has shifted decisively in favor of employers. Third, the debate over whether capitalism had become significantly more globally integrated than in the past has been resolved in favor of the globalization position. Fourth, capitalism became much more financialized, in the sense that not only has the financial sector come to represent a greater share of economic output, finance has also inserted itself in and transformed much of the

[2] For a related approach that extends the comparative analysis to Japan, see Brown et al. (1997). Jacoby (2009) provides a detailed discussion of how finance and labor fit together in different institutional contexts.

[3] The term "neoliberalism" requires some explanation for American readers. In U.S. political discourse, liberalism refers to a position that favors active government intervention in the economy to benefit ordinary people and restrain the power of business. In Europe, Latin America, and most of the rest of the world, liberalism means the opposite, referring to a policy of limited (although not a total absence of) state intervention in the economy and support for "free markets." The term neoliberalism draws on the latter meaning of liberalism.

real economy. Fifth, the severe financial and economic crisis that erupted in 2007–8 appears, at the time of this writing (June 2009), to signal the beginning of the crisis phase of the contemporary SSA.

Neoliberalism is characterized by the deregulation of business, the privatization of state enterprises and responsibilities, the dismantling of social programs, the expansion of market forces into new corners of society, a much-weakened trade union movement, the return of unrestrained competition, and the rebirth of previously rejected free-market economic theories. The SSA school has grappled with how central all the institutions associated with neoliberalism are for the contemporary SSA. For some, many of the features of neoliberalism have operated only on the margins of many countries' institutions. For example, Glyn (2001) and Jacoby (2009) argue that the scope of neoliberal reforms was quite limited in much of Western Europe and Japan. Bowles, Edwards, and Roosevelt (2005, ch. 7) argue that the role of the state has not decreased in the United States; tax revenues have risen rather than declined since 1980 as a percentage of GDP and many of the regulatory activities of the state have not diminished. In their view, and those of others such as James Galbraith (2008), although political conservatives long clamored for a smaller state (and still do in theory), once they were in power and had more influence over the nature of state spending, they found it advantageous to redirect it rather than to rein it in. Chapters 2 (Lippitt), 3 (Wolfson and Kotz), and 4 (Kotz and McDonough) in this volume argue against this view, making the case that neoliberalism has been central to a new SSA.

A consensus has emerged that a rapid decline of worker power began in the 1980s in the United States and the United Kingdom and spread to Continental Europe and Japan in the 1990s. This shift occurred partly because of employer offensives against unions and partly because of the increased threat and reality of relocating jobs offshore. As a result, labor's share of income declined in all these countries and inequality among workers increased too (Reich 2008a, b; Brown et al. 2009). In the United States, owners of capital and top executives were able to claim most of the growth in income that was generated by increased productivity. Consumption for broad sectors of the working population did increase, but only by taking on increased debt. Income growth for the very rich was not matched by a comparable growth in real investment and instead led to a series of financial bubbles.

In the 1980s and 1990s, many analysts argued that capitalism had entered a new stage of globalization. Those who initially doubted this claim cited

The extensive transnationalization of production, trade, and especially finance, complicates the prospect of nationally centered strategies of regeneration. Although Keynesian prescriptions assume relatively autonomous national economies, the last few decades of globalization have substantially reduced national autonomies. For example, with the import and export sectors forming a crucial part of even the largest economies, stimulus packages have to be coordinated internationally, but existing transnational governance structures are primarily designed to facilitate the deregulation of trade rather than the coordination of fiscal policy.

It has also become clear that efforts to reregulate finance must have an international dimension and. that participation will have to include newly more influential economies, such as China, India, and Brazil. However, as the number of players increases, it will take an extraordinarily concerted effort to put the genie of transnational finance back into the regulatory bottle.

The rise of China as a major player in the global economy may have significant implications for future restructuring. This development has injected several hundred million additional low-wage workers into the labor force of global capitalism. The axis of the United States as global consumer and China as global workshop may not be sustainable. Accommodating China's large and rapidly growing economy may be a major complication in the developing efforts to restructure global capitalism. The SSA school needs more analysis on this point.

Another recent development that needs analysis in relation to the SSA theory is the rise of various forms of religious fundamentalism, not just in the Islamic world but also in India and the Bush-era United States. Can this development be understood as a response to the marginalization of certain groups by the contemporary SSA? How will this play out in the coming period of restructuring?

One more recent development whose relation to the SSA theory is not well established concerns the increasing readiness of the U.S. government to intervene militarily far from U.S. shores. In the 1980s, following the U.S. defeat in Vietnam, U.S. military interventions were restricted to its traditional sphere in Latin America. In the 1990s a series of U.S.-led military interventions in the Middle East and Europe occurred in the elder Bush's Administration and then in the Clinton Administration. Military interventionism increased by a quantum leap with the unilateralism of the second Bush Administration after 2001.

The global dimension of an SSA appears to require a hegemonic power to back up global-level institutions. Has this interventionist trend represented an attempt to establish a clear hegemon to stabilize the global system? Or was the extreme case of U.S. unilateralism a destabilizing aberration that will be corrected under the Obama Administration? Will the Obama Administration be able to rebuild a coalition of the major world powers that can effectively restructure global capitalism? These questions call for future work within the SSA approach.

The recent leftwing upsurge in Latin America via electoral politics poses one more challenge of interpretation for the SSA theory. The politics of these changes has been wide-ranging, from social democratic regimes in Argentina, Brazil, and Chile to more radical governments in Venezuela, Bolivia, and perhaps Nicaragua. They all appear to all spring from a reaction to the negative effects of the contemporary SSA on the population of Latin America. The longevity of these movements is of course uncertain. But if they survive or increase their influence, how will these economies relate to a transnational capitalist restructuring? Were they early indications of the coming crisis of the contemporary SSA? Will they in the end become part of a new capitalist restructuring?

The international factors discussed earlier present problems for any restructuring and they are likely to prolong conflict over institutional innovation and consequently the period of crisis. Another major problem will be responding to the high levels of inequality that have developed under the current SSA. This is more than a moral or ethical question. Stagnating incomes of those at the bottom and the middle have led to a situation in which demand was sustained only through rising debt predicated on a series of asset bubbles. Financial bailouts cannot address the problem of sustained restrictions in consumer demand and pessimistic investment outlooks. Short-run fiscal stimulus programs are also not sufficient, especially if they are not explicitly directed to increase living standards and change the pattern of inequality. A permanent and substantial transfer of present and future income from the top to the middle and bottom of the income distribution can solve this problem. But such a change is highly unlikely to take place solely as a response to economic considerations. This change may only come as a response to an effective popular movement that demands it. Building such a movement out of the legacy of the long period of retrenchment and labor weakness will most likely be a lengthy task.

If we are right that the current SSA is entering a lengthy crisis period, that crisis will constitute the environment in which popular struggles for greater equity and justice will succeed or fail, which makes an understanding of this environment essential. While inevitably creating great hardship and pain for many, the crisis that is already upon us may be a time of greater opportunity for social progress. A better understanding of the character of this moment in the context of the long movements of capitalist history can contribute to better appreciating the magnitude and scope of this opportunity. Our book attempts to provide such an understanding while also pointing to controversies in the understanding of SSAs that require further inquiry.

Overview of the Book

The book is divided into four parts. Part I takes up the theory of social structures of accumulation. In Chapter 1, Terrence McDonough undertakes a comprehensive review of SSA literature published since 1994. It reviews the later work of David Gordon and his colleagues, who use the SSA approach for macroeconomic modeling. It considers the "spatialization school," which argues that current labor control strategies center around the threat of relocation or actual relocation. Since the threat of relocation can gain traction only if regions differ significantly, the spatialization school analyzes states in the United States as sub-regions of the overall SSA, each with its own particular characteristics and dynamics. A third area concerns the applications of the SSA framework to the history of the criminal justice system. This chapter also introduces a number of other theoretical and historical issues from the recent SSA literature and refers to the discussion of the economic and financial crisis in subsequent chapters of the book.

In Chapter 2, Victor Lippit develops a more rigorous definition of the concept of institution in the SSA approach and undertakes a theoretical discussion of several questions: What gives an SSA its structural integrity? Why do SSAs collapse? Why do SSAs take a long time to establish, and why do they tend to endure for extended periods? What is the relation of SSA theory to concepts of overdetermination and historical contingency? Lippit also discusses the role of class struggle in creating dynamic elements in SSAs. In an addendum, Lippit examines whether the financial and economic crisis that broke out in late 2007 represents a terminal crisis for the contemporary SSA. He suggests that a neoliberal SSA is likely to have a shorter length because the severity of its contradictions leads to an early demise.

In Chapter 3, Martin Wolfson and David Kotz propose a revised definition of an SSA, as an institutional structure that promotes profit-making and serves as a framework for capital accumulation but does not necessarily promote accumulation that is *rapid*. This reconceptualization is offered as a response to the challenge presented to SSA theory by the long persistence of neoliberalism, which seems to be part of a new SSA that has not brought rapid accumulation. They argue that liberal SSAs, which embody a high degree of capitalist domination of labor, also exhibit a slower rate of accumulation, whereas regulated SSAs, which are based on a capital-labor compromise, typically experience more rapid accumulation. Unlike Lippit, Kotz and Wolfson are agnostic on whether the two types of SSAs would experience different life spans.

Part II examines the relationship between globalization and the contemporary SSA. In Chapter 4, David Kotz and Terrence McDonough argue that a new SSA was consolidated in the early 1980s and that this SSA is best characterized as global neoliberalism. The dominant institutions in this SSA include neoliberalism, conceived of as an ideology, a set of policies, and a number of institutions, including the freer movement of capital, goods, and money over international borders, and the fragmentation of production across borders, and its reintegration through trade and the supply chain management of transnational corporations. Other elements of this SSA include a weakening of the power of labor, spatialization as a labor control strategy, financialization, the hollowing out of the domestic state, and flexible specialization and lean production on the shop floor. Kotz and McDonough argue that these institutions constitute a coherent structure that promotes profit-making and provides a framework for accumulation. This SSA also contains contradictions that have led to the economic crisis.

In Chapter 5, Michael Wallace and David Brady directly link globalization to control of the labor process. Drawing on innovations in communication and transportation, corporations have become better able to choose among multiple locations for their economic activities. This increased spatial flexibility provides corporations with a way to weaken and control labor through relocation or the threat of relocation.

As already mentioned, the financial sector has grown in size, financial profits have increased as a percentage of capital income, and financial priorities have increasingly dominated decision-making. In Chapter 6, William Tabb addresses financialization in the context of the contemporary SSA. Neoliberalism has led to a swelling of finance and to large and unsustainable increases in risk, with severe consequences that became visible in the financial and economic crisis that began in 2007. Tabb argues that this crisis spells the decline of the current SSA. In a concluding section, Tabb distinguishes his view of class-state relations in SSAs and of transnationalization in the contemporary SSA from the analyses in previous chapters.

The globalization of capitalist production relations and the emerging global character of class relations raise the question of global governance relations. In Chapter 7, Emlyn Nardone and Terrence McDonough argue that transnational state-like institutions have begun to emerge. Nation-states have not declined in importance, but their activities are now embedded in a more extensive network of international governance structures. The authors consider whether the global financial and economic crisis will lead to new global governance structures or whether some aspects of globalization will decline instead.

While some SSA theorists have discussed the contemporary SSA in global terms, others have continued the Gordon et al. tradition of analyzing SSAs in national contexts. Part III takes a close look at the contemporary SSA in the United States. In Chapter 8, Samuel Rosenberg undertakes a detailed description of the place of labor in the contemporary SSA. He first establishes the background by looking at labor-management relations and the nature of labor market segmentation in the post World War II SSA. Rosenberg then discusses the political-economic environment of the 1980s, when the contemporary SSA was created. He analyzes the "employer offensive" and the deunionization of the 1980s in detail, examines the legacy of the emergent neoliberal framework for labor and addresses the prospects for the survival of the neoliberal-era system of labor relations in light of the economic crisis.

In Chapter 9, Robert Boyer examines the explosion of CEO compensation in the last decades. He contends that this explosion is the evidence of the emergence of a finance-led SSA, or accumulation regime, to use the terms of regulation theory. The diffusion of stock options and financial market-related incentives entitled managers to convert their intrinsic power into greater compensation and wealth. Boyer argues this outcome results from a de facto alliance of executives with financiers exploiting the erosion of workers' bargaining power. He contends that this institutional compromise structured a new accumulation regime that is specific to the United States, which explains why the subprime mortgage crisis was especially severe in the United States.

In Chapter 10, Susan Carlson and her coauthors take up the role of the criminal justice system, which has not previously been given sustained attention within the SSA framework. They argue that the criminal justice system is important both directly as a market for goods and source of labor and indirectly for its role in the legitimation of the social order. Moreover, the character of the fulfillment of these roles varies from one SSA to the next. Thus, as with market organization, state policy, and other institutions discussed in the SSA literature, the character of the criminal justice system follows the rhythms of SSA construction and decay, varying not only across SSAs but also across phases of a specific SSA.

Part IV applies SSA analyses to transformations in the capitalist periphery. One criticism of SSA theory suggests that it has drawn its source material too narrowly from the U.S. experience. Nevertheless, the area of its application has steadily expanded, to Jamaica, South Korea, South Africa, Greece, India, and the Central American countries. The chapters in Part IV update previous work on South Africa and extend the analysis to Mexico and the Middle East. In Chapter 11, James Heintz contends, contrary to critics of the SSA approach as it has been applied to South Africa, that substantial empirical evidence supports the existence of an apartheid-era SSA. Moreover, the SSA framework provides an explanation of the economic crisis that contributed to the end of apartheid. After a detailed discussion of the post-apartheid era, Heintz concludes that it is too early to tell whether a new SSA has been successfully constructed in South Africa.

In Chapter 12, a contrasting analysis by Carlos Salas concludes that a new SSA was put in place in Mexico following the financial crisis of the 1980s. In contrast to the first Mexican SSA that persisted from 1930 to 1980, the current SSA is not oriented to domestic demand and looks outward to U.S. investment and the U.S. market. Consequently, the Mexican economy has become highly polarized. One sector is organized around international investment, demand, and finance and provides a relatively small number of well-paying jobs. In the absence of state policies of redistribution, a second sector, a more or less permanent informal sector of self-employment and microenterprises in urban areas, reproduces the working population.

In Chapter 13, Karen Pfeifer applies SSA theory to the Arab World, specifically to the post-World War II economies of Egypt, Jordan, and Kuwait in their regional system. Pfeifer suggests that SSA analysis makes two main contributions for understanding this region. First, the post-World War II SSA led by the United States constituted the international context within which the countries in this region undertook to develop their economies. Second, Pfeifer develops the concept of a regional SSA, with variations among the specific features in the three countries.

References

Aglietta, Michel 1979. *A Theory of Capitalist Regulation.* London: NLB.
  1998. "Capitalism at the Turn of the Century: Regulation Theory and the Challenge of Social Change," *New Left Review* 232: 41–90.

Bowles, Samuel and Robert Boyer 1988. "Labor Discipline and Aggregate Demand: A Macroeconomic Model," *American Economic Review* 78, 2: 395–400.
  1990a. "A Wage-led Employment Regime: Income Distribution, Labor Discipline, and Aggregate Demand." Pp.187–217 in Stephen A. Marglin and Juliet B. Schor eds. *The Golden Age of Capitalism.* Oxford: Clarendon Press.
  1990b. "Labor Market Flexibility and Decentralization as Barriers to High Employment? Notes on Employer Collusion, Centralized Wage Bargaining and Aggregate Employment." Pp.325–352 in Renato Brunetta and Carlo Dell' Aringa eds. *Labour Relations and Economic Performance.* London: Macmillan.

Bowles, Samuel, Richard Edwards and Frank Roosevelt 2005. *Understanding Capitalism: Competition, Command and Change.* New York: Oxford University Press.

Bowles, Samuel, David M. Gordon and Thomas E. Weisskopf 1990. *After the Waste Land: A Democratic Economics for the Year 2000.* Armonk, NY: M.E. Sharpe.

Boyer, Robert 1990. *The Regulation School: A Critical Introduction.* New York: Columbia University Press.

Boyer, Robert and Yves Saillard 2002. *Regulation Theory: The State of the Art.* Routledge, London.

Brown, Clair, Barry Eichengreen and Michael Reich eds. 2009. *The Great Unraveling: New Labor Market Institutions and the Public Policy Response.* New York: Cambridge University Press.

Brown, Clair, Yoshifumi Nakata, Michael Reich and Lloyd Ulman 1997. *Work and Employment in the U.S. and Japan.* New York: Oxford University Press.

Crouch, Colin and Wolfgang Streeck eds. 1997. *Political Economy of Modern Capitalism: Mapping Convergence and Diversity.* New York: Sage Publications.

Favereau, Olivier 2002. "Conventions and regulation." Pp.312–319 in Boyer, Robert and Yves Saillard eds (1995) *Regulation Theory: the State of the Art.* London: Routledge.

Galbraith, James 2008. *The Predatory State: How Conservatives Abandoned the Free Market and Why Liberals Should Too.* New York: Free Press.

Glyn, Andrew ed. 2001. *Social Democracy in Neoliberal Times: The Left and Economic Policy since 1980.* New York: Oxford University Press.

Gordon, David M., Richard C. Edwards and Michael Reich. 1982. *Segmented Work, Divided Workers: the Historical Transformations of Labor in the United States.* New York: Cambridge University Press.

Hancke, Bob, Martin Rhodes and Mark Thatcher eds. 2007. *Beyond Varieties of Capitalism: Conflict, Contradictions and Complementarities in the European Economy*. New York: Oxford University Press.

Hall, Peter A. and David Soskice eds. 2001. *Varieties of Capitalism: The Institutional Foundations of Comparative Advantage*. New York: Oxford University Press.

Hall, Peter A. and Kathleen Thelen 2008. "Institutional Change in Varieties of Capitalism." *Socio-Economic Review* 7, 1: 7–34.

Hollingsworth, J. Rogers and Robert Boyer 1997. *Contemporary Capitalism: the Embededness of Institutions*. New York: Cambridge University Press.

Jacoby, Sanford 2009. "Finance and Labor: Perspectives on Risk, Inequality and Democracy." Pp. 94–150 in Clair Brown, Barry Eichengreen and Michael Reich eds. *The Great Unraveling*. New York: Cambridge University Press.

Kotz, David M. 1994. "The Regulation Theory and the Social Structure of Accumulation Approach." Pp. 85–97 in David M. Kotz, Terrence McDonough, and Michael Reich, Eds. *Social Structures of Accumulation: The Political Economy of Growth and Crisis*. New York: Cambridge University Press.

Kotz, David M., Terrence McDonough, and Michael Reich eds. 1994. *Social Structures of Accumulation: The Political Economy of Growth and Crisis*. New York: Cambridge University Press.

Reich, Michael 1997. "Social Structure of Accumulation Theory: Retrospect and Prospect." *Review of Radical Political Economics* 29, 3: 1–10.

Reich, Michael ed. 2008a. *Segmented Labor Markets and Labor Mobility. Vol. I Labor Market Segmentation 1970 to 2000*. Edward Elgar.

  2008b. *Segmented Labor Markets and Labor Mobility. Vol II Flexibility, Monopsony and the New Labor Market Segmentation*. Edward Elgar.

Streeck, Wolfgang and Kathleen Thelen eds. 2005. *Beyond Continuity: Institutional Change in Advanced Political Economies*. New York: Oxford University Press.

of capital ... A great range of mechanisms relate accumulation to its institutional matrix ... No general hypothesis is advanced about the relative importance of the different elements of the structural matrix, there is no privileged list of 'crucial' institutions or forces.

This flexibility allows for the application of specific arguments to specific locational or historical circumstances without the elaboration of new and universal concepts. This is often criticized as a theoretical weakness but it is also a potential strength. The framework has proven flexible enough to provide a guide to the analysis of a wide range of situations and institutions.

Nevertheless, Victor Lippit (2005) does undertake a discussion of the basics of the SSA framework in his *Capitalism*. Invoking the concept of overdetermination, Lippit contends that the structural integrity of an SSA is created and sustained by the interrelationships among its component parts. Taking issue with this author, Lippit argues that both the length of the period of expansion conditioned by an SSA and the length of the subsequent crisis period are not contingent but rather will definitely tend to be long. This is because the sustaining interrelationships within an SSA, supported as they are by institutional inertia, will tend to change only slowly. Successful expansion creates beneficiaries who actively seek the continued stability of the SSA. Similarly the complex interrelationships that will characterize a succeeding SSA can only be assembled over an extended period of time prolonging the crisis period.

Lippit (2004: 27–8) is also more concerned than previous authors with explicitly defining what he means by the concept of institutions:

We can think of an institution in two principal ways. The first is essentially as an organization, like the World Bank or a university. The broader sense of an institution refers to the habits, customs and expectations that prevail in a particular society. While both senses of the term are used in SSA analysis, it is this second usage that is emphasized. The second usage, moreover, can be employed narrowly or broadly, and it is the broader form that is usually more helpful. A union for example, is an institution in the first sense. Collective bargaining would be an example of an institution in the second sense, employed narrowly. A national system of labor relations would also be an example of an institution in the second sense, but one employed broadly.

This definition serves to make the concept of institution clearer and to emphasize the contribution of the tradition of American institutionalist economics to the SSA framework.

Further innovations involve the application of the concept at various geographical and temporal scales. The framework has been applied over several intervals of time shorter than the "long swing." In addition, it has been applied to spaces at the subnational and the global levels.

Hamilton (1994) finds the approach still useful in analyzing a 15-year period of Jamaican economic history. Much of the work within the spatialization school is done over a similar time frame. Harriss-White (2003) uses the framework synchronically taking a kind of cross section of Indian society at a point in time, or as she puts it herself "statically, as a way of imposing an analytically useful order on the immense complexity of the Indian economy, rather than with a view to developing a thesis about its historical evolution through eras or stages" (p. 239).[7]

Michalowski and Carlson (2000) place great emphasis on distinguishing between phases *within* social structures of accumulation. Following terminology used by Gordon, Edwards, and Reich, they carefully periodize much of the U.S. twentieth century in the following (pp. 276–7):

(a) Exploration 1 from 1933 to 1947, (b) Consolidation 1 from 1948 to 1966, (c) Decay from 1967 to 1979, (d) Exploration 2 from 1980 to 1992, and (e) Consolidation 2 from 1993 to the present.

They argue that "each of these SSA phases consists of a distinct set of qualitative social relations between labor and the state that impact the strength and direction of relationships between measures of economic marginalization and patterns of crime and punishment" (p. 277). Consequently these types of factors "cannot be analyzed linearly across SSA phases because the sociological meaning of these variables may differ according to the qualitative character of each SSA phase" (p. 277).

Michelle Naples (1996) undertakes a detailed analysis of labor relations in the coal industry in the postwar period. One of her concerns in this context is to trace the impact of the construction and decay of the SSA on these labor relations at specific points in time. She draws several predictive generalizations from the SSA framework and investigates their possible expression in the postwar history of the coal industry. Among the hypotheses for which she finds evidence are the following phase-linked generalizations (Naples 1996: 112–13):

G1 Institutional innovation, change, and challenges to the meta-rules will be most widespread during the late expansion and into the long-wave crisis.

G3 Difference and challenges to the worldview are not tolerated under the newly hegemonic SSA in the early expansion.

---

[7] These shorter period analyses assume a specified SSA is in place.

G7 Labor relations in one sector are not static. The logic of the new rules is applied on an extended scale so that the full system of national union/rank-and-file/management relations only becomes fleshed out over time.

As well as being applied to differing timescales, the SSA framework has been applied at differing spatial scales as well. The spatialization school has placed special emphasis on the manner in which the impact of the existence and construction of an SSA produces differential results at local levels in explainable ways. Much of their work takes state-level government within the U.S. federal system as the spatial unit across which institutions vary in a spatialization American SSA. Perrucci (1994) undertakes a related analysis of the "Midwest Corridor," six contiguous U.S. states that have been the locations for Japanese inward investment in the auto industry. Perrucci identifies the emergence of an SSA here based on "embedded corporatism."[8]

Lobao et al. (1999) examine the effects of elements of the national SSA at the even lower level of counties within states. Specifically, they look at the effect of core manufacturing employment and state support of citizen income on levels of income inequality within localities. They find that national level arrangements are reflected in local level relationships in 1970 but that national changes are less strongly evidenced in localities in 1990 due both to inertia and the complex way in which local institutions may adjust to changes in the larger institutional context. Arena (2003) uses the SSA framework as the backdrop to a discussion of the dynamics of class conflict within the Black Urban Regime in the single city of New Orleans, Louisiana.[9]

While it has been most commonly applied at the national level, the SSA framework has been unclear whether or not it can be applied to larger, more global scales. The founders of the framework have frequently claimed no applicability beyond the United States for their particular institutional analyses. Kotz et al. (1994b: 4) argue that the SSAs in other countries in the postwar period are distinct. Nevertheless, the SSA school has often been lumped with long-wave and regulationist theories which do make international claims. Gordon (1988) does apply

---

[8] Perrucci departs from the spatialization theorists in identifying his subnational area as having an SSA rather than comprising an institutional arrangement within an overall SSA. Whether SSAs can be "shrunk" to fit a smaller than national territory must be controversial. Indeed, the spatialization school argues that under mobile capital the existence of local variation is an essential feature of the *national* SSA.

[9] See the argument in footnote 8 about whether an SSA can occupy a subnational space, in this case, a city.

the framework to "the global economy." The analyses of other countries discussed above confirm the warning of Kotz et al. The SSAs identified for Caribbean-type economies, South Korea, South Africa, Greece, and the India of the 88 percent are all quite distinct from that described for the United States in the postwar period. The question of whether these strictures will have to be maintained in analyzing the period running up to the current crisis constitutes part of the debate about the possible construction of an SSA in these years.

Was a New SSA Consolidated after the 1970s?
There is an emerging consensus within the current SSA literature that the period before the current economic crisis witnessed the consolidation of an SSA, although this position has not gone without a vigorous challenge (as is noted below). Several authors beginning with Houston (1992) have argued that the contours of a new SSA had become starkly visible (the spatialization authors; Lippit 1997; Reich 1997; Michalowski and Carlson 2000; Went 2002; McDonough 2003; Bowles et al. 2005). This new SSA was characterized by multiple institutional transformations over the period from 1973 to the present day. Each author puts forward a somewhat different list with different emphases, but the overall pattern is quite similar in each case.

It is argued that there has been a qualitative change in the globalization of economic activity. This globalization is not only one of trade but also significantly a globalization of production and investment. The global intensification of financial transfers has combined with the expansion of transnational investment and improved communication structures to give birth for the first time to a transnational, global capitalist class. The working class, too, is increasingly transnational because of the dispersal of the production process across the face of the globe, because they face a global capitalist class, and because they can be drawn into competition with one another through the hypermobility of capital.[10]

This process of globalization has perhaps its most important impact in strengthening capital in relation to labor. Corporations have restructured, downsized, and reengineered. Systems of lean production modeled on Japanese manufacturing techniques have been introduced. There

---

[10] This transnationalization of class relations is the essence of globalization from a distinctly Marxian perspective. Theorizing the rise of a transnational capitalist class in a social structure of accumulation context has been central to the work of William Robinson (2004).

has been a turn to restricted government consistent with the neoliberal vision of the desirability of unfettered markets. Supranational state organizations such as the EU, the WTO, and NATO have assumed increasing importance. The IMF and the World Bank have imposed the neoliberal agenda on borrowing countries predominantly in the Third World. Finally, the sudden restoration of capitalism in the former Soviet Union and its former Eastern European allies, followed by a more gradual capitalist restoration in China, have extended capitalist economic organization to virtually the entire world for the first time.

There is a considerable diversity of labels proposed for this SSA. A spatialization SSA is advocated by the spatialization school in that it emphasizes innovations in the method and scope of labor control. Michalowski and Carlson (2000) refer to the cybertech SSA focussing on the consequences of technological innovation. Went (2002) simply sees globalization as the new stage of capitalism. McDonough (2003) prefers global neoliberalism. Bowles et al. (2005) identify a transnational SSA.

This distinction in terminology is not entirely without significance. The spatialization school, Lippit, and Michalowski and Carlson confine the scope of the SSA discussed to the United States. This is also true of Bowles et al., although they argue that the integration of the U.S. economy into transnational economic relations is what primarily distinguishes the new SSA. Went and McDonough speak of the SSA in much broader terms but are not explicit about what geographical limits if any it might have. Robinson specifically argues in favor of the global character of the new SSA.

Is it possible to reconcile the latter view with the general consensus that SSAs are primarily national in character as confirmed by much of the work done within the tradition? Such reconciliation is possible if it is observed that this kind of transcendence of national boundaries is precisely one of the defining characteristics of the emergence of this SSA. Consequently to speak of an SSA that is larger than one national territory or region of the world is not to engage in theoretical innovation. It is rather an argument that the nature of the SSA has produced a transnational extension of the boundaries of the new social structure.

This does not require any revision of the national analyses set in the postwar period. In this (and earlier) periods, the social structures, which conditioned accumulation, took a predominantly national form. This conclusion stems directly from the insight that the economy was embedded in political, ideological, and cultural institutions that differed sometimes substantially from country to country. Went and McDonough argue implicitly and Robinson explicitly that this condition has changed with the emergence of globalization. Robinson (2004: 74–5) character- izes the changed relationships in the following way:

As capital became liberated from the nation-state and assumed tremendous new power relative to labor with the onset of globalization, nation states shifted from reproducing Keynesian social structures of accumulation to servicing the general needs of the new patterns of global accumulation and the transnational capitalist class, involving a rollback of redistributive projects. ... As the social structure becomes transformed and transnationalized in each region of the world, a new global social structure of accumulation becomes superimposed on and transforms existing national social structures.

Robinson perhaps does not emphasize enough that this hypothesized transformation of national social structures does not necessarily result in uniformity. In fact it is provocative to extend the spatialization school's argument about the role of state-level differences within United States to the global level. It is precisely the differences between nation states that are reproductive of capital accumulation when they are nested within a larger global structure.

The proposition that a new SSA was consolidated did not go without challenge. Phil O'Hara (2000, 2006) has argued vigorously that recent institutional changes do not add up to an SSA.[11] On the contrary (O'Hara 2000: 285), "they tend to deepen the extent of structural long-wave insta- bility and crisis tendencies." O'Hara pursues this argument on several fronts. He claims that some of the institutions, such as the movement toward deregulation of business and flexible production, have not been sufficiently consolidated or extensively implemented. Other institutions, most notably the deregulated financial system, are themselves sources of considerable instability. Still others combine to present the capitalist economy with new contradictions. O'Hara contends that the intensifi- cation of international competition has led to substantial overcapacity. When this is combined with constrained working-class incomes, severe chronic problems of insufficient demand have been created. Much of this analysis is prescient, but O'Hara is not *predicting* a new crisis but argu- ing that this period is more correctly viewed as one of continuing crisis of the postwar SSA rather than the opening of a new social structure of accumulation.

---

[11] The 2006 volume brings together and extends arguments from a number of articles and chapters published since 2002.

In a pair of articles, Kotz (2003) and Wolfson (2003) agree with O'Hara that the post-1970s institutional structure did not lead to a new period of rapid expansion. They use this observation, however, as the foundation of a somewhat different analysis. Wolfson (2003: 260) argues that neoliberalism is "neither a crisis of the old SSA nor a new SSA. ... the old SSA is gone." The key problem with neoliberalism according to both Wolfson and Kotz is that it was always unlikely to lead to a period of stable growth because of anarchic competition and problems of demand and realization.

Nevertheless, according to Kotz (2003: 263), neoliberalism is "a new, coherent set of institutions that impinge on the process of capital accumulation." It cannot be an SSA, however, because it has not promoted sufficient growth, nor is it likely to do so.[12] Kotz resolves the problem of the existence of a coherent set of institutions in the absence of strong growth by postulating the existence of two kinds of institutional structure (IS). A liberal institutional structure (LIS) is characterized by limited state regulation, aggressive dominance of capital over labor, high levels of competition, and liberal, free market ideology. A regulationist institutional structure (RIS) is characterized, by contrast, by an interventionist state, an element of cooperation and compromise between capital and labor, corespective behavior by corporations, and recognition of the positive role of government and other nonmarket institutions. While both institutional structures foster the effective appropriation of surplus value, only an RIS promotes rapid accumulation and growth. Thus, only an RIS can lay claim to being a true SSA, based on the traditional definition of an SSA. Kotz further hypothesizes that there is a tendency for LIS to alternate with RIS because the crises created by one type can be partially resolved through the construction and introduction of the other type of institutional structure.[13]

---

[12] It is important to note that the positions of both Wolfson and Kotz have evolved on whether a new SSA was consolidated in the neoliberal era. See Chapters 3 and 4 of this volume.

[13] This formulation of regulated structures alternating with liberal structures has a certain appeal and can be defended at a theoretical and hypothetical level as it may indeed be true that each kind of structure addresses the contradictions inherent in the other. Whether this eventuates in the more complex world of actual SSAs is more questionable. In order to sustain the hypothesized alternation historically, Kotz is forced to separate the monopoly capital period after the turn of the century into two periods, a regulated one from 1900 to 1916 and a liberal one thereafter. In order to associate the 1920s with a slow-growth liberal period, Kotz is forced to extend the period into the

Especially in light of the global crisis that emerged in 2008, it would be hard to deny the reality of some of the crisis tendencies identified by O'Hara, Wolfson, and Kotz. It is possible to argue, however, that their impact was delayed long enough so as not to forestall a long period of expansion. Much of O'Hara's discussion of the implications of these tendencies for long-run growth implicitly assumes that an institutional framework can only be said to be in place if it does not carry serious crisis tendencies immanent within it. It is true that some crisis tendencies in past institutional frameworks only became evident after a long period of expansion. On the other hand, however, the monopoly structure put into place at the turn of the twentieth century could be said to be carrying a tendency to underconsumption from its birth. This tendency originated in its suppression of working class living standards, monopolistic and oligopolistic domination of investment markets, and the imperial carving up of international markets. Further, as Lenin argued, this particular social structure carried within it a tendency toward radical international instability, a tendency that eventuated in a world war which was (at least from a North American point of view) only midway through its tenure. With this example in mind, we can see that the secure identification of crisis tendencies does not necessarily disqualify an institutional framework from underpinning a long period of expansion.

The overall tendency within the literature has been to argue that a new SSA is in place. For example, the work of Minqi Li (2004, 2005) within the SSA framework has implicitly assumed that the new neoliberal SSA was in place and has gone on to analyze the potential contradictions that may bring about its decay. In his view, the problem of inadequate demand would play a central role. The decline in the power of labor has damaged the capacity for consumer spending. This in turn encourages speculative financial activity as an alternative to investing and creating real investment demand. Neoliberal suspicion of the state and the unwillingness of capital to risk higher taxation have inhibited expansion of government demand. This has left the U.S. current account deficit as the major prop of world demand. The deficit is sustained by massive borrowing and debt that could not continue in the medium let alone the long run.

Great Depression. At the end of the day, arguing that the Roaring Twenties are central to a period of slow growth seems problematic. It is also unclear whether the Progressive Era can be unambiguously regarded as a regulated period, especially in its labor relations. See Saros (2009), despite his acceptance of this general dating scheme. While the transition from liberal to regulated institutional structures and vice versa may be suggestive in particular periods, it is not established that this dichotomy is universally sustainable or an exhaustive typology.

Li also identifies "green" concerns as some of the prime areas of threat to the continuation of the SSA. The globalization of growth and consumerist lifestyles will lead to the rapid depletion of oil reserves after production reaches a peak. Even in the absence of a peak in physical supplies of oil, the prospect of global warming will demand a reduction in energy consumption with similar consequences. The run-up in world oil prices prior to the financial crisis that broke out in 2008 and the ongoing collapse in world demand and trade have certainly lent credence to Li's analysis.

Conclusion

The last decade has seen the culmination of the joint work of Gordon with Bowles and Weisskopf in econometrically analyzing the decline of the postwar SSA. It has also seen the diffusion of the SSA perspective into American sociological studies, most particularly, and perhaps not surprisingly, in the fields of labor control and the social control mechanisms studied by criminologists. In this context, the notion of a phase within a social structure of accumulation has been further developed and investigated. At the same time that SSAs have been studied over shorter time scales, the impact of SSAs on local structures has also been investigated. SSA analysis has been extended to new geographic areas. New institutional histories have been produced. A lively debate has been conducted over whether neoliberal institutions should be characterized as the consolidation of a new SSA.

On a theoretical level, the social structure of accumulation framework has largely returned to its roots in Marxism.[14] While this has recreated a certain theoretical coherence, several issues remain unresolved. The biggest unresolved issue is the nature of the post-1970s period. Was it an extension of the crisis period, a new SSA, or something different, perhaps an LIS? While this is partly an empirical disagreement, it poses an underlying theoretical question. How rapid and consistent must accumulation be to qualify a particular institutional structure as a specifically social structure of *accumulation*? A related question is the degree to which all the inherent crisis tendencies of capitalism must be securely moderated over the medium to long term.

The identification of subnational structures that influence the business climate of particular localities and the postulation of the emergence of

---

[14] This is leavened by a certain Keynesianism.

a transnational SSA in global neoliberalism raises the question of how institutional structures relate to one another on different geographical scales. In the postwar period, different national capitalisms shared a common international environment that conditioned accumulation in each of them. Nevertheless, concrete analyses have shown that their SSAs differed from each other. Different national SSAs sharing certain common international institutions is one possible model of this relationship. On the other hand, the spatialization school analyzes regional variation within an emerging spatialized SSA in the United States. Indeed, the particular character of the new SSA conditions and even demands regional variations.

Consequently, differing local institutions can be seen to be nested within an overarching national SSA. This nesting of local variation within a singular overarching SSA is a second model of the geographical relationship of differing local structures. The question immediately arises as to whether differing national manifestations within the context of global neoliberalism can be seen in this way.

A third set of theoretical questions has also been tentatively posed. The return to Marxian roots has been accompanied by a recent interest in the application within the SSA framework of the Gramscian concept of hegemony (Arena 2003; Harriss-White 2003). Grant and Martinez (1997) argue that changes in institutional structure between SSAs and phases within SSAs alter the interpretive frames through which people understand the injustice of a situation, their own efficacy within the situation, and the nature of their opponents. These forays raise the question of the nature of the institutions that make up the SSA. The SSA framework has generally emphasized the differing character of the institutions that make up successive SSAs and the differing ways in which they condition the profit rate and the accumulation process. This tendency has preserved the flexibility of the approach in dealing with new areas and new eras. Nevertheless, it has left several questions unanswered. Are there some relations between institutions that are relatively invariant across SSAs in different times and places? Are there certain invariant principles of institutional construction, consistent with the Marxian dynamics of class conflict and capitalist competition, such as the striving for hegemony, that are more specific than the need for general state support of the accumulation process? Symmetrically, are there necessary common principles of institutional decay that are more specific than the working out of the Marxian contradictions and crisis tendencies?

Writings within the SSA framework over the past decade or so indicate that the approach is intellectually lively and is evolving in its outlook as new developments pose unexpected challenges. It is inevitable that future work will focus on placing the current economic crisis within the context of the long waves of growth and stagnation predicted by SSA theory.[15]

References

Arena, John 2003. "Race and Hegemony: The Neoliberal Transformation of the Black Urban Regime and Working-Class Resistance." *American Behavioral Scientist* 47, 3: 352–80.

Barlow, David E. and Melissa Hickman Barlow 1995. "Federal Criminal Justice Legislation and the Post-World War II Social Structure of Accumulation in the United States." *Crime, Law and Social Change* 22, 3: 239–67.

Barlow, David E., Melissa Hickman Barlow, and Theodore G. Chiricos 1993. "Long Economic Cycles and the Criminal Justice System in the U.S." *Crime, Law and Social Change* 19: 143–69.

Boushey, Heather and Steven Pressman 1997. "The Economic Contributions of David M. Gordon." *Review of Political Economy* 9, 2: 225–45.

Bowles, Samuel, Richard Edwards, and Frank Roosevelt 2005. *Understanding Capitalism: Competition, Command and Change.* New York: Oxford University Press.

Brady, David and Michael Wallace 2000. "Spatialization, Foreign Direct Investment and Labor Outcomes in the American States, 1978–1996." *Social Forces* 79, 1: 67–105.

Carlson, Susan M. and Raymond J. Michalowski 1997. "Crime, Unemployment, and Social Structures of Accumulation: An Inquiry into Historical Contingency." *Justice Quarterly* 14, 2: 209.

Gordon, David M. 1988. "The Global Economy: New Edifice or Crumbling Foundations?" *New Left Review* 68: 24–64.

    1994. "Putting Heterodox Macro to the Test: Comparing Post-Keynesian, Marxian and Social Structuralist Macroeconomic Models of the Post-War U.S. Economy." Pp. 143–185 in Mark Glick, ed. *Competition, Technology and Money: Classical and Post-Keynesian Perspectives.* Cheltenham: Elgar.

    1996. *Fat and Mean: The Corporate Squeeze of Working Americans and the Myth of Managerial "Downsizing."* New York: The Free Press.

    1997. "From the Drive System to the Capital-Labor Accord: Econometric Tests for the Transition between Productivity Regimes." *Industrial Relations* 36, 2: 125–59.

Gordon, David M., Samuel Bowles, and Thomas E. Weisskopf 1998 (1994). "Power, Profits, and Investment: An Institutional Explanation of the

---

[15] It is too early to undertake a comprehensive review of already extant efforts. For a good example, see Kotz (2009).

Stagnation of U.S. Net Investment After the Mid-1960s." *Working Paper no. 12.* New School for Social Research. Reprinted in Samuel Bowles and Thomas E. Weisskopf eds. *Economics and Social Justice: Essays on Power, Labor and Institutional Change.* Cheltenham: Elgar.

Gruneberg, Stephen and Graham J. Ive 2000. *The Economics of the Modern Construction Firm.* London: Palgrave.

Grant, Don Sherman 1995. "The Political Economy of Business Failures across the American States, 1970–1985: The Impact of Reagan's New Federalism." *American Sociological Review* 60, 6: 851–73.

——— 1996. "The Political Economy of New Business Formation across the American States, 1970–1985." *Social Science Quarterly* 77, 1: 28–42.

Grant, Don Sherman and Richard Hutchinson 1996. "Global Smokestack Chasing: A Comparison of the State-level Determinants of Foreign and Domestic Manufacturing Investment." *Social Problems* 43: 21–38.

Grant, Don Sherman and Ramiro Martinez 1997. "Crime and the Restructuring of the U.S. Economy: A Reconsideration of the Class Linkages." *Social Forces* 75, 3: 769–98.

Grant, Don Sherman and Michael Wallace 1994. "The Political Economy of Manufacturing Growth and Decline across the American States, 1970–1985." *Social Forces* 73, 1: 33–63.

Hamilton, Rosalea 1994. "Analyzing Real Wages, Prices and Productivity and the Effects of State Intervention in Caribbean-type Economies." *Social and Economic Studies* 43, 1: 1–42.

Harriss-White, Barbara 2003. *India Working: Essays on Society and Economy.* Cambridge: Cambridge University Press.

Heintz, James 2002. "Political Conflict and the Social Structure of Accumulation – the Case of South African Apartheid." *Review of Radical Political Economics* 34, 3: 319–26.

Houston, David 1992. "Is There a New Social Structure of Accumulation?" *Review of Radical Political Economics* 24, 2: 60.

Jeong, Seongjin 1997. "The Social Structure of Accumulation in South Korea." *Review of Radical Political Economics* 29, 4: 92–112.

Kotz, David M. 2003. "Neoliberalism and the Social Structure of Accumulation Theory of Long-run Capital Accumulation." *Review of Radical Political Economics* 35, 3: 263–70.

——— 2004. "The Regulation Theory and the Social Structure of Accumulation Approach." Pp. 85–97 in David M. Kotz, Terrence McDonough, and Michael Reich, eds. *Social Structures of Accumulation: The Political Economy of Growth and Crisis.* New York: Cambridge University Press.

——— 2009. "The Financial and Economic Crisis of 2008: A Systemic Crisis of Neoliberal Capitalism." *Review of Radical Political Economics* 41, 3: 305–317.

Kotz, David M., Terrence McDonough, and Michael Reich 1994a. *Social Structures of Accumulation: The Political Economy of Growth and Crisis.* New York: Cambridge University Press.

Kotz, David M. 1994b. "Introduction." Pp. 1–8 in David M. Kotz, Terrence McDonough, and Michael Reich, eds. *Social Structures of Accumulation: The*

Political Economy of Growth and Crisis. New York: Cambridge University Press.

Li, Minqi 2004. "After Neoliberalism: Empire, Social Democracy, or Socialism." *Monthly Review* 55, 8: 21–36.

2005. "The Rise of China and the Demise of the Capitalist World-economy: Exploring Historical Possibilities in the 21st Century." *Science and Society* 69, 3: 420–48.

Lippit, Victor D. 1997. "The Reconstruction of a Social Structure of Accumulation in the United States." *Review of Radical Political Economics* 29, 3: 11–21.

2005. *Capitalism.* Oxon: Routledge.

Lobao, Linda, Jamie Rulli, and Lawrence A. Brown 1999. "Macrolevel Theory and Local-level Inequality: Industrial Structure, Institutional Arrangements, and the Political Economy of Redistribution, 1970 and 1990." *Annals of the Association of American Geographers* 89, 4: 571–601.

Mihail, Dimitrios 1993. "Modeling Profits and Industrial Investment in Postwar Greece." *International Review of Applied Economics* 7, 3: 290–310.

1995. "The Productivity Slowdown in Postwar Greece." *Labour* 9, 2: 189–205.

McDonough, Terrence 1995. "Lenin, Imperialism, and Stages of Capitalist Development." *Science and Society* 59, 3: 339–67.

1999. "Gordon's Accumulation Theory: The Highest Stage of Stadial Theory." *Review of Radical Political Economics* 31, 4: 6–31.

2003. "What Does Long Wave Theory Have to Contribute to the Debate on Globalization?" *Review of Radical Political Economics* 35, 3: 280–86.

Michalowski, Raymond J. and Susan M. Carlson 1999. "Unemployment, Imprisonment, and Social Structures of Accumulation: Historical Contingency in the Rusche-Kirchheimer Hypothesis." *Criminology* 37, 2: 217–50.

Michalowski, Raymond J. 2000. "Crime, Punishment, and Social Structures of Accumulation: Toward a New and Much Needed Political-Economy of Justice." *Journal of Contemporary Criminal Justice* 16, 3: 272–92.

Naples, Michele I. 1996. "Labor Relations and Social Structures of Accumulation: The Case of U.S. Coal Mining." Pp. 109–130 In Cyrus Bina, Laurie Clements and Chuck Davis, eds. *Beyond Survival: Wage Labor in the Late Twentieth Century.* Armonk, NY: M.E. Sharpe.

Nilsson, Eric A. 1996. "The Breakdown of the U.S. Postwar System of Labor Relations: An Econometric Study." *Review of Radical Political Economics* 28, 1: 20–50.

1997. "The Growth of Union Decertification: A Test of Two Non-nested Theories." *Industrial Relations* 36, 3: 324–48.

O'Hara, Philip Anthony 2000. *Marx, Veblen and Contemporary Institutional Political Economy: Principles and Unstable Dynamics of Capitalism.* Cheltenham: Elgar.

2006. *Growth and Development in the Global Political Economy: Social Structures of Accumulation and Modes of Regulation.* London: Routledge.

Perrucci, Robert 1994. *Japanese Auto Transplants in the Heartland: Corporatism and Community.* New York: Aldine de Gruyter.

Prechel, Harland 2000. *Big Business and the State: Historical Transitions and Corporate Transformation, 1880s–1990s*. Albany: State University of New York Press.

Reich, Michael 1997. "Social Structure of Accumulation Theory: Retrospect and Prospect." *Review of Radical Political Economics* 29, 3: 1–10.

1998. "Are U.S. Corporations Top-heavy? Managerial Ratios in Advanced Capitalist Countries." *Review of Radical Political Economics* 30, 3: 33–45.

Robinson, William I. 2003. *Transnational Conflicts: Central America, Social Change, and Globalization*. London: Verso.

2004. *A Theory of Global Capitalism*. Baltimore: Johns Hopkins University Press.

Saros, Daniel E. 2009. *Labour, Industry, and Regulation during the Progressive Era*. New York: Routledge.

Went, Robert 2002. *The Enigma of Globalization: A Journey to a New Stage of Capitalism*. London: Routledge.

Wolfson, Martin H. 2003. "Neoliberalism and the Social Structure of Accumulation." *Review of Radical Political Economics* 35, 3: 255–62.

TWO

Social Structure of Accumulation Theory

Victor D. Lippit

SSA Theory and Its Origins

Social Structure of Accumulation (SSA) theory seeks to explain the long
waves – averaging about fifty or sixty years for a complete cycle – that
have characterized capitalist economic growth, and the distinct stages
of capitalism that have marked each long upswing. Thus, in the United
States, the upswing early in the twentieth century was marked by industrial consolidation, mass production, and the introduction of "scientific
management." The SSA following World War II was marked by the
growth of the state, U.S. leadership in the world economy, limited competition and tacit "accords" between capital and labor on the one hand
and between capital and the citizenry on the other. This second SSA is
analyzed in greater detail later as a means of supporting and clarifying
the theoretical argument presented here.

The focus of SSA theory is on the institutional arrangements that
help to sustain long-wave upswings. Institutions can be thought of in
a narrow sense as organizations (like universities or the World Bank),
or in a broader sense as made up of customs, habits, and expectations.
In this sense, they are typically country- or culture-specific.[1] A further
division can be made within the broader sense, which might refer to

---

[1] Several efforts have been made to treat SSAs as global phenomena, parallel to treat-
ments of the capitalist world economy (CWE). Although the CWE is quite useful for
certain purposes, focusing as it does on the linkages among economic activities that are
geographically disparate, the core conception of an SSA does not permit such treatment.
Since institutions vary widely among capitalist countries – the "lifetime" employment
system in Japan, for example, contrasts markedly with the easy dismissal of employees in
the United States – it is not meaningful to speak of a global or international SSA.

something rather specific like collective bargaining on the one hand or more broadly to the entire system of labor relations that exists within a country. Although these broader senses are generally most useful in SSA analysis, the discussion here will refer to institutions in all three senses.

Sometimes the SSA literature refers to things like "*Pax Americana*" or "U.S. hegemony" in the postwar SSA (Gordon, Weisskopf, and Bowles 1996: 233). U.S. hegemony is not strictly an institution in any of the senses described earlier, but it can be thought of as encompassing a set of institutions ranging from the nature of the relations between the United States and other countries (based on a set of mutual expectations and patterns of behavior) to an international monetary system based on the U.S. dollar, which became the principal reserve currency throughout the world.

Capitalists or enterprises require attractive profit rates to invest, but they must also have a high degree of confidence in their expected investment outcomes, a confidence that can be ensured only by a set of institutions that is both stable and favorable. The set of institutions that favors investment is the "social structure of accumulation," or SSA. The concept of the social structure of accumulation is laid out clearly by its originators, David Gordon, Richard Edwards, and Michael Reich (1982: 25):

We understand the capital accumulation process to be the microeconomic activity of profit-seeking and reinvestment. This activity is carried on by individual capitalists (or firms) employing specific workforces and operating within a given institutional environment. We wish to separate that process from its environment. ...

The inner boundary of the social structure of accumulation, then, divides the capital accumulation process itself (the profit-making activities of individual capitalists) from the institutional (social, political, legal, cultural and market) context within which it occurs.

In the other direction we specify the outer boundary so that the social structure of accumulation is not simply shorthand for "the rest of society." We do not deny that *any* aspect or relationship in society potentially and perhaps actually impinges to *some* degree upon the accumulation process; nonetheless, it is not unreasonable to distinguish between those institutions that directly and demonstrably condition capital accumulation and those that touch it only tangentially. Thus, for example, the financial system bears a direct relation whereas the character of sports activity does not.

Two distinct lines of theoretical inquiry have merged to form the basis of SSA theory. On the one hand, Marx and neoMarxian theorists have sought to ascertain the core contradictions in capitalism that ultimately drive systemic change. On the other hand, various theorists have sought an explanation for the long cycles or waves that have characterized capitalist economic growth in the past. Within this second group, we note especially the work of Kondratieff (1935) and Schumpeter (1939). Kondratieff saw long cycles in the United States as tied to the replacement needs for long-lived capital goods, while Schumpeter focused on the clustering of innovations leading to an investment boom, with activity then tapering off until a new cluster of innovations was produced.

The neoMarxian literature is richer and more complex than that focusing on long cycles, even though much of the earlier neoMarxian work followed Marx down a blind alley in presupposing an imminent collapse of capitalism and in seeking to specify the central contradictions (such as the falling rate of profit or underconsumption) that would bring about that final collapse (Weisskopf 1996). While it was developed largely by people working within this theoretical tradition, SSA theory breaks with it by focusing on the recuperative power of capitalism – its ability to revive and renew itself following prolonged periods of relative stagnation or crisis. This perspective enables SSA theory to account for the distinct stages of capitalism, as well as for the long cycles that have accompanied its development. Thus, for example, contemporary American capitalism differs dramatically from the system that prevailed half a century ago.

The two lines of theoretical inquiry that merged to form SSA theory were first brought together in the work of David Gordon. His 1978 essay, "Up and Down the Long Roller Coaster," examines the quantitative evidence for long cycles in the United States since the beginning of the nineteenth century, ties the long cycles to institutional structures that support (or fail to support) the accumulation process, and links them logically to Marxian theories of contradiction and crisis. A subsequent essay (1980) then led into the "definitive" early presentation of SSA theory in *Segmented Work, Divided Workers* (1982), a work coauthored with Richard Edwards and Michael Reich. The most comprehensive subsequent study of SSA theory is *Social Structures of Accumulation: The Political Economy of Growth and Crisis* (1994), edited by David Kotz, Terrence McDonough, and Michael Reich. It provides a rich spread of essays (including one by Gordon) assessing the state of SSA theory and the questions the theory has raised. While a number of essays addressing SSA questions have appeared before and after the publication of this latter book, its breadth and sophistication make it a logical reference point for many of the theoretical issues I address later. With slight variations, the questions I address are the ones raised by David Kotz in his thoughtful essay "Interpreting the social structure of accumulation theory" (chapter 3 in Kotz, McDonough and Reich eds. 1994).

These questions are as follows. (1) What gives an SSA its structural integrity – what makes it more than a laundry list of institutions that impinge on the accumulation process? Can we speak of core institutions in an SSA or a core organizing principle? (2) Why do SSAs collapse? What is the role of class struggle in this process? (3) Why do SSAs take a long time to establish, and why do they tend to endure for extended periods? (4) What is the relation of SSA theory to concepts of overdetermination and historical contingency, both of which suggest that institutions alone cannot account for rapid accumulation and the accompanying long-wave upswings?

To address these questions purely in the abstract is not possible. For this reason, I turn first to brief accounts of two SSAs: the postwar SSAs in the United States and Japan. These accounts should help to clarify the theoretical discussion by applying it to specific institutional frameworks. Elsewhere I have discussed in some detail a third SSA, the neoliberal SSA in the United States, to which the theoretical discussion can also be applied.[2]

It should be noted at the outset that there is no way to "prove" the importance (or even existence) of SSAs using the deductive reasoning that is so common in economic theory. In hypothesizing the role of SSAs (using *inductive* reasoning), there are two central issues to be addressed: (1) Does positing the existence of SSAs make it possible to tell a more convincing story about the economic history of capitalist countries, including especially the long cycles and distinct stages of development that have been manifest within each country? (2) Does SSA theory help us to understand current conditions and dynamics within each capitalist country, as well as the forces shaping their economic futures? I believe that the argument to follow provides a resounding affirmative response to both questions.

The Postwar SSA in the United States

For an extended period following World War II, the United States enjoyed strong growth in investment, productivity, and real wages. David Gordon, Thomas Weisskopf, and Samuel Bowles (1996; hereafter GWB)

---

[2] A complete account of this third SSA appears in Lippit (1997). See also Lippit (2005).

attribute this "golden age" to the formation of an SSA whose subsequent collapse ushered in an era of sluggish growth and real-wage stagnation. Between 1948 and 1973, the rate of growth of productivity averaged 2.8 percent per year, but it then fell sharply to an average of 1.4 percent per year between 1973 and 1995 (Baumol and Blinder 2006: 134). Between 1973 and 1995, real average hourly earnings fell by 13 percent and median family income rose by only 4 percent (*Business Week* 12/16/96: 31–32). Between 1995 and 2004, productivity growth again kicked into high gear, averaging 3.0 percent (Baumol and Blinder 2006: 134). Although SSAs can never be dated with great precision since institutions are always in the process of formation and decay, this pattern of widely disparate productivity growth rates is consistent with the presence of a postwar SSA that lasted roughly a quarter of a century, followed by its collapse and the formation of a new, "neoliberal" SSA from the mid-1990s.[3]

According to GWB, the core institutions accounting for the earlier period of prosperity consisted of (1) a capital-labor accord under which labor ceded management control of enterprise operations in exchange for rising real wages and job security; (2) *Pax Americana*, a world marked by U.S. hegemony, with a strong dollar limiting the cost of imported raw materials to American firms and facilitating their overseas expansion; (3) a capital-citizen accord in which social security, Medicare, and other accoutrements of the welfare state were accepted by business in exchange for minimal public intervention in the corporate pursuit of profit; and (4) muted intercapitalist rivalry, made possible by oligopoly at home and the weakness of foreign economies that were still recovering from wartime devastation. The capital-citizen accord implied a vastly expanded role

---

[3] Dating the new SSA from around 1995 is supported by more than the acceleration in productivity that began at that time. It is reasonable to argue that the main features of the new SSA began to take shape under the Reagan presidency in 1981, the year in which Reagan fired the air traffic controllers, and became well established by around 1995. After their sweeping victory in the 1994 elections, when they gained 54 seats in the House of Representatives, the Republicans seized control of the House for the first time in forty years. A set of conservative policies was put into place over the next few years, with President Clinton signing legislation on August 22, 1996 that "rewrites six decades of social policy, ending the federal guarantee of cash assistance to the poor and turning welfare programs over to the states" (*Washington Post* 8/23/96: A1). Moreover, 1995 was the year in which the Caterpillar strike seeking to maintain the principle of pattern bargaining finally collapsed after four years of intense conflict. The new SSA, which limits the role of government and establishes the power of capital over labor among its key institutions, was thus firmly established by the middle of the decade. As the addendum explains, the neoliberal SSA was shorter than the norm because of the intensity of its internal contradictions.

for the state in the economy, which, together with the increased defense spending that accompanied the Cold War, assured the maintenance of aggregate demand.

Although GWB do not include it in their analysis, a subsequent essay by Martin Wolfson (1994) points to the key role of (5) the financial system in the postwar SSA. A brief discussion of these five components follows, intended to indicate their relation to the theoretical issues that have been raised.

The capital-labor accord addressed one of the central contradictions in capitalist economies. As GWB put it, capital can be "too strong" or "too weak" relative to labor. If capital is too strong, wages will be kept down, but that in turn threatens the maintenance of aggregate demand, leading to a potential crisis of underconsumption. Profits will be high in production, but sales will be curtailed by limited purchasing power, discouraging new investment. On the other hand, if capital is too weak, high wages will limit profitability by raising production costs; this too will discourage new investment. A capital-labor accord is one way of assuring balance, maintaining profits in production at a satisfactory level while aggregate demand is also sustained. By facilitating labor-saving technological change (under the accord, labor focuses on the security and benefits of current workers rather than of prospective ones), it also creates scope for profit-enhancing innovation.

Pax Americana was largely an outgrowth of World War II. With much of the industrial capacity of Japan and Western Europe destroyed during the War, the U.S. economy emerged with great strength relative to its potential competitors. In addition, the fixed exchange rates agreed to at Bretton Woods in 1944 assured the strength of the U.S. dollar, and facilitated its emergence as the dominant reserve currency. This made it possible for the United States to obtain raw materials and intermediate goods cheaply abroad, and facilitated the spread of foreign direct investment by U.S. firms.

The capital-citizen accord actually had its roots in some of the New Deal policies of the 1930s when, for example, the social security system was initiated. The problem that this accord addresses was highlighted by the Great Depression, which demonstrated that an unregulated capitalism does not necessarily assure that the most basic needs of the population for employment, old-age security, and so forth will be met. Like some other institutional supports for the postwar SSA, the capital-citizen accord evolved gradually over time, supported by the Full Employment Act of 1946, under which the state assumed responsibility for macroeconomic management to sustain full employment, and subsequent extensions to the welfare state such as Medicare (signed into law in 1965). Meeting the basic needs of citizens helped secure the general acceptance of capitalism and the pursuit of profit. As the capital-citizen accord indicates, the creation and evolution of institutions is an ongoing process, so an SSA may incorporate institutions previously established or new ones that are created subsequently.

Limited competition, both domestic and international, was a natural accompaniment of the oligopolistic market structure that came to prevail in most major industries in the postwar period and the weakened state of industrialized economies abroad. This component of the postwar SSA is actually composed of two discrete elements, one of which (oligopoly) is clearly institutional and the other is actually a matter of historical contingency (the inability of industrialized economies to compete vigorously in the U.S. market for an extended period of postwar reconstruction). It should also be noted that it overlaps with the "U.S. hegemony" component. The role of historical contingency will be addressed more fully in the theoretical discussion which follows, but at this point it should be noted that the overlapping of SSA components is not unusual and in fact helps to account for the unique integrity of each SSA. This too will be elaborated in the theoretical discussion in the following.

Martin Wolfson (1994: 133–134) argues that "the financial component of the postwar social structure of accumulation contributed to strong economic growth in the United States in three important ways: by promoting stability, by enhancing profitability, and by managing class conflicts." Wolfson places special emphasis on the financial reforms of the 1930s, including the separation of commercial and investment banking, the prohibition of interest payments on demand deposits and the placing of ceiling interest rates on time deposits, the introduction of federal insurance of deposits, and the strengthening of government supervision and regulation of the financial sector. Although many of these reforms were reversed in the 1980s and 90s, that in itself does not negate the role they played in the prosperity of the postwar era. It is not at all unusual to find that institutions that play a positive role in one period do not do so in another, when changes take place in external conditions and in the other institutions with which they interact.[4]

---

[4] Various business groups in East Asia provide another example of an institution supporting an SSA during one period but proving an obstacle to SSA formation in another. The *chaebol* in South Korea and the *keiretsu* in Japan supported their postwar SSAs in numerous ways. The *chaebol*, for example, given their support by the military regimes,

International financial institutions also came to play an important role in the postwar SSA. In 1944, the Bretton Woods agreement created the basis for an international financial system that also enhanced the environment for postwar investment by establishing the U.S. dollar as a reserve currency and by supporting the expansion of international trade. It is of interest to note that these institutional changes came prior to the postwar "golden age," but having them in place helped to secure a stable financial environment with low interest rates that contributed strongly to the postwar expansion.

Japan's Postwar SSA

From 1955 to 1970, the Japanese economy grew at an average rate of 9.7 percent per year, and the growth rate continued to average between 4 and 5 percent over the next two decades (Hirata 1995: 41). Following the collapse of the stock market and real estate bubbles at the end of 1989, however, the growth rate of GDP fell off sharply to about 1.3 percent over the next eighteen years. Once again the historical pattern is consistent with a postwar SSA, in this case lasting about thirty-five years, followed by collapse. The set of institutions that composed Japan's postwar SSA was quite distinctive, and the ways in which the institutions involved were both mutually supportive and able to contribute to high rates of accumulation and economic growth is evident. The principal institutions included the following:

(1) The close relationship between corporations and the state, often referred to as "Japan Incorporated."
(2) The *keiretsu* system of business groups, typically organized around a leading bank and marked by cross-shareholdings.
(3) The "lifetime" employment (at that time until age 55) and seniority systems in the labor market.
(4) The family system.
(5) The educational system and career patterns.

The family system involved a rigid division of labor between husband and wife. Women were expected to drop out of the labor market when

made possible a high degree of leverage and thus the rapid expansion of investment. When South Korea democratized, however, and the relations between business and government changed, high levels of *chaebol* debt exposed the entire economy to severe financial risk, a risk that materialized during the Asian financial crisis of 1997.

they had children. The wives were responsible for taking care of the household and the education of the children. The husbands were free to work for their companies until late at night under this arrangement. The children, meanwhile, were being prepared for success in a brutally competitive educational system. Going to a good college and receiving favorable letters of recommendation was critical, for a lifetime job (after a two-year trial period) would typically be found right after college or high school. The meritocratic educational system, then, combined with the family system to create the next generation of dedicated employees.

The very top students at the national universities could aspire to careers in government service, careers that combined the highest social respect with the power to affect deeply the companies under their ministries' purview. Following retirement in their early fifties, most would become advisors or senior executives at these same firms, or assume leading managerial roles at public institutions. Others would go into politics and seek to become senators in the Diet. Under the marriage-arrangement system, wealthy families with daughters would seek to marry them off to government officials, seeing this as the most secure and prestigious future. The family money would then make possible a political career, which required a great deal of it.

Everyone knew that the young bureaucrats working in government ministries had to be among the very top students, that they had a great deal of power, and that their futures were very bright. Under the Japanese system, each ministry would tend to support and protect the firms in the industries for which it was responsible. When the officials reached retirement they would start a second career as senator or official in the firms they had just been supervising. Meanwhile, their places in the ministries would be taken over by the younger officials they had previously mentored. Thus, the system known as "Japan Incorporated" involved a seamless web of mutually supportive institutions, with government and corporations closely tied, but in a way that allowed for full contributions from the education, family, and lifetime employment systems.

The *keiretsu* system of business groups also played a key role in the successful formation of Japan's postwar SSA. The various member companies could support the other members of the group in various ways. Thus, for example, banks could be counted on to provide loans and trading companies to find markets or supplies abroad. The *keiretsu* relationships were cemented by interlocking shareholdings. In addition to facilitating strong economic growth, they contributed to the social standing and security that those who were successful in the educational system could expect, which in turn provided ample motivation to sustain the prevailing family system. Although this description of Japan's postwar SSA is quite brief, it should help to clarify the way in which the different institutions that compose a given SSA function in a mutually supportive fashion, enhancing its stability and helping it to endure.

The Structural Integrity of an SSA

When we speak of a social *structure* of accumulation, we imply a linkage among the various institutions that comprise a specific SSA. Moreover, when we speak of the collapse of an SSA, we imply the collapse of the entire structure rather than simply the collapse of some of its individual components. This in turn suggests as well that the various institutions must be linked together in some fashion. The question to be addressed, then, is what accounts for the structural integrity of an SSA?

There are two principal approaches to this question in the SSA literature. David Kotz (1994: 65–67) argues that a core set of institutions is established early in an SSA, a core that then interacts with and shapes the formation of the other institutions that come to constitute the full SSA (Kotz 1994: 65):

This core of institutions must be sufficient to significantly stabilize class conflicts and competition, and to assure long-term markets. For the early twentieth-century in the US, the following institutions might have made up the core: monopoly/finance capital, repression of trade unions, and an aggressively imperialist policy. The core institutions of the post World War II expansion in the US might have been peaceful collective bargaining, militarization of the economy, and US ascent to a dominant position in the world.

Terrence McDonough (1994) seeks to explain the structural integrity of SSAs in terms of either a single institution or an event that can serve as the "unifying principle" of the newly emerging SSA. Thus, he finds the early-twentieth century SSA in the United States to be based on the oligopolization of the economy that occurred in the span of a few years around the turn of the century, while World War II served as the basis for the postwar SSA. There is some similarity between the approaches of Kotz and McDonough in that both focus on a limited set of institutions or events that occur early in the formation of an SSA and contribute significantly to the formation and shaping of the other institutions that come to constitute the full SSA. There are, however, significant differences as well. While Kotz focuses on a set of institutions as the organizing principle, McDonough finds that some exogenous factor – for example,

World War II – can play a comparable role. Further, in focusing on a set of core institutions that shape subsequent institutional development, Kotz can explain the relation between the core and the "peripheral" institutions, but still cannot account for the structural integrity among the institutions that constitute the initial core. By focusing on a single organizing principle, McDonough is able to avoid this problem.

By focusing on a single organizing principle, however, McDonough distracts attention from a potentially much more robust approach that he himself cites. Referring to Gordon's 1980 article, McDonough (1994: 76–77) writes:

What is it that integrates an SSA into a coherent whole? I believe the most promising direction in which to look for the answer to this question was proposed by Gordon in one of the earliest expositions of the SSA framework. In this early article, Gordon (1980) proposes that "the interdependencies among the individual institutions create a combined social structure with a *unified* internal structure of its own – a composite whole, in effect, whose intrinsic structure amounts to more than the sum of the individual institutional relationships" (p. 17). For Gordon this unified internal structure is the reason that "changes in any one constituent institution are very likely to reverberate throughout the entire structure, creating instability in all of the other constituent institutions" (p. 17). This integral structure is thus at the heart of the SSA framework ... (and) it is likely the relationships (among) these institutions must be unique to each SSA and hence historically contingent.

Gordon's formulation is very close to the principles of overdetermination in its focus on the mutual interaction among the various institutions composing any given SSA. Perhaps the main difference is that Gordon appears to present each institution as an independent entity, which is then subject to change when another institution, an external entity, changes. The idea of overdetermination suggests that institutions are never entirely disparate entities, that each is shaped by and incorporates elements of the other institutions and social forces with which it interacts. This distinction actually strengthens Gordon's argument since it is not simply a matter of external changes influencing each institution in that the "external" institutions at least in part have been internalized.

The theoretical approaches of Kotz and McDonough are both inspired by attempts to address deficiencies they perceive in the basic presentation of SSA theory in Gordon, Edwards, and Reich's *Segmented Work, Divided Workers*. Gordon, Edwards, and Reich (GER) do not attempt to privilege any set of core institutions, and readily admit that exogenous forces – they mention World War II specifically (p. 31) – may be very important in determining the formation of an SSA. By failing to follow up fully Gordon's earlier discussion concerning the question of what accounts for the structural integrity of an SSA, however, and by presenting a listing of apparently disparate institutions in the SSAs they analyze, GER have left open the question that Kotz and McDonough attempt to address. In searching for a core organizing principle or a set of core institutions, however, Kotz and McDonough turn away from the more promising direction that Gordon himself indicated in the quotation from McDonough earlier.

In considering the question of what accounts for the structural integrity of an SSA, it is possible to build on Gordon's suggestion concerning the mutual interactions among institutions, considering this in the light of the concept of overdetermination as expounded by Resnick and Wolff in *Knowledge and Class* (1987: ch. 2). Resnick and Wolff follow Althusser's development of the Marxian insight that social processes, including economic ones, are mutually determinative. Discussing the work of Althusser, Resnick and Wolff write (1987: 88):

Each distinct social process is the site constituted by the interaction of all the other social processes, each contains "within itself" the very different and conflicting qualities, influences, moments, and directions of all those other social processes that constitute it. In this sense, argues Althusser, each social process is the site of, or "contains," the complex contradictoriness inseparable from overdetermination. Each social process exists, for Althusser's Marxism, only as a particular, unique concentration of contradictions in its environment.

Although the concept of overdetermination as developed by Resnick and Wolff focuses on the manner in which each social process is "overdetermined" by the other social processes with which it interacts, their conceptual framework can be extended readily to the interaction among institutions, that between institutions and social processes, and that between institutions and "exogenous" events or conditions. *That is to say, there is an ongoing process of institutional formation and institutional change that is brought about by the interaction among (1) the internal contradictions of any specified institution, (2) the other institutions that coexist with it, (3) exogenous events, and (4) the full range of social processes. All of these elements mutually (over)determine one another.* And just as "essentialism" (privileging the economic, for example, over the other forces that account for social processes) must be rejected in accounting for causation, any attempt to privilege a "core" set of institutions – or a core institution or event – as responsible for the structural integrity of a given SSA appears questionable.

In accounting for the structural integrity of any given SSA, then, it is critical to avoid conceptualizing institutions in isolation, and to recognize the multiplicity of forces serving to create and sustain each institution, forces that include other institutions, the full array of social processes, and exogenous events (historical contingency). In considering the forces that may ultimately undermine each institution and ultimately the entire structure of which it is a part, the interaction of these same factors must be recognized as playing a role, together with the internal contradictions that tend to arise in all institutions.

Approaching the structural integrity of SSAs in this way is much closer to the spirit of the initial work of Gordon and of GER, who do not attempt to assign priority to any particular institution and who explicitly recognize that "'exogenous' forces may be very important," citing, as I have noted, the impact of World War II on the postwar SSA (1982: 31). GER do not attempt, however, to analyze the manner in which the institutions that constitute the SSAs they address, the exogenous events with which the SSAs interact, and the various social processes overdetermine one another. Such an analysis can help to deepen our understanding of the structural integrity of SSAs and why they tend to endure for an extended period of time. Further, when the role of internal contradictions is considered together with these interactions, the forces contributing to the eventual collapse of all SSAs become more transparent.

Overdetermination and the Postwar SSA in the United States

Although it is not possible here to provide a comprehensive example of the manner in which overdetermination can account for the structural integrity of a given SSA, the approach can be applied in admittedly cursory fashion to the postwar SSA in the United States to demonstrate the logic of the argument. I have already specified five institutions as constituting the postwar SSA in the United States (the four indicated by Gordon, Weisskopf, and Bowles, and a fifth provided by Wolfson): the capital-labor accord, *Pax Americana*, the capital-citizen accord, muted intercapitalist competition, and the favorable financial framework. The discussion that follows indicates some of the ways in which these institutions interacted with one another and how they contributed to shaping one another in the process. These interactions, often mediated by exogenous events and ongoing social processes, can help to account for the structural integrity of the SSA that emerged.

the creation of a more activist generation. Given the rising concerns with environmental deterioration that followed, it was quite natural for activists to turn their attention to environmental issues. Their success in raising popular consciousness had political consequences, ultimately leading to legislation that greatly increased the regulation of business, increasing business costs, and decreasing profitability.

The era of limited competition was also unsustainable. The reconstruction of Europe and Japan initially expanded export and investment opportunities for U.S. business, but once recovery abroad had taken place, strong growth in foreign competition was inevitable. The fixed exchange rates of the Bretton Woods accord, moreover, left the U.S. dollar increasingly overvalued; the stability they initially imparted to international commerce turned into a competitive force highly inimical to U.S. business.

At home, the intensified foreign competition undermined the oligopolistic market structures. When new sources of competition emerge, firms are forced to become much more concerned with reducing production costs. As U.S. firms increasingly found themselves in this situation in the 1970s and 80s, the high costs of labor and the rising costs of regulation became increasingly intolerable. Under such circumstances, there was no way in which the capital-labor and capital-citizen accords could be sustained. In other words, muted competition, a key component of the postwar SSA, was necessary for two of the other core components to become established and to persist.

The financial institutions that played such a great part in the postwar golden age – and the low and stable interest rates associated with them – were also unsustainable when the other institutions and the external environment changed. The financial legislation of the 1930s and the Bretton Woods agreement of 1944 had created the national and international basis respectively for the low rates. With the economic recovery abroad forcing a move from fixed to floating exchange rates and a sharp decline in the value of the dollar, inflationary pressures grew strongly from the late sixties, abetted by the Vietnam War and the spikes in the price of energy associated with the rise of OPEC in 1973 and the Iranian revolution in 1979. The stagflation of the 1970s in turn gave rise to Federal Reserve Board efforts to control inflation by deliberately increasing short-term interest rates in the early 1980s, while double-digit inflation rates led to thirty-year Treasury bond rates in excess of 14 percent. Sharply rising interest rates also contributed to a sharp increase in financial crises among U.S. corporations.

Although the components of America's postwar SSA can be differentiated, it is clear that they were mutually reinforcing. The capital-labor and capital-citizen accords brought labor peace and minimized regulatory threats, enabling U.S. corporations to benefit from the expanding global economy that *Pax Americana* helped to create. Low interest rates and limited competition at home and abroad had the same effect.

In addition to the mutual reinforcement provided by the different components of the postwar SSA, the role of economic theory as ideology must also be acknowledged. Keynesianism provided the intellectual glue for America's "golden age," bringing with it widespread acceptance of a major role for government in the economy. Like everything else, of course, this acceptance was overdetermined, with the rise of the Cold War playing a major role. Even aside from military spending, however, the government took a major role in the economy through social security, the G.I. bill, the interstate highway program and other infrastructure spending. The increase in and stabilization of aggregate demand to which government spending contributed also played a leading role in the postwar SSA.[6]

This brief review should help to make it clear that the set of institutions that sustained postwar prosperity was interdependent, with each institution overdetermined by the other institutions with which it interacted, by the prevailing ideology, and by exogenous events. The postwar social structure of accumulation, then, constituted a *structure* precisely because of this process of overdetermination, and the collapse of the entire structure can readily be understood in terms of the interaction among (1) changes in the SSA's constituent institutions, (2) the development of internal contradictions in several of the institutions, and (3) the impact of exogenous events. According to the logic of this argument, then, we do not have to posit a core institution, event, or set of institutions to understand the logic underlying the structural integrity of an SSA.

Why SSAs Require Many Years to Construct and Why they Endure Many Years

According to the argument just presented, the emergence of each institution in an SSA is shaped by complex historical factors and interaction with

---

[6] While Keynesian ideology took the leading role in supporting the various elements that made up the postwar SSA, every SSA tends to generate its own economic and social ideology, an ideology that interacts with those elements in a way that supports them and contributes to their evolution.

other institutions. These same forces impart a certain durability to SSAs, a durability that is enhanced by the array of beneficiaries each institution tends to create. In the case of the capital-labor accord, for example, both parties received tangible benefits they were eager to retain. The capital-labor accord would only collapse when supportive institutions and external conditions changed in such a manner that the potential contradiction between capital and labor would rise to the surface. Such changes can take place only over an extended period of time.

Despite the solid reasons for expecting institutional changes to be a prolonged process, some authors remain unconvinced that SSAs can explain long waves. Terrence McDonough (1994), for example, argues that SSA theory "is more adequate as a theory of stages of capitalism than of specifically long waves" (p. 72), and that there is no reason why the period of expansion initiated by an SSA is necessarily long (p. 78). He finds "unsatisfying" the argument presented by Gordon, Edwards, and Reich (1982) that institutions by their very nature are durable (p. 75). While McDonough is certainly correct in agreeing with GER that each SSA represents a distinct stage in the development of capitalism, his dismissal of the argument that institutions by their very nature are durable appears questionable in the light of the discussion earlier. Although he is clearly correct in arguing that there is no reason why the period of expansion associated with the establishment of an SSA is *necessarily* long – the length of a given SSA expansion will be governed by the intensity of its internal contradictions and the impact of exogenous events – we can normally expect an established SSA to persist over a more or less extended period.

If institutions are thought of as habits and customs – and the associated patterns of behavior that people expect of others and of themselves – then of course they will be slow to change. If a specific set of institutions emerges at a particular historical juncture that encourages rapid accumulation, that set of institutions will tend to endure for a prolonged period, and thus will be associated with a prolonged period of relative prosperity. There are numerous reasons for which such institutions tend to be especially long-lived. All institutions tend to be prolonged through mutual expectations. In Japan, for example, when people meet or are introduced they bow, whereas in the United States they shake hands. Not bowing or extending one's hand is regarded as impolite, so people tend to perpetuate the respective institutions without giving it a second thought. Over time, however, institutions can and do change. On social occasions, people in the United States often greet one another with a hug or a kiss on the cheek; this institutional change has been going on for decades in the United States, but it is still far from complete and tends to exclude business greetings.

SSA institutions have additional supports. Most importantly, every SSA creates broad groups of beneficiaries; the capital-labor accord noted earlier provides just one example. Those who benefit from the existing SSA characteristically seek to sustain it and oppose public policy initiatives or any other changes that could undermine it. Moreover, the dominant ideology that characterizes each SSA – Keynesianism in the postwar United States – provides support to its component institutions. Thus the capital-citizen accord required a major role for government in assuring the lives of senior citizens and in taking responsibility for a wide range of social problems. This made it difficult to cut back dramatically on the role of government in the economy.

For all of these reasons, SSAs tend to be long-lived. They do not, however, endure indefinitely. Change is the inevitable result of internal contradictions emerging within the institutions, changes taking place in the full range of social processes, changes in historically contingent exogenous circumstances, and the overdetermination that characterizes the relations among institutions and between a given set of institutions and exogenous conditions. There is no specific time period for which an SSA will last, as its durability will depend on the strength of the individual institutions and the overall structure, as well as the counteracting strength of the forces that ultimately undermine it. Although SSAs tend to be durable, the periods for which they remain in place may vary widely.

When an SSA does collapse, the social consensus that helped sustain it is fragmented as well, and a period of intense social conflicts ensues. These conflicts include, but are not limited to, class conflicts. In seeking to restore and enhance profitability, firms seek to lay off workers and limit the wages of those who remain; workers attempt to resist this. But at the same time, in a more competitive labor environment, opportunities for women are apt to be more circumscribed and measures like affirmative action subject to increasing challenge by those who claim to be victims of "reverse discrimination." Limited tax receipts intensify competition among potential beneficiaries: should taxes be used to shore up social security, improve education, or help farmers? Or should tax reductions be implemented to benefit homeowners, those in high marginal brackets, or taxpayers in general? Such conflicts are intensified during periods of general stagnation and sluggish growth. They cannot be solved easily or quickly. Moreover, numerous elements of the institutions that comprised the previous SSA inevitably remain, together with their beneficiaries and the thought processes they engender. In the 1970s and 1980s, for example, U.S. workers perceived it as "unjust" that their real wages were not rising and unions tended to cling to bargaining tactics that were no longer viable in an era of intense global competition. Thus the establishment of a new SSA can only follow a more or less prolonged period of social conflict, during which time a new set of institutions marking a new stage in capitalist development can be established.

The foregoing discussion should help to clarify the reasons for which SSAs require many years to construct and why they endure many years. If institutions are thought of primarily as habits, customs and expectations – which properly they should be – then institutional change must require an extended period of time to come about. Although specific SSAs can vary widely in length, SSA theory can provide an explanation for the long waves that have characterized the history of capitalist development, as well as for capitalism's distinct stages.

The Role of Class Conflict in SSA
Formation and Collapse

David Kotz (1994: 55) argues that the stabilization of class conflict and competition is at the core of SSA formation. Class conflict is of course one of the main social struggles that characterize capitalist society, and we can see its impact in the example provided earlier, with firms seeking to extract the maximum value from the labor power they hire conflicting with the need of workers to meet simultaneously their own needs and the other social demands placed upon them. Privileging class conflict to the exclusion of other social conflicts, however, limits our understanding of the nature of an SSA and of the time required to form one.

Gender and racial conflicts provide obvious examples of other struggles that impact SSA formation. We should also keep in mind that society is the site of numerous other struggles, all of which impinge necessarily on its institutional structure and SSA formation. Social security and Medicare, for example, involve transfers from those presently working to the elderly, and the exploding costs of these entitlements have increased taxes on those who are working for the benefit of those who are retired (they also involve a potential shift in resources from other dependents in society such as young children). Unless substantial changes are made in these entitlement programs, tax rates can be expected to grow substantially over the course of the twenty-first century. The struggle between those who are retired (or near retirement), those who are working and (indirectly) young children is not a class conflict, but the growth of entitlements clearly affects the process of SSA formation by raising business costs and taxes, thereby reducing profitability and the resources available for accumulation.

Another example of nonclass struggle playing a role in SSA formation (or dissolution) is provided by the role of environmental movements. Environmental regulations can influence business costs and revenues in a wide range of industries – and indeed in industry in general – when they mandate treatment of factory wastes, limit carbon emissions, or increase compliance paperwork. Environmental issues may also play a role in other nonclass conflicts, such as that between urban and agricultural interests over the use of water. Thus, for example, industrial development in the city of San Diego has been constrained by the high cost of water, which is well over ten times the cost paid by agricultural users in much of California.

Just like class struggles, intergenerational, environmental, and other nonclass struggles play out over decades and are marked by partial victories for either side. When a resolution to class and nonclass struggles is reached that permits satisfactory profitability and predictability, SSA formation is enhanced. Such resolutions may involve compromise agreements (as in the capital-labor accord), or they may involve victory for one side – as in the domination of labor by capital in the neoliberal SSA that has just collapsed (see the discussion of this in the addendum) – as long as the outcome favors accumulation by making investment both profitable and predictable.

The neoliberal SSA in the United States was formed during the 1980s and 90s, and dates from around 1995 (see note 3 for an explanation of the 1995 start date). As the neoliberal SSA demonstrates, it is possible for capital to crush labor in their ongoing struggles and still retain favorable conditions for accumulation as long as the exogenous conditions are suitable. During the 1980s and 1990s, strong growth in some of the less developed countries and the growing participation of formerly communist countries in the capitalist world economy created rapidly expanding markets for U.S. companies. This meant that the demand for their products and services became less dependent on the level of domestic demand, so that stagnant real wages at home became consistent with the increasing profitability of investment.[7]

When considering the reasons why SSAs collapse, both class and nonclass struggles play major roles. As the discussion of the collapse of the postwar SSA in the United States shows, however, historical contingency (such as the rise of OPEC) and the emergence of internal contradictions within the institutions that constitute the SSA can be of comparable importance. In the case of Japan, growth based on government-supported export prowess was ultimately undermined by the inevitable floating of the yen and then its appreciation. In understanding the processes of SSA formation and collapse, it is helpful to recognize that both nonclass and class struggles play a role, and to recognize the manner in which both processes are overdetermined.

The understanding of SSAs provided here is thus antiessentialist. Each SSA – and the institutions that constitute it – is overdetermined by the broad array of extant institutions, social processes and struggles, and exogenous forces/historical contingency. SSAs tend to endure for prolonged periods of time because they tend to generate favorable changes in related institutions, because success tends to generate supporting constituencies, and because institutions are by their very nature slow to change. Ultimately, however, all SSAs do collapse, as internal contradictions emerge and as the social forces and institutions that overdetermine them change. When collapse occurs, a prolonged period of struggles, both class and nonclass, is required before a new SSA can be constituted. The long waves of expansion and stagnation that capitalist economies experience can thus be understood as an expression of SSA formation and collapse, with each SSA constituting a distinct phase in capitalist development.

Addendum: The 2007/8 Financial Crisis and the Collapse of the Neoliberal SSA

If SSA theory is to provide useful insights into the functioning of the capitalist system, it should be capable of providing a framework for

---

[7] For a comprehensive discussion of the neoliberal SSA formed in the U.S. around 1995, see Lippit (2005). As far as the dating of the neoliberal SSA is concerned, since its characteristic institutions were progressively put in place from the time of President Reagan's election in 1980, it is possible to argue that it came into being as early as that date. Whatever date for its start is accepted, it is clear that it was brought to a premature end by the global financial crisis that began in 2007/8. As the discussion in the addendum indicates, the neoliberal SSA had a shorter lifespan than might have been expected as a consequence of the intensity of its internal contradictions.

understanding contemporary developments. Beginning in 2007/8, a global financial crisis erupted, one that marked the end of the neoliberal SSA that had prevailed until that time. The term "neoliberal" refers to an ideology characterized by an exaggerated belief in the efficacy of markets. Appearing before Congress in the fall of 2008, for example, Alan Greenspan, the former chairman of the Federal Reserve Board, confessed that he did not believe it was necessary to regulate the behavior of large financial institutions because he "made a mistake in presuming that the self-interests of organizations, specifically banks and others, were such that they were best capable of protecting their own shareholders and their equity in the firms" (*International Herald Tribune* 10/24/08: 1). Just as the postwar SSA was characterized by the broad acceptance of Keynesianism, the SSA just collapsed was characterized by its own distinctive ideology, neoliberalism, which is characterized by antitax sentiment and a belief in small government, as well as in the efficacy of unregulated markets.

It is not possible here to go into detail concerning the neoliberal SSA, but a few observations concerning its nature and collapse should help to clarify the theoretical issues addressed in this chapter. I have argued here that SSAs tend to be lengthy, but that there is no specified duration. If one looks for the reasons underlying the collapse of an SSA, one should look first at its underlying contradictions, and then consider the ways that these interact with external factors. When the underlying contradictions are severe, one can expect the duration of a given SSA to be shorter than the norm. A brief consideration of the neoliberal SSA will show that it harbored contradictions of great severity, accounting for its relative brevity.

There are different ways to specify the key institutions of the neoliberal SSA, but the following set seems to capture the most significant ones: (1) the strengthening of capital relative to labor, (2) a change in financial institutions favorable to investment, (3) deregulation, (4) institutional changes in the nature of the corporation, (5) limited government, (6) an increase in international trade and investment, and (7) capital markets favorable to small, entrepreneurial companies (Lippit 1997 and 2005). Starting with the election of President Reagan in 1980 and culminating with the Republican Congressional sweep in 1994, these features increasingly characterized American capitalism. They remained dominant until the internal contradictions in several of them, interacting with external changes and the other institutions, led into the financial crisis that began in 2007/8.

Perhaps the most dominant institutional feature of the neoliberal SSA is the power of capital over labor. It is reflected in the steeply falling unionization rates in the private sector, the stagnation of real wages, the rising share of profits in national income, and the growing inequality in income distribution that characterized the entire neoliberal period (*www.marketwatch.com*, 3/30/06):

Before-tax profits reached 11.6 percent of national income in the fourth quarter of 2005, the biggest share since the summer of 1966 ... Meanwhile, the share of national income going to wage and salary workers has fallen to 56.9 percent. Except for a brief period in 1997, that's the lowest share for labor income since 1966.

By 2007, real median household income actually was lower than it had been in 2000 (Kotz 2008: 9–10). This poses a problem for an economy, a core potential contradiction: although stagnant wages make profits in production high, the purchasing power needed to buy the economy's output will be inadequate, resulting in sluggish economic growth and frequent recessions.

In fact, there are quite a few ways in which this potential problem can be circumvented temporarily: rising asset prices (enabling the wealth effect to support consumption), the expansion of credit, rising exports, and investments that do not depend on current consumption are among them. Ultimately, however, the SSA expansion becomes increasingly fragile if it is not based on rising labor income and mass purchasing power. In the neoliberal SSA, the stock market and housing bubbles created a wealth effect that helped drive household savings to negative levels.[8] Cash-out mortgage refinancings, home-equity loans, and credit card debt helped sustain consumption growth but on an increasingly shaky foundation. As David Kotz (2008: 10) observes, household debt as a percentage of disposable income rose from 59.0 percent in 1982 to 128.8 percent in 2007. Ultimately, a debt-financed SSA expansion carries within itself the seeds of crisis.

A second major contradiction is associated with the deregulation aspect of the neoliberal expansion. This of course lowered business compliance costs, raising profitability and investment. But deregulation meant that a credit default swaps market (essentially bond insurance that allowed speculation on defaults even to those who did not own the bonds

---

[8] In 2005, the U.S. personal savings rate (savings as a share of disposable income) fell to –0.5 percent, the first time it fell into negative territory since 1933, during the Great Depression (*www.msnbc.com/id/11098797/*).

in question) worth some $45 trillion by mid-2007 came into being without regulation (*Time*, 3/17/08), down payments on houses that used to be a required 20 percent fell to zero, and mortgage brokers could carry out their business (issuing mortgages) with little or no regulation. And the unregulated rating agencies could issue "AAA" ratings for mortgage-backed securities with payment for the ratings coming from the very Wall Street firms that packaged them. Like the power of capital over labor, institutions like deregulation that promoted SSA expansion embodied at the same time a virulent contradiction.

A third contradiction is the commitment to limited government that began with the Reagan era. Since complementary investment on the part of the public sector is needed to support expanded investment in the private sector, its absence is rife with potential pitfalls. The attraction of limited government to capital is the regime of low taxes that accompanies it, a regime that raises the (after-tax) return on capital. However, a decaying infrastructure, a health care system in which costs are rising out of control, and global warming/environmental decay ultimately provide severe threats to the profitability of private investment.

Finally, globalization, which is partly internal to the SSA and partly external, interacted with other institutions to support the SSA, but ultimately contributed to intensifying its internal contradictions as well. When the SSA was functioning smoothly, globalization enhanced the power of capital over labor by providing alternatives to domestic employment (through offshoring or procurement abroad), by sustaining demand even in the absence of stagnant wages, and by providing additional investment opportunities. When the financial crisis did hit, however, subprime loans were located in foreign as well as in domestic banks, and the global character of the downturn meant that foreign demand could not serve to rescue the U.S. economy from its domestic slump.

The current downturn, which at the time of this writing (May 2009) is already the most severe since the Great Depression overall, clearly marks the collapse of the neoliberal SSA. It is a genuine systemic crisis in that it will not be possible to put together the old system, the old SSA, with modest reforms in the financial system and other areas where the contradictions in the institutions that characterized it have brought about its collapse. Once again, U.S. capitalism will be forced to reinvent itself.

Just as any given SSA tends to last for a lengthy but indeterminate period, there is no fixed time in which the process of forming a new SSA can be expected to play out. It is clear that more comprehensive regulation will be needed, as well as high levels of public expenditure and eventually higher taxes. Resistance to such changes has already been registered in tax protests and the fact that the stimulus bill introduced by the Obama administration (and ultimately passed into law) garnered no Republican votes in the House of Representatives and only three votes in the Senate. Intense class and nonclass struggles over issues like labor union organizing, health care and entitlement reform, taxation, and environmental protection will have to be resolved as part of the process of creating a new SSA, and will determine the duration of the period that will be required before this can take place.

References

Baumol, William and Allan Blinder 2006. *Macroeconomics: Principles and Policy*. Mason, OH: Thomson South-Western.

Gordon, David 1980. "Stages of Accumulation and Long Economic Cycles." Pp. 9–45 in Terence K. Hopkins and Immanuel Wallerstein eds. *Processes of the World System*. Beverly Hills: Sage.

——— 1978. "Up and Down the Long Roller Coaster." Pp. 22–35 in Union for Radical Political Economics. *U.S. Capitalism in Crisis*. New York: Union for Radical Political Economics.

Gordon, David, Richard Edwards and Michael Reich 1982. *Segmented Work, Divided Workers: The Historical Transformation of Labor in the United States*. New York: Cambridge University Press.

Gordon, David, Thomas E. Weisskopf and Samuel Bowles 1996. "Power, Accumulation and Crisis: The Rise and Demise of the Postwar Social Structure of Accumulation." Pp. 226–244 in Victor D. Lippit ed. *Radical Political Economy: Explorations in Alternative Economic Analysis*. Armonk, NY: M.E. Sharpe.

Kondratieff, N.D. 1935. "The Long Waves in Economic Life." *Review of Economic Statistics* 17, 6: 105–115.

Kotz, David 1994. "Interpreting the Social Structure of Accumulation Theory." Pp. 50–71 in David Kotz, Terrence McDonough and Michael Reich eds. *Social Structures of Accumulation: The Political Economy of Growth and Crisis*. New York: Cambridge University Press.

——— 2008. "The Financial and Economic Crisis of 2008: A Systemic Crisis of Neoliberal Capitalism." *Review of Radical Political Economics*, forthcoming.

Kotz, David, Terrence McDonough and Michael Reich 1994. *Social Structures of Accumulation: The Political Economy of Growth and Crisis*. New York: Cambridge University Press.

Lippit, Victor D. 1997. "The Reconstruction of a Social Structure of accumulation in the United States." *Review of Radical Political Economics* 29, 3: 11–21.

——— 2005. *Capitalism*. London: Routledge.

McDonough, Terrence 1994. "Social Structures of Accumulation, Contingent History and Stages of Capitalism." Pp. 72–84 in David Kotz, Terrence

McDonough and Michael Reich eds. *Social Structures of Accumulation: The Political Economy of Growth and Crisis*. New York: Cambridge University Press.

Resnick, Stephen A. and Richard D. Wolff 1987. *Knowledge and Class: A Marxian Critique of Political Economy*. Chicago: University of Chicago Press.

Schumpeter, Joseph 1939. *Business Cycles: A Theoretical, Historical and Statistical Analysis of the Capitalist Process*. New York: McGraw-Hill.

Weisskopf, Thomas E. 1996. "Marxian Crisis Theory and the Contradictions of Late Twentieth Century Capitalism." Pp. 368–391 in Victor D. Lippit, ed. 1996. "Radical Political Economy: Explorations in Alternative Economic Analysis." NY: M.E. Sharpe.

Wolfson, Martin H. 1994. "The Financial System and the Social Structure of Accumulation." Pp. 133–145 in David Kotz, Terrence McDonough and Michael Reich eds. *Social Structures of Accumulation: The Political Economy of Growth and Crisis*. New York: Cambridge University Press.

THREE

A Reconceptualization of Social Structure of Accumulation Theory

Martin H. Wolfson and David M. Kotz

Introduction

Social structure of accumulation (SSA) theory is one of the most important theoretical innovations in heterodox economics. It makes sense of much of economic history. It links theoretical analysis with concrete institutional investigation. It provides a basis for understanding the evolution of capitalism over time, as well as institutional differences among capitalist systems in different countries. Not the least, SSA theory provides a basis for explaining the periodic severe economic crises that have arisen in capitalist history.

However, we believe that SSA theory has encountered difficulties in seeking to explain the economic reality of the past several decades. By most accounts, the postwar (post-World War II) SSA in the United States broke up in the late 1960s and early 1970s. After a decade of crisis and struggle, a new institutional structure was created, initially in the United States and the United Kingdom, which undermined government regulation and promoted capital mobility. This model, which soon became dominant globally, is commonly referred to as neoliberalism. In the United States, neoliberalism has meant increased income inequality, deregulation of industrial and financial markets, increased influence of financial markets over corporate decision-making, fiscal policy emphasizing tax cuts for the wealthy and cutbacks in social programs, monetary policy that puts a greater emphasis on reducing inflation than unemployment, and relatively sluggish economic growth.

How can we understand neoliberalism in the context of SSA theory? Did a new SSA emerge in the neoliberal era? Or is this era better understood as a period of crisis of the old SSA?

In our view, it has now become clear that neoliberalism is not a continuation of the crisis of the old postwar SSA, because it constituted a new, coherent, institutional structure that has been in existence since at least the early 1980s.[1] On the other hand, there is a problem with regarding neoliberalism as a new SSA because economic growth under neoliberalism has been subpar; central to SSA theory has been the idea that a new SSA promotes strong economic growth.

The growth rate of gross domestic product (GDP) in the United States during the period of the postwar SSA, from 1948 through 1973, was 3.98 percent per year, whereas growth during the crisis years of 1973–79 averaged 2.95 percent per year. Growth during the neoliberal period, which we date from 1979 to 2007, averaged 2.96 percent per year, which is not significantly different from the growth rate during the crisis period of the postwar SSA.[2] If one were to argue that a new SSA began in 1990, the result is the same. The annual GDP growth rate during 1973–90 was 2.93 percent per year, while during 1990–2007 it was 2.99 percent per year, a difference that is not significant given the lack of precision of national income account series.[3] (Data are from the U.S. Bureau of Economic Analysis, 2009.)

We are proposing a reconceptualization of SSA theory. The difficulty in using current SSA theory to explain the neoliberal era has led us to reconsider some basic aspects of the theory of an SSA. In the next two sections, we offer a critique of the current theory. We conclude that the assumption linking SSAs with rapid economic growth should be rejected.

In the section "Class Contradictions," we propose a new basis to understand SSAs, arguing that they can best be understood as institutional structures that (temporarily) stabilize class contradictions. The following section asserts that SSAs come in two varieties, "liberal" and "regulated," depending on the relative power of capital and labor.[4] Thus,

---

[1] One of the authors, David Kotz, argued in earlier works that neoliberalism represented a continuing crisis of the previous SSA.

[2] We use data through 2007 because it is the most recent business cycle peak year.

[3] Nonetheless, there are those who argue that a new SSA was established. The range of possible dates found in the literature for the beginning of a new SSA runs from 1979 to the mid-1990s. In the calculation of growth rates, however, one must be careful to use comparable stages of the business cycle. For instance, 1948, 1973, 1979, 1990, and 2007 are all peak years of the business cycle.

[4] Despite the use of the term "regulated SSA" for one of the two types of SSA, the state and other institutions do regulate economic behavior in liberal as well as in regulated SSAs. The differences between the two types of SSA are complex and multidimensional; they are explained in considerable detail later.

using this new definition of an SSA, we conclude that neoliberalism is best understood as a liberal SSA.

The section "SSAs and Capitalist Crises" analyzes the different economic problems and crises that occur in the two different kinds of SSAs. We argue that the severe financial and economic meltdown that began in 2008 represents the arrival of the crisis phase of the neoliberal SSA. The section "Liberal and Regulated SSAs and the Rate of Growth" discusses the proposition that economic growth tends to be faster under regulated SSAs than under liberal SSAs. A final section summarizes our conclusions. While our historical examples are drawn from the United States, we believe our argument applies generally to SSA theory.

The Current Theory of an SSA

Early formulations of SSA theory emphasized the stability provided by an institutional structure. Gordon, Edwards, and Reich (1982: 23) write that "Without a stable and favorable external environment, capitalist investment in production will not proceed. We refer to this external environment as the social structure of accumulation. ... The social structure of accumulation consists of all the institutions that impinge upon the accumulation process." They argue that the stability provided by the institutional structure encourages capitalist investment and economic growth.

Eventually, the SSA ceases to contribute to growth: either growth destabilizes the institutions of the SSA or the institutions provide a barrier to further growth. The economy, however, "retains the *same* social structure of accumulation once it has begun to display diminishing returns" (Gordon, Edwards, and Reich 1982: 34; emphasis in original). The prolonged period in which the SSA no longer effectively promotes accumulation is usually referred to as a crisis of the old SSA (although the term "crisis" is also used for the short-run economic recessions that occur in both phases of the life of an SSA). A crisis in the sense of a prolonged period of a poorly working SSA requires a restructuring of institutions to overcome the crisis: "we can define an economic crisis as a period of economic instability that requires institutional reconstruction for renewed stability and growth" (Gordon, Edwards, and Reich 1982: 30). In all, each SSA constitutes a specific stage of capitalism.

Later formulations of the theory focused more on ways that the institutional structure enhanced capitalist power: "The institutional structure of the postwar social structure of accumulation in the United States was consolidated in such a way as to enhance the political-economic power of the capitalist class" (Bowles, Gordon, and Weisskopf 1989: 167). Capitalist power leads to profits: "profits are made possible ... by the power of the capitalist class over other economic actors," while profits, in turn, lead to growth: "capital accumulation ... is fundamentally conditioned by the level and stability of capitalist profitability" (Gordon, Weisskopf, and Bowles 1987: 44).

There are difficulties in applying either formulation of SSA theory to the neoliberal regime, although events in the postwar U.S. economy up through the 1970s can readily be explained. In the late 1960s, with a strongly growing economy and a very low unemployment rate, labor became powerful enough to raise wages and thus contribute to reduced corporate profits. From the point of view of the earlier formulation, this eroded the capital-labor institutional relationship and the stability it had provided, and thus the postwar SSA; from the latter point of view, it was a direct challenge to the corporate power that formed the basis of the SSA.

A period of crisis emerged in the 1970s. Corporations and unions fought over the distribution of income, and the wage-price spiral of the 1970s was evidence of the inability of either party to gain the upper hand. The unanticipated inflation negatively affected the profits of financial institutions. By the 1970s, some of the institutions of the postwar SSA had eroded, and those that remained were no longer functioning to promote stability, profitability, or economic growth. The postwar SSA was in crisis, with the year 1973 commonly regarded as marking the transition from well-working SSA to crisis.

However, by the early 1980s, capital's power had been restored, and it used its influence over the state to put a new institutional structure in place. Restrictive monetary policy increased unemployment, and the rising dollar encouraged the movement of production abroad, thus reducing wages and undermining unions. The new Reagan administration was able to use "free-market" ideology to promote permanent replacement of workers, a general hostility toward unions, market deregulation, tax cuts for the wealthy, and the rollback of protective labor regulations.[5]

In the creation of the "free-market" economy in the United States, and the beginnings of a neoliberal global economy, a new institutional

---

[5] We put the words "free market" in quotes because, contrary to the conventional wisdom, the "free market" period was not one in which the government withdrew from intervention in economic affairs and left the market "free" to its own devices.

enable us to understand neoliberalism as the basis of the contemporary SSA and apply SSA theory to the institutional structure under which we have lived for more than a quarter-century.

Class Contradictions

Even if rejecting the connection between SSAs and rapid economic growth enables us to understand neoliberalism as an SSA, we are still faced with another difficulty in current SSA theory: what is the basis upon which the institutions that constitute an SSA are built? The institutions of the postwar SSA are said to be specific to the postwar period and thus not necessarily a guide to the institutional structure of neoliberalism. However, by building upon some insights in the literature, and examining them through the lens of class contradictions, we can gain greater understanding.

Gordon, Edwards, and Reich (1982: 31) argue that the emergence of "a successful new social structure ... will reflect the alignment of class forces (and other social influences) that produce it." Kotz (1994: 55) points out that "what the social structure of accumulation does is to stabilize class conflict and channel it in directions that are not unduly disruptive of accumulation."

We argue that the institutions that constitute an SSA, including those of neoliberalism, reflect the (temporary) stabilization of the contradictions of capitalism. What are these contradictions? The most important is the fundamental contradiction in capitalist society, that between capital and labor. The others include contradictions within capital and within labor, representing conflicts and the struggle for unity within each group (and may also represent international dimensions of these contradictions). By contradiction we mean a dialectical relationship between two groups, which may or may not be an antagonistic conflict. The two groups in a contradiction are always in struggle with one another, although there can be a temporary equilibrium – that is, a temporary stabilization of the struggle.

What is the relationship between the institutions of an SSA and the temporary stabilization of these contradictions? We argue that the stabilization of the contradiction between capital and labor provides the foundation for the institutional restructuring that produces a new SSA.

This contradiction can be stabilized in one of two ways. Either labor is strong enough to challenge capital and share power, or capital can overwhelm labor and dictate conditions.[7] The results of this struggle are seen most directly in the workplace and labor market. In the 1930s and 1940s, when labor was strong enough to challenge capital, it was able to win union contracts, improve workplace conditions, establish new health and retirement benefits in core industries, and force the sharing of productivity gains during the ensuing post-World War II period. By contrast, in the neoliberal era capital's greater power has meant declining union density, worsening workplace conditions, disappearing benefits, and stagnating wages.

There are also indirect implications of the stabilization of the contradiction between capital and labor, and these are of great importance to the institutional structure of an SSA. We argue that the way that this contradiction is stabilized affects the relative influence of capital and labor over the state, and that this in turn will contribute to the existence of two different types of SSAs.

Liberal and Regulated SSAs

We argue that SSAs come in two varieties. We will refer to one type as a "liberal" SSA and the other as a "regulated" SSA. The reasons for this choice of terms will become apparent as we explain our analysis of the nature of these two different types of SSA. These two types of SSA differ along five dimensions: (1) the manner in which the capital-labor contradiction is temporarily stabilized; (2) the state role in the economy; (3) the contradictions within capital; (4) the contradictions within labor; and (5) the character of the dominant ideology.

As was stated earlier, in our view the underlying difference between the two types of SSA is the different manner in which the capital-labor contradiction is temporarily stabilized. A regulated SSA embodies one form of stabilization of the capital-labor relation, in which labor has significant power, which capital is compelled to accept, producing a capital-labor compromise. A liberal SSA embodies a different form of stabilization of the capital-labor relation, in which capital does not accept compromise with labor but instead achieves a high degree of dominance over labor.[8]

---

[7] A situation in which labor dominated capital likely would go beyond capitalism and create a socialist system.

[8] Labor always has some ability to resist capital, and full domination by capital is not actually achieved. However, the active pursuit of full domination by capital characterizes liberal SSAs, in contrast to the acceptance by capital of compromise with labor in a regulated SSA.

differs according to the type of SSA.[13] In a liberal SSA, capital's ability to restrain the growth of wages and shift the distribution of income in its favor tend to result in inadequate aggregate demand and overcapacity, with companies able to produce more than they can sell. The intensified competitive environment, interacting with sluggish demand, can lead to a situation of "coercive investment" (Crotty 1993), in which companies are compelled to invest in labor-saving technology to cut costs and compete for a limited market share. In addition, liberal SSAs are typically plagued by financial crises (Wolfson 1994a). Unregulated financial markets, in a competitive environment in which wealthy investors are seeking higher and higher returns, bring heightened financial instability.

On the other hand, regulated SSAs are subject to "profit-squeeze" crises. Given an institutional context that brings a high degree of bargaining power for labor, periods of low unemployment can put pressure on corporate profits. Research on economic crises in the postwar SSA has documented this result. Weisskopf (1979) and Kotz (2009a) both found that the main cause of short-run economic crises (recessions) during the postwar regulated SSA was a profit squeeze due to rising real wages in late expansions. By contrast, Kotz (2009a) found that profit squeeze was not the cause of crises in the neoliberal period.[14]

Our analysis also suggests that the particular crisis tendencies that play a role in the decay and collapse of the two types of SSA are different. Near the end of the postwar SSA in the late 1960s, the strongly growing economy further enhanced labor's power. And as Gordon, Weisskopf, and Bowles (1987: 49–50) point out, capital's power and profits were also challenged by international competitors and domestic movements for occupational safety and health, environmental protection, and consumer product safety, among others. A stubbornly long-lasting profit-squeeze crisis was the result. After a decade of inconclusive struggle in the 1970s, capital was finally able to get the upper hand in the early 1980s, but only by the replacement of the previous regulated SSA by a new liberal SSA.

Now it appears that this liberal SSA – neoliberalism – may have entered its period of decay, with the onset of a major financial and economic

[13] Here we are using the term "crisis" in a different way from its use in describing the period of breakdown of an SSA.

[14] Kotz (2009a) found that a profit-squeeze crisis did not appear even when unemployment fell below 4 percent at the end of the 1990s. Although profits did decline from 1997 to 2000 prior to the 2001 recession, the decline was not due to a profit squeeze; real wages during that time period rose more slowly than productivity. In the context of significantly reduced bargaining power for labor in the liberal SSA, low unemployment did not have the same effect as in the preceding regulated SSA.

crisis in 2008. Neoliberalism eventually brought a financial and economic crisis so severe that it threatens the survival of the SSA. This can be understood as the result of the tendencies toward inadequate demand, overcapacity, and coerced investment, as well as the growing financial instability produced by neoliberal institutions. Kotz (2009b) presents an interpretation of the crisis that began in 2008 as the beginning of the period of decay of the neoliberal SSA.[15]

Just as capital reacted to labor's enhanced bargaining power in the postwar SSA, we would expect capital to react to the collapse of any regulated SSA by striving to create a new institutional structure that secures its domination of labor. Also, since the long-run crisis phase of a liberal SSA is likely to involve the problem of inadequate aggregate demand due to weak bargaining power of labor, a likely resolution of this crisis may be a reaction through which labor is able to increase its power. Under capitalism, this would mean a new institutional structure involving a sharing of power with capital, which could shift the distribution of income in its favor and address the aggregate demand problem, as happened in the 1930s–40s. Although there is nothing logically necessary about either of these conclusions, and indeed a transition to an institutional structure beyond capitalism remains a possibility, they are consistent with the observed tendency for U.S. history to be characterized by an alternation between liberal and regulated SSAs. Therefore, we would expect to see attempts to create a new regulated SSA in the wake of the crisis and dismantling of neoliberalism.

Liberal and Regulated SSAs and the Rate of Growth

The concepts of liberal and regulated SSAs introduce a new way to utilize SSA theory to analyze differences in the long-run rate of economic growth in various periods. There are theoretical reasons to expect that economic growth would be slower in periods of a liberal SSA than in periods of a regulated SSA. First, a liberal SSA tends to give rise to a problem of insufficient aggregate demand over the long run, because it tends to lower both real wages and public spending. Second, a liberal SSA tends to create instability on the macroeconomic level by renouncing state countercyclical spending and taxation policies, by reducing the effectiveness of "automatic stabilizers" through shrinking social welfare programs, and by loosening public regulation of the financial sector.

---

[15] See also Kotz (2008).

This renders the system more vulnerable to major financial crises and depressions. Third, the cutthroat competition of a liberal SSA tends to turn the focus of corporate managers toward short-run strategies, which typically run counter to making the long-run investments that promote a rapid rate of capital accumulation. Fourth, an independent and deregulated financial sector in a liberal SSA tends to divert investable funds from long-run productive investment to speculative activities.

Earlier in this chapter, we presented empirical evidence that the neoliberal SSA in the United States brought GDP growth that is not only slower than during the heyday of the previous regulated SSA but also not significantly faster than during the period of crisis of the previous regulated SSA. Kotz (2003) found evidence that, during the periods of two liberal and two regulated SSAs in the United States since 1900, economic growth was slower in the two liberal SSAs than in either of the two regulated SSAs.[16] However, more empirical work would be required to determine whether this relationship between growth rate and type of SSA holds in general.

Whether an SSA does or does not promote rapid accumulation, both regulated and liberal SSAs facilitate the process of profit-making. Both types tend to promote high profitability during the period when they are working effectively, before the crisis of the SSA begins. The reconceptualization of the SSA theory proposed here will make SSA theory more persuasive and more consistent with the historical evidence. It will also facilitate the use of SSA theory to analyze contemporary neoliberalism.

An interesting question for further investigation is whether either of the two types of SSA, liberal or regulated, tends to last longer than the other, including both the period when the SSA is working effectively and the following period of crisis prior to the creation of a new SSA. A related question is whether either type of SSA tends to enter its crisis phase sooner than is the case for the other. Because of disagreements about the exact starting and ending dates of the various SSAs and the starting and ending dates of the crisis phase, the historical evidence on these points is ambiguous. Also, it is not clear from a theoretical perspective whether we should expect different lifespans for the two types of SSA as a whole, or different durations before the crisis sets in. This is an interesting topic for further research.

---

[16] In Kotz (2003) the two regulated SSAs covered the periods 1900–16 and 1947–73, while the two liberal SSAs were in 1920–32 and 1980–2001. The intervals between those periods were considered periods of crisis and transition between SSAs.

Summary and Conclusion

In summary, we conclude that the concept of an SSA should be reconceptualized in the following ways:

First, the link between an SSA and rapid capital accumulation should be severed. Capitalists' objective in creating the institutions of an SSA is to promote profit-making; the institutions thus created may or may not promote rapid growth. Second, an SSA performs its role by embodying the temporary stabilization of capitalism's class contradictions, in particular the fundamental contradiction between capital and labor. The particular institutional structure that constitutes an SSA will represent the relative balance of power between the classes. Third, the nature of the SSA will depend on the way in which the class contradictions have been temporarily stabilized. Liberal SSAs emphasize a "free-market" approach and indicate a high degree of dominance by capital. On the other hand, regulated SSAs put greater restraints on capital and represent conditions of capital-labor compromise. Fourth, the nature of the economic problems and crises will tend to differ between liberal and regulated SSAs. A regulated SSA tends to exhibit profit-squeeze crises, whereas a liberal SSA is likely to suffer from inadequate aggregate demand, overcapacity, "coercive investment," and financial crises. Finally, the rate of economic growth of a regulated SSA is likely to be higher than that of a liberal SSA.

References

Bowles, Samuel, David M. Gordon, and Thomas E. Weisskopf 1989. "Business Ascendancy and Economic Impasse: A Structural Retrospective on Conservative Economics, 1979–87." *Journal of Economic Perspectives* 3, 1: 107–34.

1990. *After the Waste Land*. Armonk, New York: M.E. Sharpe.

Crotty, James 1993. "Rethinking Marxian Investment Theory: Keynes-Minsky Instability, Competitive Regime Shifts and Coerced Investment." *Review of Radical Political Economics* 25, 1: 1–26.

Dumenil, Gerard and Dominique Levy 2004. *Capital Resurgent: Roots of the Neoliberal Revolution*. Cambridge, MA: Harvard University Press.

Gordon, David M., Richard Edwards, and Michael Reich 1982. *Segmented Work, Divided Workers*. New York: Cambridge University Press.

Gordon, David M., Thomas E. Weisskopf, and Samuel Bowles 1987. "Power, Accumulation and Crisis: The Rise and Demise of the Postwar Social Structure of Accumulation." Pp. 43–58 in Robert Cherry et al. eds. *The Imperiled Economy: Book I, Macroeconomics from a Left Perspective*. New York: The Union for Radical Political Economics.

Following the Great Depression and World War II, new national social structures of accumulation (SSAs) emerged in the capitalist world in which the state actively regulated the macroeconomy as well as key economic sectors, nationalized some industries in many countries, and provided a set of social programs that is often summed up as the "welfare state." The international economy was also managed by the most powerful capitalist states to a greater extent than had previously been the case. In the decades following World War II, the old liberal ideology, theory, and policy approach came to be viewed as outmoded, relegated to an early, "immature" period of capitalist development. Even the word "capitalism" was replaced by terms such as the "mixed economy."

No one expected what came next. Time seemed to go into reverse after around 1980, as the dominant ideology, theory, and policy shifted back in the direction of the unfettered market. The emergence of the term "neoliberalism," to describe a new version of an old set of ideas, was not surprising. At first most analysts who were critical of the new (old) direction of change assumed that it was a temporary phenomenon, bred by a crisis of the old regime of state-managed capitalism. However, more than twenty-five years later it is apparent that the new direction was not a temporary lurch backward, but represented a new form of capitalism with some staying power.

We view neoliberalism as a coherent, multileveled entity whose core features include political-economic institutions, policies, theories, and ideology. We defer a discussion of the institutions of neoliberalism to later sections of this chapter, but some comment on its other dimensions is called for here. Neoliberal ideology is marked by glorification of individual choice, markets, and private property; a view of the state as inherently an enemy of individual freedom and economic efficiency; and an extreme individualist conception of society. The dominant theory is a free-market version of neoclassical economic theory, associated with such names as Milton Friedman, Friedrich Hayek, and Ronald Coase.[3]

Neoliberalism advocates a trilogy of policies known as liberalization, privatization, and stabilization. The first, liberalization, refers to freeing markets and firms from state regulation, including the removal of barriers to movement of goods and capital (although not people) across national boundaries. Privatization refers to turning state enterprises over

---

[3] This theory has come in various versions, such as Monetarism, rational expectations theory, and new classical economics, but all have shared the same basic assumptions and a vision of the capitalist "free-market" economy as an optimally self-regulating entity.

to private owners and also contracting out to private companies services that had traditionally been directly delivered by the state. The misnamed "stabilization" refers to a shift in monetary policy to focus solely on preventing inflation rather than promoting lower unemployment or economic growth. State fiscal policies are directed at reducing taxes on business and the rich while reducing or eliminating social programs.

A key point of contention surrounds the question of whether, under neoliberalism, the state reduces its intervention in the economy or rather just redirects it in ways that benefit capital. We cannot enter fully into this debate here (see Chapter 3 of this volume). It is clear that the state in the neoliberal era has reduced or eliminated many programs that had directly benefited the working class, while stepping up certain activities that directly aid capital, such as stricter enforcement of intellectual property rights. Perhaps the clearest case of increased state activism has been intervention in the class struggle to weaken the trade union movement, with British Prime Minister Margaret Thatcher's defeat of the Miners Union and U.S. President Ronald Reagan's breaking of the Air Traffic Controllers Union as seminal examples. The promotion of "competitiveness" has become the touchstone of state action in many areas of society.

However, in our view the antistate ideology and theory of neoliberalism are not just window dressing. Among the state regulatory programs that have been dismantled in the neoliberal era are some that had originated, wholly or partially, in response to the demands of business. These include regulation or public ownership in such areas as power and transportation, which are key inputs for most of capital. Another example is antitrust, which has been scaled back drastically, allowing free action by giant firms with market power, which most directly affects the firms that use their products. Public investment in the infrastructure necessary for capitalist profit-making has been reduced in the neoliberal era. It is clear that big capital, which had in an earlier era favored an active state, including state regulation and even public ownership in certain areas, came to prefer taking its chances with market forces despite the disadvantages for capital of such a path.

Some analysts prefer the term "globalization" to characterize contemporary capitalism. These two aspects of the contemporary era – globalization and neoliberalism – are closely interconnected. Neoliberal policies of free trade and the repeal of capital controls, as well as the overall "hollowing out" of the national state, fostered the globalization of production, trade, and class relations. Capital controls had emerged

Thus, according to the standard SSA theory, if global neoliberalism is a new SSA, then one should observe a more rapid pace of accumulation once global neoliberalism had been established, compared to the crisis phase of the previous SSA. Chapter 3 of this volume presents data suggesting that, in the United States, GDP growth has been no faster in the neoliberal era than it was in the crisis phase of the preceding SSA.[5] It is difficult to make a case that the neoliberal transformation accelerated economic growth in most parts of the world (see the data presented in the section "Why Global Neoliberalism Should be Considered an SSA").

In our view, the neoliberal institutional structure should be considered an SSA, but not based on its effect on the economic growth rate. We agree with the proposal for revising the understanding of an SSA put forward in Chapter 3 of this volume. That chapter argues that the early SSA literature never made a convincing case that each new coherent and long-lasting institutional structure in capitalism would necessarily promote accumulation that is rapid by some historical standard. Instead, such an institutional structure promotes profit-making and serves as a framework for the capital accumulation process, although the resulting rate of accumulation may be rapid or more moderate. Reinterpreting an SSA as a coherent, long-lasting institutional structure that promotes profit-making and serves as framework for capital accumulation, a strong case can be made that the global neoliberal institutional structure is an SSA. In the following sections, we will make that case by considering the key institutions that have arisen in the neoliberal era, on a global scale and within individual countries.

International Institutions of the Global Neoliberal SSA

Novel developments in the international economy include a significant increase in the international movement of capital, goods, and money, and a geographical extension of capitalist relations of production.

---

[5] It is possible to find data that show rapid economic growth during the neoliberal era in the U.S. economy, but only by considering the neoliberal SSA to have begun in the mid-1990s. Beginning in 1995, a speculative bubble in the U.S. stock market propelled five years of rapid economic growth. However, there is no compelling reason to date the start of the neoliberal SSA in 1995, apart from the rapid growth that began at that time. It is tautological to decide the date of a new SSA on the basis of the start of rapid growth – it should be dated on the basis of an analysis of institution creation. Furthermore, growth in the U.S. economy has not been rapid since the collapse of the stock market bubble in 2000.

Important here is the ability to fragment production across borders and to subsequently reintegrate the process through trade. From a Marxian perspective, a consequent transnationalization of class relations is of central importance. A multilayered system of transnational governance has emerged, including the World Trade Organization (WTO) and the international financial institutions. Finally, the United States has become the sole remaining superpower in the world system.

The international transformations accompanying the emergence of the global neoliberal SSA are centered around the globalization of the capitalist economy. This contention is of course controversial. Some observe that international activity is as old as capitalism itself and contend that therefore the current emphasis on globalization is misplaced, serving to discourage resistance to the implementation of neoliberal policies. This chapter argues that globalization and neoliberalism are indeed strongly related, as important and mutually reinforcing constituent parts of the current SSA.

Globalization in the contemporary period can be located in two separate but not entirely unrelated developments: an increase in the mobility of capital and an expansion of its geographic reach. Barriers to the free movement of goods, capital, and money have been greatly reduced. A key aspect of this has been the deregulation of capital movements as well as increasing state hospitality to foreign direct investment (Bryan 1995). Technological developments in information and communication technology have been important here as well as containerization and other innovations in transportation. This increase in capital mobility has taken place both at the level of physical productive capital and at the level of money capital through the massive intensification of international financial activity (Bryan 1995).

The most consequential result of this newfound mobility is fragmentation of production into multiple and often distant components across borders and then reintegration of these components into global production chains through both trade and the internal logistical operations of transnational corporations. Each part of the production process can be located in a part of the world that is capable of carrying out that process in the most profitable manner. The ability to allocate production in this manner is achieved partly through sheer size and concentration of resources. A further essential condition is the assembling of knowledge of local conditions in disparate parts of the globe. This is achieved through the creation of transnational blocs of capital through reciprocal ownership and joint venture agreements. The network organization celebrated by Manuel Castells (2000) plays a role here. The establishment of legal regimes either internationally or in the separate states that are hospitable to the cross border movement of capital investment is also an almost indispensable condition.

The second development is a subsequent dramatic geographical extension of capitalist relations of production. The collapse of the Eastern European regimes inaugurated a rapid transition to capitalism in the former Soviet sphere of influence. The post-Mao reforms started a similar but slower and more measured transition process in China. These transitions have opened up for global capitalism vast supplies of raw materials, extensive investment opportunities, massive pools of cheap labor, and large new markets. These developments also mark the end of alternative sources of support, both economic and military, for less developed states. They have a profound ideological significance in that they represent both the end of the Cold War and the end of an alternative development model for less developed areas. They also reinforce the sense that "there is no alternative" in the developed world.[6]

These developments are different from the earlier internationalization of the commodity circuit of capital that created an international division of labor. Since it is possible for commodity circulation to link the production of different modes of production, the circulation of commodities did not initially condition the globalization of capitalist class relations. Indeed, precapitalist modes of production may have been temporarily strengthened through access to international commodity circuits. The widespread relocation of capitalist production operations to previously undeveloped areas has now brought an end to this transitional era.

In conjunction with the global integration of production circuits, global integration of the money circuit has substantial consequences for the globalization of the specifically capitalist system because this globalization serves to transnationalize the capitalist class. This is the really radical significance of the globalization of finance. Globalizing the money circuit with the elimination of capital controls and the electronic linking of the world market integrates those who have a right to a

---

[6] The states ruled by European Communist Parties did not formally begin a transition to capitalism until 1989–91, and China did not clearly become capitalist until around the early 1990s, dates that are somewhat later than those for the formation of the other major institutions of the neoliberal SSA. However, by the early 1980s China had begun its integration into the capitalist world market, and the Soviet Union and its European CMEA partners had also begun to significantly reorient their economies toward trade with, and loans from, the capitalist world.

portion of the surplus produced under capitalist relations of production. This is accompanied by the global integration of the circuit of production including its extension to the less developed world. Thus, a transnationalizing capitalist class is brought into relationship with a transnational working class. The neo-Gramscian school in international political economy (Cox 1987; Gill 1994; Gill and Law 1988), the Amsterdam school (Overbeek 2001; Pijl 1997, 1998; van Apeldoorn 2004), and the political sociologist William Robinson (2004) have studied the formation of this transnational capitalist class and the establishment of its hegemony in international relations.

There is another sense, however, in which the globalization of the money circuit creates the conditions under which the economy can be said to be globalized. If financial capital is mobile enough, it can impose globalized norms of profitability in the regions in which it operates. In this way even strictly localized economic decision-making can be said to partake of the global economy in the sense that even these forms of economic calculation must be carried out with reference to global economic conditions. Increased trade liberalization has had contradictory results, leading at the same time to increased competition on the product market and increased cooperation through reciprocal share ownership, joint ventures, tight subcontracting arrangements, and the like (Castells 2000: 77–215). A merger wave has consolidated capitals across borders, leading to the creation of ever larger corporate entities.

The globalization of capitalist production and class relations inevitably raises the question of the creation of transnational institutions to govern these economic relations. Robinson (2004) has theorized the emergence of a transnational state. Unlike the traditional members of the nation-state system, the new institutions of transnational governance do not concentrate sovereignty over a particular territory. These institutions are layered and overlapping, existing at multiple geographical scales. It must be noted that they are often created by states through agreements and treaties. Although these institutions have never fully matured, nevertheless they assume some limited authority over these same states, sometimes through control over market access and sometimes through the exercise of ideological hegemony and influence. (See Chapter 7 of this volume.)

The WTO is perhaps the paradigmatic example of these developments. Created by treaty between its member states, it is able to enforce trade rules and try violators in a quasi-judicial way, imposing fines and other sanctions. Other institutions of this kind include formal organizations like the OECD and the G8. Informal organizations like the World Economic Forum and the Trilateral Commission and various NGOs also participate and are increasingly numerous. These institutions issue advice and influential policy prescriptions. Regional organizations like the European Union and NAFTA have been constructed. At the same time traditional nation-states still play an essential role, enforcing neoliberal prescriptions and pursuing "competitiveness." After all, capitalism requires political entities that can exercise coercion when needed, through such instruments as armies and prisons. Unless a truly global capitalist state emerges that both has such capabilities and is recognized as legitimate, nation-states will continue to be necessary to the reproduction of capitalism. The degree of "stateness" of the developing new complex of global institutions is contentious as it incorporates and combines state sovereignty with other forms of governance.

Aside from the WTO, the most prominent of these transnational organizations are the international financial institutions including the IMF and the World Bank. These organizations have been responsible for the imposition of structural adjustment programs on developing countries in return for loans and aid. These structural adjustment programs consisted of a package of neoliberal policies including opening the economy to foreign trade, floating exchange rates, privatizations, deregulation, an end to subsidies and reductions in social spending. The imposition of these policies marked a sharp transition in many states and an end to more active import-substitution development policies.

An important international institutional change involves the reinstatement and extension of U.S. hegemony. Despite their increasing economic power, the military capacities of Germany and Japan have remained repressed and underdeveloped. There is little evidence of a political desire in Europe to create a full military counterweight to the United States. The "Japan that could say no" evaporated in the face of economic stagnation. Indeed, at the moment, trilateralism appears to have been little more than a futurologist speculation. Thus, the collapse of the Soviet Bloc left the United States as the only remaining military superpower. This increase in relative political and military strength has led to territorial advances in the U.S. sphere of influence. Starting in the 1990s the United States has been maneuvering for political influence and control of raw materials in the central Asian and Caucasian former Soviet republics. After the attack of September 11, 2001, the United States led the occupation of Afghanistan and Iraq. Tensions have grown with Iran. An American empire has been further consolidated, most significantly through the already well-consolidated thrust to the east in Europe with the extension of NATO and the enlargement of the European Union.

Another category of institutions of global neoliberalism involves the nature of capital. First, the nature of competition between large corporations changed. Such competition had been co-respective and carefully regulated in the previous period. While large firms competed over market share, they generally eschewed price competition, which would undermine the profits of the industry as a whole. Global neoliberalism saw the breakdown of such co-respective behavior among large firms replaced by unrestrained, cut-throat competition. Sharp price competition returned to the world of large corporations.

Second, the process of selection of CEOs of large corporations changed. Previously CEOs had usually been promoted from within the firm, from among the long-serving managers who had risen within the company. This practice was replaced by the development of an external labor market for CEOs, through which the top spot was often given to an outsider. This market-based process for selecting CEOs fostered a ramping up of CEO pay, as large corporations competed for top executives. In addition to contributing to the growing income inequality of neoliberalism, this change profoundly affected firm behavior. Instead of CEOs with careers that were intimately tied up with the firm, now CEOs became aware that they might stay with the firm only for a short while before moving to a higher paying CEO job elsewhere. This promoted a shift in focus from long-run productive investments, which often take a long time to bear fruit, to gimmicks that can boost the firm's stock price over the short-run at the expense of doing what long-run success requires.

Third, the relation between financial and industrial capital changed in global neoliberalism. In the late nineteenth and early twentieth centuries, banks established a powerful position of control over many nonfinancial corporations in a number of leading capitalist countries (Kotz 1978). In the post-World War II SSA, in many countries, including the United States, financial institutions were closely regulated by the state in a way that compelled them to play a subsidiary yet supportive role in capital accumulation by nonfinancial capital. Under neoliberalism still another relation between financial and nonfinancial capital emerged, characterized by a high degree of independence of financial capital from nonfinancial capital. In the global neoliberal SSA, financial capital broke free from its close relation to nonfinancial capital and shifted to pursuing profits through purely financial activity. At the same time, many nonfinancial corporations began to engage directly in financial activities. This process had led to the introduction of the term "financialization" to describe this feature of contemporary capitalism.[7]

As Chapter 3 of this volume argues, a common thread running through most, if not all, of the institutions of global neoliberalism is the relatively full dominance of capital over labor in this SSA. The changes in the role of the state reinforced the power of capital over labor. The heightened competition among capitalists tends to put pressure on employers to drive down wages.[8]

Domestic Institutions of the
Global Neoliberal SSA

Several of the domestic institutions of global neoliberalism involve the capital-labor relation and the nature of the labor process. Others involve the role of the domestic nation-state in the economy. We will consider these in turn.

A prominent feature of global neoliberalism is the very noticeable weakening of the trade union movement in most countries. This changed the process through which wages and working conditions are determined. In the previous period, collective bargaining between trade unions and employers typically determined wages and working conditions in much of the economy. The change in the neoliberal era is often described as a shift to "market-determined" wages and conditions. However, that term obscures more than it reveals. The relative bargaining power of labor and capital is always the main determinant of changes in wages and working conditions.[9] A more accurate description of the new process of their determination is that power has shifted almost entirely to the employer. In the neoliberal era, employers are relatively free to determine wages and working conditions, constrained only by employer concerns with obtaining qualified workers. As Table 4.1 shows for four developed capitalist countries, wages rose much more slowly, if at all, in the neoliberal

---

[7] See Chapter 6 of this volume and Kotz 2010.
[8] Chapter 3 argues that the central feature of liberal SSAs – of which the contemporary SSA is one example – is the temporary stabilization of the capital-labor contradiction through relatively full capitalist dominance over labor. By contrast, other SSAs, referred to as "regulated SSAs" such as the postwar SSA, temporarily stabilize that contradiction through compromise between capital and labor.
[9] Other factors also affect wages and working conditions, including the level of development of a country's economy.

Table 4.1. *Growth Rate of Real Hourly Wages of Manufacturing Workers for Selected Countries (Annual Average Percentage Rate of Growth)*

Country	1953–73	1973–79	1979–2000
France	4.45	3.31	1.05
Japan	5.91	1.74	1.20
UK	2.04	1.44	1.03
USA	1.71	0.02	–0.47

Note: Data for all four countries prior to 1953 were not available. The third period goes through the year 2000, which was a business cycle peak year in the global economy. The first period is from the era of regulated capitalism, the third that of neoliberalism, and the second represents the crisis-ridden transition between the two.
Source: United Nations, various years.

era than they had in the period of regulated capitalism. The institution of employer-determined wages and working conditions is of course favorable for profit-making.

Second, in the previous SSA there was a system of labor segmentation, in which some jobs were in the "primary sector" and others in the "secondary sector." Primary sector jobs had relatively high pay, good fringe benefits, pay that rose with seniority, and significant job security, in contrast to jobs in the secondary sector. A part of the primary sector jobs consisted of unionized jobs, although some were nonunion managerial, professional, and technical jobs. In the neoliberal era, many of the primary sector jobs were transformed into jobs resembling secondary sector jobs under the previous SSA. Pay declined, benefits became less favorable or disappeared, pay increases became less certain, and job security disappeared. In many sectors employers substituted temporary and contingent workers for regular employees. Employers imposed such conditions under the banner of "labor market flexibility," an ironic name since the desired flexibility was only for those on one side of the labor market, namely employers, but not for workers. Employers gained the "flexibility" to treat workers as they wished, while workers lost the ability to protect their interests.

Third, new production systems were introduced in the neoliberal era. In place of the relatively rigid, yet low-cost, mass production technology of the previous SSA, many industries shifted to such new systems as flexible specialization and just-in-time production.

Fourth, a shift in production location patterns, known as "spatialization," arose in the period of global neoliberalism (see Chapter 5). Taking advantage of improved communication and transportation technologies, capital became much more effective at using the threat of moving production, or the actual moving of production, from one location to another as a means to more effectively control labor. While there has always been a tendency in capitalism for firm location to shift from high-wage to low-wage regions and countries, this tendency became much more pronounced in the neoliberal era. It has become a major means of establishing capital's power to control wages and working conditions.

Many of the domestic institutions of global neoliberalism involve the role of the state. We will identify six such institutions. First, the state renounced the use of Keynesian aggregate demand management techniques that had been aimed at achieving faster economic growth and a low level of unemployment. In the previous SSA, in most of the industrialized capitalist countries, both fiscal and monetary policies were generally directed to that end.[10] This contributed to a low average rate of unemployment in the developed capitalist countries during that period. In the neoliberal era states renounced stimulatory fiscal policy, instead aiming for a balanced budget, while monetary policy was redirected toward the aim of preventing inflation. This approach was justified by the new neoliberal economic theories, which held that neither fiscal nor monetary expansion could bring faster growth or lower unemployment in the long run but would instead just produce a higher inflation rate.[11] However, as Table 4.2 shows, the result was significantly higher average unemployment rates in the neoliberal era than in the era of regulated capitalism.

Second, there has been a sharp reduction in the "social wage" provided through the state, by cutting or eliminating such programs as guaranteed retirement pensions, unemployment compensation, disability insurance, and educational subsidies. Individual workers have had to rely on their own means to a much greater extent to finance such needs.

---

[10] In some countries during that period, if the unemployment rate fell so low that the resulting rise in labor's bargaining power began to seriously erode profits, the state would shift gears and use aggregate demand management to slow the economy and restore capital's ability to extract profits (Boddy and Crotty 1975).

[11] There is some controversy about the large fiscal deficits in the United States in the 1980s and the 2000s. Some view them as a cynical use of Keynesian techniques to expand the economy to improve the Republican Party's re-election chances. In our view, the large fiscal deficits of those two periods were driven by several other factors: (1) supply-side theories, which held that tax cuts would stimulate private investment; (2) a determination to shift income to the rich through tax cuts; and (3) growing military expenditures in both periods.

Table 4.2. *Average Unemployment Rate in Five Countries*[12]
(Percentage of the Labor Force)

Country	1950–73	1974–79	1980–2000
France	2.0	4.6	10.0
Italy	6.1	6.7	10.7
Japan	1.7	1.9	2.9
UK	1.8	4.8	8.5
USA	5.0	6.7	6.4

Source: OECD 2008.

Third, there has been a shift in the distribution of the financial burden of paying for public services. Taxes on capital and on the rich have been reduced, shifting the burden to wage earners and other groups.

Fourth, there has been a shift in the provision of a wide range of public services from state agencies and state employees to private companies operating under state-funded contracts. While accepting the principle that there exist "public goods" that cannot simply be sold by profit-seeking firms to individual users, private for-profit firms have come to play a greatly expanded role in the process of providing such publicly funded goods. This has taken place in a wide range of public services, including transportation, social welfare programs, education and job training, meal provision in public agencies and public schools, incarceration of prisoners, and various coercive services including guards, police, and the military.[13]

Neoliberal ideology, which holds that states are inherently inefficient while capitalist firms are optimally efficient, provides the justification for such contracting out of public services. At the same time, the hunger on the part of influential corporations for the opening of new sectors to profit-making assures a hefty lobbying push for the introduction of such programs. It is difficult to understand why a private firm, which must pay dividends to its shareholders as well as very high salaries to its executives, should be able to deliver the same public service more cheaply than

---

[12] Unlike for average GDP growth rates, the average unemployment rates must be for nonoverlapping periods. Hence, the second period in Table 4.2 starts in 1974 and the third period, in 1980.

[13] In 2007, the Bush Administration even proposed contracting out some federal tax collection responsibilities. However, the resulting charges of a return to medieval "tax farming" practices buried that proposal.

a well-run government agency. If there are any cost savings, it appears that they stem from the lower wages, inferior benefits, and worse working conditions of the private sector workers who actually deliver public services under such contracts. Such cost savings are not economic efficiencies but rather a shift of income from labor to capital. However, neoliberal economic theories regard the relatively good wages, benefits, and working conditions in the state sector as "monopoly rents" extracted by "greedy" public sector workers and their unions from the hapless taxpayers, with the connivance of elected officials. According to that view, turning public services over to private companies and the resulting shrinkage of the state workforce returns wages to their appropriate "market-determined" level.

Fifth, in many cases natural monopolies and sectors considered central to national economic welfare and progress, which had typically been subject to state regulation or state ownership in the previous SSA, were deregulated and privatized. In the various industrialized capitalist countries, this has applied to such sectors as transportation, communication, power, key metals (such as steel), military hardware, and financial institutions.[14] Neoliberal economists argued that regulation or public ownership of natural monopolies generates more costs than benefits, with the former including holding back technical progress that would otherwise erode the natural monopoly. For key sectors, they argued that state regulation or ownership had no justification, since private ownership and market forces always take the best care of national economic welfare.[15] As in the case of contracting out public services, a hidden agenda was driving down workers' wages and benefits in sectors where workers previously had significant bargaining power. As these sectors were deregulated and privatized, a new harsh competition quickly drove down wages and benefits, particularly in the transportation sector.

---

[14] In some developing countries even the water supply has been privatized under pressure from the international financial institutions. In the developed countries a similar result has been achieved through persuading millions of people to buy water in bottles, at a price higher than that of gasoline, instead of getting it from the tap at a fraction of the cost.

[15] Actual deregulation did not always proceed as far as neoliberal economists recommended. For example, in the United States in the early 1980s economists argued that federal insurance of bank deposits was unnecessary and should be eliminated, but Congress never took such a foolish step.

Sixth, the neoliberal era has seen the implementation of more repressive policies of social control (see Chapter 10 of this volume). In the United States, the prison population skyrocketed, as sentences for the types of infractions committed by poor and working people were extended. These policies, while of course not libertarian, are necessitated by neoliberalism through the rise in social dislocation, tension associated with rising levels of inequality, and the exclusion of marginalized populations and groups from the political process.

Why Global Neoliberalism Should be Considered an SSA

Presenting lists of institutions that characterize global neoliberalism does not suffice to show that it constitutes an SSA. In order to consider global neoliberalism an SSA, we must be able to make a case that it is a coherent, long-lasting set of institutions that promotes profit-making and forms a structure for the capital accumulation process. That neoliberalism has been long-lasting is now clear, since it has tenaciously held on for more than a quarter-century, although as is noted at the end of this chapter, its future is now uncertain. It is also clear that global neoliberalism is a coherent set of institutions. All of the key institutions are consistent with each other. They are also consistent with neoliberal ideology and neoliberal theories, which promote and glorify markets, private property, and individual choice, while vilifying collective actions, collective provision, and collective choices that tend to predominate when trade unions and states play a more active role.

Global neoliberalism promotes profit-making in several ways. First, its institutions increase the bargaining power of capital relative to that of labor. This results in slower wage growth and avoidance of the costs of providing good benefits and good working conditions. It also enables capital to exercise greater control over the labor process. Second, deregulation of business provides greater freedom of action for capital in pursuit of profits. The social costs of the pursuit of profit, which may be charged to capital in a regime of state regulation of business, can be pushed onto society as a whole. Third, the necessary social costs of maintaining society in general, and capitalist society in particular, which require government programs that must be paid for through taxes, are shifted from capital to labor and other groups in society. Fourth, whole new sectors have been opened to profit-making activity through privatization, deregulation, and

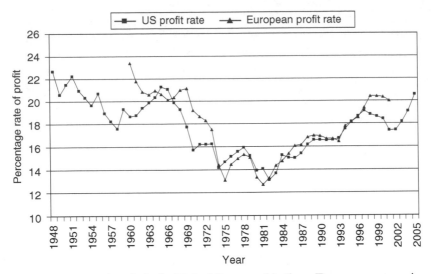

Figure 4.1. Rate of profit in the United States and in three European economies.
Note: The "European profit rate" is a combined rate of profit for Germany, France, and the U.K.
Source: For the U.S., Wolff (2001: 318, Figure 1 – extended series provided by Wolff to the authors). For Europe, Dumenil and Levy (2004: 24, Figure 3.1, data provided by Dumenil and Levy to the authors).

contracting out of public services. Fifth, the geographic scale of profit-making activity has been greatly expanded by opening the entire world to relatively free movement of goods, services, and capital. This generates economies of scale and specialization.

There is empirical evidence that global neoliberalism has been favorable for profit-making. As Figure 4.1 shows, in the U.S. economy, the rate of profit declined in the later part of the previous SSA, starting in the late 1960s. By the mid-1980s the profit rate had begun to recover, rising to its highest level since the 1960s by 2005. The profit rate for a combination of Germany, France, and the U.K. followed a similar pattern (Figure 4.1).

As the institutional structure of capitalism since the early 1980s, global neoliberalism has formed the structure within which capital accumulation has taken place, and it has shaped that process in particular ways. There are several ways in which global neoliberalism has shaped capital accumulation.

Global neoliberalism has affected the channels through which funds are obtained for capital accumulation. Under neoliberalism big corporations have paid out a large share of profits in the form of dividends

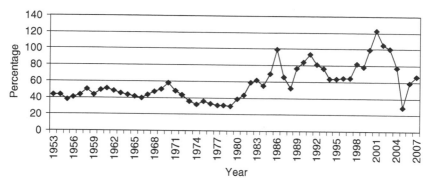

Figure 4.2. Net dividends as a percentage of after-tax profits for U.S. nonfinancial corporations.
Source: U.S. Federal Reserve System 2008, Flow of Funds Table F.102.

and stock buybacks, as Figures 4.2[16] and 4.3[17] show.[18] This reduces the internal funds available for accumulation, which tends to increase reliance on borrowing to finance accumulation. Neoliberal theory argues that financial market-based allocation of capital is more efficient than re-investment of retained earnings. However, that assumes that outside investors somehow possess knowledge about the real economic prospects of firms, which is not realistic. Outside investors follow fads and are easily taken in by skillful promoters and unscrupulous burnishers of corporate account books. This gives to the capital accumulation process a highly speculative, unstable character.

While the high rate of profit tends to encourage capital accumulation, there remains the problem of how the growing output resulting from accumulation can be sold. By constricting the growth of wages and state spending, global neoliberalism makes the sale of increased output dependent on some combination of rising luxury consumption, debt-financed

[16] Figure 4.2 shows a significantly higher dividend payout ratio after the early 1980s. The sharp one-year decline in that ratio in 2005 reflects both a very large increase in profits and a decline in dividend payouts that year.

[17] As Figure 4.3 shows, net new stock issued was almost always greater than zero before the late 1970s, indicating that nonfinancial corporations as a whole were raising funds from the sale of new stock. The usually negative value of net new stock issued after the early 1980s shows that nonfinancial corporations were sending funds out rather than raising funds in the equity market. In 2007, net stock buybacks rose to a remarkable 58 percent of cash flow.

[18] Large dividend payouts and stock buybacks are driven by corporate managers' obsession in the neoliberal era with the short-term performance of the company's stock, rather than the long-term economic performance of the company.

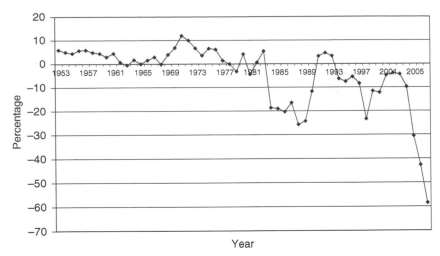

Figure 4.3. Net new stock issued as a percentage of cash flow for U.S. nonfinancial corporations.

Note: A negative value for net new stock issued means that nonfinancial corporation buybacks of their own stock exceeded new stock issued during that year. Cash flow is total internal funds plus dividends paid out.

Source: U.S. Federal Reserve System 2008, Flow of Funds Table F.102.

working class consumption that rises faster than wages, and/or purchases of means of production based on inflated expectations of future profits and demand growth. In the neoliberal era the new rich do not hide their lavish spending on luxury goods, unlike the less showy ethic of the rich in the previous SSA. The waves of speculative bubbles, which are associated with neoliberalism, have the effect of promoting exaggerated expectations about the growth of profits and demand in the future.[19]

On the level of theoretical analysis, it is not clear that global neoliberalism would tend to promote a rapid rate of capital accumulation, by comparison to earlier SSAs or even by comparison to the crisis period of past SSAs. On the one hand, a high rate of profit tends to promote a high rate of accumulation, since the profit rate is the incentive for accumulation, and profits are a major source of funds for accumulation. On the other hand, a high rate of profit does not guarantee a high rate of accumulation. Profits are not automatically used for accumulation. They may instead flow into various forms of consumption, or they may flow into

---

[19] The high profits and the pronounced shift of income toward wealthy households create a large pool of investable funds relative to productive investment opportunities. This gives rise to speculative asset bubbles, as the excess funds find their way into such assets as corporate securities and land.

Table 4.3. *Growth Rates of Real Gross Domestic Product for Selected Countries (Annual Average Percentage Rate of Growth)*

Country	1950–73	1973–79	1979–2000
France	5.0	2.8	2.1
Germany	6.0	2.4	2.1
Italy	5.6	3.5	2.0
Japan	9.2	3.5	2.7
UK	3.0	1.5	2.3
USA	4.0	3.0	3.1

Sources: OECD 2000; U.S. Bureau of Economic Analysis 2000; Maddison 1995: 83; World Bank 2005.

financial investments that do not ultimately contribute to real accumulation. There are various ways in which the institutions of global neoliberalism tend to limit the pace of capital accumulation. These are discussed in Chapter 3 in this volume, involving several features of neoliberalism: a tendency toward insufficient aggregate demand growth, macroeconomic instability, unrestrained competition that discourages long-run productive investment, and an independent financial sector that tends to divert funds from productive investment.[20]

We referred earlier to evidence found in Chapter 3 of this volume that GDP growth in the U.S. economy has been no faster in the neoliberal era than it had been in the crisis phase of the previous SSA. Table 4.3 shows the growth rates of real GDP for six leading capitalist countries. For all six the GDP growth rate was significantly slower in the neoliberal era than it had been in the postwar era of regulated capitalism. Only in the United Kingdom was growth significantly faster in the neoliberal era than it had been in the crisis phase preceding the neoliberal SSA. It is noteworthy that the fastest GDP growth in the neoliberal era has been in China, which, while it has liberalized its economy over time, has not adopted the neoliberal model. Instead, it has retained a combination of state ownership and planning with marketization and the pursuit of private profit.

The Uneven Spread of Neoliberal Institutions and Globalization

In the postwar era the capitalist countries, despite some differences in their particular domestic institutional configuration, had institutions

---

[20] The cited discussion in Chapter 3 concerns liberal institutional structures in general.

that embodied in some form the state-regulated character of SSAs in that period. In much of Western Europe the domestic SSA had a social-democratic character, while in Japan the SSA was more corporatist. The United States had still a different type of state-regulated SSA, based on what has been called "military Keynesianism." In the developing countries, import-substitution industrialization regimes were common. Despite the differences, all involved strongly statist domestic institutions, and all fit in well with the international-level institutions of that period.

In this respect the global neoliberal SSA is qualitatively different from the SSA that preceded it. The development of neoliberal institutions has been quite uneven across countries. The most complete introduction of neoliberal institutions took place in the formerly state socialist countries of central and eastern Europe. As they dismantled their old system and rapidly installed capitalism, most of them thoroughly adopted new neoliberal institutions, particularly Russia and some of the other former Soviet republics. The working class in those countries had been completely demoralized and deactivated, and it was unable to put up any effective resistance to neoliberalism. Some developing countries were also forced to undergo substantial neoliberal restructuring as they came under the sway of the IMF and World Bank in the 1980s and 1990s. This was particularly prevalent in Latin America.

However, in some countries resistance from the working class and other groups prevented the complete neoliberal restructuring of domestic institutions. Among the developed capitalist countries, the shift in the neoliberal direction was greatest in the United States and United Kingdom, where working class resistance was largely defeated, and a major neoliberal restructuring was possible. However, even in those two countries the state retained some regulatory and social welfare roles from the previous SSA.

In some major Western European countries, a kind of "social neoliberalism" emerged, in which some features of neoliberalism were installed, including privatization, a reduction of state regulation of business, and a neoliberal shift in fiscal and monetary policy, but the welfare state was only marginally reduced and trade unions retained significant power at work. In some of the Nordic countries, the support for social democracy from the working class and other groups prevented its dismantling. Social-democratic institutions largely remained in place, with only marginal shifts in the direction of neoliberalism.

A number of Asian countries largely resisted the shift toward neoliberal domestic institutions. Japan made only very partial moves toward domestic neoliberal restructuring, despite periodic talk about undertaking "reforms." While the previous lifetime job guarantee system has weakened and a previously unknown level of unemployment emerged, the corporatist model remained relatively intact. Several Asian countries developed rapidly in the 1980s–90s with a state-directed development model, including South Korea, Indonesia, Malaysia, Taiwan, and Singapore.

Perhaps the most important exception to the neoliberal trend has been China, which in 1978 started its break with state socialism through a gradual replacement of central planning and state property by market forces and private enterprise, along with an opening to the world capitalist market. However, contrary to the neoliberal model, in China the state retained control over the development process, through such means as activist macropolicy aimed at rapid growth, a high rate of public investment in infrastructure, state ownership of the major banks, a well-defined industrial policy, and state regulation of trade and capital movements. The main features of neoliberalism introduced in China have been the dismantling of social welfare programs and state-funded education and the privatization of most, although not all, state enterprises.

The uneven spread of neoliberal domestic institutions, which is explained by differing particular histories in each country, is an important feature of the global neoliberal SSA. This variation even has certain benefits for profit-making and capital accumulation under this SSA. The global organization of production, which characterizes global neoliberalism, benefits from local differences so that different phases of capital accumulation and different stages of production can be apportioned to the most profitable locations. Head offices and research and design facilities can be located in countries whose social democratic institutions provide a suitable environment for them, while moderately labor-intensive production can take place in the wide-open economies of Eastern Europe with their educated yet relatively cheap labor. The most labor-intensive production can be shifted to China, where wages are very low while the regulatory state keeps order and builds the necessary infrastructure. In addition, China's state guided development brings very rapid growth, which helps fuel global growth while supplying cheap consumer goods and much-needed financing for U.S. capitalism.

It appears that the relation between the global and national aspects is different in the contemporary SSA compared to the previous era. The postwar state-regulated SSAs can be thought of as a series of national state-regulated SSAs that were linked internationally by an appropriate set of international institutions, such as the Bretton Woods system and a particular form of U.S. hegemony. By contrast, the global neoliberal SSA exists in its most pure form at the transnational level, where neoliberal principles became fully dominant in such institutions as the WTO, IMF, and World Bank.[21] Global neoliberalism is a transnational structure with local structures nested within it, with variation in the extent to which local structures conform to the neoliberal model.

Contradictions and Crisis of the Global Neoliberal SSA

No SSA under capitalism lasts forever. Every SSA has contradictions that eventually tend to sharpen. The intensification of the contradictions of an SSA eventually leads to a structural crisis. During the period of crisis, conflict among groups and classes is the means by which the old SSA is dismantled and something new is put in its place. The possible sequels are a new SSA within capitalism or the supersession of capitalism and the building of an alternative system.

The contemporary global neoliberal SSA has a number of contradictions. First, the sharp imbalance between rapidly rising profits and stagnating wages tends to create a problem of inadequate aggregate demand. This is made more severe by the limited growth in state spending and the renunciation of expansionary macropolicy. Second, the increasingly speculative character of the financial sector, due to financial deregulation and the short-run view that comes from unrestrained competition and the market in CEOs, tends to bring growing financial fragility over time. Third, there is a tendency for asset bubbles to emerge as rising profits and growing household incomes of the rich chase after limited productive investment opportunities. When such bubbles collapse, as they eventually must, this can wreak financial and economic havoc. Fourth, the high degree of global economic and financial integration tends to synchronize the business cycles of the major countries. As a result, any financial crisis or severe recession spreads rapidly around the globe, becoming more severe and more difficult to manage.

Fifth, there is a contradiction between the role of the U.S. dollar as the global trading and reserve currency on the one hand and the large

---

[21] When the World Bank's chief economist, the renowned Joseph Stiglitz, began to criticize some aspects of neoliberalism in the late 1990s, he was unceremoniously fired from his post.

and persistent U.S. trade and current account deficits associated with its role as consumer of last resort in the global economy on the other hand, with the latter tending to undermine the former. Sixth, capital's dominance over labor, and the resulting degradation of the condition of the working class and other popular groups, poses a potential problem. The huge rise in inequality under neoliberalism, the increase in insecurity for ordinary people, and the decline of public services have developed alongside the fattening of the already rich, partly at the public trough, and the appropriation of unprecedented incomes by unproductive financial wheeler-dealers. This enormous contrast may at some point spark a serious rebellion. Seventh, the unplanned and chaotic type of economic growth under global neoliberalism leads to rapid depletion of natural resources and, as has now become well understood, a growing threat of global climate change. The demand that these threats to the sustainability of human civilization be addressed may require a shift to a different economic model from that of global neoliberalism.

As of January 2009, it appears that a subset of the earlier contradictions has now sharpened to the point of initiating the crisis phase of the global neoliberal SSA. It is too early to provide a definitive analysis of this process, but some tentative observations can be made at this time. The first sign of a coming breakdown in global neoliberalism may have been the wave of left-wing electoral victories in Latin America in recent years, in countries where global neoliberalism had caused particularly severe and widespread popular suffering. This has led to a range of new paths, from the moderate efforts to break from the most extreme aspects of global neoliberalism in Brazil and Argentina to more radical attempts to supersede capitalism entirely in Venezuela and Bolivia.

In 2007 the giant housing bubble in the United States began to deflate, followed in 2008 by a severe financial crisis starting in the United States and spreading quickly to the global financial system. With remarkable speed, some of the largest financial institutions hurtled toward insolvency, as trillions of dollars in mortgage-backed securities and financial derivatives that they held suddenly collapsed in value. The central banks and treasuries of the major capitalist powers quickly abandoned their former free-market stance to rescue the tottering banks and insurance companies. Many leading financial institutions have been kept alive with huge injections of public funds while others have been de facto or de jure nationalized. By late 2008 the financial crisis was joined by a rapidly developing recession in the real sector of the global economy, which all analysts quickly pronounced the worst in memory. The United States, Western Europe, and China announced plans for huge government spending programs, resurrecting a Keynesianism long dead in the West although never abandoned in China.

This financial and economic crisis appears to mark a turn to the crisis phase of the global neoliberal SSA. As of this writing, the first four contradictions of global neoliberalism referred earlier seem be directly responsible for the immediate crisis – the imbalance between profits and wages, the speculative financial sector, the tendency for asset bubbles to emerge, and the highly integrated global financial and economic system that spreads a crisis rapidly across the globe.[22] As the crisis develops, the other contradictions mentioned earlier may also come into play. As economic conditions worsen and neoliberal ideology stands discredited, we may see popular rebellion spreading beyond Latin America. The imbalances in the global trade and financial system may cause problems. The advocates of new economic directions to combat global climate change may be politically strengthened, although opponents will doubtless insist that in a time of economic crisis nothing should be done that would add costs for business.

Talk of economic restructuring is everywhere at the time of this writing. The SSA theory cannot predict the course that economic restructuring will take. However, the SSA theory does suggest that sustaining the global neoliberal SSA is not a viable option and that, in the years ahead, out of the struggles of various classes and groups will emerge a new path for the global system. Whether that will be a new form of capitalist-dominated SSA, or a new compromise between capital and popular constituencies – or even the end of the capitalist era – cannot yet be determined.

References

Boddy, Raford and James R. Crotty 1975. "Class Conflict and Macro-Policy: The Political Business Cycle." *Review of Radical Political Economics* 7, 1: 1–19.

Bryan, Dick 1995. *The Chase across the Globe: International Accumulation and the Contradictions for Nation States*. Boulder, CO: Westview.

Castells, Manuel 2000. *The Rise of the Network Society*. Oxford: Blackwell.

Chang, Ha-Joon 2002. *Kicking Away the Ladder: Development Strategy in Historical Perspective*. London: Anthem Press.

---

[22] The main role of inequality, which is not always mentioned in accounts of the crisis, has been to spur a rapid and unsustainable growth in household debt, particularly mortgage debt. For an analysis of the crisis of neoliberalism based on the SSA theory, see Kotz 2009.

Cox, Robert 1987. *Production, Power and World Order.* New York: Columbia University Press.

Dumenil, Gerard and Dominique Levy 2004. *Capital Resurgent: Roots of the Neoliberal Revolution.* Cambridge, MA: Harvard University Press.

Gill, Stephen 1994. "Knowledge, Politics, and Neo-Liberal Political Economy." Pp. 75–88 in Richard Stubbs and Geoffrey R. D. Underhill, ed. *Political Economy and the Changing Global Order.* New York: St. Martin's Press.

Gill, Stephen and David Law 1988. *The Global Political Economy: Perspectives, Problems and Policies.* Hemel Hempstead: Harvester and Wheatsheaf.

Gordon, David M., Richard Edwards, and Michael Reich 1982. *Segmented Work, Divided Workers.* New York: Cambridge University Press.

Kotz, David M. 1978. *Bank Control of Large Corporations in the United States.* Berkeley: University of California Press.

1994. "Interpreting the Social Structure of Accumulation Theory." Pp. 50–71 in David M. Kotz, Terrence McDonough, and Michael Reich, eds. *Social Structures of Accumulation: The Political Economy of Growth and Crisis.* New York: Cambridge University Press.

2002. "Globalization and Neoliberalism." *Rethinking Marxism* 14, 2: 64–79.

2009. "The Financial and Economic Crisis of 2008: A Systemic Crisis of Neoliberal Capitalism." *Review of Radical Political Economics* 41: 3: 305–17.

2010. "Financialization and Neoliberalism." In Gary Teeple and Stephen McBride, eds. *Global Rule in Crisis.* Toronto: University of Toronto Press, forthcoming.

Maddison, Angus 1995. *Monitoring the World Economy 1820–1992.* Paris: Organization for Economic Cooperation and Development.

McDonough, Terrence 1994. "The Construction of Social Structures of Accumulation in US History." Pp. 101–32 in David M. Kotz, Terrence McDonough, and Michael Reich, eds. *Social Structures of Accumulation: The Political Economy of Growth and Crisis.* New York: Cambridge University Press.

OECD. 2000. *World Economic Outlook.* www.oecd.org/.

2008. Organization for Economic Cooperation and Development website.

Overbeek, Henk 2001. "Transnational Historical Mechanism: Theories of Transnational Class Formation and World Order." Pp. 168–183 in Ronen Palan, ed. *Global Political Economy: Contemporary Theories.* London: Routledge.

Pijl, Kees van der 1997. *The Making of an Atlantic Ruling Class.* London: Verso.

1998. *Transnational Classes and International Relations.* New York: Routledge.

Robinson, William I. 2004. *A Theory of Global Capitalism: Production, Class and State in a Transnational World.* Baltimore: Johns Hopkins University Press.

United Nations various years. *United Nations Monthly Bulletin of Statistics*, Number 13 (January to June 1959) through Number 57 (January to April 2003).

U.S. Bureau of Economic Analysis 2000. *National Income and Product Accounts.*

U.S. Federal Reserve System 2008. Website http://www.federalreserve.gov/datadownload/. Statistical Release of June 3, 2008.

van Apeldoorn, Bastiaan 2004. "Transnational Historical Materialism: The Amsterdam International Political Economy Project." *Journal of International Relations and Development* Special Issue 7, 2: 110–12.

Wolff, Edward N. 2001. "The Recent Rise in Profits in the United States." *Review of Radical Political Economics* 33, 3: 315–24.

World Bank 2005. *World Development Indicators*. Washington, DC: The World Bank.

FIVE

Globalization or Spatialization?

The Worldwide Spatial Restructuring of the Labor Process

Michael Wallace and David Brady

Introduction

Since the 1990s, scholarly accounts of globalization and its consequences have become prevalent throughout the social sciences (see Brady et al. 2007 for a review). While some view globalization as a centuries-long process of world system integration (Sklair 2002), others focus on recent changes in the last several decades. Although conceptualizations of globalization vary widely, they share a common insight that many phenomena previously centered in the local, sub-national, or national levels are increasingly interconnected on a global scale. Globalization implies increasing interpenetration and interdependency among societies, cultures, and peoples of the world often accompanied with a concern that the autonomy and sovereignty of the local setting is being diminished.

The changes created by globalization resemble the transformations discussed by those who advance social structures of accumulation (SSA) theory. Various scholars in this tradition place primary emphasis on the emergence of finance capital, neoliberalism, or other manifestations of globalization as the primary face of the new SSA. While having made numerous advances in SSA theory (Kotz, McDonough, and Reich 1994), we contend that SSA scholarship has strayed from Gordon, Edwards, and Reich's ([GER] 1982) central premise that the transformation of the labor process is a defining feature of each SSA (Wallace and Brady 2001). With the aim of restoring the centrality of the labor process, we extend the SSA approach in three ways. First, we argue that since the turn of the century, the U.S. economy has been in a consolidation phase of a new SSA. We call this SSA spatialization, which is premised on the spatial restructuring of the labor process and a technocratic control system. Second, following Edwards (1979), we contend that each SSA carries with it a system of labor control, which is essential to fully understanding the SSA. Third, we seek to forge a connection between globalization and SSA literatures.

Despite what these two streams of research can offer each other, they often talk past each other. To students of globalization, we contend that spatialization provides the inner logic for the rise of globalization. To students of SSA theory, we argue that GER's central premise – that the driving force of SSA structuration is located in the labor process – provides a distinctive perspective on changes to contemporary capitalism that should be retained. By returning to and reinvigorating this core premise, SSA theory can provide a unique and necessary corrective to globalization theory. We organize this chapter in three parts. First, we examine complementarities between and the relevance of globalization for SSA theory. Second, we review the historical development of previous SSAs and their control systems in the United States. Third, we provide a description of the latest SSA, spatialization.

Globalization's Place in SSA Theory

In a previous collection of articles on SSA theory by Kotz et al. (1994), one of the more influential pieces was Gordon's (1994) incisive critique of globalization arguments. Gordon challenged the novelty of globalization, dismantled the evidence about globalization's impact on workers, and expressed deep skepticism about the potential for globalization to alter the U.S. economy. In the decade and a half since Gordon's essay, a great deal has changed. In some ways his critique was probably premature. After all, globalization experienced its most significant expansion, and peaked several years after his article was published. Across affluent democracies, for example, trade openness grew from a mean of 43.8 percent of GDP in 1960 to a mean of 80.6 in 2000. Though far below West European levels, trade openness increased substantially in the United States from 9.6 in 1960 to 26.3 in 2000 (Brady et al. 2007). Moreover, trade plus investment openness in the United States was only 22.9 percent of GDP in 1990, but rose to over 37 percent of GDP by 2000.[1] Of

---

[1] Mean trade plus investment openness rose from 53.4 percent of GDP in 1975 to a peak of 136.1 in 2000 before declining to 100.5 in 2003. This mean was driven partly by extremely high levels of investment flows in small West European countries, such as Belgium, the Netherlands, and Ireland. Trade plus investment openness started lower and rose more

course, some claims of the globalization literature are overblown – for example, international economic exchange still disproportionately occurs between affluent democracies (Alderson 2004) – but the reality of rising international trade, investment, and migration is now difficult to dispute (Brady et al. 2007). While it is understandable that Gordon echoed the skepticism of many economists, the dramatic increase in international trade, investment, and migration that followed his essay could certainly have led to different conclusions (but see Sutcliffe and Glyn 1999).

The concept of globalization has diverse connotations, including cultural, political, and economic globalization; what Sklair (2002) calls "generic globalization;" the longer history of international economic integration since the rise of the modern capitalist system; and the early 20th century wave of globalization. This literature cuts across at least six major realms of social life. First, in the *economic* realm, globalization implies the openness of markets, interpenetration of capital across borders, and freer access to a global pool of workers. Discussions of economic globalization sometimes center on transformations in the labor process, that is, changes in the organization of work and the relative power of workers and capitalists (e.g., Bonacich and Appelbaum 2000). Second, in the *sociocultural* realm, globalization creates more opportunities for cross-cultural contact, cultural diffusion of products, ideas, and behaviors, and the emergence of a global consciousness on many issues (such as multiculturalism and environmentalism). Third, in the *political* realm, globalization implies the transcendence of national governments by international organizations, nongovernmental organizations, and institutions of world governance (e.g., Frank et al. 2000). Fourth, in the *technological* realm, improvements in transportation and telecommunications technologies have led to the "death of distance" and a hyperintegration of global life. Fifth, in the *financial* realm, there has been a trend toward the restructuring and consolidation of financial markets, a deregulation of foreign exchange, and the emergence of finance capital, as opposed to entrepreneurialism and business acumen, as the driving force of accumulation. Finally, in the *ideological* realm, there has been a growth of a neoliberalism that espouses the virtues of free markets, privatization and individualism, an antipathy toward the state as the nemesis of economic efficiency, and an exclusively monetarist approach for economic stabilization (Harvey 2004). Changes in these six realms are intertwined

slowly outside Western Europe. Nevertheless, the United States doubled from 18.2 in 1960 to 37.0 in 2000 (31.9 in 2003).

with innovations in legal/criminal institutions, health care and medicine, entertainment, the environment, and even sports.

To put the significance of globalization in context, we briefly review a few of the major areas of research. A number of studies investigated whether globalization was triggering deunionization. Generally, these studies conclude that globalization cannot really explain cross-national differences in unionization – since that is overwhelmingly driven by institutions – but international trade and migration have contributed to within-country declines in unionization (e.g., Baldwin 2003; Lee 2005; Sassoon 1996). For example, Magnani and Prentice (2003) argue that the bulk of unionization decline in U.S. manufacturing cannot be explained by globalization, and Kay (2005) shows that globalization can actually foster transnational labor organizing. However, Brady and Wallace (2000) find that increased foreign direct investment has undermined union organizing and union density in the United States. Western (1997) finds that trade openness triggered union declines in the 1980s. Employers often globalize production to avoid high labor costs and inflexible work arrangements and, explicitly, to counter unionization (Alderson 2004). As Western (1997: 195) remarks, "The unity of nation-class organizations rooted in national institutions was outflanked by an emergent international institutional context." Perhaps equally important, managers and employers use the threat of globalization to extract concessions from organized labor and to undermine the organizing and recruitment of workers into unions (Brady and Wallace 2000).

One of the older debates about globalization's consequences concerned deindustrialization (Bluestone and Harrison 1982). Since Harrison and Bluestone (1988) called attention to deindustrialization and the "Great U-turn" of increasing inequality, and linked those trends to the "globalization gambit," many have analyzed the influence of trade and investment for manufacturing jobs. Some find evidence that increasing globalization coincided with an unmistakable decline in manufacturing employment in all affluent democracies. For example, Alderson (1999: 718) shows that: "Globalization has played an important, independent role in the deindustrialization of advanced industrial countries." Others claim that globalization has at most a modest effect on manufacturing employment in affluent democracies. The level of globalization, especially for the United States, is considered too low to be the main cause of deindustrialization. Also, globalization has mainly involved trade and investment among affluent democracies, so the economic impact from developing countries such as Mexico or China is rather limited. Ultimately, technology, rising worker productivity, and economic development were found to be more influential than globalization in driving deindustrialization (Alderson 1999). Responding to such studies, Brady and Denniston (2006) propose a curvilinear relationship between globalization and manufacturing. Initially, globalization causes a growth of manufacturing employment through differentiation, which involves a specialization of industries and employment across countries. Subsequently, however, greater globalization causes deindustrialization. As economies move from moderately to highly globalized, saturation will undermine manufacturing because of competition among countries, mimetic isomorphism[2] of firms relocating production facilities (DiMaggio and Powell 1983), and the spatialization of production (Brady and Wallace 2000). Ultimately, both productivity gains and globalization appear to contribute to deindustrialization (Alderson 1999; Brady and Denniston 2006).

A related literature analyzes the influence of globalization on specific industries and corporate practices (e.g., Anderson et al. 2001). This work provides convincing evidence that globalization is not a myth and is actually occurring. Sklair (2002), for example, interviewed members of global firms in California to illustrate the uses and meanings of "globalization" in corporate vocabularies and practices. Also, Kurdelbusch (2002) demonstrates that large companies in Germany increasingly implement variable pay schemes as a result of growing internationalization of product and capital markets. Such studies link to literatures on the broader question of how globalization affects inequality. Economists contend that globalization contributes to the increasing skill premium, the significant decline in the blue-collar payroll share, and the increasing gap between nonproduction and production workers in U.S. industries (Bardhan and Howe 2001; Dasgupta and Osang 2002). Sociologists tend to be more empirically critical of globalization, arguing that globalization undermines the position of labor, and magnifies the power of managers and capitalists to search for cheaper wages (Brady and Wallace 2000). Alderson and Nielsen (2002) find that outward direct investment, manufacturing imports from developing countries, and immigration contributed to the great U-turn of increased inequality that many affluent democracies have experienced since the 1970s. Some show that the globalization of the U.S. economy has led to increased inequality and

---

[2] Mimetic isomorphism refers to the herd behavior that exists when organizations in uncertain environments model themselves after other organizations that they perceive as successful.

reduced worker earnings (Brady and Wallace 2000; Dasgupta and Osang 2002). Ultimately, the consensus appears to be that differences among nations or varieties of capitalism in inequality tend to persist under heightened globalization, but globalization has probably contributed at least modestly to increased inequality within affluent democracies since the 1970s. Partly, this is because of the original claim that globalization contributes to a displacement of workers from well-paid jobs (Harrison and Bluestone 1988). Equally important for the argument about spatialization we develop below is how globalization alters power relations between workers and capitalists[3] and triggers institutional changes favoring flexibility.[4] Unfortunately, the precise mechanisms by which this occurs are only beginning to be studied in globalization literatures.

Beyond these literatures, many aspects of labor and work have received surprisingly less attention in the globalization literature (Brady et al. 2007). A few studies examine how globalization affects workers' experiences, especially within multinational firms (e.g., Blair-Loy and Jacobs 2003; Ono 2007). For example, Scheve and Slaughter (2004) find that FDI increases employee perceptions of insecurity in Britain in the 1990s. Yet, globalization studies have generally neglected the subjective aspects of employment such as satisfaction, autonomy, and alienation (but see Gille and O'Riain 2002; Graham 1995). To its detriment, the globalization literature has largely ignored the SSA literature and GER's (1982) central concern with the labor process. This is a missed opportunity since SSA theory provides a useful perspective for placing globalization in historical context, and making sense of globalization's consequences for workers relative to other influences on work. In our view, globalization's influences on work and the labor process originate in the spatial restructuring of labor.

Social Structures of Accumulation and Systems of Labor Control

Before proceeding to our account of spatialization, we discuss the historical trajectory of previous SSAs to provide historical context for the

---

[3] For example, Choi (2006: 78) remarks, "Firms' enhanced locational mobility as a result of the globalization process is effective in pressuring workers who fear losing their jobs to concede at the bargaining table and accept a lower share of the rent."

[4] Globalization-triggered institutional changes create greater volatility, uncertainty, and insecurity for workers, and undermine the social contract of management-labor relations (Ono 2007).

rise of spatialization. In their path-breaking book *Segmented Work, Divided Workers*, GER (1982) described SSAs as a complex of integrated institutional arrangements facilitating the accumulation of capital. These include core technological systems, the ways in which markets are organized, the monetary and credit systems, the pattern of government involvement in the economy, mechanisms for limiting inter-capitalist rivalry, and the role of military force in securing access to capitalist markets. Importantly, GER focused on the creation and demise of mechanisms for managing conflict. Indeed the names of the three successive long swings they identified – initial proletarianization, homogenization, and segmentation – centered on the extensive reorganization of the labor process involved in class struggle.

SSAs are marked by successive periods of exploration, consolidation, and decay of institutional features as each SSA emerges and eventually plays itself out. Each period of decay is simultaneously a period of exploration as the obstacles to continued capitalist expansion under the old SSA give way to experimental strategies and arrangements for renewed accumulation. Each new SSA consolidates around the experimental arrangement that provides the most promising route for rejuvenating capitalist accumulation while addressing the key problems of controlling and pacifying labor. Despite this original focus on labor process and class struggle, we suggest that this emphasis on the labor process has perhaps become less visible in the subsequent SSA literature (Wallace and Brady 2001).

Edwards (1979) added a convincing account of workplace control systems that evolved historically to mediate the "contested terrain" between workers and capitalists. Edwards contends that different systems of control periodically emerged to address contradictions inherent in the growth of capitalism and the diminishing effectiveness of previous control systems. When control systems were in ascendance, labor was relatively weak; as control systems began to decay, worker resistance to capitalist prerogatives became more likely and had greater prospects for success. Edwards' depiction of the ebb and flow of capitalist control systems coincides approximately with the wax and wane of the SSAs. Indeed, we argue that control systems are one of the pivotal mechanisms in managing the capital-labor conflict under a prevailing SSA, even though this was not explicitly stated in GER (1982). Each of the SSAs was anchored by a dominant control system that sought to address a fundamental crisis of labor control in capitalist production by devising a strategy for eliciting optimal cooperation from workers. We articulate this implicit but pivotal bridge between SSAs and control systems as we review each of the prior SSAs.

In what follows, we provide a historical synthesis of the concepts of SSAs and control systems to provide the foundation for a discussion of the new era of spatialization and technocratic control. Table 5.1 depicts the historical sequence of the argument.

As the first SSA, *proletarianization* sought to elicit more reliable and intensified work effort by bringing workers under more constant supervision in the capitalist's shop or factory. This SSA and its *simple control system* entered an exploratory period in the 1820s–40s, a consolidation period in the 1840s–70s, and a period of decay in the 1870s–90s. The key change during this period was that workers now labored under the roof of the capitalist and at its direction. Most workers retained their craft methods of production and often owned their own tools. Still, this new relationship was inherently conflictual, subjecting workers to a new industrial regimen. In a variant of simple control that Edwards (1979) calls "entrepreneurial control," the capitalist-entrepreneur, who was typically a craftsman himself, supervised day-to-day operations directly. Entrepreneurial control was arbitrary, capricious, and sometimes clumsy but usually effective because the hard work and personal involvement of the capitalist-entrepreneur inspired loyalty from workers and obscured the class character of the production process. Sustained growth led to the expansion of the firm, which created new challenges for entrepreneurial control since it became more difficult for capitalist-entrepreneurs to oversee day-to-day operations. As firms outgrew their entrepreneurial origins, authority was delegated to a wider stratum of foremen and supervisors leading to a new form of simple control known as "hierarchical control." While providing a temporary resolution to the problem of firm growth, the increasing distance between capitalists and workers undermined the bond of loyalty.

As proletarianization declined, two realities produced a renewed crisis of control in the workplace. First, the harshness of factory conditions and the blatant exercise of arbitrary power by factory managers made the class character of capitalist production transparent. Second, workers acquired a virtual monopoly of knowledge about shop floor production that tilted the balance of power in their favor. These two factors – along with the economic crises of the late 1800s – signaled the demise of the first SSA of proletarianization and launched exploratory efforts to construct a new SSA. Several "experimental" control systems vied for the attention of capitalists in the early 1900s and attempted to resolve the crisis

Table 5.1 *Historical Overview of Social Structures of Accumulation and Dominant Control Systems*

SSA	Initial Proletarianization	Homogenization	Segmentation	Spatialization
Dominant control system	Simple: entrepreneurial hierarchical	Technical	Bureaucratic	Technocratic
Approximate timing				
1790–1820				
1820–mid-1840s	Exploration			
Mid-1840s–1873	Consolidation			
1873–late 1890s	Decay	Exploration		
Late 1890s–WWI		Consolidation		
WWI–WWII		Decay	Exploration	
WWII–early 1970s			Consolidation	
Early 1970s–present			Decay	Exploration
2000–???				Consolidation

Definitions

Social structures of accumulation: The specific institutional environment within which the accumulation of capitalist profits takes place; includes such things as core technological systems, the way markets are organized, the monetary and credit systems, the pattern of government involvement in the economy, and the character of class conflict over the accumulation process.

Dominant control systems: The "contested terrain" of capitalist-worker relations: the dominant system of control used by capitalists to elicit compliance by workers to a prevailing system of production; a core component and a dynamic feature of the social structure of accumulation.

control systems that pushed workers to their limits, corporations utilizing bureaucratic control "survive and prosper on their ability to organize the routine, normal efforts of workers, not on their ability to elicit peak performances" (Edwards 1979: 146). Bureaucratic control, with its specialized and routinized jobs, reigned supreme in an era of standardized products and mass consumer markets.

By the writing of *Contested Terrain*, the contradictions of bureaucratic control revealed "a pact with the devil that, while offering temporary respite from trouble, spells long-term disaster" (Edwards 1979: 157). First, the increased security of jobs under bureaucratic control meant that workers could turn their attention to venting frustration about jobs that were alienating, boring, or dissatisfying. Second, bureaucratic control – aided by long-term labor contracts and cost-of-living agreements – accelerated the process of transforming labor costs from a variable to a fixed cost of production, putting the squeeze on capitalist profits, especially during downswings in the business cycle. Hence, bureaucratic control presented a contradiction between the desire for loyal workers with high job security and the need for flexibility in the allocation of labor. From the 1970s to the 1990s, this contradiction could no longer be put off by modest internationalization of labor. Third, bureaucratic control potentially politicized class struggle by making conflicts over rules and procedures within the corporation part of a broader movement for economic democracy and citizen rights.

Spatialization and Technocratic Control

As the segmentation SSA decayed from the 1970s to the 1990s, the exploratory stage of the next SSA was occurring. Since about 2000, we propose that the new SSA of *spatialization* has been experiencing consolidation (Wallace and Brady 2001).[5] Much of this period has been marked by experimentation with alternatives to the inefficiencies of bureaucratic control (e.g., worker participation, quality circles, and profit-sharing), which sought to humanize the face of bureaucratic control but did not fundamentally alter its core. In contrast, the current SSA of spatialization employs a spatial division of labor and the threat of spatial relocation to defuse potential workers' resistance and fragment their interests along regional and national lines. Spatialization is accompanied by *technocratic*

---

[5] For empirical applications of spatialization theory, see Brady and Wallace (2000); Grant (1995); Grant and Hutchinson (1996); and Grant and Wallace (1994).

control (Burris 1993), which involves the use of computers, information technology, and technological expertise to organize and direct the labor process across spatially distant networks of organizations.

Spatialization prioritizes employers' quest for the optimal geographic arrangement of their business operations in order to maintain the desired proximity to labor markets, natural resources and raw materials, and consumer markets. Moreover, spatialization involves the restructuring of the labor process so that different work tasks can be done in different locations with no loss in profitability or control. Less bound by temporal and spatial constraints, employers can use relocation or threats of relocation to discipline workers, erode wages, and maintain a supply of quiescent labor. Simply put, spatialization affords capitalists wider access to cheaper and weaker labor in the new global economy.

The onset of spatialization is made more viable by: (1) the increasing modularization of work tasks (i.e., fragmentation of work into discrete components and a highly integrated division of labor that allows different modules to be carried out in different locations); (2) advanced transportation technologies; (3) advanced information and telecommunication technologies; and (4) new geopolitical agreements addressing economic integration and liberalization. Having sufficiently routinized work tasks in many manufacturing and service industries (point 1), technological innovations in transportation, telecommunications, and trade (points 2, 3, and 4) have made entire segments of work geographically fungible.

We argue, however, that employers' ultimate goal in pursuing spatialization is not only spatial relocation as an end itself, but is equally about the realization of a mature system of flexible accumulation (Rubin 1996). The *threat* of spatial relocation may often be as effective as actual relocation itself in achieving a compliant labor force conducive to flexible accumulation. Hence, spatialization is a very efficient process for re-introducing the three major aspects of labor flexibility identified by Rosenberg (1991): *wage flexibility* (adjusting wages to meet labor market conditions); *employment flexibility* (altering the number of workers or number of hours as needed); and *functional flexibility* (varying the work tasks performed by individual workers in response to production needs).

Three decades of fundamental economic change marked the decay of segmentation and the exploratory period of spatialization. The 1970s was the "decade of deindustrialization" in which millions of blue-collar jobs were lost as plants closed, and/or moved operations (Bluestone and

Harrison 1982). Deindustrialization signaled the beginning of a new "hypermobility of capital" (Bluestone and Harrison 1982) in which capital could flow quickly toward low-wage labor pools first in the American "Sunbelt" and then in developing countries or even other developed countries (Brady and Denniston 2006; Brady and Wallace 2000; Grant and Wallace 1994). Meanwhile, sophisticated communications technologies permitted U.S. companies to monitor their global operations on a daily basis from the comfort of their U.S.-based headquarters. In the early 1980s, U.S. workers who were fortunate enough to keep their jobs faced the prospects of accepting declining economic rewards and job security (Wallace 1998). The long-term effect was to seriously undercut the wage structure for middle-class workers, reassert capitalists' claims for labor process flexibility, and send a sobering message to workers.

Although deindustrialization continued into the 1980s, it also set the stage for the "decade of deunionization" in the 1980s, which witnessed an expanded employer assault on labor unions. The watershed moment of this assault – President Reagan's crushing of the Professional Air Traffic Controllers Organization (PATCO) strike in 1981 – signaled once and for all the demise of the capital-labor accord and fundamentally altered the rules of the game for employer-worker relations in the emerging regime of flexible accumulation. New employer strategies for weakening unions were replete with signs of spatialization: whipsawing (pitting two distant unionized plants, or a unionized and nonunionized plant against each other); two-tiered wage structures (offering new employees lower wages and benefits than long-time employees doing the same jobs); outsourcing (lower-paying nonunionized plants do part of the work formerly assigned to unionized employees); and industrial homework (a special type of outsourcing where work is hired out on a contingent basis to workers in their homes).

Deunionization gave way to the "decade of downsizing" in the 1990s in which major corporations swept aside the remnants of bureaucratic control by drastically cutting their work forces and adopting various forms of contingent work (*New York Times* 1996; Wallace 1998). Sennett (1998: 49) estimates that between 13 and 39 million U.S. workers were downsized by 1995. Downsizing, contingent labor, and job insecurity are hallmarks of the new, flexible corporation and are clear manifestations of the spatial restructuring of work in which permanent workers are constantly reminded by the temporary workers alongside them how contingent their own employment really is (Budros 1997; Smith 1997). In the wake of downsizing over 120,000 workers at AT&T, one manager's statement spoke volumes: "We need to recognize that we are all contingent workers in one form or another" (Andrews 1996: D1, D6). Ethnographic studies of contingent work during the 1990s suggest that both permanent and temporary workers are victims of a "divide and conquer" strategy whereby both groups experience distrust and resentment of each other, an intensification of work effort, greater job insecurity, and tighter managerial control (Henson 1996; Parker 1994; Rogers 1995).

Although spatialization implies a multilayered (i.e., local, regional, national, transnational, global) spatial division of labor, it is inextricably linked to globalization. In fact, numerous extant visions of globalization explicitly incorporate key features of spatialization. Giddens (1990: 64) identifies the key feature of globalization as the "space-time distancia-tion"; in other words, globalization can be defined as "the intensification of worldwide social relations which link distant localities in such a way that local happenings are shaped by events occurring many miles away and vice versa." Others note that globalization implies a "shrinking" of the world through the compression of time and space (Harvey 1989; Mittleman 1996). Castells (1996: 92) succinctly defines the essence of a spatialized, global economy as "an economy with the capacity to work as a unit in real time on a planetary scale." Castells envisions a global-ized network of production in which information and capital flow freely without boundaries of time and space. In this network, a host of new organizational forms are emerging (Dimaggio 2001).

By their very nature, numerous aspects of flexible accumulation sys-tems such as outsourcing and just-in-time inventory systems require greater interorganizational coordination and cooperation. Partnerships, joint ventures, subcontracting, and temporary relationships with inde-pendent contractors – along with traditional mergers – increasingly blur organizational boundaries. Many of these new arrangements – such as joint ventures in the international automobile industry – intentionally transcend national boundaries in order to exploit market advantages held by one partner or the other, achieve economies of scale, pool information or know-how, or simply share the risk of uncertainty in quickly changing or turbulent markets (Hollingsworth 1998). These new organizational arrangements further deepen the web of transnational relationships among owners of capital and their managers and agents. In this scenario, individual organizations become simply nodes in a globalized network of production and conduits for the international flow of capital and information. As such, capitalism in the era of spatialization increasingly approaches Harrison's (1994) "concentration without centralization" in which capitalist power is enhanced despite decentralization.

As we argued in the previous section, a vital component of any SSA is a system of labor control. Spatialization requires a fundamentally new control system in order for capitalists to maintain effective control and coordination even as it becomes more decentralized and spatially dispersed. Following Beverly Burris's (1993) *Technocracy at Work*, we contend a system of technocratic control has allowed both the flexibility and the coordinating features necessary to facilitate work under spatialization (for earlier discussions of technocracy, see Akin 1977 and Alvesson 1987). While technocratic control may incorporate elements of earlier systems, it centers on the use of computerized technologies in the workplace and technical expertise in the creation, dissemination, and interpretation of computerized information. Computers in the workplace can be simultaneously a tool for unimaginable autonomy, creativity, and spontaneity (Hirschhorn 1984) or an instrument for mind-numbing routinization (Shaiken 1984). Perhaps the only certain conclusion to be drawn from the vast literature on computerization in the workplace is that the real possibilities and limitations of computerized work are determined not so much by the machine itself but by the capitalists, entrepreneurs, and managers in whose interests computerized work is organized. Burris (1998) contends that computer technologies are both more flexible and more variable than previous workplace technologies, leading to a wider range of applications and consequences for the organization of work.

Four aspects of technocratic control coincide with prevailing tendencies in spatialization. First, there is an underlying centralization of control despite physical decentralization of computers and related technology, a feature epitomized by telecommuting and teleconferencing. In some cases, workers may operate in an aura of relative autonomy and exercise discretion over the pace and flow of day-to-day activities, retaining the unity of conception and execution of work that prevailed under craft technologies. In more routinized jobs, however, the execution of tasks is essentially carried out by computerized processes, and the worker is reduced to a machine tender who monitors the performance of the system and the quality of the output and reports breakdowns or malfunctions (Burris 1993).

Some argue that technocratic control tends toward "algorithmic control" characterized by the reduction of "decision-making as much as possible to a set of self-contained rules (algorithms) implementable by a computer" (Applebaum and Albin 1989: 252; cf. Vallas 1999). Algorithmic control is prevalent among occupations as diverse as medical technicians, automobile mechanics, bakers, insurance adjusters, machinists, travel agents, bank tellers, stockbrokers, and UPS delivery persons (Sennett 1998). In extreme cases, technocratic control threatens to undermine traditional proprietary rights to intellectual property, to compromise confidential information exchanged with clients or customers, or to undermine the autonomy and professional judgment that has been the hallmark of many professions. Consequently, technocratic control is premised ultimately on routinizing nonroutine work activities to the extent possible but also of bringing them under closer, more omnipresent managerial supervision than is possible under previous systems of control.

Second, just as spatialization is transforming relationships between the haves and have-nots in the global economy, technocratic control contributes to a polarization between the haves and have-nots of technical expertise (Burris 1993). This new polarization involves a dichotomy between those who analyze, manipulate, and interpret information contained in computerized systems or design and repair the system itself versus clerical workers or data entry personnel who merely collect, store, and perform routine (algorithmic) operations on computerized information (Kraft 1977). This expertise dichotomy is the pivotal axis of the reconstituted core and periphery of the contemporary workplace in which essential personnel are retained as permanent employees and nonessential personnel are downsized and rehired as contingent workers. As a result, technocratic control is not only a key force in sculpting the lean and mean look of the modern capitalist enterprise but also an important feature shaping the informal culture of the workplace.[6]

Third, technocratic control has facilitated a new level of social networking that reinforces the prevailing pattern of inter-organizational networks that characterizes spatialization. E-mail, the Internet, and other computerized systems of communication defy the rigid, hierarchical boundaries that constrained social interaction in the bureaucratic firm, and are spawning denser, more dynamic, more fluid lines of social interaction that cut both laterally and vertically within the organization as well as spilling over

---

[6] Kunda (1992) suggests subtle distinctions in the form of control exercised over workers in these two sectors: experts are subjected to "normative control" whereby they are expected to demonstrate their identification and internalization of the goals of the organization by working extra hours, volunteering for more challenging work assignments, socializing with influential insiders in the workplace while non-experts are subjected to more coercive, utilitarian forms of control and are excluded from informal interactions with influential workers.

with various degrees of authority, status, economic rewards, and prospects for advancement as a way to elicit the "routine performances" that would allow the firm to prosper. Technocratic control centers on the use of sophisticated computer systems and technical expertise to organize and direct the labor process across networks of organizations.

SSA theory posits that as each system of accumulation reaches a level of maturity, it carries the potential for creating new crises of accumulation and control. It is therefore appropriate to ask what crises might emerge for the spatialization SSA in the next half-century. While social forecasting can be perilous, certain broad patterns can be anticipated. First, while spatialization currently is rife with signs of the global consolidation of capital and the fragmentation of labor, it is altogether possible that the passage of time will create new opportunities and strategies for labor to organize collectively against capitalists if nationalistic and ethnic divisions among workers can be overcome. Second, the synchronization of the accumulation process around a single common technology – computers – poses potential opportunities for workers themselves to communicate, organize collectively, and challenge the authority of technocrats and capitalists. Third, the re-intensification of work effort among both high-end and low-end workers and the growing disparity between the experience of citizens in their roles as consumers and workers will bring quality of working life and workers' rights into sharper focus. Fourth, the growing contradiction between society's technological capacity to produce enough food, shelter, and comfort to support the global population and the inequalities of an economic system that create legions of poor, hungry, and desperate people around the globe will potentially create a crisis of legitimacy for the current system (Przeworski 1991).

In any event, workers in the twenty-first century will increasingly work in an economy without borders – neither the borders of national boundaries, nor the less obtrusive boundaries of space and time that have structured human interaction through the centuries. This will undoubtedly create new frontiers in the world of work for workers and scholars alike.

References

Akin, William E. 1977. *Technocracy and the American Dream*. Berkeley, CA: University of California Press.
Alderson, Arthur S. 1999. "Explaining Deindustrialization: Globalization, Failure, or Success?" *American Sociological Review* 64: 701–21.

2004. "Explaining the Upswing in Direct Investment: A Test of Mainstream and Heterodox Theories of Globalization." *Social Forces* 83: 81–122.

Alderson, Arthur S. and Francois Nielsen 2002. "Globalization and the Great U-Turn: Income Inequality Trends in 16 OECD Countries." *American Journal of Sociology* 107: 1244–99.

Alvesson, Mats 1987. *Organizational Theory and Technocratic Consciousness.* New York: Walter de Gruyter.

Anderson, Cynthia D., Michael D. Schulman, and Phillip J. Wood 2001. "Globalization and Uncertainty: the Restructuring of Southern Textiles." *Social Problems* 48: 478–98.

Andrews, Edmund L. 1996. "Don't Go Away Mad, Just Go Away." *New York Times* (February 13): D1, D6.

Applebaum, Eileen and Peter Albin 1989. "Computer Rationalization and the Transformation of Work." Pp.247–65 in Stephen J. Wood, ed. *The Transformation of Work? Skill, Flexibility, and the Labor Process.* Boston, MA: Unwin Hyman.

Arsen, David D. 1991. "International and Domestic Forces in the Postwar Golden Age." *Review of Radical Political Economics* 23: 1–11.

Baldwin, Robert E. 2003. *The Decline of U.S. Labor Unions and the Role of Trade.* Washington DC: Institute for International Economics.

Bardhan, Ashok Deo and David K. Howe 2001. "Globalization and Restructuring during Downturns: A Case Study of California." *Growth and Change* 32: 217–35.

Blair-Loy, Mary and Jerry A. Jacobs 2003. "Globalization, Work Hours, and the Care Deficit among Stockbrokers." *Gender and Society* 17: 230–49.

Bluestone, Barry and Bennett Harrison 1982. *The Deindustrialization of America.* New York: Basic Books.

Bonacich, Edna and Richard P. Appelbaum 2000. *Behind the Label.* Berkeley: University of California Press.

Bowles, Samuel, David M. Gordon, and Thomas E. Weisskopf 1983. *Beyond the Wasteland: A Democratic Alternative to Economic Decline.* Garden City, NY: Garden Press.

Brady, David and Michael Wallace 2000. "Spatialization, Foreign Direct Investment and Labor Outcomes in the American States, 1976–1996." *Social Forces* 79: 67–100.

Brady, David, Jason Beckfield, and Wei Zhao 2007. "The Consequences of Economic Globalization for Affluent Democracies." *Annual Review of Sociology* 33: 313–34.

Brady, David and Ryan Denniston. 2006. "Economic Globalization, Industrialization, and Deindustrialization in Affluent Democracies." *Social Forces* 85: 297–329.

Braverman, Harry 1974. *Labor and Monopoly Capital: The Degradation of Work in the Twentieth Century.* New York: Monthly Review Press.

Budros, Art 1997. "The New Capitalism and Organizational Rationality: The Adoption of Downsizing Programs, 1979–1994." *Social Forces* 76: 229–49.

Burris, Beverly H. 1993. *Technocracy at Work.* Albany, NY: State University of New York Press.

1998. "Computerization of the Workplace." *Annual Review of Sociology* 24: 141–57.

Castells, Manuel 1996. *The Rise of the Network Society*. Cambridge, MA: Blackwell.

Choi, Minsik 2006. "Threat Effects of Capital Mobility on Wage Bargaining." Pp. 64–86 in Pranab Bardhan, Samuel Bowles, and Michael Wallerstein, eds. *Globalization and Egalitarian Redistribution*. Princeton, NJ: Princeton University Press.

Dasgupta, Indo and Thomas Osang 2002. "Globalization and Relative Wages: Further Evidence from U.S. Manufacturing Industries." *International Review of Economics and Finance* 11: 1–16.

Dimaggio, Paul 2001. *The Twenty-First Century Firm*. Princeton, NJ: Princeton University Press.

DiMaggio, Paul J. and Walter W. Powell 1983. "The Iron Cage Revisited: Institutional Isomorphism and Collective Reality in Organizational Fields." *American Sociological Review* 48: 147–60.

Edwards, Richard 1979. *Contested Terrain: The Transformation of the Workplace in the Twentieth Century*. New York: Basic Books.

Frank David J., Ann Hironaka, and Evan Schofer 2000. "The Nation-State and the Natural Environment over the Twentieth Century." *American Sociological Review* 65: 96–116.

Giddens, Anthony 1990. *The Consequences of Modernity*. Stanford: Stanford University Press.

Gille, Zsuzsa and Sean O'Riain 2002. "Global Ethnography." *Annual Review of Sociology* 28: 271–95.

Gordon, David M. 1994. "The Global Economy: New Edifice or Crumbling Foundations?" Pp. 292–305 in David M. Kotz, Terrence McDonough, and Michael Reich, eds. *Social Structures of Accumulation: The Political Economy of Growth and Crisis*. New York: Cambridge University Press.

1996. *Fat and Mean: The Corporate Squeeze of Working Americans and the Myth of Managerial "Downsizing."* New York: Free Press.

Gordon, David M., Richard Edwards, and Michael Reich 1982. *Segmented Work, Divided Workers*. New York: Cambridge University Press.

Graham, Laurie 1995. *On the Line at Subaru-Isuzu*. Ithaca: Cornell University Press.

Grant, Don Sherman 1995. "The Political Economy of Business Failures across the American States, 1970–1985." *American Sociological Review* 60: 851–73.

Grant, Don Sherman and Richard Hutchinson 1996. "Global Smokestack Chasing: A Comparison of the State-Level Determinants of Foreign and Domestic Manufacturing Investment." *Social Problems*. 43: 21–38.

Grant, Don Sherman and Michael Wallace 1994. "The Political Economy of Manufacturing Growth and Decline across the American States, 1970–1985." *Social Forces* 73: 33–63.

Harrison, Bennett 1994. *Lean and Mean: The Changing Landscape of Corporate Power in an Age of Flexibility*. New York: Basic Books.

Harrison, Bennett and Barry Bluestone 1988. *The Great U-Turn*. New York, NY: Basic Books.

Harvey, David 1989. *The Condition of Postmodernity.* Oxford: Blackwell.
2004. *A Brief History of Neoliberalism.* New York: Oxford University Press.
Henson, Kevin D. 1996. *Just a Temp.* Philadelphia: Temple University Press.
Hirschhorn, Larry 1984. *Beyond Mechanization.* Cambridge, MA: MIT Press.
Hollingsworth, J. Rogers 1998. "New Perspectives on the Spatial Dimensions of Economic Coordination: Tensions between Globalization and Social Systems of Production." *Review of International Political Economy* 5: 482–507.
Kay, Tamara 2005. "Labor Transnationalism and Global Governance: The Impact of NAFTA on Transnational Labor Relationships in North America." *American Journal of Sociology* 111: 715–56.
Kotz, David M., Terrence McDonough, and Michael Reich, eds. 1994. *Social Structures of Accumulation: The Political Economy of Growth and Crisis.* New York: Cambridge University Press.
Kraft, Philip 1977. *Programmers and Managers: The Routinization of Computer Programming in the United States.* New York: Springer-Verlag.
Kunda, Gideon 1992. *Engineering Culture: Control and Commitment in a High-Tech Corporation.* Philadelphia: Temple University Press.
Kurdelbusch, Antje 2002. "Multinationals and the Rise of Variable Pay in Germany." *European Journal of Industrial Relations* 8: 325–49.
Lee, Cheol-Sung 2005. "International Migration, Deindustrialization and Union Decline in 16 Affluent OECD countries, 1962–1997." *Social Forces* 84: 71–88.
Magnani, Elisabetta and David Prentice 2003. "Did Globalization Reduce Unionization? Evidence from U.S. Manufacturing." *Labour Economics* 10: 705–26.
Mittleman, James H. 1996. "The Dynamics of Globalization." Pp. 1–19 in James H. Mittleman, ed. *Globalization: Critical Reflections.* Boulder, CO: Lynne Rienner.
New York Times 1996. *The Downsizing of America.* New York: Times Books.
Ono, Hiroshi 2007. "Careers in Foreign-Owned Firms in Japan." *American Sociological Review* 72: 267–90.
Parker, Robert E. 1994. *Flesh Peddlers and Warm Bodies: The Temporary Help Industry and Its Workers.* New Brunswick, NJ: Rutgers University Press.
Powell, Walter and Laurel Smith-Doerr 1994. "Networks and Economic Life." Pp. 368–402 in Neil Smelser and Richard Swedberg, eds. *The Handbook of Economic Sociology.* Princeton, NJ: Princeton University Press.
Przeworski, Adam 1991. "Could We Feed Everyone? The Irrationality of Capitalism and the Infeasibility of Socialism." *Politics and Society* 19: 1–38.
Rogers, Jackie Krasas 1995. "Just a Temp: Experiences and Structure of Alienation in Temporary Clerical Employment." *Work and Occupations* 22: 137–66.
Rosenberg, Sam 1991. "From Segmentation to Flexibility: A Selective Survey." *Review of Radical Political Economics* 23: 71–9.
Rubin, Beth A. 1996. *Shifts in the Social Contract: Understanding Change in America Society.* Thousand Oaks, CA: Pine Forge Press.
Sassoon D. 1996. *One Hundred Years of Socialism.* London: Fontana Press.

Scheve, Kenneth and Matthew J. Slaughter 2004. "Economic Insecurity and the Globalization of Production." *American Journal of Political Science* 48: 662–74.

Sennett, Richard 1998. *The Corrosion of Character: The Personal Consequences of Work in the New Capitalism.* New York: W. W. Norton.

Shaiken, Harley 1984. *Work Transformed.* New York: Holt, Rinehart & Winston.

Sklair, Leslie 2002. *Globalization: Capitalism and Its Alternatives.* New York: Oxford University Press.

Smith, Vicki 1997. "New Forms of Work Organization." *Annual Review of Sociology* 23: 315–39.

Sutcliffe, Bob and Andrew Glyn 1999. "Still Underwhelmed: Indicators of Globalization and Their Misinterpretation." *Review of Radical Political Economics* 31: 111–32.

Vallas, Steven P. 1999. "Rethinking Post-Fordism: The Meaning of Workplace Flexibility." *Sociological Theory* 17: 68–101.

Wallace, Michael 1998. "Downsizing the American Dream: Work and Family at Century's End." Pp. 23–38 in Dana Vannoy and Paula J. Dubeck, eds. *Challenges for Work and Family in the Twenty-first Century.* Hawthorne, NY: Aldine de Gruyter.

Wallace, Michael and David Brady 2001. "The Next Long Swing: Spatialization, Technocratic Control, and the Restructuring of Work at the Turn of the Century." Pp. 101–33 in Arne L. Kalleberg and Ivar Berg, eds. *Sourcebook on Labor Markets: Evolving Structures and Processes.* New York: Plenum Press.

Wellman, Barry, Janet Salaff, Dimitrina Dimitrova, Laura Garton, Milena Gulia, and Caroline Haythornthwaite 1996. "Computer Networks as Social Networks: Collaborative Work, Telework and Virtual Community." *Annual Review of Sociology* 22: 213–38.

Western, Bruce 1997. *Between Class and Market.* Princeton: Princeton University Press.

Williamson, Oliver E. 1975. *Markets and Hierarchies: Analysis and Antitrust Implications: A Study in the Economics of Internal Organization.* New York: Free Press.

SIX

Financialization in the Contemporary Social Structure of Accumulation

William K. Tabb

Introduction

Social structures of accumulation (SSA) have life cycles. They are born in an antagonistic relation to the exhaustion of the previous SSA. Conceptually, they may be seen to start in the negative moment of undoing the already weakened institutional accommodations, norms and expectations that had prevailed before and whose internal contradictions can no longer be contained. The institutional solutions of the new SSA allow for renewed accumulation under stable conditions. This does not mean that SSAs should be defined by rapid economic growth (a perspective endorsed by Kotz and Wolfson in Chapter 3), but rather by stability over a period of decades and by the manner in which the institutions that define it form a coherent overdetermining totality (see Chapter 2).

Reacting to the financial excesses and crises of the 1920s, the SSA that was built in the 1930s and that was consolidated in the postwar period constrained the role of finance in the economy. This SSA decayed in the great stagflation of the 1970. The SSA that replaced it, beginning in the early to mid-1980s, soon generated a much greater and ultimately unsustainable role for finance. I concur with the general agreement that a national Keynesian SSA was consolidated in the postwar period and came to an end in the great stagflation of the 1970s.

A global neoliberal SSA can be dated from Ronald Reagan's 1980 electoral victory (of course, not all SSA dating correspond as cleanly with turning point elections). The new SSA was characterized by a weakening of labor relative to capital, with a corresponding gap between productivity and wages; by a qualitatively different globalization of competition, setting the terms of a transnational economy of complex commodity chains and diversification of manufacturing venues rather than the previous international economy characterized by differential manufacturing in the core and commodity production in the periphery; the upsetting of the previously settled position and prospects of oligopolies and national champions formerly protected within nation states; and by movements of loan and investment capital.

In this chapter, I privilege domestic and global level financial innovations and the growth of finance in a climate of aggressive deregulation as aspects of this global neoliberal SSA. As Kotz and Wolfson (Chapter 3) argue, the period of neoliberal dominance generated a boom for the wealthy although the rapid growth in productivity did not benefit the mass of the population, who fell deeper in debt as the SSA proceeded. This imbalance, the fragility of debt leverage and therefore the fragility of aggregate demand and macroeconomic stability, lent a particular character to this period, which in historical retrospect may have ended in the last years of the first decade of the new century. It is too early to be sure, of course, and I expect there will continue to be debates among SSA theorists as to how to periodize neoliberalism. There are also matters of how class and state relations should be theorized in an SSA perspective and whether a transnational SSA has emerged in the current period. I shall return to these questions in the conclusion of the chapter.

The Nature of the Neoliberal SSA

Neoliberalism had both a negative moment of destruction of the old national Keynesian order and a positive moment of the creation of new institutional forms and social relations. The former can be seen as a period of crisis; the latter as the establishment of a coherent regime of accumulation. Observers living through transitional periods can lack an appreciation of the dialectical nature of change and so fail to see how tension inherent in the collapse or undoing of seeming enduring accommodations is a necessary prelude to the incorporation of new social elements into a fledgling SSA.

Thus, many analysts initially saw neoliberalism as an effort to turn the clock back to a kind of capitalism that no longer existed. There was, and is, a reluctance to see the harsh new world of greater risk and destabilization of the postwar SSA accommodations as anything but an era of crisis. Yet it has had decades of durability. Andrew Gamble (2006: 21) has noted that it took some time to appreciate that neoliberalism "did have some distinctive new features as the prefix 'neo' implied, and was an integral part of the re-organization of capitalist relations which was taking place."

Neoliberalism is globally coherent. Its dominant elements, attitudes, and practices are mutually reinforcing. With regard to the state-citizen relationship the new dispensation rejected previous entitlement presumptions of welfare state provisioning and the regulatory role and participation of the state in favor of deregulation, contracting out and privatization. The new capital-labor discord is one of flexibility, higher cost of job loss, downward pressure on wages and benefits; and of individualism in place of solidarity, acceptance of unionism, and greater degree of job security. The previous core-periphery relation between the richer countries of the world system and the rest in which the former are industrialized and the latter providers of raw materials is replaced by the emergence of newly industrializing economies and significant deindustrialization of much of the former manufacturing core where the growth of business services and high technology sectors has become characteristic. Capital-capital relations are therefore globalized and complex commodity chains indicate production with complex cooperation-competition patterns among technologically sophisticated firms and unremitting pressure on suppliers and contractors.

The Transition from a National Keynesian SSA to a Global Neoliberal SSA

The growth of the financial sector results in part from the need to lubricate such developments. The decay of this SSA, within which financialization was so central, was fairly abrupt, as the subprime meltdown in the United States triggered global crisis. The shaping of a new SSA is now underway. To gain insight into this next transformation it is useful to review the transition from the SSA of National Keynesianism to Global Neoliberalism. From an SSA perspective, the end of the latter is not unexpected, even if the depth of the crisis its passing unleashed is profound.

Unlike the postwar SSA, with its close long-term working relations between banks and manufacturing firms that favored European corporatist and Japanese state-led banking patterns, global neoliberalism privileges Anglo-American finance, with its focus on short-term maximizing, better suited to the needs of dramatic redeployment of capital, rapid sectoral restructuring, downsizing, plant closings, and focus on shareholder value. The slowing of the global economy and greater volatility in the final decades of the twentieth century led profit seekers deeper into an array of financial speculations made potentially quite profitable by such departures as floating exchange rates and rapid growth in new centers of the semiperiphery. Finance, which is central to each of the accommodations of the new conjuncture, provides an avenue of insight into transformative elements, raising two important questions regarding the new era's regime of accumulation.

The first is: How does neoliberalism allow the greater appropriation of surplus created in production to be appropriated by the financial sector? We see in this regard the importance of U.S.-based financial institutions (including their subsidiaries in the City of London and elsewhere) along with competitors based in global money centers in reorganizing corporate structures to maximize shareholder value, benefiting from buyouts, mergers, acquisitions and financial hedging strategies. Second, this regime is now decades old and showing definite signs of strain. Its very successes promote a logic of expansion that now threatens its continued viability. How are we to understand its internal contradictions?

While it would be possible to privilege other milestones as the crucial markers in the development of finance as central to the social structure of neoliberalism, I stress the importance of (1) the reorganization of production stemming from dramatic innovation and reduction of costs in transportation and communication, which has increased the scope of business horizons and so encouraged major restructuring that needs to be financed; (2) the development of computer-assisted number crunching and data processing, which allows carrying out sophisticated calculations in market evaluation and risk assessment at low cost and a high degree of complexity and parses risk to develop new financial instruments; (3) the end of the Bretton Woods system of fixed exchange rates has been the occasion for financial innovation to hedge increased foreign exchange risk; and (4) the triumph of shareholder value maximization as the dominant ideology of corporate governance which paved the way for the transition from managerial capitalism to finance capitalism.

The first of these developments revalued assets everywhere, opened markets, encouraged consolidations and complex supplier networks and commodity chains. The second and third developments led to financial engineering and the development and rapid expansion in the use of innovative financial products. The explosion of derivative instruments allowed speculation on price movements in a wide range of assets and leverage beyond what outright purchase would have allowed. Thanks to high gearing ratios, sophisticated quant strategies that realized small gains on transactions could still generate huge profits. These opportunities inspired the search for all manner of means to unlock asset values. In conjunction with the fourth shift enumerated, these developments put pressure on firms that had signed contracts with strong labor unions during the era of managerial capitalism and made political accommodation with social partners to abandon prior understandings.

Greta Krippner (2005), who presents measures of increased financialization, notes that it is difficult to escape the reality that we live in a world of finance. There is wide agreement that "The management of American corporations, large and small, moves to the rhythm of Wall Street." (Krippner 2005: 173) In theorizing this development I argue that financialization is the central feature of the contemporary social structure of accumulation, that the Anglo-American model of capitalism has grown dependent on financial innovation as a major, if not the major source of economic growth, and that financialization has dramatically changed the way capitalist production is organized and imparts a systematic risk of great significance.

Financialization joins globalization and neoliberalism as the key words of the new SSA. It is the dominance by the financial industry of the other economic activity so that it is financial markets that powerfully determine the state of the overall economy and centrally characterize the new SSA. It means that stock prices, currency values, and interest rates shape the economic prospects of working people and these in turn are at the mercy of speculators who increasingly constrain and shape corporate strategies and the choices of politicians. It is the predominance of financial activities over production of goods and services that powerfully characterizes the new SSA.

In exploring these issues the rest of the paper is divided into three sections. The first describes the transition from a national Keynesian SSA to one of global neoliberalism highlighting the central role finance has played. The second part considers how finance continues to restructure markets in the contemporary era. The last considers vulnerabilities and dangers inherent in this finance driven stage of capitalist development bringing in the global dimension.

The Central Role of Finance in the Global Neoliberal SSA

As the importance of globalization and the importance of the shift from the national Keynesian social structure of accumulation to one of global neoliberalism came into general awareness, attention at first focused on the impact of trade in the restructuring of national economies. It took some time for the awareness to grow that globalization and the deregulation that both accompanied it and made it possible followed a three stage sequence, in which different aspects dominated the process: first, trade in 1950–70; second, foreign investment from the late 1960s; and finally financial liberalization from the early 1980s. The importance of the third financial stage, as Nayyar (2006: 145) writes,

had two dimensions: the deregulation of the domestic financial sector in the industrialized countries and the introduction of convertibility on capital account in the balance of payments. ... The globalization of finance, at a scorching pace since the mid-1980s, is not unrelated to the dismantling of regulations and controls.

Actually, the trend to financialization was evident before financial deregulation moved into full swing in the 1980s and 1990s. As national Keynesianism and the (relative) domestic quiet life under oligopolistic competition came under pressure from foreign firms, domestic producers (often the owners of foreign producer subsidiaries or contracting from foreign suppliers) profits were more likely to be reinvested in financial assets than in plant and equipment. Weisskopf, Bowles, and Gordon (1983: 389), noted that increases in financial assets, as a percentage of all corporate uses of funds had increased from less than 20 percent in the period 1959–66 to 25.8 percent during 1973–79.

The epochal defining shift was captured by Paul Sweezy (1994: 11) in a passage worth quoting at some length:

The locus of economic and political power has shifted along with the ascendancy of finance capital. It has long been taken for granted, especially among radicals, that the seat of power in capitalist society was in the boardrooms of a few hundred giant multinational corporations. While there is no doubt about the role of these entities in the allocation of resources and other significant matters as well, I think there is an added consideration that needs to be stressed. The occupants of these boardrooms are themselves to an increasing extent constrained and controlled by financial capital as it operates through the global network of financial markets. In other words, real power is not so much in corporate boardrooms as in the financial markets.

Sweezy went on to say that what holds for these CEOs also applies to elected officials; they too are controlled in what they can and cannot do by financial markets. This applies not only to the leaders of developing economies under IMF and World Bank tutelage, but also to the stronger economies of the core, including the United States. Elected officials generally have not sought to question the efficiency of financial markets.

Indeed, they have let the financial sector, a major contributor to all politicians with any prospect of electoral success, indicate which policies they can pursue and which reforms are not to be discussed. Sweezy offered the example of not only the Clinton Administration's fiscal policies, but also its health care reform, which failed muster in financial markets.

Over the decades of global neoliberalism, finance has grown at a rate far in excess of that of the real economy (Tabb 2007). In the United States the financial sector at its peak generated forty percent of all corporate profits. In the United Kingdom, financial services generated twenty-five percent of gross domestic product. In other countries finance is less prominent but growing in importance as Anglo-American institutions bring their innovative financial products to local markets, and domestic institutions copy these strategies. Central to all of this activity is the increase in debt, a deterioration in safety margins and standards for loans, higher leverage, and the increase in the proportion of financial assets that are relatively far more illiquid and, as it turned out, far riskier than initially presumed, producing losses exceeding $100 billion for major banks by mid-2008.

There were a number of aspects to debt creation in the neoliberal era. One source of debt creation was stagnant real wages and the high cost of job loss (Farber 2005), which encouraged borrowing to maintain consumption levels facilitated by the banking industry's targeting of low income households with poor credit ratings. The stagnation of wages and loss of purchasing power from labor market churning came in part as a result of restructuring pressures imposed by financial markets on U.S. companies. Firms that built up large cash reserves became targets for private equity firms, which by paying a premium price to take control are able to purchase and reorganize corporations, selling off or closing units, downsizing and in other ways withdrawing money, and loading them up with debt before taking them public again.

Globalization and offshoring put further pressure on workers. The share of U.S. national income going to wages and salaries reached its lowest recorded level in 2005. Corporate profits, which were seven percent of U.S. GDP in 2001 (at the start of the upturn, rose to 12.2 percent at the beginning of 2006, while real median incomes were three percent lower. American families added to their debt between 2001 and 2005 at a rate 60 percent greater than the growth of the overall economy. The financial sector grew for other reasons as well. Merger and acquisition activities, nationally and cross-border, relied on financing and assumption of debt; internationally oriented businesses learned to hedge foreign exchange exposure and securitize accounts receivable, and banks offered a host of new products. Each of these developments raised the profits and increased the size of the financial services sector.

One of the first gambits that proclaimed a new era of financialization was the expansion of securitization, the process of turning illiquid assets into liquid capital. By bundling an expected cash flow (credit card receivables or perhaps airplane leases) and packaging them as an asset that is sold, the buyer gets a future cash flow of payments and the seller gets a lump sum payment. Securitizing mortgages allows banks to sell off loans they originate and make new loans. The ready availability of buyers of such securities, the upward trajectory of real estate markets, the low default rates, and the low cost of raising funds encouraged financial institutions to expand into the sub prime market in a big way making loans to low income people whose objective credit status was weak.

The major banks are large players in this market, usually through subsidiaries, extending loans, bundling them, and selling off most of them in securities that earn high credit ratings and are bought by institutions such as pension funds and insurance companies. Those originating the loans sell them, and neither the buyer nor seller of the securities is doing a great deal of due diligence or worried about what happens when interest rates go up, and the variable interest mortgages borrowers are obligated to pay can easily become unaffordable. As a result, the collapse of the sub prime market in 2007 did a great deal of damage.

Financial wizards figured out one could sell a brand, say "Dunking Donut," as a special purpose entity (SPE), which owns the brand while the company continues to run the business (with some restrictions such as on advertising spending, so that the new owner's investment is protected). Returns to the owner of the SPE are isolated from the rest of business in this way allowing such corporate securitizations to achieve a triple-A rating even though the company as a whole is poorly rated. The company raises money at lower cost and the purchaser has a secure investment given the protections put in place. There is a legal separation of assets even if the company itself were to go bankrupt. The idea is a simple one. Soon, collateralized debt obligation packages of assets, containing, for example, mortgage-backed securities allowed for selling derivatives of derivatives that appeared safe in a period of easy credit and low default rates. However, because the real asset base of such packages was small, and the great majority of what was being held involved pyramided debt, a small loss of value could turn into huge losses to their holders, as became all too evident when the subprime real estate market collapsed in 2007.

A similar process was underway in the ownership of corporate America. The shorter time horizon in the era of financialization was also manifest in the behavior of stockholders, the growing importance of private equity and hedge funds, and in the dramatic increase in the use of derivatives and other high leverage vehicles. In the United States in the 1950s, households owned 90 percent of stock and held shares as long-term investments. As institutional investors, pension funds and mutual finds became more important, and their performances scrutinized comparatively in league tables every quarter, they, and so company managers as well, were pressured to maximize share price in the short run. By the 1980s turnover had increased dramatically as shareholder value came to dominate.

If shareholders are no longer behaving like owners in the sense that they have decreased interest in the long-term future of a company, but rather only in short-term stock price movements, fast buying and selling, they become speculators, and that is very different. The head of the British employers' organization, John Sanderland, who was also head of Cadbury-Schweppes, which was feeling the pressure to break up its own holdings to raise shareholder value, told the CBI's 2006 annual gathering (Stern 2006: 11):

It may be old-fashioned but I view a shareholder as a shareholder – someone whose interests in the success and prospects of the company last more than three weeks. ... I have real concerns about promoting the use of my company's stock as hedge-fund plays – just as I would if they were chips in a casino.

While under managerial capitalism the firm was understood as integrated unit dedicated to long-term growth, with finance capitalism the firm was understood as a bundle of assets, the pieces of which could be bought and sold to maximize investor returns. Buyout firms that thought they could extract more value from company assets increasingly stepped in to buy companies seen as underperforming, a term that could mean simply that they held large cash reserves and so could be in effect bought up with their own money. A buyout firm would take control and then use excess company reserves, sell off pieces of the firm, restructure other parts, and then resell the company. The leverage allowed private equity firms, and indeed hedge funds and investment banks in the deregulated financial system that repealed or allowed violation of basic tenets of the postwar SSA, to increase risk to the system in so extreme a fashion that it was only a matter of time until it collapsed.

Even after the new owners had extracted large fees, dividend payments, and returns from selling off noncore assets, companies had to use their available cash reserves and capacity to borrow to take out loans to make them a less likely takeover target or face takeover. While in the managerial capitalist model high debt levels were a sign of poor management, the new norm was to take all assets and turn them into liquid capital that could be withdrawn from the company, leaving high levels of debt requiring management to rigorously cut costs. Nonfinancial corporations came to have fewer employees in-house and less money to spend on physical plant or research and development.

As financial engineering came to dominate corporate decision-making, leveraged recapitalizations became more common. A private equity firm would buy up a company and then the company they owned would borrow money that would be used to pay large dividends to its new owners. The default rate for such companies rose, but the private equity firm sponsoring the buyout often walked away with large short-term profits. By cutting the labor force, pension costs, and other business expenses, when the company, went public again, presumably as a better run, cost-efficient firm, it was often worth more than the purchase price.

There is much irony in a situation in which pension funds desperate for higher returns to meet mushrooming commitments to retired workers in underfunded plans invested in hedge funds and the hedge funds bought up companies, putting the screws to workers to reduce wages and pension costs to pay off the loans taken out to gain control of the firm. Such activities by hedge funds, which famously squeezed costs, put pressure on competitors to do the same; hence the wider phenomena of a sea change in the status of pensions. Coinciding with the rise of leveraged buyouts was acceleration in the number of companies "freezing" their pension plans (so that members stop accruing benefits). In 2007, around a quarter of pension plans in the United States had been frozen, with the expectation that the number would more than double in the next five years. In the United Kingdom, where financialization dominated the economy to even a greater extent than in the United States, about 70 percent of pension plans had been frozen or simply terminated. A similar development is evident in the provision of health care by employers, where companies rid themselves of such obligations and unions were forced to accept special purpose vehicles that take over obligations for a lump sum payment by the company. Should that vehicle fail to meet health benefit liabilities in years to come, such as promises to retirees, the company is not liable (Wighton 2007: 3).

In 2006, there was $150 billion in companies taken private in such "de-equitization" public-to-private transactions, in which companies listed on the stock markets were bought by private equity firms. While most of this took place on the New York and London exchanges, the phenomenon was going global (Smith and Cohen 2007: 1). These deals depended on the availability of funds that could be borrowed at low cost and the deductibility of the interest cost of borrowing the money to buy, with very little, relative to the total cost of the buyout, of the private equity firms' own capital. This tax shelter added value to the company.

How much value is added depended on the likelihood the market gave to possible default on the large debt. Since default rates were historically very low, banks were ready to lend to finance these undertakings. So, it increasingly turned out, were pension funds and insurance companies. Lenders were relaxed about terms and offered low-cost loans since they had funds needing to be placed. Because private equity firms are able to raise huge amounts of money for these activities, and LBO funds join together in "club deals" to share risk, ever bigger takeovers transformed the corporate landscape – at the cost of creating extremes of leverage that could not survive an increase in interest rates and a reversal of expectations leading to insistence on debt repayment and refusal to roll over debt.

Hedge funds, a dangerous U.S. contribution to the growth of financialization, were the fastest growing segment of the industry, accounting for half of all trading on the New York and London stock exchanges in 2007 and a major force in the less transparent debt markets that were one and a half times larger than the stock market itself. In both markets, hedge funds are seen as trading on nonpublic information and as moving markets in violation of insider trading rules, but they do not face the same sort of regulatory oversight as other major market players. Their horizons are also shorter and they are more highly leveraged. The typical "2 and 20" compensation scheme (2 percent fees go to managers plus 20 percent of the profits) encourages and generously rewards risk taking. The large and increasing numbers of such funds, which according to the SEC controlled $2.4 trillion in assets in 2006, pursue similar strategies. The growth of participants has therefore pushed down returns and encouraged still riskier behavior as more money piles into these vehicles, creating the potential for serious systemic risk. Because of the existence of deep financial markets, there was a general belief that their positions can be sold if need be, so hedge funds bet using lots of leverage and often unhedged credit derivatives. Hedge fund borrowers became an important source of bank revenues. As Morris Goldstein (2005: 8) writes,

In an environment where flows into hedge funds are strong, where banks face strong competition from other suppliers of services to hedge funds, and where hedge funds are very important clients to banks, how heavily can we count on a regulatory model where banks are the agents primarily responsible for exercising oversight over the risk-management practices of hedge funds?

While speculators are believed by mainstream financial theorists to be exploiting market inefficiencies and anticipating market movements (Paredes 2006), the potential for herd error is often ignored until a major widely shared misjudgment occurs. As successful hedge funds attract entry by less skilled, opportunistic players and their less sophisticated customers, the potentially successful opportunities for high returns may not match the amounts being thrown onto the market. It is not only highly leveraged players who then face the prospect of serious losses when hedge financing turns into Ponzi financing, borrowing to pay interest on existing debt (Minsky 1992). The "Minsky Moment" inevitably was to come.

The expansion of the financial instruments described in this essay can be seen as a dramatic increase in what Karl Marx called fictitious capital, paper claims to ownership of capital that does not (or does not yet) exist in material form. The financial system can be said to work on the basis of rewards that are to be realized in the future, expectations that may not be realized. As gearing ratios have increased, there is more fictitious capital being supported by such expectations. At a time when the cost of borrowing was low, default rates modest by historical standards, and purchase of assets at what seemed to be inflated prices common, hopes were not disappointed that risk would be rewarded. At a certain point – a point that is never clear beforehand even if warnings often multiply in its anticipation – investors come to question the security of such investments. At that point, money is less forthcoming or only under conditions of greater assurances and higher interest. That point came in 2007 and was widely evident in the disastrous global economy of 2008.

Fear of serious asset valuation loss led to a spectacular growth in credit derivatives, which (in theory) allow investors to buy protection against defaults and other downside risks. These are sold mostly by the giant banks. JP Morgan Chase was said to hold some 2.2 trillion of credit derivative exposure as of mid-2006. The existence of derivative contracts produces moral hazard. Greater risk is undertaken because the investor is insured. Lenders don't worry because they believe they are protected. As a result they may not monitor closely, or at all. Neither may those who sell the derivatives that can be quite complex. For the issuers these instruments may prove highly risky, especially when speculative activity is in remote markets and arcane products like credit default swaps and catastrophe bonds. These are highly illiquid. They cannot easily be sold off as many of the earlier innovations in securitization could. While losses to individual investors and local issuers may not be a major policy concern for international regulators, the scale of speculation has increased dramatically, raising questions of systemic weakness when some of the insurers of risk were discovered in 2008 to lack the capital to meet their obligations, and themselves collapsed.

The growing amount of capital that sought investment opportunities reflected little provision for risk. There were warnings. The International Monetary Fund declared the possibility of illiquid market conditions for some of the new and complex financial instruments, which could act to amplify a market downturn (International Monetary Fund 2006: 7). Emily Thornton (2006: 54), while expressing the reasonable conclusion that 'so far' the rewards had justified the risks – indeed booked profits and their stock prices had performed admirably, they raise the stakes and are "arguably the biggest game of risk ever to play out on Wall Street." The wreckage of the collapse of such leverage would be considerable, triggered not only by a change in market sentiment but also by a failure to settle trades with knock-on effects in highly leveraged interdependent markets (as the collapse of Long-Term Capital Management in 1998 threatened to do, and as happened with Bear Stearns a decade later).

These phenomena generalized in the closing years of the decade. The rapid rise of debt and high leverage raised serious questions for systemic stability despite the presumed more sophisticated risk-management tools employed by major banks, as a reading of the increasingly agitated *Global Stability Report; A Report by the International Capital Markets Department on Market Developments and Issues* (released twice a year by the International Monetary Fund) suggests (see also Schinasi 2005). Warnings were ignored.

An instrument that grew dramatically in importance is the collateralized loan obligation. CLOs are packaged loans pooled and sold in segments (or tranches) on the basis of the degree of risk. This broadens the market for such debt since the safest tranches receive a high credit rating and so can be easily placed. This effectively turns junk loans into triple-A securities. CLOs were a great success and their use expanded dramatically. Those investors holding the bottom tranches absorb losses and those at the top are protected since the loss is unlikely to be total even in the case of failure of the enterprise. David Henry (2006: 90–1) explains the significance of the scale of collateralized loan obligations:

In fact, unbeknownst to many, CLOs are pumping up the entire economy. Because their loans are secured by the assets of the borrowing companies, which means they'll retain more of their value in bankruptcy than unsecured bonds like those wiped out in 2001 and 2002 during the wave of defaults. By refinancing existing corporate debt on better terms and by supplying money for companies to heal and grow again after the last recession, CLOs have helped drive default rates down to 20-year lows. Hedge funds have added to the enthusiasm by loading up on junk loans. And the economy has grown, allowing companies to pay down debt and adding to the confidence of CLO investors. It's a virtuous circle.

But as Henry was aware, the availability of such huge amounts of money was driving deals that were more and more questionable and "payback time may be coming." Risk analysts at the Federal Reserve warned that many piling into CLOs did not understand the risk they were taking since in a downturn losses could be significant. By 2008 some debt claims found no takers and others could not be refinanced or could not support their higher carrying charges.

In a world where banks no longer retained the credit risk on the bulk of the loans they originated and distributed, or where banks are bypassed entirely in credit markets where loans are resold, there was less worry about risk by those who originate the creation of credit. Then there are also incentives to increase the volume of such credit without worrying about loan quality. While hedging reduces risk for individuals, it increases risk to the financial system as a whole. This occurs because distributing risk among more holders brings more players into the game. In a downturn these players may be unable to honor their obligations, imparting weakness to the system globally, as it is not clear who is holding what amount of dangerous levels of risk and therefore who can or cannot be trusted to meet obligations. Individuals believing they are protected become less risk adverse.

Unlike under the previous SSA's norms, in which banks could be persuaded to either roll over debt or renegotiate terms, dispersion of debt holders makes such workouts far more difficult. Banks confidently insured some of these collateralized debt obligations by guaranteeing (quite foolishly as it turned out) to take them back on their books if they incurred losses. When this happened at the beginning of 2007, there were major losses for the large players. In 2008 Citigroup and other U.S.

banks were bailed out to the tune of hundreds of billions. The Swiss bank UBS and other banks around the world each lost hundreds of billions and were saved by huge infusions of taxpayer monies. Global losses from the collapse were between one and two trillion dollars.

There had been a concentration of risk. The U.S. Office of the Comptroller of the Currency (2004) Bank Derivatives Report reveals that five commercial banks accounted for 96 percent of the total notional amount of derivatives; for four of these five, exposure equaled 230 percent or more of their risk-based capital. For banks and hedge funds, higher leverage has become the general rule, which is worrying (Geithner 2006). Whatever the systemic risk, there was just too much money to be made for speculators to turn cautious until fear grew to exceed greed. Even in the face of widespread loss after a pause the game is likely to resume. The question that remains to be answered by history is whether financialization, which has been so much the economy's driving force, means the amounts involved in a meltdown will bring the era of global neoliberalism itself to an end and cause a new SSA emerge. I assert that this is the case.

The End of a Finance-Dominated SSA?

Is there reason then to believe the current regime may be reaching its limits or is the global neoliberal SSA, which is tied so closely to financialization, expanding globally, extending the use of innovative financial instruments and ownership claims? In this concluding section I suggest that (1) the systematic risks from uncontrolled financialization are substantial; (2) its liberal institutional framework of redistributive growth, in which the overall growth rate is hardly impressive and benefits accrue overwhelmingly to those at the top at the expense of the majority, is becoming increasingly politically unacceptable; (3) the underlying logic of neoliberalism as an SSA is increasingly in question; and (4) we are likely to see the emergence of new regulationist institutional structures.

The rupturing of the neoliberal regime came about as a result of financial crisis, and a swing back to a regulated institutional structure is inevitable. The political resistance to neoliberalism's inherent tendency to create deeper income and wealth inequalities and slower growth grew to a revolt against the system as the crisis deepened and elected officials became bolder in the measures they considered for the creation of a new economic model. While some continued to believe they could fix the old model by throwing money at banks, success in extending the global neoliberal SSA can be doubted.

David Kotz (2003) and Kotz and Wolfson (Chapter 3) has proposed the existence of two kinds of institutional structures – a regulationist institutional structure characterized by elements of the postwar SSA – a positive role for an activist government, interventionist to preserve stability and promote growth and to address market failures, cooperation between labor and capital and so on – and contrasts it with a liberal institutional structure, featuring free market ideology, limited government regulation, and harsh capital-labor relations – here called global neoliberalism. Growth is slower under a liberal institutional structure than under a regulationist institutional structure. What we see is a process of what I have called redistributive growth, or what David Harvey (2005) has usefully described as accumulation by dispossession. Harvey uses the term to describe the process by which somebody is divested of their assets or their rights. He has in mind privatization of water, health care, and education through privatization of public goods, which had been entitlements and came to be bought and sold increasingly on the private market, dispossessing those who could not afford the market price of what had been common property or a matter of citizenship rights. The term is *apropos* of what has happened under a regime of global neoliberalism.

A liberal institutional SSA has a number of inherent built-in problems. Such free market periods are characterized by underconsumption tendencies, as financial managers downsize enterprises and squeeze wages and benefits to make debt payments, and government favors regressive taxation. The upward redistribution of income is mistaken for beneficial growth, since what is actually happening to ordinary working people is ignored. There is a close correlation between the growth of finance and a decline in accumulation, as measured by aggregate business investment in the United States, the United Kingdom, France, and Germany (Stockhammer 2004).

Since the presumption that financial markets are always efficient and that interference by government slows growth is so deeply embedded in the thinking of mainstream economists, the financial press, and compliant politicians, there is a general failure to ask why overall growth slows compared to periods in which regulationist institutional structures dominate. When the downturn comes there is likely to be greater recognition of the prevalence of asymmetric information and financial market imperfections and exploration of heterodox institutional perspectives on finance that stress more critical understandings (Arestis and Stein 2005;

Wolfson 2003). It has even led the Institute for International Finance, representing the major financial institutions, to accept blame for their irresponsible actions and to propose better self-regulation as the answer and for U.S. Secretary of the Treasury Paulson, fresh from leading a major Wall Street investment bank, to propose expanding the Fed's remit (but without greater enforcement powers). Both acted to head off serious financial regulation.

At the societal level, the central issue is: what is the consequence of growth dependent on financialization when the capacity to carry debt declines further and new panic sets in? By pushing stockholder value logic to the point of extracting every ounce of surplus and loading firms with debt, not allowing them the reserves traditionally held against bad times, financialization has tempted large-scale bankruptcies in a downturn. In 2000, looking at some of the features of the U.S. economy stressed in this chapter that were visible then, Richard Freeman (2000: 20) suggested that "The US economy could just as readily come back to earth as the exemplar capitalist models of the 1970s and 1980s, Japan and Germany, and the 1960s third way ideal, Sweden, as continue along its new full employment prosperity." While the tech boom did crash shortly after this forecast, the process of financialization continued after a brief interlude.

More recently, we have seen the rise of new centers of accumulation. In 2008, the International Monetary Fund's *World Economic Outlook* estimated that over the previous five years China accounted for a quarter, Brazil, India, and Russia for almost another quarter, and all emerging and developing countries together for about two-thirds of world growth (in purchasing power parity terms). Given the vast surplus savings available on a global scale and opportunities for expanding the Anglo-American financial regime to the rest of the world, it seemed imprudent to declare the neoliberal SSA to have reached its zenith, despite the severe losses in the financial sector and the spreading impacts on the rest of the economy. Funds from these fast-growing economies had flowed into the U.S. economy.

This flow has stopped, however, as the crisis spread and these economies got into similar troubles. Their own financial sectors became problematic and their exports fell. One possibility is that somehow all of this could be overcome and financialization will expand globally and continue to grow as a proportion of the total world economy, with the ownership of major financial institutions and assets more widely distributed globally. This possibility cannot be dismissed, but it appears unlikely given the damage financialization has caused.

It is possible as well that even if this does occur, the logic of overextension inherent in financialization will lead to even larger globally encompassing bubbles. In a 2007 interview, as storm clouds were visible, the chief executive of Citigroup, Chuck Prince, remarked "When the music stops, in terms of liquidity, things will be complicated. But as long as the music is playing, you got to get up and dance. We're still dancing." It was not much later that the music had indeed stopped and Prince was no longer CEO, Citigroup was announcing losses of incredibly large magnitudes, and the financial sector was announcing major layoffs and dragging the stock market down.

The serious losses generated by over-leveraged U.S. financial institutions, with knock-on effects globally for those who had innocently bought the securitized assets sold by Wall Street with their "toxic waste" (uncollectible collateral), raised uncomfortable questions for the future of American-style financialization and even broader questions of the future balance between U.S.-based financial institutions and those of emerging market economies. Indeed, the changing balance of national capitalisms as the era of globalization of the world system economy proceeds raises issues not only of the damage caused by relatively unregulated financialization and the continued viability of neoliberalism as an SSA. It also raises issues of how SSAs are to be theorized in a far more integrated world political economy in which new centers of accumulation are shifting the global balance of power away from U.S. hegemony. Next generation SSA theorizing will have to pay great attention to the world system context, in which current account surplus countries, newly important transnational corporations, sovereign wealth funds, and other actors will be more closely integrated into core country economies.

Conclusion

The analysis of this chapter allows for reflecting on the reconceptualization of SSA theory as suggested by other contributions to this collection as well as the nature of the global neoliberal SSA and where we are in history. In this conclusion I will discuss class and state relations in relation to the financialization of the neoliberal SSA. In particular I will discuss how SSA theorists might want to understand globalization – or as some prefer, transnationalization – in class and state terms, whether there is a single emergent global SSA, and the role of the state in midwifing a new SSA and in defending the power relations of the existing neoliberal SSA.

Class Analysis in the New SSA

I begin with class analysis. In Chapter 3, Kotz and Wolfson frame the discussion of how a new SSA is constructed by focusing on the typical capitalist:

> one would expect the individual capitalist to favor institutions that support each step in the profit-making process. Furthermore, institutions which support a high rate of profit, or a higher one than has prevailed previously, would gain the support of the individual capitalist.

In my view, however, the higher profits accruing to newly empowered financial capital come at the *expense* of productive capital in other sectors. Redistribution in the sphere of circulation is central to explaining the growth of financialization. It is the hegemony of financiers over producers and the impact of rising debt that drove expansion in the SSA (Tabb 2007). This possibility is outside the framework proposed by Wolfson and Kotz, which focuses on the profits of capital as a whole.

One of the central aspects of SSA theorizing is that of contradictions or conflictual tensions within an SSA, in the institutions that initially provide stability but eventually break down. As discussed, it was the rise of transnational corporations and later financialization that led to a new balance among the fractions of the capitalist class. When maximizing shareholder value replaced the previous SSA's greater regard for other stakeholders, including workers, short-term thinking came to dominate over the long-term health of firms. As banks were freed of income ceilings, restrictions on their geographic mobility and functional restraints, they responded with the development of new financial products, not only derivatives but also credit arrangements with working class families in the form of home equity loans and easier access to credit card debt.

While financial sector debt and asset inflation reached previously unimagined heights, the SSA was built upon a sharp disjuncture between the interests of finance capital, on one side, and the overall growth rate of the economy and the incomes of most nonfinancial companies and working people, on the other. Manufacturers, as I have suggested, were quite unhappy with these developments. To speak of "the capitalist" agreeing to changes that benefit them is to miss the centrality of the intra-class conflict and of course a parallel division between the professional classes associated with and benefiting from the distribution of income in their favor in the new SSA and those who lost out.[1]

---

[1] I discuss the use of the construct class in these contexts in Tabb 2004b and 2009b.

The Role of the State in the Neoliberal SSA

I agree with Kotz and McDonough (Chapter 4) that a transnationalization of class relations is a central aspect of both the global neoliberalism
and any successor SSA. I take issue, however, with their suggestion that
this transnationalization may be leading to the formation of a transnational capitalist class and even to the emergence of transnational state-
like structures. Countries are rarely eager to give up their sovereignty
to some Kautskian superstate institution. The competition between
national capitalist classes remains keen and in the current crisis has led
both workers and capitalists to lean more heavily on their governments
for protection against competitors. Tensions between European corporatist states and Anglo-American financialization and between the sys-
temically important states of the former periphery and those of the core
reluctant to cede power, evident at international negotiations, suggest
the superiority of framing the IMF, World Bank, and WTO in terms of
struggles to determine soft law governance frameworks in global state
economic governance institutions (GSEGIs), in which coercion by strong
states over weaker ones is possible, rather than by a framing of a global
state (Tabb 2004a).

As to efforts by historically U.S.-dominated GSEGIs to become a
transnational state formation, previous success in forcing Washington
Consensus policies on developing countries must be set against the
examples of numerous Latin American governments (which had the longest experience of domination by neoliberalism) and which have reduced
the influence of the GSEGIs on their destinies. The buildup of foreign
currency reserves by the East Asian developmental states has increased
their independence as well. While the global financial crisis from 2008
on led to renewed dependence on the IMF and other lending agencies
by some of the poorest governments, those especially in Eastern Europe
with large foreign currency denominated debt, these are developing with
less controlling structural adjustment requirements than in the past. It is
not at all obvious that the GSEGIs are able to act as a transnational state
in the contemporary conjuncture.[2]

Kotz and McDonough present the global neoliberal SSA as characterized by "the limited growth in state spending and the renunciation
of expansionary macropolicy." In the United States, and to different

---

[2] Contributors to two journals' special issues on TCC/TCS literature have been skeptical
of this approach: Symposium, *Science & Society* 2001–2002; and Symposium, *Theory and
Society* 2001. For my own view of the use and limitations of the TCC/TCS perspective, see
Tabb 2009a.

extents elsewhere, there was a renunciation of Keynesian macroeconomics and a shift in policy toward the reduction of the size and scope of the Welfare State. However, while the rationale differed, tax cuts to stimulate economic growth from Reagan to Bush the younger were a dominant macroeconomic policy in the neoliberal SSA. Rather than limiting state spending, the neoliberal SSA fiscal policies downsized social programs while increasing military expenditures, a difference in priorities and not a reduction in federal spending. Also, budget deficits increased dramatically. What is more to the point, the particular growth paradigm of the global neoliberal order, and hardly only in the United States, was characterized by debt dependence and the weakness of the expansions produced as a result of the vast increase in national, personal, and corporate sector debt as well as the growth model's generating systemic instability.

Because the employment and economic stimulus that the financial sector contributed must be replaced by a new leading sector or sectors (not yet obvious), the role of government stimulus aimed at direct job creation will be more important in the transition. Certainly, addressing the current crisis will require a greater role for state spending on social consumption to meet immediate survival needs of the unemployed as well as the attraction of increased social investment for employment creation and to rebuild infrastructure and human capital slighted in the neoliberal SSA. Less clear is the extent to which a continued federal role in providing incentives and guidance of possible leading sectors of the future to replace and restructure exhausted basic industries indicate a greater state role on a continuing basis in a new SSA. The popular press and the scholarly literature appreciate that the period 1980–2009 was the time of the global neoliberal SSA – even if this was not the designated label, that it has come to an end, and that a post neoliberal period has begun (Demirovic 2009).

References

Arestis, Philip and Howard Stein 2005. "An Institutional Perspective on Finance and Development as an Alternative to Financial Liberalization," *International Review of Applied Economics* 19, 4: 381–98.

Demirovic, Alec 2009. "Postneoliberalism and Post-Fordism – Is There a New Period in the Capitalist Mode of Production?" *Development Dialogue* January.

Farber, Henry S. 2005. "What Do We Know About Job Loss in the United States? Evidence from the Displaced Worker Survey, 1984–2004." *Economic Perspectives*, Federal Reserve Bank of Chicago, Second Quarter.

Freeman, Richard B. 2000. "The US Economic Model at Y2K: Lodestar for Advanced Capitalism?" Working Paper 7757, National Bureau of Economic Research.

Gamble, Andrew 2006. "Two Faces of Liberalism." Pp. 20–35 in Richard Robison, ed. *The Neo-liberal Revolution: Forging the Market State.* Houndsmills: Palgrave Macmillan.

Geithner, Timothy F. 2006. "Hedge Funds and Derivatives and Their Implications for the Financial System." Distinguished Lecture, Hong Kong Monetary Authority and Hong Kong Bankers Association. September 14.

Goldstein, Morris 2005. "What Might the Next Emerging-Market Financial Crisis Look Like?" *Working Paper* WP 05-7. Washington, DC: Institute for International Economics.

Harvey, David 2005. *A Brief History of Neoliberalism.* New York: Oxford University Press.

Henry, David 2006. "Danger – Explosive Loans." *Business Week* October 23.

International Monetary Fund 2006. *Global Financial Stability Report; Market Developments and Issues*, September. Washington, DC: International Monetary Fund.

Kotz, David M. 2003. "Neoliberalism and the Social Structure of Accumulation Theory of Long-Run Capital Accumulation." *Review of Radical Political Economics* 29, 3: 263–70.

Krippner, Greta R. 2005. "The Financialization of the American Economy." *Socio-Economic Review* 3, 2: 173–208.

Minsky, Hyman P. 1992. "The Financial Instability Hypothesis." Working Paper No. 74. Jerome Levy Economics Institute.

Nayyar, Deepak 2006. "Globalization, History and Development: a Tale of Two Centuries." *Cambridge Journal of Economics* 30, 1: 137–59.

Paredes, Troy 2006. "On the Decision to Regulate Hedge Funds: The SEC's Regulatory Philosophy, Style, and Mission." Faculty Working Paper Series 06–03–02. School of Law, Washington University.

Schinasi, Garry J. 2005. "Safeguarding Financial Stability." *Economic Issues* no. 36. Washington, DC: International Monetary Fund).

Smith, Peter and Norma Cohen 2007. "Record $150 bn of delistings." *Financial Times* January 2.

Stockhammer, Engelbert 2004. "Financialization and the Slowdown of Accumulation." *Cambridge Journal of Economics* 28, 5: 719–41.

Stern, Sefan 2006. "The Short-Term Shareholders Changing the Face of Capitalism." *Financial Times* March 28.

Sweezy, Paul M. 1994. "The Triumph of Financial Capital." *Monthly Review* 46, 2: 1–11.

Symposium 2001. "Responding to William Robinson's `Social theory and global-ization." *Theory and Society* 30: 2.

Symposium 2001–2002. "Responding to William I. Robinson." *Science & Society* 65: 4.

Tabb, William K. 2004a. *Economic Governance in the Age of Globalization.* New York: Columbia University Press.

2004b. "The Two Wings of the Eagle." Pp. 95–101 in John Bellamy Foster and Robert W. McChesney, eds. *Pox Americana: Exploring the American Empire*. New York: Monthly Review Press.

2007. "The Centrality of Finance." *Journal of World Systems Research* 13, 1: 1–11.

2009a. "Globalization Today: At the Borders of Class and State Theory." *Science & Society* January.

2009b. "The Transnational Capitalist Class and the Politics of Capitalist Globalization." Pp. 98–115 in Samir Gupta, and Jan Nderveen Pieterse, eds. *Politics of Globalization*. New Delhi: Sage.

Thornton, Emily 2006. "Inside Wall Street's Culture of Risk," *BusinessWeek* June 12.

U. S. Office of the Comptroller of the Currency 2004. *OCC Bank Derivatives Report:* Fourth Quarter 2004.

Weisskopf, Thomas E., Samuel Bowles and David M. Gordon 1983. "Hearts and Minds: A Social Model of U.S. Productivity Growth." *Brookings Papers on Economic Activity* 2: 381–441.

Wighton, David 2007. "Pensions Worry CEOs." *Financial Times* July 25.

Wolfson, Martin 2003. "Neoliberalism and the Social Structure of Accumulation." *Review of Radical Political Economics* 35, 3: 255–62.

SEVEN

Global Neoliberalism and the Possibility of Transnational State Structures

Emlyn Nardone and Terrence McDonough

In Chapter 4, David Kotz and one of the present authors argue that the resolution of the crisis of the1970s and early 1980s involved the construction of a new social structure of accumulation (SSA). This new SSA is best characterized as one of global neoliberalism. Kotz and McDonough argue that neoliberalism in this period constituted a multileveled phenomenon that included neoliberal institutions, neoliberal policies, neoliberal theories, and neoliberal ideology. Among neoliberal policies, the aggressive attempt to remove any barriers to the free movement of goods and capital across borders was especially prominent. This provides one of the many links between neoliberalism and globalization. Neoliberalism promoted globalization, and globalization in a dialectical fashion was also at the root of support by capital for the new neoliberal orientation. Increasing international competition undermined profitability. Capital began to pursue a program of deregulation and capital flight as a means to recover profitability. Further, the resultant globalization of production weakened labor and strengthened capital's ability to effectively pursue its newly preferred strategy.

Transformations at the level of the state must be counted among the prominent institutions of this global neoliberalism. Indeed the contemporary changes in domestic state structures and policy have attracted a great deal of analysis. Globalization is easily identified as an influence on these changes. International "competitiveness" has become the stated rationale for government policy in all areas of social life. It is also clear that several institutions of an international character such as the World Trade Organization, the European Union, and the International Monetary Fund have assumed increasing importance.

This is hardly surprising in the context of an institutional reorganization of capitalism where its transnational nature has assumed a central significance.

It is the central purpose of this chapter to interrogate the specific character of these latter developments. It is natural to hypothesize that an internationalization of the SSA would be accompanied by the development of state institutions of a transnational character. The existing nature and conception of state institutions, however, makes this thesis difficult to sustain. The nation-state model of legitimate political institutions has become literally ubiquitous in the modern period. There are obvious problems with extending this model to understand global or even regional political institutions.

The current conception of state sovereignty is defined by its territorially delimited nature. The state's writ runs only within well-defined boundaries.[1] This does not mean that *inter*-national institutions cannot exist. It is just that they derive their form and force from agreements between preexisting and sovereign nation states and are not independent of these states. Indeed, international institutions of this type were prominent in the post World War II SSAs. The Bretton Woods institutions provided a framework for international economic relations for many nations in this period. It would indeed be more natural to expect that this category of international arrangement should persist into the global neoliberal SSA. The specific international institutions would change in the transition from one SSA to another, but the basic character of these institutions would not be transformed.

Further, it has been pointed out that it is easy to exaggerate the extent to which the traditional nation state has been disempowered by the globalization of economic activities. The nation state is still the most powerful political actor within its borders, establishing the legal framework of economic activities among other measures needed to secure the mode of production. Central to the exercise of political power is the ability to project effective force within and frequently outside the boundaries of the state. It is generally nation states which have the capacity to organize such force in the contemporary world. The argument of this chapter will not seek to minimize the importance of today's nation states. Rather it will argue that the role, not the importance, of the nation state in the overall international political framework has changed.

[1] This perspective tends to ignore the difficulties involved in the extension of imperial power.

Despite the force of the foregoing arguments, it is the thesis of this chapter that those institutions that participate in the governance of the international economy have been assuming a transnational character. While various national state structures remain a necessary part of this process, the territorial aspect of states and therefore the nation-state has indeed been problematized by capitalism's growth beyond national boundaries. We will not, however, try to establish the construction of transnational state institutions on the basis of the traditional model of the sovereign nation state. Indeed it is the reorganization of political and regulatory institutions on a novel basis which underlines the transitional character of the emergence of global neoliberalism.

In service of this argument, the remainder of this chapter is divided into a number of sections. The first section discusses the theoretical basis on which a novel conception of the transnational state can be developed. It begins with a description of the relationship between the nation-state and SSAs as traditionally understood within SSA theory. The next subsection discusses in general terms the Marxian conception of the state, the relationship of states to markets, and Polanyi's double movement in the history of the state. We next take up the "Italian" school of international political economy, which has applied Gramscian insights to international institutions and discussed the emergence of the transnational capitalist class. This approach has been further developed by William I. Robinson in the conception of the transnational state apparatus (TNS). Finally in this section we employ the "new medievalism" in suggesting more concretely the novel character of this TNS.

The next section first sketches out the broad contours of the actually emerging elements of this TNS. We then develop the relationship of the TNS and the persistence of the traditional nation-state. A further subsection links the emergence of an international human rights discourse to Polanyi's second movement. This section concludes by developing the connections between this TNS and the global neoliberal SSA. A concluding section will discuss the relationship of these new state structures and the emergence of what appears to be the first stages of the crisis of global neoliberalism.

Theorizing the Transnational State

The goal of this section is first to reevaluate the traditional SSA approach to the role of the state in the international context. Second, it seeks to bring to bear Marxian state theory, Polanyi, and a number of innovative contemporary approaches to the transnational state.

SSA Theory and States

Much of the work undertaken within the SSA school has tended to focus on the economic aspects of the "accumulation" process, rather than on the more social and political aspects of the "social structures" that underpin and facilitate the accumulation processes. On the other hand, SSAs have been most frequently located at the level of the nation-state. Treating the boundaries of the SSA as contiguous with those of the nation-state was justified through an appeal to the basic structure of the theory. Justifying this initial preference for a nation-centric analysis, McDonough (1994: 79) argued as follows:

> Since political and ideological institutions are an important part of any SSA, and politics and ideology are often specific to particular regions or even nations, it seems appropriate to consider SSAs as national or regional phenomena rather than as ones encompassing the whole of the capitalist world.

The international setting of these national SSAs was not ignored. International institutions and arrangements existed but they were considered as shared aspects of the different national SSAs. Such country-specific approaches have been fruitful in an historical setting in which a system of nation-states was the predominant state form (Kotz et al. 1994: 308–09). However, this type of analysis may be in need of revision in order to better conceptualize the emergence of global and transnational (as opposed to national and international) patterns of production and consumption and consequently the global scale of accumulation that increasingly characterizes the contemporary political economy. This reconsideration would argue that SSA theory originally, and justifiably, articulated country-specific cases, with particular but not exclusive emphasis placed upon the United States. Contemporary developments, however, place new emphasis on those elements of capitalism that have a tendency to transcend national boundaries.[2]

The fundamental elements of national capitalisms (class relations, production, commerce, finance) have *over-spilled* national institutional confines. Following from this, the "inter" national economy framework that governed economic and political activity among nation-states has also evolved beyond previous institutional constraints. These tendencies, which can be viewed as "trans" and "supra" national outgrowths from

---

[2] The idea of capitalist production transcending national boundaries is of course not new. "The need of a constantly expanding market for its production chases the bourgeoisie over the whole surface of the globe. It must nestle everywhere, settle everywhere, establish connexions everywhere" (Marx 1978 [1888]: 476).

previously nationally articulated SSAs, therefore cannot be explained by the type of nation-centric study originally carried out within the SSA school. An emerging global SSA can no longer be appropriately theorized as the culmination of nationally sited SSAs, with their individual logics of accumulation driving the world's economy.

While territorial state units are still arguably the most important elements in governing the world economy, their role and function have been problematized by the globalization of capital, the increasing influence of non-state actors, and various advances in technology and communication that have compressed space and time and created an increased ability to organize production on a global scale. All of these developments, which can be described as symptoms of the process known as globalization, have challenged the functioning of nationally determined social structures relating through *inter*national (rather than *trans*national) institutions.

States and Markets

While globalization may not yet exist as a finished project, it is most certainly a process of change that challenges our traditional conceptions of the relations between economy and society. In any attempt to capture the complexity of the global SSA, it is important to consider the dialectic of states and markets:

Since the middle of the nineteenth century, the development of the international (and now increasingly global) political economy has been associated with the dialectical interplay of the rivalries between more integral nation-states on the one hand and the forces of globalising capitalism on the other (Gill 1994: 75).

Throughout the history of capitalism the interplay between these two pivotal elements has been a major determining force of both the growth and decline of capital accumulation (Schwarz 2000). However, states and markets cannot be analytically isolated from each other. The success of capitalist accumulation relies on mediating the relationship between economic logics and pressures on the one hand and social requirements and demands on the other.

This mediation process can be described in terms drawn from Karl Polanyi's *The Great Transformation* (2001 [1944]). Polanyi identified a two-fold movement in the development of capitalism. The first movement was the state's diminishing role in core economic activity, ironically through intervention to allow market forces to take over many functions previously carried out by states in the realm of production and distribution. The second aspect of this movement was the opposing reaction that society developed to the negative effects of a more purely market-driven economy, thus forcing the state to intervene again to soften the harsh effects of *laissez faire*.

In the late 1970s, following a period in which the Keynesian-inspired postwar economy experienced seemingly intractable problems of rapid inflation and rises in unemployment as well as the rising cost of social programs, states began to emphasize the first aspect of Polanyi's two-fold movement. Part of the consequences of this policy shift can be seen in the emergence of the neoliberal "global" economy. While Polanyi's movement described the process of regulating capitalism in a nation-state system, the effect of the globalization of production poses a different set of problems for states attempting to carry out Polanyi's movement in the current period. It is much more difficult to implement rules to govern a transnational capitalism, thus requiring innovative sets of structures and institutions.

These factors provide the impetus for the creation of new forms of governance for capitalism. In the classical Marxist tradition the modern state is fundamentally a capitalist state. It is the outcome and partial embodiment of a particular configuration of class relations engendered by the capitalist mode of production, and represents, among other things, the domination of one class by another. Following in this tradition a globalization of production relations can be seen as at the same time a globalization of class relations.

Gramsci and the Transnational Capitalist Class
The neoGramscian school (Cox 1987; Gill and Law 1988; Gill 1990) and the Amsterdam school (Pijl 1984, 1998; Overbeek 2001; van Apeldoorn 2004) in international political economy have examined the formation of an emerging transnational capitalist class (TNCC) and its effects on production relations. Cox's work is the most ambitious attempt to apply a Gramscian historical materialism to international relations theory (Linklater 1996).[3] Essentially he applies Polanyi's ideas about state regulation and re-regulation to the "internationalization" of the state, which necessarily involves the reconstruction of state structures in line with

---

[3] Cox is concerned with various historical hegemonic orders existing in three main time periods. He contends that the dominant modes of production within these specific periods determine interactions between states. The Liberal International Order dominated by Pax Britannica, the Imperialist Age up to 1945, and then the neoliberal world order after that period.

the expansion of capitalist production relations. This process resulted in the eroding of the power of labor in a global context, in contrast to the increasing structural power of capital. The Gramscian aspect of his work emphasizes that the most prominent forces within the interstate system achieve a form of ideological consensus through both coercive and non-coercive methods, which then dictate how best to proceed to restructure domestic economies. Thus for (Cox 1987: 254): "the internal structures of states are adjusted so that each can best transform the global consensus into national policy and practice."

Cox argues this process of the internationalization of the state is broken into three stages. In the 1930s the state was predominant over its economy, followed by the postwar system, which achieved a compromise in which domestic populations' desires were balanced with the needs of international capital, as embodied in the welfare state systems mediated through international institutions such as Bretton Woods. In many places these welfare states were then, in the current phase, partly dismantled as transnational sources of power began to take precedence over domestic states' authority.

The sources of this transformation in the relationship between state and world economy are not part of a teleological triumph of global capitalism or a technological inevitability but arise more from a political agenda designed to reconfigure the balance of power between capital and labor and other fetters on the globalization of production. Central to this, according to Cox (p. 32) is that

key aspects of economic management are therefore to be shielded from politics, that is to say, from political pressures. This is achieved by confirmed practices, by treaty, by legislation and by formal constitutional provisions.

In Cox's view, these processes are associated with the globalization of national classes and class fractions in line with internationalizing capital and economy. The internationalization of various configurations of class relations involves the internationalization of the state. As national classes increasingly interpenetrate one another, the need for state structures that capture this activity becomes prominent. Transnational classes first rise out of the more dominant states, but their defection from states leads to a loss of hegemony for the state and a transfer of that authority to the agents of transnational production and capital. Hence, instead of there being anarchy in the international system, Cox argues that transnational governance and hegemony exist through capitalist class interactions on a global basis.

The Transnational State Apparatus

Drawing from these insights, political sociologist William Robinson has examined the possible emergence of a Transnational State (TNS) apparatus to embody the TNCCs' political interests (Robinson 2001, 2004, 2005). Robinson (2001: 166) describes this TNS as an apparatus that

> is multilayered and multifaceted. It links together functionally institutions that exhibit distinct gradations of "stateness," which have different histories and trajectories, and which are linked backward and forward to distinct sets of institutions, structures and regions. The supranational organisations are economic and political, formal and informal ... [t]hese supranational planning institutes are gradually supplanting national institutions in policy development and global management and administration of the global economy.

According to Robinson this emerging structure is an attempt to replace the role previously played by hegemonic nation-state powers in earlier epochs of capitalism by providing the necessary instruments to allow for the reproduction of class relations within global accumulation processes.

We wish to emphasize that Robinson's and especially our use of the term TNS should not be confused with or be associated with the demise of nation-states or with the idea of a global state in the traditional sense. The TNS concept is a qualitatively different form of state with different roles and competencies from those in the heretofore national variants. It can be seen as more of an emerging network of bodies, forums, institutions, and regions, *including* preexisting national state structures that are in the process of being transformed.

The New Medievalism

While these international structures have been ceded a certain amount of sovereignty by states, they are not necessarily themselves state structures in the traditional sense, that is, they do not rely for their authority on monopolizing the political exercise of force. While Robinson observes that we need to conceive of the TNS in a way different from that of the traditional nation-state and gestures toward the multileveled and varied nature of this new structure or set of structures, he does not provide a unifying framework within which to understand these new developments.

International relations theorist Hedley Bull coined the phrase "New Medievalism" in the late 1970s to describe certain parallels between contemporary developments in the modern state system and the system of governance loosely applied by overlapping powers and authorities in medieval Europe (Bull 1977). Bull recognized a number of trends in the international system that led him to apply this metaphor: (1) regional integration as exemplified by the EU (but including other forms of regional integration); (2) disintegration of existing states into smaller regions of local governance, for example, devolution in the United Kingdom or regional autonomy in Spain; (3) increases in private (terrorist, criminal) violence, which challenges the states' monopoly on violence; (4) the increase in influence of international and transnational organizations; and (5) the technological unification of the world, especially in forms of production, transport, and communication (Gamble 2001).

The New Medievalism assumes that the world is experiencing the end of strict national sovereignty (for critiques of this position see Krasner 1999). It sees the nation-state being supplanted by horizontal networks of states, NGOs, and international institutions. These theorists envision a world of multiple allegiances and responsibilities replacing the undivided loyalty formerly owed by the citizen to the sovereign state. In this new-medieval world, sub-national, national, and supranational institutions share authority over individuals. There is here a heuristic claim that by understanding the pre-international world, we can begin to understand a post-international world.

This provides a route through which to break the modern identification of the state and the nation-state. While historians have not hesitated to discuss "the state" in medieval society, this has carried with it no assumption that the state in this sense closely resembles the modern state. Governance in medieval Europe functioned through elaborate hierarchies. Authority was multiple and boundaries were overlapped in changing configurations. Many areas were subject to various systems of law and governance. There was no center of universal competence in the way that has come to traditionally exist in the nation-state. So in a sense sovereignty was distributed rather than concentrated. Governance within the medieval period was determined by the relationships between Church and Emperors, between rival Kings, between Kings and feudal lords, and between feudal lords and their vassals, and so on down the line. Hence there were different spheres of influence making it impossible to posit a single authority or power in specific locations, resulting in overlapping claims and various simultaneous loyalties. These centrifugal tendencies were countered by two powerful organizational patterns with universalistic aspirations – the Holy Roman Empire and the Roman Catholic Church. At the same time these claims, both rival and complementary, undermined the prospect of unitary authority.

Similarly within the current period, that is within New Medievalism, we have two rival and complementary sources of authority – the nation-state system and the transnational market system. This helps to explain how and why in the global neoliberal world, like in its medieval counterpart, a certain degree of stability and coherence has been maintained despite the loss of the hegemony of one all-encompassing organizing principle. Hence, the New Medievalism is a system of overlapping authority and multiple loyalties held together by a duality of competing universalistic claims from the state system and market economy. Friedrichs (2001), for instance, sees the New Medievalism as a macro-analytical tool for understanding a post-Westphalian[4] world and as an alternative to the discourse of globalization. The persistence of states, the transformation of existing structures and institutions, and the emergence of new ones can be partially understood through this framework of New Medievalism.

It is perhaps necessary here to return to Robinson's suggestion about institutions taking part in varying degrees of "stateness". Many of the components of this new framework (those which are not themselves states) are similar to the traditional state in that they exercise governance over areas of social activity that have been traditionally governed by states. Most of the functions covered are generally considered economic (see the next section). They depart from the traditional state in not being able to back up their governance directly with the threat of the exercise of legitimate force. They can, however, enforce their decisions in two other potential ways. The first is through the action of the nation-states which participate in the TNS. The second way is through the sanction of the withdrawal of the benefits of participation. This is the threat exercised by the IMF for instance. This is analogous to the source of the coercive power of the Church in the medieval system of power. The WTO combines both of these strategies in withdrawing the benefits of trade through authorizing sanctions to be carried out by member states.

The Evolving Transnational State Apparatus

William Robinson (2001, 2004) identifies the emergence of a form of a transnational state structure that carries out a governance role in the transnational sphere. However, very little work has been done on actually describing the scope of the components of such a structure and the

---

[4] The Treaty of Westphalia (1648) is viewed as the inauguration of the modern state system.

extent of its power or capacity to fulfill this role. Robinson focuses more on the ideological capacity of these structures, emphasizing, for example, the role the World Economic Forum plays "as the most comprehensive transnational planning body of the TCC and the quintessential truly global network binding the TCC together in a transnational civil society" (Robinson 2004: 127). Robinson does, however, also describe how transnational networks and global structures transgress the ability of nation-states to mediate distribution, for example within the capital accumulation process (Robinson 2004: 102). But concretely, what is the actual scope and extent of this condensation (a term Robinson uses in reference to Poulantzas' concept of state) of state-like structures that have formed in conjunction with the new global class relations? What capacities now inhere in this transnational institution, or set of institutions, which can facilitate a global structure of accumulation? In this section we will examine some of the potential components of this structure that have actually emerged on the global scene.

Regional Trading Blocs
The growth of regional organizations through the formation of trade blocs has been enormous. Every continent now has some form of regional forum with varying degrees of competencies. These regional arrangements sometimes function as quasi states in certain policy areas and at other times function as completely new forms of structural organization, in that their internal coherence is based upon shared or pooled sovereignty and compromise between many states rather than on the concept of homogeneity through nationality. While regional forums have developed at difference paces and their functionality varies widely, there is an undeniable movement towards the pooling of regional sovereignty, especially in matters pertaining to trade. These various organizations can be termed Regional Economic Communities (RECs).

While the European Union (EU) is the most widely known regional arrangement, its creation has often been influential in regional integration efforts in others areas of the globe (Cameron 2005). For non-EU European states such as Iceland and Norway, who are both members of the European Free Trade Association (EFTA), the European Economic Area Agreement allows them to partake in the EU internal market. The African Union (AU), for example, draws together a whole myriad of regional and subregional arrangements through the African Economic Community (AEC). Contained within the AEC are various subgroups, which are all integrating at different speeds. For example, the East

African Community, the West African Monetary Union, the Economic and Monetary Community of Central Africa, and the Southern African Customs Union all have fully functioning free trade areas and customs unions, while some even have a common currency area. There are currently proposals and interregional negotiations to further integration in other ways, such as visa-free travel and the creation of single markets. As progress is made on a regional level, the AU tries to coordinate policy on a continental level by integrating regional arrangements into broader African agreements. There are proposals to develop an All African Central Bank, an African Monetary Union, and so on.

Similar arrangements exist in other areas of the globe. The Association for South East Asian Nations operates a free trade area through the Asia Free Trade Agreement. UNASUL/UNASUR in South America operates a customs union and free trade area in most of its member states while CARICOM in the Caribbean has a free trade area, a customs union, a single market, and an almost fully functioning currency area. The Gulf Area Free Trade Agreement and North American Free Trade Agreement (NAFTA) are free trade arrangements, in the Persian Gulf region and North America respectively, which may lead to further economic integration efforts. Furthermore, regional organizations often interact with one another and negotiate over specific matters representing common positions for all the constituent states. These organizations also work with other global institutions such as the World Bank (WB) and International Monetary Fund (IMF), since sometimes policy initiatives either contradict or complement arrangements made by individual states with these global institutions. These negotiations sometimes help forge common positions when dealing at the global level with trade agreements within the WTO, for example.

Global Finance

One of the most important issues in integrating different regions into a global accumulation process concerns the provision of finance and capital for the development of products and markets. This is often facilitated on a global level through the international financial institutions (IFIs). Located within the United Nations system, but with independent mandates, the IMF and the World Bank Group (WBG) play key roles, especially in the area of development. Through its use of structural adjustment programs (SAPs), the IMF can determine domestic economic policy in states requiring its assistance. Usually such policies are meant to facilitate the relatively seamless integration of states into the global marketplace. This is accomplished through programs of privatization and the opening up of domestic markets. The WBG operates through five constituent organizations. It provides capital for infrastructure projects to sovereign states through the International Bank for Reconstruction and Development and the International Development Association, capital to private firms in developing states through the International Finance Corporation, investment risk insurance through the Multilateral Investment Guarantee Agency, and investment dispute resolution mechanisms between private interests and states through the International Centre for Settlement of Investment Disputes (ICSID).

Through all these instruments these global financial institutions can facilitate the integration of developing states into various circuits of accumulation. For example, the legal mechanisms as defined by ICSID have been adopted in many trade contracts and treaties, and many bilateral investment treaties between states have built-in recourse to ICSID should a dispute arise. This instance perhaps illustrates a point made by Hardt and Negri (2000), who observe that "through its contemporary transformation of supranational law, the imperial process of constitution tends either directly or indirectly to penetrate and reconfigure the domestic law of the nation states, and thus supranational law powerfully overdetermines domestic law" (p. 17), although this perhaps overstates the case.

Underlying these global institutions are a whole array of regional and subregional financial institutions and Multilateral Development Banks with links to the global level IFIs. They often work in tandem with global institutions, and many of the same precedents and structures are replicated. Where these institutions operate there tends to be a high degree of regional integration. There are development banks in Europe, Africa, Asia, the Caribbean, and the Americas, which in turn have smaller banks dealing with specific areas within each continent.

The World Trade Organization

On a global scale, trade is governed by the World Trade Organization (WTO), which is an outgrowth of the General Agreement on Tariffs and Trade (GATT) agreements. The formation of the WTO is an example of a practice known as *forum hopping*. This occurs when one forum fails to resolve issues due to a restrictive mandate or because it insufficiently privileges the more powerful states. The trade organization originally envisaged under the UN system through Bretton Woods was the

International Trade Organization, but the most powerful members used the GATT vehicle instead. The WTO has truly global oversight in matters of trade and can permit member states to implement sanctions over other states if they fail to adhere to trade agreements. The body also has a judicial mechanism and uses the power of states to enforce its rulings. Often its jurisdiction is underpinned by national state constitutional amendments that are required for membership. However, agreement must be reached by member states for progress to be made on various regulations regarding tariffs and subsidies. Since developing nations have more recently organized and acted with one voice, Western states have found it more difficult to force agreements. In addition, Western domestic policies (e.g., agricultural subsidies and tariffs) have been put under greater public scrutiny.

NGOs

Aside from the organizations that originate as outgrowths of the official governance mechanisms of states, there are many organizations from the private sphere that make up a global civil society. Of course, many of these organizations exist in opposition to globalism and seek to put forward their own alternatives to global neoliberalism, for example, Greenpeace, the World Social Forum, and so forth. Others act as forums to facilitate globalization. Often these bodies have a predominantly ideological or policy formulation function. One example is the International Chamber of Commerce (ICC), which claims to keep national governments, global bodies, and the UN system apprised of issues deemed important to international business. The ICC also holds a meeting with the G8 host country before each summit and meets with the WTO. It also operates an International Court of Arbitration for disputes on international contracts.

Policy Forums

There is also an ever-increasing trend toward coordination of policy by developed states through forums and organizations such as the G8 and the Organization for Economic Cooperation and Development (OECD). The G8 meets annually and discusses matters ranging from trade, economy, and security to social policy, human rights, and environmental policy. Since the mid-1980s, separate biannual and triennial meetings have been held by each country's finance ministers; more recently environment, employment, and education ministers have met annually as well. The G8 does not have any permanent secretariat and is still largely an informal forum, but nonetheless it serves as an important arena to put forward agendas deemed important by the countries that participate. The OECD, on the other hand, is a formal international organization with a permanent secretariat that proposes initiatives to member states. It proposed the Multilateral Agreement on Investment (MAI), for example, which was never implemented due to large-scale opposition from civil society groups, NGOs, and developing states. This case demonstrates that there are global economic processes and oppositions that take place on a transnational level.

Through these forums there are also interactions between developing and developed states. The G20, for instance, expands participation to countries such as Brazil, China, and Indonesia, but also includes the heads of the IMF and World Bank and the EU President, among others. It was recently convened to discuss global financial regulation.

The Nation-State and the Transnational State Apparatus
It is important to return at this point to the role of the nation-state in the TNS. Much of the discussion of the role of the nation-state in the global neoliberal era has emphasized the decline of its power and maneuverability. It is easy to over-emphasize this. Indeed it was the pursuit of particular policy objectives by nation-states themselves that has driven the globalization of the economy. Global neoliberalism grew out a set of policies; it was not an inevitability. It is our contention here not that the nation-state is less powerful along some abstract metric but that the power of the nation-state is increasingly exercised in the context of the larger framework of the TNS. In the absence of the still important part played by the nation-state, the TNS could claim little effectiveness.

According to Robinson (2001: 183), the nation-state in this context is increasingly acting as the "neo-liberal state," or as Cerny (1990: 53) calls it, a "competition state." Thus, the nation-state is increasingly administering economic and political reforms, sometimes requiring constitutional redrafting, which emanate from transnational forums, with fundamental consequences for production relations. These policies have often been formulated in supranational institutions representing a TNCC interest.

This class's influence is not limited, however, to expression through transnational channels. This elite influence is deeply ideological in that it has found means of consensually controlling decisions made within national states through advisors, experts, or by straightforwardly financing various administrations on both the left and right of the political spectrum. This top-down strategy is further buttressed by similar efforts at the regional and state levels, where pressures exerted by industry and organizations with a global outlook challenge those of domestic labor movements and local industry. The ensemble of transnational institutions, with its underlying neoliberal ideology, in some ways *transcends* but it also *transforms* states. Robinson (2001: 188) sums this up:

> But far from the "end of the nation-state," as a slew of recent studies have proclaimed, we are witness to its transformation into neo-liberal states. These neo-liberal states as component elements of a TNS provide essential services for capital. National governments serve as transmission belts and filtering devices for the imposition of the transnational agenda.

Robinson's point need not be taken to indicate that states inevitably play this role in the current period. These state actions are the result of concrete struggles at the local level. In this context, conflicts of interest can exist between local and transnational capitalists within indigenous domestic settings and also between local and transnational capitalists in transnational settings.[5] The state must try to mediate this conflict by assuaging local interests, while at the same time enforcing agreements made on the transnational level. This division between local and transnational capital, operating both with the nation-state and transnational institutions, has the potential to replace more traditional divisions between financial, industrial, and commercial capital. Further it is certainly still possible for states to respond to initiatives from local progressive forces as is evident in Venezuela and Bolivia.

While nation-states have retained or even increased their importance in locally implementing transnational initiatives, it must be recognized they have also begun to cede authority in certain areas, especially over macroeconomic issues, to "trans" and "supra" national bodies. In the case of currency and interest rates within the Euro-zone, the European Central Bank has taken over many of the roles of national central banks. In North America, NAFTA signatories have delegated authority over labor and trade disputes to the formulations and authorities agreed upon in that treaty. Economic institutions such as the WTO, have, as Biersteker (2002) has pointed out, "begun to extend their intrusiveness into the previously sacrosanct domain of the 'domestic' by criticizing some labor policies, consumer product safety standards and environmental accords as non-tariff barriers to free trade" (p. 169). Loan recipients from the

---

[5] Struggles between capital and working class and other popular forces also play a role.

IMF and WB have surrendered control of wide areas of domestic policy to these organizations.

The extra-territorializing of sovereignty has been accompanied by increased regionalization, such as that practiced by the EU (discussed earlier). These regions are sometimes seen as a buffer against global forces (Telò 2001: 13) but more often serve as a way station to further globalization. Paradoxically, regionalization supports the participation of small nations in the global economy as independent states. Such areas aspiring to independence can claim economic viability in a restructured global economy, as the traditional large-scale heavy industries of manufacturing and resource extraction are no longer prerequisites for national survival. Service industries such as banking and finance can now compensate for the lack of more traditional manufacturing industries and make smaller states viable.[6]

These new countries also provide competition for more established countries by challenging them for the capture of foreign direct investment. This new-found viability of small states serves an important role for capitalist interests. The more traditional European nation-states have experienced increased competition from newer states, which have brought less "baggage" to forming institutions that underpin capital accumulation under the new conditions. This trend towards emerging-nation nationalism can also lend globalization a sense of legitimacy. While established democracies may feel they are ceding sovereignty, newer states are feeling increasingly enabled and empowered, at least initially.

The Second Part of Polanyi's Movement and International Human Rights

States have increasingly disengaged from explicit involvement in national economies, especially with regard to any form of nationalized production (steel and auto industries), many services (national airlines and postal services), and finance (national banks), hence allowing them to be more fully integrated into global circuits and thereby subjected to global accumulation logics operated by various private interests. This is analogous to the first part of Polanyi's movement. These developments have had profound implications for the legitimacy of the liberal democratic state as the principal form of representation for citizenry. As Axtmann (1996: 131) notes:

---

[6] The case of Iceland in the current financial crisis underlines that there are risks to this strategy as well.

Extraterritorial global forces both invade the space of the nation-state and, because of their extraterritoriality, are operating outside the controlling reach of the nation-state. Both as space invaders and space evaders do they challenge the democratic polity.

This raises the question of how bodies not territorially sited and not having a direct sovereign mandate can be legitimized and be seen to be acting democratically, thus forestalling any inclination to roll back the effects of global capitalism. One answer is in the spread of the rhetoric of "democracy, freedom and human rights," forwarded hand in hand with economic restructuring, thus lending the emerging global framework a sense of legitimacy. These principles influence policy in nation-states by acting either as a "guiding hand" or as a "moral compass" in both developed and developing states, while also serving to shape national aspirations in emerging states.

The area of human rights is an especially important discourse relating to the development of transnational governance structures. This is at least weakly analogous to the second part of Polanyi's movement. The universalization of human rights has become so institutionalized and diffused within the international system that it has become one of the prerequisites of new state recognition. States must now not only satisfy the requirement of being domestically acceptable to their own populations (which was the previous criterion for full state recognition); they must also be globally acceptable through ensuring "requirements such as the establishment and consolidation of democratic institutions, the treatment of the rights of minority populations, and even the management of the economy" are met, and furthermore by ensuring that international standards on property rights, gender, and other areas previously regarded as "private" are consistent with global "norms" (Biersteker 2002: 169).

In other areas, bodies such as the International Court of Justice deal with cases between states regarding areas such as cross-border pollution, while the International Criminal Court deals with issues such as war crimes and genocide. By dealing with concerns outside the remit of national states, these bodies can help maintain a sense of authority and belief in a global system, which is a vital ideological aspect of any emerging transnational state-like structure.

The TNS and the Global Neoliberal SSA
An argument for the consolidation of a global neoliberal SSA was made in Chapter 4. Here we wish to expand on the role that the new transnational governance institutions have played in this SSA.

An international political economy can be defined as one that consists of a collection of nationally distinctive SSAs. As Kotz et al. (1994: 1–2) noted in relation to earlier periods:

[w]hile Japan, Germany, the United States, Sweden, and South Africa are all market-orientated capitalist economies, their structures and performances also differ considerably from one another. To explain these outcomes we need a theory that incorporates the institutional differences among the capitalist countries.

Such national SSAs were connected through "inter" national institutions, in which states made efforts to govern what was essentially a congregation of nationally sited capitalisms. Circuits of accumulation and production were mediated by borders that were policed and regulated by the system of states utilizing a set of international governance mechanisms to assist in this process.

However, in the current period, states have shifted their emphasis from relatively tightly regulated domestic systems to more deregulated open systems that would attract investment and enable their own nationally sited productive forces to compete more effectively in global markets. This new approach represents an ideological shift towards a new strain of liberalism and it has led to the transformation of existing national SSAs and the international regimes of accumulation that had previously complemented but ultimately limited capital's capacity to expand.

This new program for capitalism has been pursued partly through new trans-national institutional frameworks to govern capitalism's expansion outside of the traditional and limited remits of nation-states. So while states continue to exist and perform functions under their original national titles, their roles are condensing and are increasingly led by determinations at a global level. This attenuation of state action and initiative is consistent with the neoliberal project of restricting the role of the state in the economy and society. These developments are also congruent with other elements of global neoliberalism (see Chapter 4 this volume).

In previous periods different national SSAs were linked by common sets of international institutions. Global neoliberalism has transformed this relationship. Global neoliberalism has constituted a transnational SSA. This transnational SSA is not, however, homogenous across national boundaries. This transnational framework is limited in its scope. It has been primarily concerned with the liberalization of the movement of goods and capital across national boundaries.[7] The so far limited remit of transnational governance allows the creation of national differences, which paves the way for capital to site various parts of the accumulation process in the most profitable locations. In the current period, when state action is examined at the national level, differences in form, policies, and operation may be still very apparent. However, the significance of these differences has been transformed. These sets of policies and bodies may be viewed as drawn from a more or less extensive menu of instruments, which is itself part of the emerging global SSA and effectively determines production, competition, regulation, and consumption within both domestic and global spaces.

The Current Crisis and the TNS

The globalization of economic activity facilitated by innovative governance arrangements has obviously played a central role in the genesis of the current crisis. Most prominently the internationalization of finance contributed strongly to the now-burst asset bubble and the propagation of the crisis across the globe. Less immediately, globalization has played an important part in generating the underlying demand crisis that will prolong the downturn. The dismantling of economic borders has contributed to the excess capacity that is crippling many industries, most prominently auto at the time of writing. More importantly, the globalization of production has weakened labor producing stagnant wages leaving consumption overly dependent on unsustainable borrowing, the possibility of which has now collapsed. The particular character of the TNS is also going to prove important in determining the prospects for the economy. While oriented to the elimination of barriers to trade and the free movement of capital, the institutions of the TNS are much less suited to address the economic crisis. Because of the differing interests involved, the opening of trade and capital flows is a complex and protracted political problem, but the object of the exercise is relatively clear and transparent, at least in the abstract. Devising policy to address an unfolding and unexpected global economic crisis is considerably more challenging.

International governance is presented with two immediate problems, and the current institutional structure is suited to neither. The

---

[7] The complexity of the process and institutions demanded by this liberalization should not, however, be minimized.

first immediate task is addressing the financial crisis and devising an appropriate and much more interventionist, regulated, and transparent international financial architecture. The second is producing a coordinated fiscal stimulus of sufficient size and extent to meet the sheer size of the current downturn in production and demand. The vehicle for the discussion of these issues has been recently expanded to the G20, a forum that in contrast to the G8 also includes the larger of the "less developed economies" including, for instance, Brazil, India, and China. While inclusion of a broader range of countries is certainly appropriate to the scale of the problems, there is little indication that this expansion of participants will not make eventual agreement correspondingly more difficult.

The declaration after the November 2008 Washington summit listed many of the problems but was short on detail.[8] It was anxious not to make a clean break with neoliberalism, declaring a commitment to "free market principles, including the rule of law, respect for private property, open trade and investment, competitive markets. ..." Amazingly, given the context, the report also worried about "over-regulation."

The following April 2009 London summit tackled issues of banking regulation and fiscal stimulus more explicitly. However, U.S. opposition limited the impact of changes in financial regulation demanded by Germany and France, while German opposition meant that a more ambitious program of coordinated fiscal stimulus was not approved. More money was supplied to the IMF but no brakes were put on the Fund's contractionary conditions for granting loans. The G20 remained committed to a global neoliberal agenda. The meeting endorsed the completion of the World Trade Organization's Doha Round. Significantly, it pledged itself to "promote global trade and investment" and not to take measures that "constrain worldwide capital flows." Perhaps most tellingly it "resolved to ensure long-term fiscal sustainability and price stability and will put in place credible exit strategies from the measures that need to be taken now to support the financial sector and restore global demand."[9]

The G20 has been unable to take decisive action in the face of the global economic crisis. It has undertaken a number of initiatives, but in

---

[8] Summit on Financial Markets and the World Economy. The White House, Office of the Press Secretary, November 15, 2008.
[9] G20 Leaders Statement The Global Plan for Recovery and Reform – London, 2 April 2009.

each area these have been restricted to the lowest common denominator. Effective vetoes were exercised by several of the developed economies. The inclusion of the larger economies outside the "rich man's club" of the G7 has been hailed as a progressive step forward in global governance. Despite the integration of the "emerging market" economies, the G20 has, however, been anxious not to break out of the neoliberal consensus forged over the last three decades. The G20 is still more comfortable in the pursuit of free trade and greater capital mobility than it is in addressing the global financial and fiscal crises.

The larger task facing the TNCC and hence the TNS is the construction of a new SSA that can deal with the contradictions of global neoliberalism. It is far from clear that the TNS state form is capable of addressing these problems. Just as the TNS emerged along with and as part of global neoliberalism and represented a break with previous state forms, the construction of a governance system adequate to a new SSA could involve a further development of the TNS, but could also involve a break with the TNS. This break could involve a departure from the relatively diffuse and distributed nature of sovereignty under the TNS. This would involve a global concentration of power and decision-making.

At the same time, it is not obvious that the contradictions of the current system – inequality, excess capacity, sluggish accumulation, and financial instability – are amenable to solutions that maintain or intensify transnational economic activity. It is therefore not inevitable the current transnational character of the economy will be maintained in any eventual institutional resolution of the current downturn. If populations return to state policy in search of a resolution of the crisis, this could well prompt a withdrawal from the transnationalization of sovereignty and governance.[10] If this proves to be the case, the significance of the TNS will be limited to the global neoliberal era, which began to come to an end in the crunch of 2008. One of the points of SSA theory, however, is precisely this. Institutional forms, including state forms, are finite, limited to particular stages of capitalism, and are transformed in response to capitalist crisis.

References

Apeldoorn, Bastiaan van 2004. "Transnational Historical Materialism: The Amsterdam International Political Economy Project." *Journal of International Relations and Development*, Special Issue 7, 2: 110–12.

---

[10] For an argument that domestic state policy is more likely to be an effective response to the current economic problems see Weisbrot (2009).

Axtmann, Roland 1996. *Liberal Democracy into the 21st Century, Globalization, Integration and the Nation-State*. Manchester: Manchester University Press.

Biersteker, Thomas J. 2002. "State, Sovereignty and Territory." In Walter Carlsnaes, Thomas Risse and Beth Simmons eds. *Handbook of International Relations*. London: Sage.

Bull, Hedley 1977. *The Anarchial Society: A Study of Order in World Politics*. London: Macmillan Press.

Cameron, Fraser 2005. "The EU Model of Integration-Relevance Elsewhere?" *Jean Monet/Robert Schuman Paper Series* 5, 37.

Cerny, Philip G. 1990. *The Changing Architecture of Politics. Structure, Agency and the Future of the State*. London: Sage.

Cox, Robert 1987. *Production, Power and World Order, Social Forces in the Making of History*. New York, Columbia University Press.

Friedrichs, Jorg 2001. "The Meaning of New Medievalism." *European Journal of International Relations*, 7, 4: 475–501.

Gamble, Andrew 2001. "Regional Blocs, World Order and the New Medievalism." In Mario Télo ed. *European Union and New Regionalism, Regional Actors and Global Governance in a Post-Hegemonic Era*. Aldershot: Ashgate.

Gill, Stephen 1990. *American Hegemony and the Trilateral Commission*. New York: Cambridge University Press.

1994. "Knowledge, Politics, and Neo-Liberal Political Economy." In Richard Stubbs and Geoffrey R.D. Underhill eds. *Political Economy and the Changing Global Order*. New York: St. Martin's Press.

Gill, Stephen and David Law 1988. *The Global Political Economy, Perspectives, Problems and Policies*. Hemel Hempstead, Harvester and Wheatsheaf.

Hardt, Michael and Antonio Negri 2000. *Empire*. Cambridge, MA: Harvard University Press.

Krasner, Stephen 1999. *Sovereignty: Organised Hypocrisy*. Princeton: Princeton University Press.

Kotz, David M. 1994. "*The Regulation Theory and the Social Structure of Accumulation Approach.*" Pp. 85–97 in David M. Kotz, Terrence McDonough and Michael Reich eds. "*Social Structures of Accumulation: The Political Economy of Growth and Crisis.*" New York: Cambridge University Press..

Linklater, Andrew 1996. "Marxism." In Richard Burchill and Andrew Linklater eds. *Theories of International Relations*. London: MacMillan Press.

Marx, Karl. 1978 [1888] "Manifesto of the Communist Party." In *The Marx-Engels Reader*, Second Edition, ed. Robert C. Tucker. New York: W.W. Norton.

McDonough, Terrence 1994. "*Social Structures of Accumulation, Contingent History, and Stages of Capitalism.*" Pp. 72–84 in David M. Kotz, Terrence McDonough and Michael Reich eds. "*Social Structures of Accumulation: The Political Economy of Growth and Crisis.*" New York: Cambridge University Press.

Overbeek, Henk 2001. "Transnational Historical Mechanism: Theories of Transnational Class Formation and World Order." Pp. 168–183 in Roland Palan ed. *Global Political Economy: Contemporary Theories*. London: Routledge.

Pijl, Kees van der 1984. *The Making of an Atlantic Ruling Class*. London: Verso.
 1998. *Transnational Classes and International Relations*. New York: Routledge.
Polanyi, Karl 2001 [1944]. *The Great Transformation: The Political and Economic Origins of our Time*. Boston: Beacon Press.
Robinson, William I. 2001. "Social Theory and Globalization: The Rise of the Transnational State." *Theory and Society* 30: 157–200.
 2004. *A Theory of Global Capitalism, Production, Class, and State in a Transnational World*. London: University of Baltimore Press.
 2005. "Gramsci and Globalisation: From Nation-State to Transnational Hegemony." *Critical Review of International Social and Political Philosophy* 8, 4: 1–16.
Schwartz, Herman M. 2000. *States versus Markets, the Emergence of a Global Economy*. New York: St. Martin's Press.
Telò, Mario 2001. "Reconsiderations: Three Scenarios." In Mario Télo ed. *European Union and New Regionalism, Regional actors and global governance in a post-hegemonic era*. Aldershot: Ashgate.
Weisbrot, Mark 2009. "It's the Global Economy, Stupid (Or Is It?)" *The Guardian Unlimited*, April 8.

PART THREE

THE CONTEMPORARY SOCIAL STRUCTURE OF ACCUMULATION IN THE UNITED STATES

Labor in the Contemporary Social Structure of Accumulation

Samuel Rosenberg

After the end of World War II, an institutional framework – the post-war social structure of accumulation (SSA) – gradually evolved, setting the stage for renewed prosperity in the United States. Domestically, this structure included two important elements. First, the federal government played a more important role in stabilizing and fostering the growth of the economy and in protecting, to a degree, individuals and businesses from competitive forces in the economy. Second, while labor and management continued to be in competitive conflict, there was a shared set of understandings about the nature of the conflict with "management's rights" and "labor's role" becoming more clearly defined. Internationally, the postwar institutional framework was characterized by the economic and political dominance of the United States.

Strains in this postwar SSA began to appear in the late 1960s and continued in the 1970s. Stagflation, one of the outward manifestations of such strains, reflected the economic and political stalemate over which groups in the United States would bear the burden for the relative decline in the economic and political hegemony of the United States. The stagflation was broken in the early 1980s, and a "neoliberal" SSA was created.[1]

---

[1] While David Kotz and Terence McDonough argue in their chapter ("Global Neoliberalism and the Contemporary Social Structure of Accumulation") that the term "global neoliberalism" best captures the contemporary SSA, the term "neoliberal" is utilized here instead to describe the contemporary SSA in the United States. This chapter focuses on the United States – where the shift in a neoliberal direction was the greatest among the developed capitalist countries. It does not investigate the extent to which neoliberal institutions have come to characterize other capitalist countries, both developed and less-developed.

While not explicitly discussed in these terms, the Reagan administration attempted to create a new institutional framework, a new SSA, for economic prosperity based on neoliberalism, or deregulated capitalism. Ideologically, the federal government was attacked as the most important cause of the economic problems faced by the United States. Monetarism, as practiced by the Federal Reserve, took on a greater role in macroeconomic policy. Business, as well, was questioning the previously accepted set of understandings regarding "management's rights" and "labor's role."

Employer strategy and government policy were closely aligned and focused on eliminating labor market "rigidities" thereby fostering labor market "flexibility." Government deregulatory policies weakened the minimal social protection policies already in place and weakened labor in previously regulated industries. Union power was reduced through governmental policy and aggressive antiunion management behavior, resulting in a sharp trade union decline. While employers compromised to a degree with labor during the postwar SSA, now under the "neoliberal" SSA, they achieved a high degree of dominance over labor. As a result, during the 1980s, labor standards declined, the wage structure was lowered, wage inequality grew as did the amount of low-wage employment. Job insecurity became more widespread. The burden for the relative decline of the United States in the world economy was borne by those workers, both organized and unorganized, with weakened bargaining power and by the poor.

The prolonged economic expansion of the 1990s was built on the emergent "neoliberal" SSA. Deunionization continued apace thereby enabling greater employer freedom in setting pay and personnel policies. Wage gains continued to lag productivity increases. The increasing presence of contingent employment relationships fostered job insecurity as did corporate downsizing in the face of strong profitability and a strong economy. Productivity growth was fueled by investments in information technology and by the intensification of work effort, the latter being based on worker insecurity.

Wage inequality diminished and the floor of the wage structure rose only in the second half of the 1990s, when the unemployment rate was low and the federal minimum wage was increased. Following the short, relatively mild recession of 2001, however, wage and income inequality once again increased. The legacy of the neoliberal restructuring of the 1980s remained. The conservative "free market" restructuring of the economy, the ascendancy of business, the deunionization of the private sector, and the overall growth of inequality and insecurity all point to the following question. What is the role of labor in the contemporary SSA?

This chapter is divided into four main sections. The first, focusing on labor-management relations and the nature of labor market segmentation in the post World War II SSA, will serve as historical background for the analysis of labor in the contemporary "neoliberal" SSA. The second discusses the political-economic environment of the 1980s, a time of the creation of the contemporary "neoliberal" SSA. The third analyzes the "employer offensive" and the deunionization of the 1980s. The fourth treats the legacy of the emergent neoliberal framework.[2]

Business-Labor Relations in the Post World War II Social Structure of Accumulation: Conflict amid Stability

Those working within a SSA framework argue that two central components of the post-World War II institutional framework were peaceful collective bargaining, characterized as a "capital-labor accord," and segmentation of labor (Gordon, Edwards, and Reich 1982). However, labor-management relations were more conflictual than an "accord" or a "truce" would suggest. While unions and many of the major corporations accepted the legal boundaries of collective bargaining set by the National Labor Relations Act of 1935, the Taft-Hartley Act of 1947, the rulings of the National Labor Relations Board (NLRB) and the courts, serious conflict did not disappear.

Employers chose to live with unions where they existed. A large share of nonagricultural workers were unionized. In 1954, 34.7 percent of non-agricultural workers were union members (Blum 1968: 45). More than 60 percent of production workers in manufacturing were covered by union contracts. And the collective bargaining contracts signed in the major manufacturing industries influenced wage setting throughout the economy. In 1948, General Motors (GM) and the United Auto Workers (UAW) reached agreement on a contract containing important innovations in wage payments – automatic wage adjustments over the life of the two-year contract. Wages would be adjusted on the basis of an Annual

---

[2] The analysis presented in this chapter is developed more fully in Rosenberg (2003).

Improvement Factor (AIF) reflecting labor's share of expected productivity increases and a Cost of Living Adjustment (COLA) designed to protect workers' real wages from inflation.

By the end of the 1950s, automatic wage adjustments along the lines of the UAW-GM agreement became the most common form of labor contract. Pattern bargaining generalized wage agreements within and across industries. The "threat effect" forced nonunion employers to provide compensation packages in line with those negotiated by unions or else face the threat of unionization. The interindustry wage structure was relatively stable with minimal variation in the rate of wage changes across industries (Piore and Sabel 1984: 83). Furthermore, workers' wages were rising in step with the productive capacity of the economy helping to maintain an adequate demand for goods and services, thereby facilitating capital accumulation.

Labor markets were segmented into primary and secondary sectors. Primary jobs were characterized by relatively high wages, relatively good working conditions, employment stability, and opportunities for advancement. Secondary jobs paid relatively low wages, had relatively poor working conditions, and provided minimal job security and few opportunities for advancement. Wage setting within the primary sector was much less affected by forces of competition than was wage setting in the secondary sector.

Many explanations have been advanced for the process of labor market segmentation. The social SSA literature emphasizes a duality within the structure of the economy and the strategies of employers and unions. Primary jobs were more likely to be found in the monopolistic "core" of the economy while secondary jobs predominated in the competitive "periphery." Furthermore, employers were the driving force behind the imposition of "simple control," synonymous with secondary jobs, and "bureaucratic control," synonymous with independent primary positions. "Technical control" and the subordinate primary jobs that came along with it, emerged out of negotiations between large firms, with product market power, and their unions. Employers and their managerial representatives would retain control over the basic operations of the firm while workers would gain primary job rights including higher living standards and improved job security (Edwards 1979). To some degree, the labor market was segmented along the lines of those who benefited from collective bargaining and those who did not. This bargain between labor and management constituted the "accord" or the "truce."

However, the terms "accord" and "truce" imply more peaceful relations than were actually the case. While there was a sense of stability in the collective bargaining relationship, and such stability promoted productivity growth and capital accumulation, serious conflict did not disappear. Not surprisingly, nonunion firms fought strongly to stay nonunion. More importantly for the notion of an "accord" or "truce," many, though not all, unionized firms often opposed union-organizing drives in newly constructed plants they located in nonunion areas. The relocation of economic activity first became apparent in the late 1940s. It grew more prevalent in the 1950s and 1960s. For example, many textile and clothing manufacturing firms with unionized workforces in the northern states opened new plants in the South and fought hard to keep them nonunion. The same held for firms in the electrical equipment industry, whose managements were convinced by the strikes of 1946 that the large existing manufacturing plants in the Northeast and Midwest had become hotbeds of labor militancy. Unions would have difficulty in organizing new production workers in this industry, particularly in the South. Decentralization of economic activity did not guarantee that unions would be avoided, but it made organizing new workers more difficult. The share of the unionized workforce in the country as a whole peaked in 1954 and then began a steady decline.

The sharpest decline in business activity since World War II, until that time, had begun toward the end of 1957. Profit margins were under pressure and foreign competition was becoming stronger. Management, interested in slowing wage gains and increasing their control over the work process, took a "harder line" in their dealings with their workers. In 1958 and 1959, over 30% of the workers in manufacturing, under contracts covering bargaining units of 1000 or more workers each whose contracts expired, went on strike. These figures were never reached in later years (Kaufman 1978: 423). Though rare, some major employers such as the American Oil Company, Standard Oil of Indiana, United Aircraft Corporation (in 1960), and General Electric (in 1960) kept their plants operating during strikes.

Mass production union leaders were convinced that management "at the very least looks to a drastic cutting down of union power and, at the most, offers a challenge to union existence" (Barbash 1961: 25). In retrospect, although employers did not challenge the existence of unions, they did try to reduce union power. Thus, even at the time that the "capital-labor accord" was said to be the strongest and collective bargaining relatively peaceful, union leaders were less than fully secure in their relations with management.

The second half of the 1960s and the first half of the 1970s represented a time of strong bargaining strength for the labor movement. Yet, while labor was doing well at the bargaining table, a managerial resistance to new unionism was strengthening. The share of the private sector workforce unionized continued to shrink. While unions in the most highly organized industries were still relatively protected by their bargaining strength from the nonunion model, the roots of the nonunion model were being laid. They would take hold by the 1980s when a new "neoliberal" SSA would be created.

The Deregulatory Government Policy Regime of the 1980s: A Component of the Contemporary "Neoliberal" Social Structure of Accumulation

Seeking to reverse the economic decline of the 1970s, which represented a crisis of the postwar SSA, to raise the average rate of profit, and to improve the overall productive efficiency of the economy, the Reagan administration pursued deregulatory policies in the name of furthering labor market flexibility thereby improving labor market efficiency. Programmatically, this attack on the state led to a weakening of the minimal social protection policies benefiting workers, in general, and the poor, in particular. Two thrusts of state labor market policy were apparent. The first was to increase competition in the labor market at a given level of unemployment by reducing the social wage and lowering the effective minimum wage. The second was to reduce union power through higher aggregate levels of unemployment, increased labor market competition, the reinterpretation of existing industrial relations legislation in a pro-business manner, and the deregulation of the transportation and communications industries.

While the Reagan program did represent a more conservative direction in government policy, it was following steps taken under the Carter administration. Continuing with its policy approach toward the end of the Carter administration, the Federal Reserve, under the guise of monetarism, pursued an austerity policy designed to lower the rate of inflation by raising unemployment and eroding the power of labor. Restrictive monetary policy, together with falling world prices for food and energy, resulted in the rate of inflation dropping from 13.5 percent in 1980 to 3.2 percent in 1983. But the unemployment rate rose to 9.7 percent in 1982 and 9.6 percent in 1983, levels not experienced since the Great Depression of the 1930s. Although unemployment rose throughout the economy, it was centered in mining, construction, and manufacturing, those areas where unions have traditionally been the strongest.

The growth in the number of unemployed constitutes in, and of itself, an increase in competition in the labor market. A decline in the real value of the federal minimum wage has the same effect on low-wage workers. Throughout the eight years that Ronald Reagan was in office, the minimum wage remained at $3.35 per hour, the value set in 1981. At that time, this represented the longest elapsed time without a minimum wage increase since the passage of the Fair Labor Standards Act of 1938, enacting the federal minimum wage for the country as a whole. After hovering around 50 percent of average hourly earnings in the private nonagricultural industries during the 1950s and 1960s, the minimum wage averaged 45 percent of average hourly earnings in the 1970s. By 1985, it had declined to about 39 percent of average hourly wages (Mishel, Bernstein, and Allegretto 2007: 190–92).

At the same time as the number of unemployed was rising, the federal government was cutting back on unemployment insurance (UI). The weakening of the UI system began during the Carter administration with the taxing of unemployment benefits. The Reagan administration continued with this policy thrust by increasing the effective rate of taxation of UI and shortening the effective duration of these benefits. Subject to minimal federal standards, states set qualifying requirements for UI benefits and benefit duration. Changes at the state level made it more difficult to qualify for UI. The share of the unemployed collecting UI declined during the 1980s. In 1975, when the unemployment rate was 8.5 percent, 76 percent of the unemployed received UI. During 1982, with a higher unemployment rate than in 1975, only 45 percent received compensation (Levitan, Carlson, and Shapiro 1986: 165). Later, in 1987 and 1988, approximately 32 percent of the unemployed received a benefit, compared to 40 to 45 percent of the jobless during similar periods in the 1960s and 1970s (Baldwin and McHugh 1992: 2).

The cutbacks in UI were designed to provide an incentive to the unemployed to accept jobs, albeit ones that may initially pay lower wages than they were used to receiving. Similarly, government policy changes regarding Aid to Families with Dependent Children (AFDC) were designed to provide incentives to recipients to search for and accept low-paying positions. Initially, the Carter administration tried to expand the welfare program. However, they were unsuccessful and by the end of its term in office, the administration began calling for cuts in AFDC outlays. This about-face foreshadowed the approach to be taken when the Reagan administration did cut the welfare program. Programmatic changes limited the number of people eligible for assistance and the amounts they received. Welfare caseloads declined and many families still collecting AFDC saw their benefits reduced.

The large number of unemployed and the cutbacks in the minimum wage and the social wage hurt unions. Government policy, setting a union busting tone, did the same. In 1981, its first year in office, the Reagan administration fired the striking air traffic controllers and had the Professional Air Traffic Controllers Organization decertified. They were able to do this because federal employees are legally forbidden to strike. This action sent a clear message to employers; they should feel free to bash unions.

The Reagan administration's appointments to the National Labor Relations Board (NLRB) were designed to create a majority that would roll back many of the gains made by the labor movement. By June 1984, according to one estimate, the NLRB had recast nearly 40 percent of the decisions made since the 1970s that conservatives had found objectionable (*Business Week* 1984: 122). The antiunion perspective of the NLRB made it more difficult for union-organizing drives to succeed and for unions to achieve their goals at the bargaining table. Employers were now more able to engage in unfair labor practices designed to stop a union victory in a representation election without suffering negative consequences. In addition, employer rights during a union-organizing drive were expanded. It was now easier for employers to move union jobs to nonunion locations. It was now more difficult for a union to succeed with a strike.

The transportation and telecommunications industries, union strongholds, were deregulated during the Carter and Reagan administrations. In 1978, during the Carter administration, the U.S. Congress passed the Airline Deregulation Act. The telecommunications industry was deregulated as a result of a divestiture of AT&T demanded by the Reagan administration's Justice Department in 1984. The trucking and railroad industries were also deregulated during this period. With the introduction of increased competition in these industries, unions faced more difficult bargaining environments.

Employer Domination and Deunionization in the 1980s: Components of the Contemporary "Neoliberal" Social Structure of Accumulation

Government policy served to weaken union and nonunion workers alike, just what many employers desired. Facing a rising wage premium of unionized labor, increased foreign and domestic competition, and pressure on profits, employers sought increased "flexibility" to lower labor costs, improve labor productivity, and have workers bear more of the cost of economic uncertainty. As did the government, employers wanted to diminish the insulation of some more privileged workers from market forces. During the first half of the 1980s and beyond, many though not all companies, profitable and unprofitable alike, took the "low road" to improving profitability. They were aided by an enabling environment of antilabor government policy, weak and soon to be weaker unions, and a general excess supply of labor.

The 1980s represented a period of deunionization of the U.S. labor force and declining union density was one sign of the weakening bargaining power of organized labor. In 1980, 23 percent of the workforce was unionized, including 22 percent of private sector workers. By 1989, union density had declined to 16 percent; in the private sector only 12 percent of the workforce was unionized. Union coverage shrunk in traditional union strongholds such as manufacturing, mining, construction, and transportation (Freeman 1988). Aggressive antiunion management behavior was a factor behind union decline. Furthermore, labor was much less able to use the strike to further its goals. There was a sharp decline in the number of strikes. During the 1980s, there were approximately 1250 work stoppages annually, in contrast to 2660 a year during the 1970s (U.S. General Accounting Office 1991: 3). In addition, many employers heeded the message sent by President Reagan in the air traffic controllers' dispute. A U.S. General Accounting Office (1991) study found that many union representatives and employers believed there was a growing willingness of employers to hire permanent replacements for striking workers. This shift in employer strategy had a chilling effect on workers' willingness to strike.

Changes in labor market institutions pushed wage setting in a more "market oriented" direction. Many companies gained wage and benefit concessions from their workers. Wage settlements were low, two-tier wage arrangements became more common as did pay for performance, previous wage bargaining patterns were eroded, and wage settlements became more firm and plant specific. A central feature of collective bargaining prior to the 1980s had been the AIF and COLA clauses, initially negotiated between General Motors and the United Auto Workers in 1948. During the 1980s, however, both of these clauses diminished in importance as companies were, in essence, questioning previous understandings made with their unionized workforces. During the first half of the 1980s, unprecedented numbers of union members received modest wage increases or experienced no increases, or even wage reductions. Between one-third and one-half of workers covered by major collective bargaining agreements experienced a wage cut or wage freeze. Initially, in 1981–82, the wage and benefit concessions began in a narrow range of companies facing economic difficulties. By 1984–85, the situation had changed. Concessions were now being granted in virtually every industry with a unionized labor force. The concessions were most severe in the recently deregulated industries. Even profitable firms were getting on the bandwagon and pressing their workers for givebacks (Mitchell 1985, 1994). While the extent of wage cuts and wage freezes did decline in the second half of the 1980s, as the economy grew and unemployment declined, unions were still unable to negotiate substantial improvements in pay.

Within ·the unionized sector, industry-wide wage standards were eroded in tires, trucking, meatpacking, airlines, and automobiles, among others. Multiemployer bargaining in steel ended, and some firms withdrew from multifirm agreements in trucking and underground coal mining. Nonunion employers, as well, set pay based more on local labor market conditions. As part of the trend toward more company specific agreements, COLA clauses were eliminated from many contracts. In the second half of the 1970s, approximately 60 percent of the workers under major contracts had COLA clauses in their contracts, compared to only about 40 percent by the late 1980s, and approximately 20 percent by 1992. Overall, firm- and plant-specific wage differentials increased in the 1980s, at least within manufacturing. This growth in firm- and plant-specific wage differentials was an important source of growth in the dispersion of earnings.

Company working time policy was also revised to lower labor costs. Many employers responded to the more difficult economic environment by lengthening weekly or annual working time without necessarily increasing pay accordingly and pushing for more flexibility in scheduling work. Weekly and annual working time of full-time workers increased in the 1980s. Workers also received less time off for vacations and holidays. In the early 1980s, paid holidays and paid vacation time were reduced, for example, in auto, steel, rubber, and retail food stores. Airline pilots provided airline companies with a variety of working time concessions increasing the proportion of flight time to paid hours. Truckers agreed to being paid for time spent actually driving rather than for a specified number of hours per trip. In terms of work scheduling, workers, at times, experienced a decline in overtime pay and/or the elimination of premium pay for Saturday and Sunday work, and more inconvenient work schedules. This change occurred in such industries as tire, aluminum, retail food stores, steel, trucking, textiles, paper, and mining (Rosenberg 1994).

In addition to pushing for longer and more flexible hours from their full-time workers, American companies also tried to increase the utilization of a "just in time" cheaper workforce. While there are no consistent longitudinal data sources making it difficult to measure trends in contingent and nonstandard work over time, it does appear that growth in contingent and nonstandard work occurred during the 1980s (Rosenberg and Lapidus 1999). Furthermore, temporary jobs were growing more rapidly than overall employment. Employment growth in the temporary help supply industry was directly related to the decreasing ability of unions to block the increasing usage of temporary workers (Golden and Appelbaum 1992). Although the proportion of employed persons working part-time grew slowly in the 1980s, the increase was accounted for totally by those working part-time involuntarily (Mishel, Bernstein, and Schmitt 2001: 251). While part-time jobs are not necessarily bad, expanding part-time employment was concentrated in "bad" secondary labor market type part-time jobs (Tilly 1992).

Overall, there was a rapid growth in very low-wage employment and increased inequality of wages and income, partly due to the "push for flexibility" (Harrison and Bluestone 1990).[3] Job quality, as measured by real earnings, employer-provided health insurance benefits, union coverage, and involuntary part-time employment declined in blue-collar, subordinate, primary jobs and the secondary labor market (Gittleman and Howell 1995).

The Legacy of the Emergent Neoliberal Framework

By some measures, the Reagan administration's version of supply-side economics together with the employer offensive did not lead to a better functioning, efficient economy. The rate of economic growth did not accelerate, and an investment boom did not materialize in the 1980s. What the conservative economic agenda did lead to was growing economic inequality. About 40 percent of the increase in inequality can be attributed to changes in federal governmental tax and transfer

---

[3] See Congressional Budget Office (2006) for data on the overall widening of the wage distribution in the 1980s.

payment programs with the rest being the result of increasing inequality of market income (Gramlich, Kasten and Sammartino. 1993) et al. 1993). Nevertheless, the emergent neoliberal framework did lay some groundwork for future economic growth. With the exception of the mild recession in 2001, the economy grew continuously from the early 1990s until the end of 2007, the beginning of the deep recession.[4]

The Reagan legacy strongly influenced the Clinton administration policy program and the nature of the economic expansion in the 1990s. Clinton's macroeconomic and social policies were constrained, perhaps too strongly, by the large federal budget deficits of the previous decade. Clinton's social policy carried out the Reagan attack on welfare benefits to its conclusion. Clinton's labor policy was the least pro-union of any Democratic administration in the post World War II period, reflecting the decline in the economic and political strength of labor, a legacy of the Reagan era. Collective bargaining relationships remained conflictual and even in long-term collective bargaining relationships unions were often on the defensive.

Arguing that misguided government policy during the Reagan and Bush administrations contributed to stagnation in average incomes and the greatest increase in inequality since, at least, before World War II, the Clinton policy program was, to a degree, aimed at raising the floor of the overall pay structure, diminishing wage inequality, and diminishing after-tax income inequality. The minimum wage had been raised to $4.25 per hour in 1991 during the George H.W. Bush administration. The Clinton administration succeeded in having the U.S. Congress pass legislation raising the minimum wage to $5.15 per hour in 1997. This increase notwithstanding, in 1999, the minimum wage was still just 39 percent of average hourly earnings in private nonagricultural industries, the same level as in 1985, during the middle of the Reagan years (Economic Report of the President, 2001: 330). The Earned Income Tax Credit (EITC) serves as a wage subsidy for the working poor. The administration expanded the EITC by making more families eligible and improving the payments to recipients. At the top of the income scale, the Clinton administration increased the income tax rate on the highest earners.

During the Clinton years, changes in the unemployment insurance system potentially increased this benefit for those who lost their jobs. The major policy initiatives occurred at the state level, but the Clinton administration set an enabling environment for such changes. Many

---

[4] This chapter was completed in May 2009.

states eased eligibility requirements and raised both the maximum benefit and the average level of benefits. Nevertheless, less than 38 percent of unemployed workers received UI in 1999, the same percentage as in 1990 (Wenger 2001: 12). However, the unemployment rate was 4.2 percent in 1999, lower than the 5.6 percent level in 1990.

While the approaches taken during the Clinton administration to the minimum wage, the EITC, and UI were counter to Reagan administration policy thrusts, the Clinton administration did carry the Reagan attack on Aid to Families with Dependent Children (AFDC) to its conclusion. In 1996, with the passage of the Personal Responsibility and Work Opportunity Act, the "entitlement" to welfare was ended and a strong work requirement was imposed. Welfare recipients who failed to engage in "work activities" were to be denied benefits. In most instances, people would not be able to receive welfare benefits for more than five years over the lifetime.

Clinton's capitulation to Congressional conservatives on welfare reform represented a major defeat for liberal (utilizing the twentieth century American definition of the term) Democrats and their supporters, including the labor movement. While President Clinton did appoint individuals to serve on the NLRB who were likely to be more sympathetic to the arguments of the labor movement, important parts of the labor movement's legislative agenda went down to defeat. The North American Free Trade Agreement was approved. The Workplace Fairness Act, prohibiting the hiring of permanent replacement workers during strikes, received only tepid support from the Clinton administration and was defeated in Congress.

Driven by rising investment spending, particularly on information technology, and rising consumption spending arising out of increased household wealth due to a spectacular stock market boom, the economic expansion of the 1990s was the longest, though not the strongest, in the history of the United States. Labor productivity grew more rapidly in the second half of the 1990s than it had in the two preceding decades. Between 1973 and 1995, labor productivity growth in the nonfarm business sector averaged 1.4 percent annually. In contrast, between 1996 and 1999, the annual average rate of labor productivity growth was 2.7 percent (*Economic Report of the President* 2001: 333). As the economy expanded, more people were hired, and the unemployment rate fell to levels not seen since the late 1960s. The unemployment rate steadily declined from 7.5 percent in 1992 to 4.2 percent in 1999, while the labor force participation rate rose to 67.1 percent in 1997–99, the highest level of the post World War II period (*Economic Report of the President* 2001: 321, 325).

Even though the rate of labor force participation was high and the rate of unemployment was steadily falling, implying stronger worker bargaining power, many workers, particularly production and nonsupervisory workers, union and nonunion alike, were accepting modest wage increases. Unions remained weak, and the share of the workforce unionized continued to decline. By 1999, only 13.9 percent of wage and salary workers were unionized. In the private sector, the figure stood at 9.4 percent. Many unionized workers were quite reluctant to strike to achieve their goals. Major work stoppages – those involving 1,000 workers or more – were extremely rare, there being only 17 in 1999, the fewest in the post World War II period (U.S. Bureau of the Census 2000: 444–45). With rare exception, nonunion workers were also reluctant to push for higher wages. Many workers felt increasingly insecure as they were exposed more, though not necessarily fully exposed, to the vicissitudes of the market. Evidence from the General Social Survey confirms that the 1990s were a period of relative pessimism about job security (Schmidt 2000).

The focus on worker insecurity raises the issue of whether the internal labor market, a central concept of labor market segmentation theory, is still operating. The complete demise of the internal labor market seems overstated though it is likely diminishing in importance. While half of all new jobs end in the first year (Farber 2005), long-term employment relationships still exist. In 2006, 30.0 percent of workers twenty-five years of age and older had job tenure of more than ten years, just slightly below the comparable figure of 31.9 percent in 1983. However, the share of men with such lengthy job tenure declined from 37.7 percent to 31.1 percent, while the comparable share among women rose from 24.9 percent to 28.8 percent. In fact, older men who would have been more likely to be protected by internal labor markets in the 1960s and 1970s and earlier experienced sharp declines in median job tenure. From 1983 to 2006, median job tenure fell for men ages 45–54, from 12.8 years to 8.1 years, and for men ages 55–64 from 15.3 years to 9.5 years (U.S. Bureau of Labor Statistics 2000, 2006).

Even though the unemployment rate fell to low levels in the second half of the 1990s, widespread bottlenecks did not arise. First, there was enough additional labor supplied by existing workers to meet the needs of most employers. A rising sense of job insecurity leads workers to work as long as possible when jobs are available in anticipation of the time when they would be unemployed. Second, women have been steadily entering the labor market. The employment rate of women increased from 47.5 percent in 1979 to 57.5 percent in 2000, while the employment rate of men diminished only slightly over this period, from 73.8 percent to 71.9 percent (Economic Report of the President, 2005: 257). Third, many women previously receiving AFDC entered the labor market as a result of the changes in the welfare program. The number of families receiving public assistance fell from 4,791,000 in 1995 to 2,582,000 in 1999 (U.S. Bureau of the Census 2000: 391). The labor force participation rate of single women with children rose from 57.5 percent in 1995 to 73.9 percent in 2000 (U.S. Bureau of the Census 2009: 376). Fourth, there was significant immigration, both legal and undocumented. Between 1994, the first year for which government data are available, and 2004, foreign born workers accounted for more than half of the growth of the entire labor force (Congressional Budget Office 2005: 3).

Only after several years of low unemployment did real earnings begin to rise. Their slow rate of growth meant that it was not until 1998 that average real weekly earning exceeded the level in 1989, the end of the previous economic expansion (Economic Report of the President, 2001: 330). While average real wages were not much improved over 1989 levels, the low unemployment rates of the second half of the 1990s and the increase in the federal minimum wage did benefit low-paid workers. From 1995 to 2000, real hourly wages of workers in the bottom quintile of the wage distribution rose by more than 11 percent, faster than the earnings of more highly paid workers (Mishel, Bernstein, and Allegretto 2007: 121). Not only did real hourly wages of the low-paid rise in the second half of the 1990s, their hours of work increased as well.

However, the lessening of wage inequality was only temporary, as the recovery from the short and shallow recession of 2001 bypassed many people. Overall, average real wages grew more slowly from 2001–2005 than from 1997–2001 (Dew-Becker and Gordon 2005: 79). Real wages increased most rapidly at the top of the wage distribution and least rapidly at the bottom (Congressional Budget Office 2006: 5). The federal minimum wage was not raised for ten years, the longest time since the creation of the federal minimum wage in 1938.[5] In fact, in 2005, the minimum wage was worth just 32 percent of what an average worker earned

---

[5] The federal minimum wage was finally increased from $5.15 per hour to $5.85 per hour in 2007.

per hour, the lowest point in forty years (Mishel, Bernstein, and Allegretto 2007: 190). Deunionization continued, with the unionization rate in 2006 falling to 12 percent overall and 7.4 percent in the private sector (U.S. Bureau of Labor Statistics 2007).

With labor so weak, the rapid productivity growth of the early 2000s occurred in large part because of an intimidated labor force. Typically, employment declines are associated with weak productivity growth. However, that was not the case from 2001–2003. Companies facing intense competition and pressure on profits were restructuring. They were cutting costs, including labor costs, reducing employment, and keeping investment expenditures low. In fact, the job loss rate rose sharply after 1997–99 through to 2001–03, despite the onset of the economic expansion in late 2001 (Farber 2005). At the same time, companies were raising output and labor productivity with their remaining workers (Oliner, Sichel, and Stiroh 2007).

As did the Reagan administration two decades earlier, the Bush (George W.) administration attacked labor. The Bush NLRB more often than not decided cases in favor of employers and often reversed rulings of the Clinton NLRB. The rulings of the Bush NLRB made it harder for workers to form unions through card check agreements, more difficult for workers who were illegally fired for union activity to recover back pay, and easier for employers to refuse to hire union supporters. Furthermore, they reclassified vast numbers of workers as supervisory, thereby prohibiting them from joining unions. And the U.S. Department of Labor issued a rule redefining who is eligible for overtime pay with the likely effect that fewer workers will receive overtime pay.

Conclusion

The contemporary "neoliberal" SSA represents the resolution of the economic and political stalemate of the 1970s arising from the relative decline in the worldwide economic power of the United States. This economic and political stalemate was a manifestation of the crisis phase of the postwar SSA. Beginning in the early 1980s and building on the policies of the Carter administration that preceded it, the Reagan administration, together with business, pursued strategies and polices that resolved the stalemate largely on business' terms. Deregulation, deunionization, and labor flexibility are components of the contemporary "neoliberal"

SSA. Increased economic inequality and stagnant wages and benefits for many workers are the results.

Owners of capital and exceedingly well-paid professionals and managers have been the main beneficiaries. The richest 1 percent of American households received 21.5 percent of all household income in 2000, a share not seen since the late 1920s. While their income share did drop with the bursting of the stock market bubble in 2000, it has begun to increase once again. Households in this group increased their shares of both capital income and labor income. Overall, the share of income going to the top fifth of households was 48.1 percent in 2005, in contrast to 41.4 percent in 1979. This rise in the top fifth's share of income occurred almost entirely within the share of income accounted for by the top 5 percent of families (Mishel, Bernstein, and Allegretto 2007: 59, 62).

On the other hand, average hourly earnings of production and nonsupervisory workers have virtually stagnated since 1979, while labor productivity has risen (Dew-Becker and Gordon 2005: 79). Furthermore, private sector workers as a whole were less likely to receive employer-provided health benefits and employer-provided pensions in 2004 than they were in 1979 (Mishel, Bernstein, and Allegretto 2007: 135, 138).

Excessive consumer debt and asset bubbles preceded the onset of the current recession, the most severe of the post World War II period. Debt and asset bubbles were the direct result of the "neoliberal" SSA. Due to stagnating real earnings and declining employer-provided health benefits, many families were forced to take on excessive debt to maintain their desired standard of living or to meet unexpected medical expenses. The rise in profits relative to wages and the increasing concentration of household income at the top of the income distribution resulted in a large and growing volume of funds seeking investment opportunities, be they productive or speculative. With a shortage of available investment opportunities relative to available funds for investment, conditions were ripe for asset bubbles in real estate and securities. The collapse of these asset bubbles led to the current recession.

The economic crisis constitutes, at minimum, a serious strain within the contemporary "neoliberal" SSA. Whether it will lead to the replacement of the contemporary "neoliberal" SSA by a new postwar SSA remains to be seen. The Obama administration is willing to redress, at least to a degree, the imbalance of power between labor and capital, improve the social wage, utilize government action to rebuild the economy, and restructure firms and industries in crisis. But whether it will pursue an aggressive labor agenda or place significant constraints on the actions of owners of capital is not yet clear. Furthermore, recalcitrant owners of capital may not be willing to compromise with labor, while labor may not be strong enough to force such a compromise. It is likely that a new SSA will emerge, a hybrid between the "neoliberal" and postwar varieties.

References

Baldwin, Mark and Richard McHugh 1992. *Unprepared for Recession: The Erosion of State Unemployment Insurance Coverage Fostered by Public Policy in the 1980s.* Washington DC: Economic Policy Institute.

Barbash, Jack 1961. "Union Response to the 'Hard Line'". *Industrial Relations* 1, 1: 25–38.

Blum, Albert A. 1968. "Why Unions Grow." *Labor History* 9, 1: 39–72.

Business Week 1984. "NLRB Rulings that are Inflaming Labor Relations." June 11:122–130.

Congressional Budget Office 2005. "The Role of Immigrants in the U.S. Labor Market." November.

2006. "Changes in Low-Wage Labor Markets between 1979 and 2005."

Dew-Becker, Ian and Robert J. Gordon 2005. "Where did the Productivity Growth Go? Inflation Dynamics and the Distribution of Income." *Brookings Papers on Economic Activity* 2: 67–127.

Economic Report of the President 2001. Washington DC: U.S. Government Printing Office.

2005. Washington DC: U.S. Government Printing Office.

Edwards, Richard C. 1979. *Contested Terrain: The Transformation of the Workplace in the Twentieth Century.* New York: Basic Books.

Farber, Henry S. 2005. "What Do We Know About Job Loss in the United States? Evidence from the Displaced Workers Survey, 1984–2004." *Economic Perspectives* 2Q: 13–28.

Freeman, Richard B. 1988. "Contraction and Expansion: The Divergence of Private Sector and Public Sector Unionism in the United States." *Journal of Economic Perspectives* 2, 2: 63–88.

Gittleman, Maury B. and David R. Howell 1995. "Changes in the Structure and Quality of Jobs in the United States: Effects by Race and Gender, 1973–1990." *Industrial and Labor Relations Review* 48, 3: 420–440.

Golden, Lonnie and Eileen Appelbaum 1992. "What was Driving the 1982–88 Boom in Temporary Employment? Preferences of Workers or Decisions and Power of Employers." *American Journal of Economics and Sociology* 51, 4: 473–93.

Gordon, David M., Richard Edwards and Michael Reich 1982. *Segmented Work, Divided Workers: The Historical Transformation of Labor in the United States.* New York: Cambridge University Press.

Gramlich, Edward M., Richard Kasten and Frank Sammartino 1993. "Growing Inequality in the 1980s: The Role of Federal Taxes and Cash Transfers." Pp. 225–49 in Sheldon Danziger and Peter Gottschalk eds. *Uneven Tides: Rising Inequality in America*. New York: Russell Sage Press.

Harrison, Bennett and Barry Bluestone 1990. "Wage Polarization in the US and the 'Flexibility' Debate." *Cambridge Journal of Economics* 14, 3: 351–73.

Kaufman, Bruce E. 1978. "The Propensity to Strike in American Manufacturing." *Proceedings of the Thirtieth Annual Meeting of the Industrial Relations Research Association*. Madison, WI: Industrial Relations Research Association: 419–26.

Levitan, Sar A., Peter E. Carlson and Isaac Shapiro 1986. *Protecting American Workers: An Assessment of Government Programs*. Washington DC: Bureau of National Affairs.

Mishel, Lawrence, Jared Bernstein and John Schmitt 2001. *The State of Working America: 2000/2001*. Ithaca, NY: Cornell University Press.

Mishel, Lawrence, Jared Bernstein and Sylvia Allegretto 2007. *The State of Working America 2006/2007*. Ithaca, NY: Cornell University Press.

Mitchell, Daniel J.B. 1985. "Shifting Wage Norms in Wage Determination." *Brookings Papers on Economic Activity* 2: 575–99.

　1994. "A Decade of Concession Bargaining." Pp. 435–74 in Clark Kerr and Paul D. Staudohar eds. *Labor Economics and Labor Relations: Markets and Institutions*. Cambridge MA: Harvard University Press.

Oliner, Steven D., Daniel E. Sichel and Kevin J. Stiroh 2007. "Explaining a Productive Decade." *Brookings Papers on Economic Activity* 1: 81–137.

Piore, Michael J. and Charles F. Sabel 1984. *The Second Industrial Divide: Possibilities for Prosperity*. New York: Basic Books.

Rosenberg, Sam 1994. "The More Decentralized Mode of Labor Market Regulation in the United States." *Economies et Societes* 18, 8: 35–58.

　2003. *American Economic Development Since 1945: Growth, Decline and Rejuvenation*. Basingstoke: Macmillan Press.

Rosenberg, Sam and June Lapidus 1999. "Contingent and Non-Standard Work in the United States: Towards a More Poorly Compensated, Insecure Workforce." Pp. 62–83 in A. Felstead and N. Jewson eds. *Global Trends in Flexible Labor*. Basingstoke: Macmillan Press.

Schmidt, Stefanie R. 2000. "Job Security Beliefs in the General Social Survey: Evidence on Long-Run Trends and Comparability with Other Surveys." Pp. 300–31 in David Neumark ed. *On the Job: Is Long Term Employment a Thing of the Past?* New York: Russell Sage Press.

Tilly, Christopher 1992. "Dualism in Part-Time Employment." *Industrial Relations* 31, 2: 330–47.

U.S. Bureau of the Census 2000. *Statistical Abstract of the United States: 2000*. Washington, DC, U.S. Government Printing Office.

　2009. *Statistical Abstract of the United States: 2009*. Washington, DC, U.S. Government Printing Office.

U.S. Bureau of Labour Statistics 2000. "Employee Tenure in 2000." News Release, August 29.

　2006. "Employee Tenure in 2006." News Release, September 8.

2007. "Union Members in 2006." News Release, January 25.

U. S. General Accounting Office 1991. "Strikes and the Use of Permanent Strike Replacements in the 1970s and 1980s." January.

Wenger, John B. 2001. *"Divided We Fall: Deserving Workers Slip through America's Patchwork Unemployment Insurance System."* Washington, DC: Economic Policy Institute.

NINE

The Rise of CEO Pay and the Contemporary Social Structure of Accumulation in the United States

Robert Boyer

Introduction

Social structure of accumulation (SSA) theory has contributed to our understanding of contemporary capitalist economies by pointing out the basic social relations and economic mechanisms that were at the origin of the post-World War II golden age (Bowles, Gordon, and Weisskopf 1983) and then detecting the emerging crisis of this regime: the previous mechanisms were unable to overcome the nonreproductive cycle during the 1970s. The first wave of this research showed the key role of the transformation of work and capital/labor relations in the emergence of the post-World War II SSA (Gordon, Edwards, and Reich 1982). A second wave investigated the impact of conservative strategies upon the overcoming of this structural crisis and the absence of a clear alternative to the previous SSA regime (Gordon, Weisskopf, and Bowles 1989). This is a clear contribution to a political economy of contemporary capitalism (Kotz, McDonough, and Reich 1994).

Regulation theory has followed a parallel strategy. First, it coined the concept of a Fordist accumulation regime as an explanation of the high and stable growth observed not only in the United States but in France as well after World War II (Aglietta 1982; Boyer, and Saillard 2002). Second, it argued that this regime, built upon an unprecedented capital/labor compromise, entered a structural crisis in the early 1970s (Boyer and Juillard 2002) and since then, collective actors have struggled in order to redefine the basic institutional forms according to their interests. Many emerging institutional configurations that would support a new accumulation regime, an alternative to Fordism, have been diagnosed, including competition-led, service-propelled, or information and communication technologies-led.

The last two decades also brought forward another hypothesis about the restructuring of capital accumulation under the aegis of finance (Aglietta 1998). Clearly, the insertion of financial flows into the world economy has become a leading force in the redesign of the capital/labor relation, competition and economic policy. Nevertheless, the viability of a finance-led regime has long been a matter of controversy among *regulationist* researchers: some perceived the process of financialization as irreversible and quite general (Aglietta 1998), whereas others considered that it was quite specific to the United States and UK and ultimately bound to enter into a major crisis, as have any previous accumulation regimes (Boyer 2000a). Nowadays history has delivered its assessment, and everybody agrees that with the successive bursting of the Internet and real estate bubbles, this regime has shown its fragility (Aglietta and Rebérioux 2004).

The innovation of the present chapter is to start a much more micro analysis of the role of managers, the transformation of their remuneration and their shifting alliances from a fraction of wage-earners to financiers, and to investigate the social and political processes that made possible such a structural change. It also explores a political approach to the organization of the firm and the significance and role of stock-options, inasmuch as the stylized facts challenge the conventional economic theories, especially the consequences derived from the seminal paper of Jensen and Meckling (1976), somewhat revised subsequently (Jensen and Murphy 1990).

The chapter is organized as follows. Is the CEO remuneration boom justified by an unprecedented performance of the firms they run? Empirical studies conclude that the surge of CEO compensation in the United States does not correlate with an equivalent increase of rate of return of corporate capital. The bulk of the chapter aims at explaining this discrepancy by the intrinsic power of top managers and its conversion into wealth in the era of financialization (Section "Corporate Governance and Shareholder Value"). It then provides a short survey of the empirical evidence from the abundant literature about managers' compensation. Numerous converging statistical analyses confirm the rather large autonomy and significant power of managers at the firm level (Section "The Power of Managers at the Firm Level"). The highly specific social and macroeconomic context of the 1990s has given a renewed power of managers in political arena. Many policies concerning labor, competition, and finance have been redesigned according to this new distribution of power between corporations, institutional investors, and wage-earners (Section "Power of Managers"). This significant change in institutionalized compromises is therefore the origin of the transformation of the accumulation regime toward a typically finance-led configuration: top mangers allied de facto with financiers under the "defense of shareholders" motto. Consequently, the explosion of CEO remuneration is the revealing factor of this structural change (Section "An Emblematic New Accumulation Regime"). Such an SSA might prevail under specific conditions, and actually fulfilled in the United States, but its very success breeds destabilizing forces and increases the probability of a structural crisis. Although abstract, a simple model puts into perspective the subprime crisis (Section "An Exclusively American Model that Entered into a Structural Crisis in 2007"). A short conclusion summarizes the major findings and suggests that the heyday of financialization is over (Section "Conclusion").

Corporate Governance and Shareholder Value: The Conventional View Does Not Fit with Observations

Align the Interests of Managers and Shareholders: The Motto of the 1990s

In the epoch of *value creation*, and then *shareholder value*, the divergence of interest between managers and owners pops out as a crucial issue. Why not to try to align the strategy of top managers with the objectives of stock market value maximization on behalf of the shareholders? The use of stock options therefore widely diffuses, not only to the traditional corporation operating in mature industries, but also in the start-ups of the information and communication technology industry (Figure 9.1).

In the former industries, stock options are conceived as an incentive for good management and shift the strategy of CEOs from extreme diversification to concentration on their core business, and the economizing of capital. In the later industries, a large fraction of the personnel receive a modest wage but a significant number of stock options that can be cashed when the expected profits will manifest themselves. This reduces production costs and makes higher profits, since the American accounting principles in the 1990s did not require stock options to be included into the costs. The search for radical innovations and stock options as a form of remuneration is closely associated in the vision of

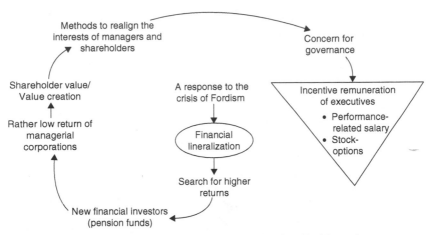

Figure 9.1. Disciplining the managers by shareholder value.

the "new economy." Stock options are therefore central to American business in the 1990s: they are supposed to *control* the managers of mature corporations and *reward* the professionals and managers of the sunrise sectors.

The Joint Stock Corporation in the 1990s: Good Financial Performance but Moderate Improvement of Economic Efficiency

The 1990s boom of U.S. stock markets (the New York Stock Exchange and Nasdaq) was initially interpreted as an evidence for an unprecedented efficiency of production, specially in information and communication technologies. In retrospect, the national account data do not confirm diagnosis suggested by the financial results as presented by American corporations' CEOs and CFOs (Figure 9.2). On one side, the rate of return on equity of the 100 S&P larger corporations actually increased from 10 percent to nearly 17 percent. But a closer look shows that such an impressive boom results from a declining interest rate paid on corporate debt and a typical leverage effect based upon the difference between this interest rate and the rate of return of total capital. On the other side, when one computes the economic rate of return according to the national account methodology, the recovery of large corporations profitability is far less impressive: the slow decline from 1985 to 1992 is interrupted and the economic rate of return increases by only 3 percent from 1993 to 2000 and then declines with the bursting out of the Internet bubble. In retrospect, the prosperity of American corporation that was supposed to be attributed to the impact of ICT and a new management

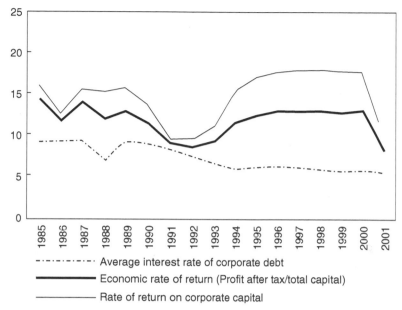

Figure 9.2. S&P 100 American corporations: high financial profitability due to the leverage of debt.
Source: Plihon 2002: 90.

style was largely due to the quality of the policy of the Federal Reserve Board and a clever management of credit and bonds by corporations.

Top Executives Remuneration Explosion, Far Ahead of Performance Improvement and Average Wage Evolution

Thus, the contribution of managers to better financial performance of quoted American corporations is likely to be quite modest indeed. Their remuneration should have experienced a similar, hence modest, increase. But on the contrary, they benefited from an unprecedented boom of their total remuneration (Figure 9.3). In the early 1970s, the average compensation of top 10 CEOs was about $1.3 million (in 1999 dollars), whereas average salaries were about $40,000. Since 1975, the trends of these two variables have been diverging: quasi stagnation of average salaries and fast and quasi-continuous increase of the average compensation of top 100 CEOs, reaching $40 million in 1999. One notes again an acceleration of their total compensation after 1995, that is, at the beginning of the internet financial bubble in the United States.

These figures seem to confirm the core hypothesis of this chapter: benefiting from the competitive threat exerted by foreign competition and

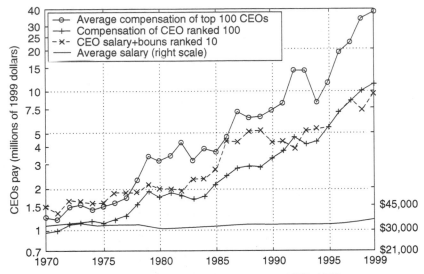

Figure 9.3. U.S. CEOs' pay versus the average wage, 1970–1999.
Source: Piketty and Saez 2003: 33, figure 11.

still more of the consequence on corporate governance of financialization, the American CEOs no longer consider themselves as the elite of
permanent wage-earners. Nevertheless, in Germany or Japan, CEOs
continue to see themselves as the upper strata of wage-earners. But not
any longer in the United States, where they are part of an implicit alliance with financiers.

Under the Aegis of Shareholder Value, the Hidden Alliance between Managers and Financiers

Since the mid-1980s, financial liberalization, the multiplicity of financial
innovations, and their diffusion from the United States to the rest of the
world have drastically changed the conception of corporate governance
and the conduct of economic policy as well. Conventional wisdom states
that the joint stock corporations that operate in the manufacturing and
service sectors have been subordinated to the strong requirements of
institutional investors. The power of these new actors precisely derives
from financial deregulation and the high mobility of capital and entitles
them to ask for new rules of the game: higher rates of return on invested
capital, conformity of actual profits to previous forecasts and financial
analysts' expectations, and the stability of the flow of profits generated by
the corporations. In the United States, and to a minor extent in the UK,

a finance-led growth regime has replaced the Fordist one. The relevance of this model was not warranted in countries such as Germany or Japan (Boyer 2000a). In spite of this divergence in national growth regimes, the ideal of shareholder value, or at least its rhetoric, has been diffusing all over the globe.

Nevertheless, a more precise investigation suggests a more nuanced appraisal. Given the fad promoted by financial investors concerning of stock options and the support of many experts in corporate finance, the objective of realigning the interests of shareholders and managers has been widely diffused, first in the United States, and then in many other OECD countries. Cleverly, without necessarily admitting it openly, the managers have used the demands of institutional investors to redesign their own compensation. On top of their wage, many forms of remuneration have developed on the basis of profit and stock market valuation, and they have drastically increased the total income of CEOs (Piketty and Saez 2003: 16). Top executives have been practicing the art of judo: converting the pressure of the financial community into a countermove that benefits them and continues to erode the bargaining power of wage-earners (Froud and al. 2000).

Thus, beneath the tyranny of investors, an implicit alliance between *managers* and *investors* takes place, and wage-earners have to comply with a new wave of labor market deregulation (Figure 9.4). For instance, in order not to be fired, they have to bear a larger share of risk, just to stabilize the rate of return of the corporation. The wage labor nexus itself is transformed accordingly. First of all, the shift from pay as you go pension schemes to pension funds generates a huge inflow of saving into the stock market (Montagne 2003), and in the United

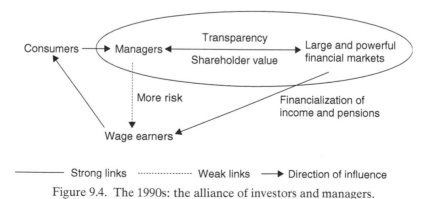

Figure 9.4. The 1990s: the alliance of investors and managers.

States this propels a finance-led growth regime. Second, in order to try to compensate modest wage increases, permanent workers accept various forms of profit-sharing and even they have access to the corporate shares via special schemes. Thus, managers have been reorienting their alliances, with definite consequences for macroeconomic patterns – *regulation* modes – of income inequality and even economic policy formation.

The Power and Informational Asymmetry in Favor of Executives
How to explain this pivotal role of managers? A political economy approach suggests one interpretation: given their position in the firm, structurally, managers are able to exert a power within the economic sphere. Power relations are not limited to the political sphere they exist under other forms in the economy (Lordon 2002). Many factors may explain a clear asymmetry both with respect to labor and to finance.

- A mundane observation first: executives make decisions on an *everyday basis* and directly affect the strategy of the firm. By contrast, the control of the boards has a *low frequency*, the control by financial analysts is only *indirect* and in most OECD countries wage-earners have *not any say* about the management of the firm they work for.
- Therefore, managers built up *special knowledge* and competences that need not be revealed to financial markets, competitors, or labor representatives. External financial analysts may gather statistical information about the firm and its competitors, but the real sources of profitability may still be mysterious because of lack of familiarity with the intricacies that make the success of a given corporation.
- By definition, all *insider information* is not to be revealed nor provided to outsiders since it might well be the source of extra profits. There is therefore a clear incentive to use this information strategically and opportunistically. Of course, insider trading on stock market is illegal but not the everyday use of insider information and knowledge.
- There is *a strong asymmetry of power and information* between the top managers and the various boards and committees. Their members are appointed by the executives, the information they are provided is elaborated by the staff of corporations, and finally, the members of the board tend to belong to the same social network. Thus, the probability of accepting the agenda and the proposal put forward by the

CEOs is quite high. Similarly, during the general assembly of share-holders, minorities do not have the resources to propose alternative nomination and proposals (Bebchuk 2004). Therefore, the control of managers by auditors, financial analysts, shareholders' organizations, is operating *ex post* and generally when the financial situation has become dramatic. A fine tuning of the control of managers is quite difficult indeed.

All these arguments derive from the same, central feature of profit generation. The *patrimonial conception of the corporation* assumes that profit derives from the mix of substitutable and generic factors of production, according to the prevailing system of prices. The basic hypothesis is that each factor is paid according to its marginal productivity. This model breaks down as soon as one adopts an organic conception: the corporation is defined by a set of complementary competences that are difficult to replicate (Biondi et al. 2009). This is the origin of the net profit of the firm, once the capital has been paid at the ongoing interest rate. Therefore, the entrenched power of executives is the mirror image of the ability of the firm to generate profits (Bebchuk and Fried 2003; Bebchuk 2004). It is therefore illusory to think that the traders on the financial markets know better than the managers the origin and causes of the success of a given corporation. Their informational advantage derives from statistical analysis of the macro and sectoral determinants of a sample of firms belonging to the same sector.

The Power of Managers at the Firm Level: Converging Empirical Evidence

In previous configurations, top managers have a pivotal role since they develop alliances with other social groups and these alliances vary according to the institutional, political, and economic context. The previous hypothesis about the intrinsic power of managers, both at the micro and macro level, is difficult to test fully and directly, but scattered evidence suggests the existence and permanence of such power.

Clear Windfall Profits for Managers Benefiting from Stock Options

The intensive use of stock options in the United States was supposed to align the strategies of CEOs with the interest of shareholders. It has already been argued that, at the *micro level*, such alignment of interests

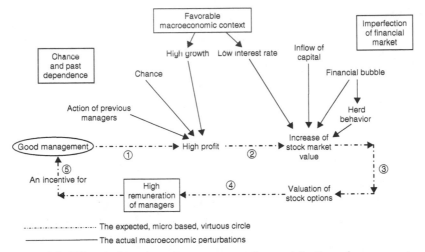

Figure 9.5. Why stock options do not sort out the contribution of managers to the performance of the corporation.

can never be perfect. New sources of discrepancies emerge when the firm is embedded into the *macroeconomic context* (Figure 9.5).

- First, the contemporary financial performance of a firm is largely shaped by the decisions taken by previous CEOs, given the large time lag between investment (and still more for R & D expenditure) and its impact on the competitiveness of the firm. Actually, the *time of financial valuation* by stock markets is far shorter than the *time of maturation of innovation* and productive investment. The car industry and even more the biotech sector are good examples of such time lags that might cover nearly one or two decades.

- There is a second source of discrepancy between stock options and actual merits of CEOs. During the second half of the 1990s, a fast and stable growth with almost no inflation enabled very *low interest rates*, thus generating and diffusing *a speculative bubble* that had no direct correlation with the quality of management (Boyer 2004). Bad and good managers benefited equally from the common belief that a new growth regime had emerged and that profit could only grow and thus sustain unprecedented rates of return for invested capital.

- A third limit of stock options derives from the fact that financial markets are generally *micro efficient* (in valuing the relative price of stocks) but *macro inefficient* in the sense that they are not immune from a bad intertemporal allocation of capital: overconfidence and her behavior are the responses to the typical uncertainty of highly liquid financial markets, thus generating speculative bubbles (Orléan 1999). During such speculative periods, the compensation of CEOs no longer has any relation with their contribution to the performance of the company they run.

These three mechanisms (path dependence and chance, impact of macroeconomic context, and imperfection of financial markets) totally distort the core virtuous circle contemplated by the proponent of stock options (Figure 9.6).

These divergences between the incentive mechanism of stock options at the micro level and their macro determinants have had a major impact on the skyrocketing of CEOs' remuneration from 1995 to 2000 (Table 9.1). If financial markets were perfect, the distribution of dividends would be the only relevant performance index and source of remuneration of shareholders and CEOs benefiting from stock options. Actually, since the early 1980s, the increase of share prices has represented between two-thirds and three-fourths of the total return for shareholders. This provides a rough estimate of the overvaluation of CEOs compensation during this period (Erturk et al. 2004: 25).

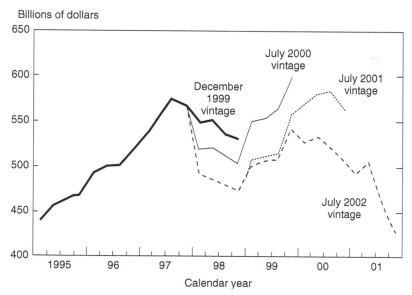

Figure 9.6. The systematic overstatements of profits after 1997: a slow process of adjustment in the United States.
Source: Himmelberg and Mahoney 2004: 10.

Table 9.1. *Two Evaluations of the Impact of Stock-Options on Corporate Profits in the United States*

a. Stock options exercised as a percent of after corporate profit				
	1997	1998	1999	2000
1. Stock options exercised	68.61	100.08	139.29	197.37
2. Profit estimated by Bureau of Economic Analysis	552.1	470.0	517.2	508.2
Stock options exercised compared to profit	12.4 percent	21.3 percent	26.9 percent	38.8 percent

Source: Himmelberg and Mahoney (2004: 10)

b. Options expenses as a percent of net earnings for S & P companies			
1996	1998	2000	2002
2 percent	5 percent	8 percent	23 percent

Data: The analyst's accounting observer in Business Week, July 20, 2003: 38.

Since 1997, a Favorite Corporate Strategy: Distorting the Profit Statements

The relative autonomy of top executives also affects the information provided to capital markets. In this respect, the American system entitles a significant freedom to the interpretation of the Generally Accepted Accounting Principles (GAAP). During the Internet bubble, many firms used and abused this opportunity (Himmelberg and Mahoney 2004). In retrospect, the overestimation of corporate profits was so large that the *ex post* accurate figures show a *reduction* of corporate profit after 1997, whereas *ex ante* until July 2001, the corporations generally reported *upward revisions* of their profits (Figure 9.6).

Such a discrepancy between real time private information and *ex post* public evaluation by American national accounts may have many sources. First, the accounting rules are not the same for corporations and for national accounts. But this cannot explain the discrepancy shown by Figure 9.6, which shows only Bureau of Economic Analysis estimates elaborated according to unchanging rules. A second and quite important source of discrepancy relates to an *unexpected surge of employee stock options exercised* during the second half of the 1990s. During this period, stock options were not considered to be a cost by corporations. This feature contributed to the spiraling of stock markets: the shift of employee compensation from basic wages to stock options increases corporate profits, hence a higher valuation of the shares of the corporation and finally a new incentive to grant stock options to a wider category of personnel. Of course, the CEOs and CFOs have been the key beneficiaries of this trend.

Two independent surveys show that the share of stock options exercised in total corporate profit steadily increased from the mid-1990s to the early 2000s. For the Bureau of Economic Analysis, they represented 12.4 percent in 1997 and continuously grew until the 2000s, when they represented nearly 39 percent of corporate profits. According to *Business Week* (2003: 38), option expenses as a percent of net earnings of S&P companies represented only 2 percent in 1996, 8 percent in 2000, and finally 23 percent in 2003 (Table 9.1).

A third and more problematic strategy has to be put into the picture to explain the diverging evaluations in Figure 9.6: publicly quoted corporations intentionally inflated their profit statements, largely by using the flexibility of GAAP, playing the game of *creative accounting* and in some extreme cases lying in order to sustain the rise of their shares (Enron, Worldcom, Ahold). This is the unintended fallout of the conjunction of shareholder value and the convention of a required ROE of 15 percent. Such a target cannot be reached on a permanent basis by the majority of firms and sectors; thus, it is not really a surprise if creative accounting became in the 1990s one of the favorite disciplines taught in prestigious business schools and practiced by CFOs. As a result, CEOs, CFOs, and other top executives became rich, potentially or really when they had the opportunity to exercise their stock options before the crash of the stock market. This provides additional evidence concerning the discretionary power that benefits top management in modern corporations.

Power of Managers: From the Corporation to the Political Arena

It is now time to go out of the inner *micro structure* and functioning of the large corporation that generated significant autonomy and power for the top executives and explore how the insertion of the large publicly-quoted corporations into the social and political system has changed since the mid-1980s (Fligstein 1990; Fligstein and Shin 2004). The rise of CEO compensation and especially the surge of stock options may have a series of relevant explanations at the *macro level*.

Financial Liberalization has been a Prerequisite for CEO Compensation Explosion

The internal shift in the hierarchy of the departments of the large firm is closely related to the transformation in the American growth regime. Clearly, the explosion of CEOs compensation and the rise of CFOs could not have happened under the Fordist regime, since finance was strictly regulated, and the major issue was the mutual adjustment of production along with (largely domestic) demand, in accordance with the then over-whelming reference to Keynesian-style monetary and budgetary policies. But the crisis of Fordism in the late 1960s opens a period of major structural change: basically, penetration of imports, labor market dereg-ulation, and financial innovation and liberalization. The wage-earners' bargaining power is therefore eroded and symmetrically the managers have to respond to the demands of financial markets and not as much to those of labor.

The reform of pensions plays a crucial role, since it links the evolution of the wage labor nexus along with the transformation of the finan-cial regime (Montagne 2003). On one side, the inflow of pension funds into the stock market increases its *liquidity* and thus makes the market prone to financial bubbles. On the other side, financial intermediaries and institutions put forward the idea that *shareholder value* should be the only concern of quoted corporations. Financialization (Palley 2007) and the explosion of CEO compensation are the logical outcomes of the interaction of these two mechanisms (Figure 9.7).

When Economic Power is Converted into Political Power

A political economy explanation usefully complements a micro grounded analysis of the power of managers within the corporation (Roe 1994). This explanation explores how managers convert their economic power into the ability to partially shape economic policy according to their interests. During the last two decades, large corporations have used both *exit and voice* in order to be influential in the political arena. First, with the large opening of national economies and the free movements of capital, the managers of multinational corporations have been able to redesign domestic labor contracts according to the requirements of the competitiveness of their domestic sites of production (see Figure 9.6). Second, they asked for lower taxation of profits, arguing that they could

Figure 9.7. The main episodes and factors in the financialization of executive remuneration.

benefit from preferential treatment abroad. Thus, the managers have been combining the threat of delocalization, that is, *exit*, along with *voice* via the lobbying in direction of lawmakers.

The business and financial communities have vigorously expressed their demands to politicians, and they have been heard: governments have adopted pro-business policies: they deregulated labor markets, slimmed down the welfare benefits provided by the state, they lowered taxation of high incomes, and they adopted an accommodating conception of fair competition. Furthermore, lobbies have explicitly required the absence of regulation of the new financial derivatives, from the Enron energy derivatives to the subprime derivatives. This has played a definite role in the emergence of successive financial crises in the United States.

Benefiting from a Tax System Redesigned in Favor of the Richest

Top managers and financiers benefit furthermore from a long-term evolution of the American tax system. Since rich individuals do participate more in the political process than the poorer fraction of the population, they have succeeded in obtaining an alleviation of the high income bracket marginal tax rates. The effective federal tax rate for the median American family is nearly constant since 1980, after a significant increase since the 1960s. But the shift is in the opposite direction for millionaires and the top 1 percent of households (Table 9.2). Similarly, while the payroll tax and welfare contributions are up to 31 percent in 2000 from 6.9 percent in 1950 (Table 9.3), corporate taxes have been declining to very modest levels (10 percent).

Robert Boyer

Table 9.2. *Contrasting Evolution of Tax Rates for Middle Class and Rich Families*

	Effective Federal Tax Rate	
	Median Family	Millionaire or Top 1 Percent
1948	5.30	76.9
1955	9.60	85.5
1960	12.35	66.9
1965	11.35	68.6
1970	16.06	
1975	20.03	35.5
1977		31.7
1980	23.68	
1981	25.09	
1982	24.46	
1983	23.76	
1984	24.25	
1985	24.44	24.9
1986	24.77	
1987	23.21	
1988	24.30	26.9
1989	24.37	26.7
1990	24.63	

Source: Phillips 2002: 96.

Thus, at the *societywide level*, the rise of entrepreneurial income (Piketty and Saez 2003), the evolution of the conception of social justice (market allocations are fair), the revision of the income tax, and finally the reduction of the share of the corporations in total state receipts confirm the hypothesis of a *renewed political power of large corporations*, and especially of their top executives.

An Emblematic New Accumulation Regime

It is now clear that the explosion of American CEO compensation is not merely a local and transitory curiosity but the symptom of a structural transformation of contemporary capitalism.

Table 9.3. *The Declining Share of the Federal Tax*
Burden Paid by Corporations and the Rising
Share of Payroll Taxes

	Share of Total Receipts (Percent)	
	Corporate Taxes	Payroll Taxes*
1950	26.5	6.9
1960	23.2	11.8
1970	17.0	18.2
1980	12.5	24.5
1990	9.1	35.5
2000	10.2	31.1

Source: Phillips 2002: 149.
*Social security and Medicare.

The Core of a Finance-led Accumulation Regime: A New
Alliance between Managers and Financiers

Actually, the whole architecture of institutional forms has been redesigned under the aegis of a de facto social compromise: the top managers
accept the principle of shareholder value, while financiers recognize the
power of managers. Wage-earners are excluded from this arrangement,
unless they agree to link a significant part of their remuneration to the
financial success of the firm they are working for, and if they enrol in
pension funds and thus might benefit from stock market booms. This alliance puts the financial system as the dominant institutional form, since
its very functioning implies the quite definite transformations of others
(Figure 9.8).

- The publicly quoted corporation looks for a high and *stable rate of*
  return in order to comply with the demands of the shareholders.
  Thus, a new pattern emerges for investment. Productive investment
  becomes more sensitive to profit than to expected demand, whereas
  the high liquidity of the stock market makes mergers and acquisitions
  as well as LBOs easier.
- This new configuration of the financial system has definite consequences
  for the evolution of the *wage labor nexus*. During the Golden Age,
  firms used to grant the equivalent of insurance to wage-earners because
  their remuneration was not directly affected by the uncertainty typical
  of a market economy. With the rise of shareholder value, a fraction

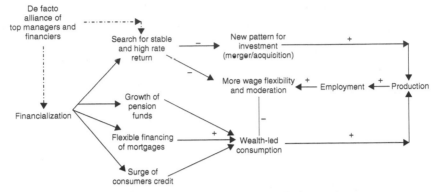

Figure 9.8. A new finance-led accumulation regime.

of this uncertainty is now borne by labor, via more *rapid employment adjustments,* wage *flexibility,* and less generous welfare benefits. Consequently, the wage bill becomes more reactive to macroeconomic shocks, and the household consumption profile is affected negatively.

• Financialization partly or totally compensates this adverse trend because it brings a transitory relaxation of households' budget constraints. The transition from a pay as you go system to *pension funds* alters the wealth of wage-earners, and financial assets tend to become a significant determinant of consumption. Simultaneously, the ability to revise mortgages opens new source of financing when interest rates are declining, and easy access to credit helps to sustain consumption in spite of the wage moderation induced by the search for labor flexibility deployed by corporations.

This *new alliance* therefore brings *a shift in the hierarchy of institutional forms* (Boyer 2000b) and, at least potentially, makes possible a genuine accumulation regime, implicitly based on a coalition of managers and core wage-earners, and at odds with the Fordist regime.

The Components of a Finance-Led Accumulation Regime

The central variable of this regime is stock market valuation, since it is this market that governs the strategies of firms and the behavior of individuals, and it socializes expectations of all actors (Orléan 1999). Direct finance tends to overtake bank credit as the key component of the financial system: generous access to credit is conditioned by the valuation of the stock market. A careful management of productive investment

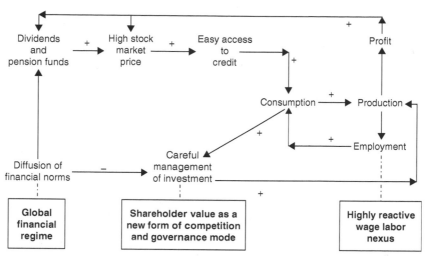

Figure 9.9. The main macroeconomic relations of a finance-led accumulation regime.

drives a new pattern for macroeconomic variables and simultaneously stock market wealth is taken into account by banks when they grant credit to households (Figure 9.9).

Consequently, the levels of production and employment are no more the consequence of the interaction of production and consumption norms independently of any major role of the financial markets, that is, the Golden Age regime of the post-World War II era (Aglietta and Rebérioux 2004). Basically, the stock market is the focal point that all actors consider when they make decisions, since it provides a coordination of expectations. Growth is thus governed by these expectations.

This Regime is Possible but Requires Specific Conditions

Previous research has proposed a simple model of finance-led growth using these hypotheses (Boyer 2000a). Although such a model, built upon forward-looking and somewhat risky behavior (households consume today because the stock market tells them that they will be rich tomorrow), *seems structurally nonviable*, it may have a dynamic equilibrium. The very possibility of such a regime requires *a precise configuration* for the parameters of the investment and consumption functions. It is more likely, the higher the ratio of wealth in shares/disposable income, the more important is the impact of wealth upon consumption, and the higher the propensity to invest profit with respect to accelerator effects.

An Exclusively American Model That Entered
into a Structural Crisis in 2007

This simple model delivers two interesting results, concerning respectively the universality and the long-run stability of a finance-led SSA.

This Model Cannot Diffuse Easily to the Rest of the World

A rough calibration of the model for some OECD countries delivers a first interesting result (Table 9.4): the U.S. economy is the only clear candidate for such a finance-led regime, followed by the UK. In contrast, all the other economies do not experience superior performance if shareholder value principles are introduced. The reason for such a result is simple enough: when the wage is the main source of income, financial portfolios are small and investment reacts essentially to demand and not directly to profit, then financialization is detrimental since it implies a loss in production, profit, and employment. Furthermore, the explicit or implicit alliances among financiers, industrialists and wage-earners are quite different indeed, compared with those prevailing in the United States.

The U.S. configuration shows a *remarkable congruence* among financial deregulation, the transformation of corporate governance, the diffusion of stock options within CEOs' compensation schemes, and finally the financialization of the wage labor nexus. In the United States the alliance between financiers and top managers has contributed to the coalescence of a brand new finance-led accumulation regime, and this has not happened elsewhere.

The Success of this Regime Propels it into Financial
Fragility and the Subprime Structural Crisis

But even starting from a stable finance-led SSA, the economy can be destabilized by three types of evolutions. First, there is a *limit threshold* for the target rate of the Return on Equity (ROE): if it is too high, the equilibrium might disappear. Thus, the permanent pressure for upward ROE cannot go on forever. Second, if *wages become too flexible* due to the continuous erosion of the bargaining power of wage-earners, the equilibrium turns out to be unstable. Third, the very success of financialization, that is, a permanent increase of *financial wealth more rapid than earned income*, may trigger a brusque shift from a stable to an unstable regime. Therefore, even in the absence of financial bubbles that are not captured by the model, there is an internal barrier to the process of financialization.

Table 9.4. *The Finance-Led SSA Is Typical of the United States. Few*
Chances of Diffusion to the Rest of the World, with the
Exception of the United Kingdom

Countries Parameters	United States	United Kingdom	Canada	Japan	Germany	France
Average propensity to consume (1996)	0.95	0.926	0.956	0.869	0.884	0.908
Wealth in shares as a percent of disposable income (1997)	145	75	95	30	25	20
Capital gains as a percent of disposable income	35.5	15	11	−7	7	5
Shares and bonds as percent of households' financial assets	28.4	52.4	n.a.	25.3	21.3	14.5
Interest rate	5.34	7.38	5.20	0.32	3.5	3.46
Return on bonds	6.51	5.59	7.30	1.06	3.97	4.23
Reference profitability (%)	12–16	12–16	12–16	5	6–7	9

Sources: Line 1: Japan 1998, Keizen Koho Center, An international comparison, p. 97.
Lines 2, 3 and 4: *The Economist*, September 19–25, 1998, p. 129.
Lines 5 and 6: Japan Almanac, Asahi Shimbun 1998, p. 26.
Line 7: *The Economist*, September 19–25, 1998, p. 129.

This explains why the United States and to some extent the UK economies were the most severely struck by the 2007–2008 crises. They are
more than typical boom and recession adjustments, since they display
most of the features of a *structural crisis* (Guttman 2008, Crotty, Epstein
2008). A succession of financial innovations has allowed a cumulative
rise of the stock of credit relative to the disposable income of American
households. This increase first supported growth, but now it is a brake
to the recovery of consumption. Besides this macroeconomic limit, the
pricing mechanism for over-the-counter derivatives is no longer working, which creates a *systemic challenge* to the viability of the pyramid
of derivative products. Finally, *exceptional interventions* by the Federal
Reserve and the public budget have been necessary to prevent the complete meltdown of the U.S. financial system and a 1929-type cumulative
depression (Boyer 2008).

Conclusion

The main objectives of this chapter have been threefold.

First, it proposes a *political economy* explanation for the explosion of U.S. CEO compensation far ahead of and frequently quite independently from the actual performance of their corporations. By their position, they have an *intrinsic power* that cannot be easily monitored by outsiders, however powerful the financial community might seem.

Second, this local economic power has been extended by political lobbying into an ability to convert it into *wealth appropriation*. The irony is that the *shareholder value* movement that was supposed to align the interests of managers and shareholders has helped the CEOs to succeed in this strategy.

Third, all these transformations coalesce into a new *finance-led accumulation* regime. It was first successful and contributed to the macroeconomic dynamism of the United States, but it entered a zone of financial fragility in the 2000s, and finally it experienced a structural crisis with the meltdown of the subprime derivatives market. Consequently, the sources of the *2007 crisis* are to be found in the *most sophisticated financial system*, the United States being the one, and not at all in emerging countries, in contrast to the financial crises of 1997.

For the first time, *the legitimacy of financial liberalization* is challenged by American citizens, and the remuneration of top managers is under scrutiny. A new epoch opens over a quite uncertain New "New Deal."

References

Aglietta, Michel 1982. *Regulation and Crisis of Capitalism*. New York: Monthly Review Press.

Aglietta, Michel 1998. « Le capitalisme de demain », *Note de la fondation Saint-Simon*, no. 101, Novembre.

Aglietta, Michel and Antoine Rebérioux 2004. *Dérives du capitalisme financier.* Paris: Albin Michel.

Bebchuk, Lucian Arye 2004. "The Case for Shareholder Access: A Response to the Business Roundtable." SEC Roundtable, March 10.

Bebchuk, Lucian Arye and Jesse M. Fried 2003. "Executive Compensation as an Agency Problem." *The Journal of Economic Perspectives* 17, 3: 71–92.

Biondi, Yuri, Vincent Bignon and Xavier Ragot 2009. "Une analyse économique de l'évolution des normes comptables européennes: le principe de 'juste valeur'." Paris: Prisme, Centre Cournot, Updated from 2004 draft.

Bowles, Samuel, David Gordon and Thomas Weisskopf 1983. *Beyond the Waste Land: a Democratic Alternative to Economic Decline*. New York: Anchor Press.

Boyer Robert 2000a. "Is a finance-led growth regime a viable alternative to Fordism? A preliminary analysis." *Economy and Society* 29, 1: 111–45.

2000b. "The political in the era of globalization and finance; focus on some Régulation School Research." *International Journal of Urban and Regional Research.* 24, 2: 274–322.

2004. *The Future of Economic Growth. As New Becomes Old.* Cherltenham UK: Edward Elgar.

2008. *History Repeating for Economists. An anticipated Financial Crisis,* Prisme no. 13, November, Cournot Centre for Economic Research, Paris. http://www.centrecournot.org/prismepdf/Prisme_13_EN.pdf

Boyer Robert and Michel Juillard 2002. "The United-States: Good bye, Fordism!" Pp. 238–256 in Robert Boyer and Yves Saillard eds. *Régulation Theory: The State of Art.* London: Routledge.

Boyer, Robert and Yves Saillard eds, 2002. *Régulation Theory: The State of Art.* London: Routledge.

Crotty James and Gerald Epstein 2008. "The costs and contradictions of the lender-of-last resort function in contemporary capitalism: the sub-prime crisis of 2007–2008", WP Political Economy Research Institute (PERI) University of Massachusetts, Amherst, May 2–3.

Erturk, Ismail, Julie Froud, Johal Sukhdev and Karel Williams 2004. "Pay for corporate performance or pay as social division: re-thinking the problem of top management pay in giant corporations." *Working Paper.* Manchester University.

Fligstein, Neil 1990. *The Transformation of Corporate Control.* Cambridge, MA: Harvard University Press.

Fligstein, Neil and Taekjin Shin 2004. "Shareholder Value and the Transformation of the American Economy, 1984–2001" IRLE Working Paper. University of California, Berkeley.

Gordon, David, Richard Edwards and Michael Reich 1982. *Segmented Work, Divided Workers.* New York: Cambridge University Press.

1989. "Business Ascendancy and Economic Impasse: A Structural Perspective on Conservative Economics, 1979–1987." *Journal of Economic Perspectives* 3, 1:107–34.

Guttmann, Robert 2008. A Primer on Finance-Led Capitalism and Its Crisis *Revue de la Régulation,* n°3/4, 2nd seæester. http://regulation.revues.org/index5843.html

Himmelberg, Charles P. and James M. Mahoney (2004), "Recent revisions to corporate profits: What we know and when we knew it." Federal Reserve Bank of New York.

Jensen, Michael and William Meckling 1976. "Theory of the Firm: Managerial Behaviour, Agency Costs and Ownership Structure." *Journal of Financial Economics* 3: 305–60.

Jensen, Michael and Kevin Murphy 1990. "Performance Pay and Top-Management Incentives." *Journal of Political Economy* 98, 2: 225–64.

Lordon, Frédéric 2002. *La politique du capital.* Paris: Éditions Odile Jacob.

Kotz, David, Terrence McDonough and Michael Reich eds. 1994. *Social Structures of Accumulation: The Political Economy of Growth and Crisis.* New York: Cambridge University Press.

Montagne, Sabine 2003. *Les métamorphoses du trust: les fonds de pension américains entre protection et spéculation.* Thèse Université Paris 10-Nanterre.

Orléan, André 1999. *Le pouvoir de la finance.* Paris: Odile Jacob.

Palley, Thomas I. 2007. "Financialization: What it is and Why it Matters." *Working Paper 525.* Washington DC: The Levy Economics Institute.

Phillips, Kevin 2002. *Wealth and Democracy.* New York: Broadway Books.

Piketty, Thomas and Emmanuel Saez 2003. "Income inequality in the United-States, 1913–1998." *Quarterly Journal of Economics*: 1–39.

Roe, Mark 1994. *Strong Managers, Weak Owners: the Political Roots of American Corporate Finance.* Princeton NJ: Princeton University Press.

TEN

Social Structures of Accumulation and the Criminal Justice System

Susan M. Carlson, Michael D. Gillespie, and Raymond J. Michalowski

Introduction

Social structure of accumulation (SSA) theory posits that at particular historical moments a unique set of economic, political, and social institutions come together to provide the conditions necessary for a period of sustained, vigorous capital accumulation, particularly by regulating class conflict and competition (Kotz 1987). Gordon, Edwards, and Reich (1982: 25) further suggest that "... different social structures of accumulation may incorporate (or exclude) differing sets of social institutions" with a tendency of the institutional ensemble to become more complex and include more institutions over time.

To date, SSA analyses of the post-World War II SSA in the United States have been limited to the four pillars that comprise the SSA – limited capital-labor accord, capital-citizen accord, pax Americana, and containment of inter-capitalist rivalry (Bowles, Gordon, and Weisskopf 1990) – or "core institutions" (Kotz 1987; McDonough 1994) that impinge most directly on the accumulation process. Scant attention has been given to other institutions that may play an important supportive role in facilitating capital accumulation.

This chapter provides an analysis of one such institution – the criminal justice system – across phases of the post-World War II SSA in the United States.[1] Several SSA authors have discussed prisons and the new

---

[1] The "criminal justice system" in the United States is made up of 51 separate systems – one at the federal/national level, and one in each of the 50 states. Each has its own set of criminal laws, and law enforcement, judicial, and corrections components. The U.S. Constitution limits the jurisdiction of the federal system to crimes that cross state

"garrison state" (Bowles, Gordon, and Weisskopf 1990; Gordon 1996), rising expenditures on the criminal justice system (Lippit 1997), and the war on drugs (Houston 1992) as characterizing the most recent phase of the post-World War II SSA, but none have theorized the role of the criminal justice system in the capital accumulation process. We offer such an analysis here.

Research by two of the authors of this chapter has demonstrated a relationship between changes in the U.S. post-World War II SSA and crime and its control. Carlson and Michalowski (1997) first examined the relationship between official unemployment and crime rates across SSA phases. Consistent with expectations based on SSA theory, we found that the relationship between unemployment and crime differs across SSA phases. The relationship was only strong, positive, and statistically significant for all crimes during the decay phase (1966–1979), while being negative but not statistically significant in the ensuing decay/exploration phase (1980–1992). We interpreted these results as indicating that the statistical relationship between unemployment and crime is sensitive to changes in the social meaning of unemployment across SSA phases, as the official measure of unemployment increasingly failed to capture the surplus population at the margins of the economy as unemployment became more structural. Thus, while crime trended upward as members of the surplus population turned to crimes associated with the underground (particularly drug) economy, the proportion of the population actually counted in official unemployment statistics trended downward.

In a second study, combining SSA theory and the work of Rusche (1978 [1933]) and Rusche and Kirchheimer (1967 [1939]), Michalowski and Carlson (1999) examined historical contingency in the unemployment-imprisonment (U-I) relationship across SSA phases.

lines (i.e., contain any element that falls under the umbrella of "interstate commerce"; Article 1, Section 8, Clause 3), but federal jurisdiction over criminal cases has increased over time due to court rulings that have broadened the interpretation of "interstate commerce." For example, use of interstate telephone or mail services in the commission of a crime can bring the case under federal jurisdiction. In 2004, 17.7 percent of total criminal justice expenditures were at the federal level, 31.9 percent at the state level, and 50.3 percent at the local (county or city) level (U.S. Bureau of Justice Statistics 2007b). Policing is primarily a local function (67.8 percent of all law enforcement expenditures), and corrections a state function (59.7 percent of all corrections expenditures), with only 12.1 percent of all prisoners housed in federal facilities (U.S. Bureau of Justice Statistics 2007b). Despite the lesser role of the federal system, we focus mostly on changes in federal criminal justice policy because federal legislation marks the culmination of changes that occur within the state systems over time – that is, it represents the consolidation of penal and law enforcement practices at the national level.

Consistent with theoretical expectations, the positive, significant relationship between official unemployment and new court admissions to prison rates grew in strength across the initial exploration, consolidation, and decay phases. However, after peaking in the second half of the decay phase (1967–1979), the U-I relationship turned very strong, significant, and negative during the most recent decay/exploration phase (1980–1992). Once again we argued that the strong, negative U-I relationship in this latter period reflected the intersection of a sharp rise in admissions to prison coupled with an increasingly inadequate measure of unemployment that obscured the growth in those living at the margins of the economy.

Taken together, these studies suggest a connection between crime, the criminal justice system, and historical shifts in the post-World War II SSA. However, the exact nature of the relationship between the criminal justice system as a political institution and the capital accumulation process has not been analyzed theoretically.

SSA Theory, Capital Accumulation, and the Criminal Justice System

Gordon, Edwards, and Reich (1982: 19) see the state as performing "some critical supportive functions" for capital accumulation. James O'Connor's (1973) theory of the capitalist state is consistent with this view (see e.g., Kotz 1987: 25–6). He argues that the institutions within the capitalist state perform two often contradictory functions – accumulation and legitimization. That is (O'Connor 1973: 6), "the state must try to maintain or create the conditions in which profitable capital accumulation is possible. However, the state also must try to maintain or create the conditions for social harmony." This raises the question of how the criminal justice system might contribute to (or hamper) the state's accumulation and legitimization functions.

Even the most avid supporters of free markets see the maintenance of law and order as a necessary and legitimate function of the state (e.g., Friedman 1962). This involves controlling crime and civil disorder, which is essential for accumulation and legitimization in two broad ways. By defining and controlling property crime, the criminal justice system creates a legal and security framework that underscores the sanctity of private property. By minimizing violent crime and social disorder, the criminal justice system also creates the social harmony necessary for system legitimacy and investor confidence, core requirements for capital accumulation.

The criminal justice system also has a potential role to play in two of the three steps of the capital accumulation process. In the first step of the accumulation process (i.e., investment in means of production and labor power), criminal justice penal policy can provide capitalist investors with access to exploitable labor, either directly through a contract or lease system where access to convict labor is provided either free or at below market wages, or indirectly by providing job training and flexibility in sentencing that allows opening the prison doors when the labor market is tight.

Second, in the profit realization step of the capital accumulation process, the criminal justice system and its employees serve as markets for goods and services produced by the private sector. As a purchaser of the latest technology and weaponry for law enforcement, building supplies for prison construction, other goods and services necessary for the day-to-day maintenance of prison populations, and private corrections and security services, the criminal justice system serves as a lucrative market for profit realization. Likewise, criminal justice system employees constitute an important market for consumer durable and nondurable goods, and services.

We propose that the particular way the criminal justice system facilitates the state's accumulation and legitimization functions will vary historically depending on two factors: (1) the size, content, and perceived or real threat of the surplus population, which in turn depends on (2) labor market conditions. Specifically, we contend that as tightening labor markets in periods of consolidation threaten accumulation by increasing capital's wage bill, the criminal justice system will respond by decriminalizing some offenses, lowering penalties for others, and creating punishment strategies that will return all but the most dangerous convicted offenders to the labor market in relatively short periods of time. Conversely, as periods of decay and exploration generate increases in the surplus population and attendant crimes, criminal justice system strategies will seek to restore system legitimacy by increasing the severity of penalties in ways that will keep significant portions of the now, no longer needed, surplus population behind bars.

The Criminal Justice System across Phases of the Post-World War II SSA in the United States

According to Bowles and his colleagues (1990), the post-World War II SSA includes a consolidation phase from about 1948 through 1966, a decay phase from about 1966 through 1979, followed by a phase of over-lap between decay and initial exploration for institutional alternatives, a period of decay characterized by "business ascendency" from about 1979 through the early 1990s. Our historical analysis of changes in the criminal justice system begins with the decay/exploration phase between the two world wars that produced the post-World War II SSA (Gordon et al. 1982: 12). We then discuss each of the phases in the post-World War II SSA, and end our analysis with the most recent phase beginning roughly in 1992. This has been an intense period of institutional exploration and change, resulting in what Kotz (2003) refers to as a "liberal institutional structure" that falls short of being a new SSA.

Decay/Exploration Phase between the World Wars
In the years between World War I and World War II, a new penal philos-ophy and set of practices developed that would eventually coalesce in the mid-to-late 1940s into the "treatment model" of corrections, along with a professional model of policing. Prior to World War I, the goals of pun-ishment were deterrence and retaliation. Punishment was by hard labor, either in contract or state account prison industry systems where prisoners produced nondurable consumer goods that were sold in the free market (the profits from which benefitted the labor contractor and/or state while prisoners were paid little if at all), in public works (e.g., chain gangs in the South), or in the prison to maintain and run the facility (Barnes 1921; Weyand 1926; Gill 1931; McKelvey 1934, 1935). Determinate sentencing was the norm where the convicted went to prison for a fixed number of years with no possibility for early release.

The goals of punishment changed in the post-World War II years to emphasize social protection by incapacitation of dangerous offend-ers, and rehabilitation of offenders who did not pose a risk to society and returning them as productive workers and law-abiding citizens to the community (Barnes 1922: 256). This new "treatment" model of cor-rections combined an emphasis on "reforming" or "rehabilitating" the convicted felon with use of indeterminate sentences, parole, and pro-bation. The use of indeterminate sentences, along with the possibility of early release, was designed to provide individualized treatment for the offender, and to supply the prisoner with a positive incentive – early release for "good behavior" – for acquiring the attitudes and behavior patterns to live as a productive worker and law-abiding citizen on the outside. Indeterminate sentencing also gave the parole board the author-ity to make "incorrigible" prisoners serve the full maximum sentence.

The use of probation as an alternative to imprisonment also became widespread (McKelvey 1977: 310–15). Another feature of the treatment model of corrections was an end to the direct exploitation of prison labor by labor contractors in the private sector, or via the state allocation system. Instead, prisoners received basic education and job training to prepare them for reentry into the labor force (MacCormick 1931).

A more professional policing model developed during this SSA phase that emphasized increased efficiency via departmental reorganization, the development of state and regional policing agencies, use of scientific crime detection, formal training of law enforcement officers, and crime prevention (Tibbitts 1933: 899–901). In addition, the Federal Bureau of Investigation was established as a domestic policing agency that provided training to local law enforcement officers through its national academy (Federal Bureau of Investigation 2007). Police officers were peace officers whose role was to protect and serve the public, not to fight crime.

Consolidation Phase
From the late 1940s until the mid-to-late 1960s, economic output and real wages trended steadily upward while unemployment drifted downward, despite short-term fluctuations in the business cycle (Bowles et al. 1990: 35–46). Under these booming economic conditions, the unemployed drifted in and out of the portion of the surplus population Marx (1967[1867]) referred to as the "floating form" concomitant with movements in the business cycle, posing no threat to the capitalist order. For the few who came under the control of the criminal justice system, the institutional arrangements put in place during the previous phase – the rehabilitative ideal, probation, indeterminate sentencing combined with early release on parole, work-release programs, job training, and education – were sufficient to facilitate capital accumulation by providing a steady stream of trained labor from behind prison bars. As Thorsten Sellin (1965: 251) stated at the time,

Since the First World War, and especially since the last one, there have been tremendous changes in correctional practices. Our best prison systems today are seriously endeavoring to rehabilitate offenders and are earnestly seeking for the most effective methods of doing so. In that connection, the labor of prisoners plays a role but not one that exploits them solely for profit; it rather aims to train them for jobs that will be available to them on their release.

The labor supply was often tight and well-paying; lower-skilled jobs were plentiful. Offenders returning to the community were able to find gainful, legitimate employment. Not only were capitalist employers eager to employ these workers, but their presence slowed wage growth by increasing labor supply. As Assistant Director of the U.S. Bureau of Prisons, H.G. Moeller (1969: 83) observed,

[w]ork opportunities for the probationer and the parolee in private industry are increasingly available. The National Association of Manufacturers has publicized the importance of work-release programs. Industry has co-operated with correctional authorities in introducing into institutions training programs specifically designed to provide the offender with skills which are scarce in the labor market.

While this situation held during the consolidation phase, it would not last after the first few years in the decay phase.

In sum, the consolidation phase of the post-World War II SSA in the United States was a time of economic prosperity facilitated by the professional policing model and a penal regime that supplied trained labor to industry. The surplus population was small and posed little, if any, threat, so releasing prisoners did not threaten social order or state legitimacy. Crime rates were low, as were imprisonment rates.[2] However, the ability of the criminal justice system to facilitate accumulation and legitimization began eroding during the subsequent period of economic decay, necessitating changes, first in law enforcement, and then in corrections.

Decay: By 1966 the growth engine of the previous twenty years of consolidation was losing steam. The reemergence of strong industrial economies in countries previously devastated by World War II, combined with profit-eroding pressures from labor and other social claimants, as well as the deficit-inducing escalation of the Vietnam war, slowed the growth of the U.S. economy. Unemployment turned increasingly structural as good jobs began disappearing from the economy more rapidly than new ones being created, with the share of U.S. manufacturing jobs falling 22.1 percent during the decay phase, 1966 to 1979 (Executive Office of the President 1995: 324). In response to these conditions, crime rates increased, and public disorder in the form of civil rights demonstrations, ghetto rebellions, and anti-Vietnam war protests

---

[2] During the consolidation phase, official U.S. mean rates of homicide/nonnegligent manslaughter, aggravated assault, robbery, and burglary were 5.0, 83.9, 56.7, and 442.0 per 100,000, respectively, while the mean prison population rate in state and federal prisons was 111.9 per 100,000. See Carlson and Michalowski(1997) and Michalowski and Carlson (1999) for data sources. As we will see, crime rates have never returned to these historical lows, and there has been nearly a fivefold increase in imprisonment rates.

signaled a significant decline in social harmony. The consolidation-phase criminal justice policies no longer served to facilitate accumulation and legitimization.

Bowles and his colleagues note that the decay in the social institutions of the post-World War II SSA was not uniform across the entire 1966–1979 period. Instead, decline occurred in two identifiable subphases, 1966–1973 and 1973–1979. We suggest that each of these subphases resulted in corresponding adjustments within the criminal justice system.

The first phase of decline was characterized by low and then rising unemployment, rising inflation, and falling rates of profit (Bowles et al. 1990: 96), and, most importantly, mass uprisings on the streets of urban ghettoes and on college campuses. Local and state police, operating under the professional policing model, with their emphasis on protecting and serving citizens, were ill-equipped to restore social order. In a number of instances, states had to call up National Guard troops to quell these disturbances.

Increasing crime rates and mass protest in the mid-to-late 1960s threatened state legitimacy by creating an image of public insecurity and social disharmony. They threatened accumulation by further eroding investor confidence at a time when the old SSA was increasingly unable to deliver expanding profit margins. In an effort to reinvigorate legitimacy and accumulation, the U.S. Congress passed the Omnibus Crime Control and Safe Streets Act in 1968 (P.L. 90–351), establishing the Law Enforcement Assistance Administration (LEAA) under the U.S. Department of Justice. Through LEAA, local law enforcement agencies received federal funds to improve their ability to fight street crime and quell civil disorders. Most of this money was spent on the "hard side" to arm local police with the latest technology in the areas of weaponry, surveillance, and communications, and to develop new methods of police work modeled on the U.S. military (Kraska and Kappeler 1997), while the "soft side" of police education and improving police-community relations received less support (Michalowski 1985: 181–2). Overall, the breakdown in order maintenance during the first decay phase, coupled with loss of productive capital in areas affected by mass disturbances, and increased costs for restoring order likely would have had a dampening effect on capital accumulation.

The second subphase of decay, lasting roughly from 1973 through 1979, witnessed rising unemployment, runaway inflation, and continuing low rates of profit (Bowles et al. 1990: 96). Although crime rates continued their upward climb, with average rates being double to more than triple those during the consolidation phase, the average imprisonment rate increased only about 7 percent.[3]

The combination of increased law enforcement capacity and the still-dominant "treatment model" in corrections was ill-suited to control the increasingly large surplus population. Success of rehabilitation programs depends on the availability of jobs that pay a living wage as an economically viable alternative to crime as a way of life. As Greenberg and Humphries (1980: 218) observe:

In the three decades following 1940, the treatment model made a certain amount of sense. Unemployment remained fairly low, so that there seemed to be a place in the economy for those who wanted it ... The deterioration of the economy in the 1970s, with its seemingly intractably high levels of inflation and unemployment, had destroyed the material base for the rehabilitative ideal ... The hope that all who want a job can have one ... is no longer even remotely believable.

In the context of rising joblessness in the 1970s, increasing the strength of local law enforcement was not sufficient to control the growing population of potentially criminal surplus workers as long as prisons operated according to the treatment model. By the end of the decade, many individual states had begun to replace rehabilitation as the primary goal of imprisonment with strategies to maximize incapacitation and presumably increase deterrence. An increasing number of U.S. states enacted determinate sentencing, habitual offender statutes, felony firearm laws, and other repressive measures designed to reduce crime by keeping convicted offenders locked up for longer periods. For example, in 1976 the Michigan legislature enacted a felony firearm law (MCL §750.227b) that made possession of a firearm in the commission of a felony a separate felony subject to a mandatory two-year sentence to be served prior to, and consecutive with, the sentence for the underlying felony for a first offense, and stiffer mandatory sentences for subsequent offenses (Loftin and McDowall 1981; Loftin, Heumann, and McDowall 1983). Then in 1978, the Michigan legislature passed the harshest drug law in the nation (MCL §333.7401), popularly referred to as the "650-lifer law" because it mandated a sentence of life in prison without the possibility of parole for possession, possession with the intent to deliver, manufacturing, or delivering 650 grams (22.9 ounces) of cocaine and/or Schedule I or II

---

[3] During the second decay phase, official U.S. mean rates of homicide/nonnegligent manslaughter, aggravated assault, robbery, and burglary were 9.3, 238.8, 202.1, and 1,428.7 per 100,000, respectively, while the mean prison population rate in state and federal prisons was 120.0 per 100,000 (see note 2 for data sources).

narcotics (Affholter and Wicksall 2002). Michigan's drug law prescribed sentences even more harsh than the "Rockefeller Drug Laws," most of which were enacted as part of the 1973 New York Substance Control Act revisions (Tinto 2001: 906). As a result of these changes, particularly harsh mandatory sentences for drug crimes, imprisonment rates began to increase during the second period of SSA decay, but would jump sharply in the exploration phase as more states and the federal government followed suit.

Turning to facilitation of capital accumulation, it is unlikely that the criminal justice system played much of a role during the second decay phase. The correctional system continued to release offenders on parole into the community where they were less likely to find jobs. Recidivism increased, and crime rates rose, as did the costs associated with increased crime. In addition, the criminal justice system did not expand its direct demand for more goods and services produced in the private sector, nor did it indirectly increase demand via increasing employment of law enforcement, correctional, and other workers.

Further Decay and Initial Exploration for Alternatives

SSA theorists argue that exploration for new institutional arrangements begins to occur within the context of economic crisis as the old SSA continues to decay (Gordon et al. 1982). This phase, which we have labeled as both decay and exploration, encompasses the Reagan and the first Bush administrations. The beginning years were characterized by "stagflation," the unprecedented occurrence of high official unemployment rates and double-digit inflation. Profits eroded and misery increased. The surplus population in impoverished inner cities grew, as did the underground economy, particularly the crack cocaine market, providing employment opportunities for young men and women rendered unemployable in the mainstream economy, as well as necessary goods and services at lower cost (Wilson 1987; Anderson 1990, 1999; Bourgois 1995). Sharp increases in violent crime accompanied the growth of the underground economy, particularly the illicit drug trade, as guns were used to enforce sales territories and keep workers in line, as well as in the commission of crimes for money to buy drugs (Taylor 1990; Currie 1993).

During this phase, individual states followed New York and Michigan in adopting harsh penalties for drug crimes and violent felonies, while the federal government waged a war on drugs. Four pieces of federal legislation contain progressively repressive strategies for controlling the inner-city poor, and reflect the abandonment of the treatment model of punishment, in favor of one founded on deterrence and incapacitation.

The Comprehensive Crime Control Act of 1984 (P.L. 98–473) abolished one of the cornerstones of rehabilitation, the parole system, at the federal level. It also established a commission to develop sentencing guidelines to limit the discretion of judges on the federal bench, overhauled the federal bail system, and endorsed pre-trial detention of "dangerous" defendants in the federal system. The law increased penalties for drug trafficking, and revised forfeiture of property procedures in drug-related and racketeering cases. Taken together, these provisions increased prison terms of federal prisoners and made pre-trial detention more possible.

The Anti-Drug Abuse Act of 1986 (P.L. 99–570) increased fines and prison terms for drug-related offenses, appropriated funds to build more federal prisons, ordered the military to identify unused facilities that could be used as federal prisons, and increased spending for federal, state, and local drug-related law enforcement efforts. The harshness of this law is revealed by the relative appropriation of funds between repressive and placative strategies – nearly 65 percent of the $1.7 billion went for law enforcement and corrections, while about 12 percent and 22 percent went for preventative education and drug treatment, respectively. Moreover, one of the provisions of the 1986 law makes clear which group was being targeted – the surplus population in inner cities. This law stipulated a five-year mandatory minimum sentence for *selling* 5 grams of crack cocaine (the drug of choice in inner-city neighborhoods), while it would take selling 500 grams of powdered cocaine (a drug popular among those from the middle and upper classes) to earn a five-year sentence.

The Anti-Drug Abuse Act of 1988 (P.L. 100–690) contained provisions to coordinate the national effort against drugs and mandated more efforts in the area of drug interdiction along the nation's borders and internationally. Two provisions were directed at the surplus population. First, conviction of simple possession of 5 grams of crack cocaine with *no intent to sell* was punishable by a mandatory five-year sentence. Second, the law created "one-strike eviction" where public housing tenants, or persons under their control, would be evicted for engaging in criminal activity in or near the premises.

Finally, the Crime Control Act of 1990 (P.L. 101–647) provided mandatory minimum sentences for drug-related crimes involving minors and near schools. It also established grant programs to assist states with developing new incarceration programs, such as boot camps for young offenders. These programs tended to widen the incarceration net because they typically placed young, first-time offenders, who would have received probation under the treatment model, in secure custody (MacKenzie et al. 1995).

Taken together, this shift to a repressive penal strategy at both the state and federal levels helped facilitate capital accumulation in two direct and one indirect ways. First, by 1992, policies such as lengthy, mandatory minimum sentences dramatically increased the imprisonment rate to a historical high of 332.2 prisoners per 100,000 behind bars in federal and state correctional facilities in 1992. Increasing the proportion of the surplus population behind bars aided profit realization in two ways. First, it expanded employment in the criminal justice system, particularly in courts and corrections. In the judicial/legal part of the system, the number of employees increased by 50.8 percent between 1982 and 1992 (U.S. Bureau of Justice Statistics 2007a), employing over a third of a million by the end of the decay/exploration phase. Similarly, employment in corrections more than doubled between 1980 and 1992, reaching over half a million employed by the end of the phase. Employment growth in these areas increased the number of consumers to purchase durable and nondurable goods, and services, and hence, profit realization.

Second, as the incarcerated population grew, state and federal prison systems became an increasingly lucrative market for goods and services produced/provided by private corporations. From the building supplies used to construct more prisons to prison phone services provided by corporations like AT&T, to health services, to high-tech surveillance equipment, the corrections system became an important exploitable market. Between 1980 and 1992, the proportion of total corrections expenditures for expenses other than payroll rose from 38.4 percent to 47.4 percent (U.S. Bureau of Justice Statistics 2007a, see Appendix). The other parts of the criminal justice system also served as increasingly large markets as the proportion of nonpayroll policing expenditures increased from 21.5 percent in 1980 to 30.4 percent in 1992, while those in the judicial/legal area increased from 36.2 percent in 1982 to 42.1 percent in 1992.

Third, the increased severity of the criminal justice system facilitated capital accumulation by creating the image of a return to social harmony. This, in turn, contributed to restoring investor confidence that had been badly eroded by the social and economic disruptions of the decay phase. By reasserting the primacy of law and order, the criminal justice system contributed to capital accumulation through the vector of increased state legitimacy. In addition, high rates of incarceration among working-age men reduced official unemployment rates, creating the illusion that the economy was more robust in providing jobs than it actually was, thus further boosting investor confidence and system legitimacy. For example, Western and Beckett (1999: 1043, Table 5) show that the average official unemployment rate for 1985–89 would have increased 1.2 percentage points, from 5.5 to 6.6 percent, for all men if the incarcerated had been counted among the unemployed, while the average rate for African American men would have increased 5.3 percentage points, from 11.6 to 16.9 percent.

In sum, the decay/exploration phase of the post-World War II SSA witnessed major changes in criminal justice policy resulting in dramatic increases in prison populations. In turn, the role of the criminal justice system in capital accumulation shifted from supplying trained labor to industry to being a more important player in profit realization. In the most recent exploration phase, these trends continued, with an increasing solidification of the criminal justice system's role in profit realization.

Exploration

When signing the Violent Crime Control and Law Enforcement Act (P.L. 103–322) into law on September 13, 1994, President Bill Clinton stated, "People who commit crimes should be caught, convicted, and punished," and "'three strikes and you're out' will be the law of the land" (Clinton 1994: 1540). This sums up the key elements of the new repressive penal regime that is part of an emerging liberal institutional structure (Kotz 2003). The bill's balance of punitiveness is shown by the relative allocation of funding. Law enforcement received the largest share of 44.4 percent of the $30.2 billion, most of it going to state and local agencies for the much-touted hiring of 100,000 additional officers to patrol the streets, as well as other initiatives. Most telling is the $9.7 billion allocated to four grant programs for state construction of an additional 100,000 prison beds. Each of these grant programs provided financial incentives for states to lock up more violent offenders for longer lengths of time.

The 1994 law also increased the number of federal offenses subject to the death penalty to 60, and did indeed mandate life sentences without the possibility of parole for those convicted of three violent or drug trafficking crimes. The bill provided new and stiffer penalties for violent and drug trafficking crimes committed by gang members, and authorized prosecution of juveniles 13 and older for particular serious violent offenses. It also required states to set up sex offender registries, and establish notification systems. It created new offenses or enhanced penalties for drive-by shootings, sex offenses, crimes against the elderly, firearms theft and smuggling, firearms trafficking, use of semiautomatic weapons, interstate domestic violence, and hate crimes.

Finally, the 1994 law prohibits awarding of Pell Grants for higher education to prisoners, a provision that had been proposed nearly on an annual basis between 1982 and 1994 (Ubah 2004: 76). Since these grants had provided much of the funding for higher education programs in prisons, this provision effectively ended the opportunity to earn a college degree while behind bars, an opportunity that once served as an important source of successful rehabilitation (McCollum 1994; Ubah 2004).

Taken together, this capstone piece of legislation, and state laws that contain similar provisions guaranteed that prison populations would continue to grow (despite dropping crime rates), employment in the system would increase, and the criminal justice system would continue to facilitate the accumulation function of the state in the realization phase of the circuit of capital. By 2004, the prison population rate had reached an unprecedented high of 488.2 per 100,000, with 1.43 million people held in state and federal prisons (Harrison and Beck 2005).

The unprecedented rates of incarceration during this phase had an even stronger impact on male official unemployment rates. Western and Beckett (1999: 1043, Table 5) estimate that official unemployment rates of all men would have been 1.7 percentage points higher (7.6 versus 5.9 percent) if those incarcerated were counted among the unemployed, while the rate for African American men would have been 18.8 percent compared with the official rate of 11.3 percent, a difference of 7.5 percentage points. Again, this creates the illusion that the economy is performing better than actually is the case, increasing both investor confidence and legitimacy of the system.

Employment in the criminal justice system also increased. Between 1992 and 2004, the number of jobs increased by 30.6 percent in policing, 33.2 percent in the judicial/legal part of the system, and 32.2 percent in corrections, with 2.37 million employed in the criminal justice system overall. This growth of employment in the system once again increased the size of the market for consumer goods and services and profit realization over and above the preceding SSA phase.

The proportion of nonpayroll criminal justice expenditures in this SSA phase increased, suggesting more profits flowing into corporate coffers. Between 1992 and 2004, police budgets witnessed the largest increase in nonpayroll expenses, rising from 30.4 percent to 37.5 percent. The judicial/legal and corrections parts of the system saw more modest increases between 1992 and 2004 in their budgets covering nonpayroll items, with judicial/legal increasing from 42.1 percent to 43.3 percent, and corrections, 47.4 percent to 50.1 percent.

The most recent SSA phase was marked by the passage of the final piece of legislation that brought punitive penal practices to the federal level, practices that had developed gradually at the state level beginning in the second decay phase of the post-World War II SSA, and made them the law of the land. These practices also changed the role of the criminal justice system in the accumulation process as the system and its employees became an increasingly lucrative market for profit realization. No longer is the labor power of prisoners viewed as a valuable commodity to be retrained, rehabilitated, and restored to the labor market. Instead, increased prison populations are the means to the end of profit realization.

Empirical Evidence of Historical Contingency in the U.S. Capital Accumulation-Criminal Justice System Relationship

We have argued that the role of the criminal justice system in the accumulation process in the U.S. post-World War II SSA has changed from a primary emphasis on retraining, rehabilitating, and restoring offenders to jobs in the industrial labor market under the tight labor market conditions of the consolidation phase, to the criminal justice system and its employees playing an important role in the profit realization stage of the accumulation process. We also suggested that the efficacy of the criminal justice system would be undermined during the decay phases of the post-World War II SSA as the treatment model broke down, and the new criminal justice institutional arrangements had yet to be put in place.

If these arguments are plausible, we would expect to find a positive association between criminal justice expenditures and capital accumulation during the consolidation, decay/exploration, and second exploration phases. A negative association should hold during the decay phase as the treatment model lost its ability to facilitate capital accumulation. Finally, the relationship should be weak to nonexistent in the second decay phase when the new punitive model of criminal justice was just beginning to develop at the state level.

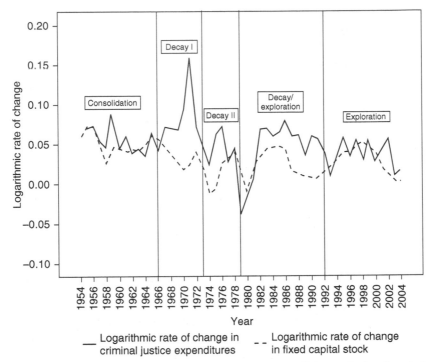

Figure 10.1. Change in criminal justice expenditures and change in fixed capital stock across post–World War II SSA phases, 1954–2004.

Figure 10.1 shows the relationship between the logarithmic rate of change in nonfinancial, corporate business sector net fixed nonresidential private capital stock and the logarithmic rate of change in total direct criminal justice expenditures (see Appendix for data sources). Consistent with our institutional analysis, the two series move together during the consolidation phase of the post-World War II SSA. Then as expected, in the decay phase the two series diverge, with criminal justice expenditures escalating due to the cost of restoring order, while capital accumulation drifted downward suggesting that productive property loss and increased costs of crisis containment acted to dampen capital accumulation. By the end of the second decay phase, the series begin to trend together again, and do so markedly in the final two phases when the new set of institutional arrangements in the criminal justice system was in place.

Table 10.1 presents the zero-order correlations between capital accumulation and criminal justice expenditures series for the criminal justice system as a whole, and each of its separate parts. The pattern of results for the criminal justice system as a whole is consistent with our expectations

Table 10.1. Bivariate *Correlations between the Logarithmic Rate of Change in Fixed Capital Stock and the Logarithmic Rate of Change in Criminal Justice Expenditures*

	Consolidation 1954–1966*	Decay I 1966–1973	Decay II 1973–1979	Decay/ Exploration 1979–1992	Exploration 1992–2004
Change in total criminal justice expenditures	0.468†	−0.516†	0.099	0.569*	0.440*
Change in police expenditures	0.561†	−0.448	0.093	0.576†	0.110
Change in corrections expenditures	0.239	−0.491	−0.172	0.574†	0.409†
Change in judicial/legal expenditures	0.077	−0.171	0.369	0.459†	0.399†
(*N*)	(12)	(8)	(7)	(14)	(13)

* Due to data limitations in the criminal justice expenditure series, the consolidation phase covers only 1954–1966.

† Correlation is significant at p < 0.10 level (one-tailed).

based on our institutional analysis, and with our observations about Figure 10.1 – a moderate positive relationship between capital accumulation and criminal justice expenditures during the consolidation phase, a moderate-to-strong negative relationship during the first decay phase, a weak positive relationship during the second decay phase, and moderate-to-strong positive relationships in the two most recent phases.[4] The remaining results in Table 10.1 conform to our expectations with two notable exceptions.

During the consolidation phase, the relationship between corrections expenditures and capital accumulation is positive but weak. This may be due to the corrections expenditure series measuring the market potential of the corrections system and its employees, not the flow of offenders into the labor market. Other measures need to be examined that more

---

[4] Here we focus on effect sizes, not statistical significance, for two reasons – the series contain only a small number of time points, and the correlations measure the strength of the relationship between the two series in the population of time points, not a sample thereof.

adequately tap this role of the corrections system in the capital accumulation process that was of primary importance during the consolidation phase. In addition, it may have cost less to rehabilitate and return offenders to the labor market during the consolidation phase than it did to expand prison populations and provide markets during more recent phases, hence explaining the weaker correlation between corrections expenditures and capital accumulation during the consolidation phase.

The second somewhat unexpected finding is the weak positive relationship between police expenditures and capital accumulation during the most recent exploration phase when the relationship was moderate for the total system and the other parts thereof. An examination of a graph of the two series reveals that the weak relationship is due to a single spike in police spending in 2002. This may indicate that the spending on law enforcement in the immediate aftermath of the 2001 terrorist attacks did not benefit capital accumulation.

These empirical results, while not definitive, do suggest that the hypotheses we developed in our institutional analyses are plausible. We now turn to our discussion of the implications of our analysis for SSA theory and directions for future research.

Conclusion

In this chapter, we have offered an historical institutional analysis of the changing role of the criminal justice system in the capital accumulation process. In the nineteenth and early twentieth centuries, the criminal justice system facilitated capital accumulation through the direct provision of low-cost convict labor to capitalist manufacturers of nondurable goods. As an increasingly strong labor movement challenged this practice, it was replaced by a state accounting system designed to reduce the costs of imprisonment. In the post-World War II SSA, as labor markets tightened, prisons facilitated capital accumulation by training convicts in skills and work habits, and releasing them as potential workers for industrial capitalist firms. Finally, in the most recent phases, an "imprisonment binge" has served capital accumulation indirectly by restraining large segments of the surplus population from posing public problems in the form of crime, and directly by serving as a vehicle for private profit realization.

Recent policy developments in 2008–2009 reducing prison populations and the size of the corrections labor market, might be construed as minimizing the role of the criminal justice system in profit realization.

First, several states have eliminated mandatory minimum sentences for lower-level drug offences and restored judicial discretion in sentencing drug offenders, including sentencing nonviolent, first-time offenders to treatment rather than prison. Most recently, New York dismantled the infamous Rockefeller drug laws in this manner and made it possible for an estimated 45–55 percent of convicted drug offenders behind bars to apply for resentencing, albeit with no guarantee of a sentence reduction (NY L2009, ch. 56; Correctional Association of New York 2009). Second, several states, most notably Michigan and Kansas, and the federal government via the Second Chance Act (P.L. 110–199) have instituted prisoner reentry programs in prison and in the community that include substance abuse treatment, mentoring, and job training (Federal Sentencing Reporter 2008; Scott-Hayward 2009). If successful, these programs may indicate a return to the rehabilitative ideal. Third, a recent report reveals that 26 of 37 states surveyed have slashed corrections budgets for 2010 in response to the current fiscal crisis, with seven of these states cutting these budgets by over 10 percent (Scott-Hayward 2009). Prison closures, downsizing and elimination of recently created prisoner reentry programs, cutbacks in salaries and benefits, and personnel reductions are to result from these budget cuts.

On their face, these policy developments should reduce prison populations, the number of prisons, and the number of correctional employees, thus reducing the role of the criminal justice system in the profit realization phase of the circuit of capital. However, there is evidence that these policy changes will not have this end result. First, changes in drug laws also contain many exclusions and include increased penalties for "drug kingpins," which are likely to slow the growth of, but not reduce, prison populations (Correctional Association of New York 2009). For example, despite many states having enacted drug reform laws since 2001, federal and state prison populations have continued their upward march as of the end of 2007, although at a slower pace than in the 1990s. The prison population increased an average of 6.6 percent per year in 1990–1999, 2.14 percent in 2000–2006, 1.8 percent in 2006–2007, and there was a .77 percent increase in the six months ending June 30, 2008 (Bureau of Justice Statistics 2009; West and Sabol 2009). Second, as noted earlier, successful rehabilitation of offenders requires a robust job market, which does not exist in the context of the present recession, thus prisoner reentry programs that do survive budget cuts are unlikely to reduce prison readmissions due to parole violations and recidivism. Finally, states have moved quickly to offset corrections budget cuts with federal stimulus dollars.

Kansas, for example, used stimulus dollars to reduce its corrections budget cuts from 23.0 percent to 7.3 percent, while the states of South Dakota and Nebraska used stimulus monies to transform substantial cuts into budget increases (Scott-Hayward 2009: 5).

These actions suggest that once the economy improves, states will restore and perhaps increase corrections budgets, as occurred after the 2001–2002 recession (Wilhelm and Turner 2002). Moreover, there is strong resistance to closing prisons by correctional worker unions and rural communities, where prisons often became the largest employers during the 1980s and 1990s (Huling 2003; Gramlich 2009a), and marked public opposition to releasing prisoners in some locations (Gramlich 2009b). Thus, should they pursue these actions to reduce prison populations and contain corrections costs, state lawmakers likely will be faced with legitimacy crises, and few will want to appear "soft on crime."

In conclusion, for SSA theory, we contend that our analysis demonstrates the importance of analyzing other social institutions beyond those considered to be the core institutions of a particular SSA. While SSAs do not contain all of "the rest of a society" (Gordon et al. 1982: 25), there are social institutions that play important roles within particular SSAs. The criminal justice system is one such institution that plays both a role in capital accumulation, and in legitimization via social control of the surplus population. Other institutions such as the family, military, and education likewise should be examined.

For sociologists and other social scientists who conduct institutional analyses, our analysis demonstrates the utility of the SSA framework in explaining change in social institutions across long stages of history. The SSA perspective offers a unified approach for analyzing such change, by allowing for historical contingency in the processes that lead to institutional change and its empirical effects.

Further analysis of the role of the criminal justice system in capital accumulation also is warranted. In particular, while the empirical evidence we presented here offers tentative support for the plausibility of our hypothesized scenario, further econometric analyses are necessary to develop more definitive support. In addition, this chapter has given relatively little attention to the role of the criminal justice system in SSAs before World War II. For the sake of completeness, this analysis should be expanded to include all of the capitalist era in the United States. Finally, we suggest that such analyses should be conducted in other nations. With the highest imprisonment rate among industrialized nations, the role of the criminal justice system in the United States in the capital accumulation process may be the exception rather than the rule internationally.

Appendix Data Sources

Criminal Justice Expenditures, Employment, and Payrolls

Annual data on total criminal justice system, police, and corrections expenditures by all governments for 1954–1996 came from Carter et al. (2006, series Ec1159, Ec1160, and Ec1163, respectively). More recent expenditure data were from U.S. Bureau of Justice Statistics (2007a, Table 6) for 1997–1999, and U.S. Bureau of Justice Statistics (2007b; cjee0001.wk1, jeeu0101.wk1, cjee0201.csv, cjee0301.csv, cjee0401.csv) for 2000–2004. Data for judicial expenditures only were available for 1954–1968 (Carter 2006, series Ec1162). Therefore, we calculated the proportion of judicial and legal expenditures that were judicial in 1969 and used this proportion to estimate judicial and legal expenditures for 1954–1968. The judicial and legal series for 1969–1996 was obtained from Carter et al. (2006, series Ec1161), from U.S. Bureau of Justice Statistics (2007a, Table 6) for 1997–1999, and U.S. Bureau of Justice Statistics (2007b; cjee0001.wk1, jeeu0101.wk1, cjee0201.csv, cjee0301.csv, cjee0401.csv) for 2000–2004. All expenditure series were converted to constant billions of U.S. dollars (1982–1984 = 100) using the consumer price index from the Federal Reserve Bank of Minneapolis (2007). We took the first difference of the natural logarithm of each of these series to obtain the logarithmic rate of change in expenditures used in Figure 10.1 and the correlations in Table 10.1.

We obtained data on the number of employees in the criminal justice system by activity for 1980 (1982 for judicial/legal and total employment) and 1992 from U.S. Bureau of Justice Statistics (2007a; eetrnd07. wk1). Data for 2004 came from U.S. Bureau of Justice Statistics (2007b; cjee0402.csv).

Data on one-month payroll expenditures in the criminal justice system by activity were obtained for 1980 (1982 for judicial/legal and total employment) and 1992 from U.S. Bureau of Justice Statistics (2007a; eetrnd08.wk1), and for 2004 from U.S. Bureau of Justice Statistics (2007b; cjee0402.csv). We multiplied the one-month figure by 12 to obtain an estimate of annual payroll expenditures for each part and the system as a whole. We then subtracted the annual estimates from their respective total expenditures (see above) to obtain nonpayroll expenditures, which is an estimate of expenditures on goods and services other than labor, and thus, a proxy for involvement of the criminal justice system in the profit realization process.

Measure of Capital Accumulation
For our measure of capital accumulation, we used a measure consistent with, but not identical to, that used in Bowles et al. (1989, 1990). We obtained the nonfinancial corporate business sector net fixed nonresidential private capital stock at historical cost in billions of U.S. current dollars from the *National Income and Product Accounts,* Table 4.3, line 28. This series was converted to constant billions of U.S. dollars (1982–1984 = 100) using the consumer price index from the Federal Reserve Bank of Minneapolis (2007). For the measure of capital accumulation, we took the first difference of the natural logarithm of this series to obtain the logarithmic rate of change of fixed capital stock.

References

Affholter, Patrick and Bethany Wicksall 2002. "Eliminating Michigan's Mandatory Minimum Sentences for Drug Offenses." Michigan Senate Fiscal Agency.

Anderson, Elijah 1999. *Code of the Street: Decency, Violence, and the Moral Life of the Inner City.* New York: W.W. Norton.

1990. *Street Wise: Race, Class, and Change in an Urban Community.* Chicago: University of Chicago Press.

Barnes, Harry Elmer 1921. "The Economics of American Penology as Illustrated by the Experience of the State of Pennsylvania." *Journal of Political Economy* 29, 8: 617–42.

1922. "Some Leading Phases of the Evolution of Modern Penology." *Political Science Quarterly* 37, 2: 251–80.

Bourgois, Phillipe 1995. *In Search of Respect: Selling Crack in El Barrio.* New York: Cambridge University Press.

Bowles, Samuel, David M. Gordon and Thomas E. Weisskopf 1989. "Business ascendency and economic impasse: A structural retrospective on conservative economics, 1979–87." *Journal of Economic Perspectives* 3, 1: 107–34.

1990. *After the Waste Land: A Democratic Economics for the Year 2000.* Armonk, NY: M.E. Sharpe.

Bureau of Justice Statistics 2009. "Adults on Probation, in Jail or Prison, and on Parole." *Sourcebook of Criminal Justice Statistics Online* http://www.albany.edu/sourcebook/csv/t612006csv.

Carlson, Susan M. and Raymond J. Michalowski 1997. "Crime, Unemployment, and Social Structures of Accumulation: An Inquiry into Historical Contingency." *Justice Quarterly* 14, 2: 101–33.

Carter, Susan B. et al. 2006. *Historical Statistics of the United States Millennial Edition Online.* New York: Cambridge University Press.

Clinton, William J. 1994. "Administration of William J. Clinton, 1994." GPO Access.

Correctional Association of New York 2009. "Analysis of Rockefeller Drug Law Reform Bill." Correctional Association of New York http://droptherock. ipower.com/wp-content/uploads/2009/03/analysis-of-rockefeller-reform-bill.pdf.

Currie, Elliot 1993. *Reckoning: Drugs, the Cities, and the American Future.* New York: Hill and Wang.

Executive Office of the President 1995. *Economic Report of the President.* GPO.

Federal Bureau of Investigation 2007. "FBI History: Timeline of FBI History." Federal Bureau Investigation.

Federal Reserve Bank of Minneapolis 2007. "Consumer Price Index, 1913-." Federal Reserve Bank of Minneapolis.

Federal Sentencing Reporter 2008. "Summary of Provisions of the Second Chance Act." *Federal Sentencing Reporter* 20, 4:279–80.

Friedman, Milton 1962. *Capitalism and Freedom.* Chicago: University of Chicago Press.

Gill, Howard B. 1931. "The Prison Labor Problem." *Annals of the American Academy of Political and Social Science* 157: 83–101.

Gordon, David M. 1996. *Fat and Mean: The Corporate Squeeze of Working Americans and the Myth of Managerial 'Downsizing'.* New York: The Free Press.

Gordon, David M., Richard Edwards, and Michael Reich 1982. *Segmented Work, Divided Workers: The Historical Transformation of Labor in the United States.* New York: Cambridge University Press.

Gramlich, John 2009a. "Tracking the Recession: Prison Economics." http://www. stateline.org/live/details/story?contentId=403563.

2009b. "Strapped States Eye Prison Savings." http://www.stateline.org/live/details/story?contentId=365279.

Greenberg, David F. and Drew Humphries 1980. "The Cooptation of Fixed Sentencing Reform." *Crime and Delinquency* 26, 2: 206–26.

Harrison, Paige M. and Allen J. Beck 2005. "Prisoners in 2004." *Bureau of Justice Statistics Bulletin,* NCJ 210677.

Houston, David 1992. "Is there a New Social Structure of Accumulation?" *Review of Radical Political Economics* 24, 2: 60–67.

Huling, Tracy 2003. "Building a Prison Economy in Rural America" Pp. 197–213. In Marc Mauer and Meda Chesney-Lind eds. *Invisible Punishment: The Collateral Consequences of Mass Imprisonment.* New York: New Press.

Kotz, David M. 1987. "Long Waves and Social Structures of Accumulation: A Critique and Reinterpretation." *Review of Radical Political Economics* 19, 4: 16–38.

2003. "Neoliberalism and the Social Structure of Accumulation Theory of Long-Run Capital Accumulation." *Review of Radical Political Economics* 35, 3: 263–70.

Kraska, Peter B. and Victor E. Kappeler 1997. "Militarizing American Police: The Rise and Normalization of Paramilitary Units." *Social Problems* 44, 1: 1–18.

Lippit, Victor D. 1997. "The Reconstruction of a Social Structure of Accumulation in the United States." *Review of Radical Political Economics* 29, 3: 11–21.

Loftin, Colin, Milton Heumann, and David McDowall. 1983. "Mandatory Sentencing and Firearms Violence: Evaluating an Alternative to Gun Control." *Law & Society Review* 17, 2: 287–318.

Loftin, Colin, and David McDowall 1981. "'One with a Gun Gets You Two': Mandatory Sentencing and Firearms Violence in Detroit." *Annals of the American Academy of Political and Social Sciences* 455, 1: 150–67.

MacCormick, Austin H. 1931. "Education in the Prisons of Tomorrow." *Annals of the American Academy of Political and Social Science* 157: 72–7.

MacKenzie, Doris Layton, Robert Brame, David McDowall, and Claire Souryal 1995. "Boot Camp Prisons and Recidivism in Eight States." *Criminology* 33, 3: 327–57.

Marx, Karl 1967. *Capital: A Critique of Political Economy*. New York: International Publishers.

McCollum, Sylvia G. 1994. "Prison College Programs." *The Prison Journal* 73, 1: 51–61.

McDonough, Terrence 1994. "The Construction of Social Structures of Accumulation in US History" Pp. 101–32. In David M. Kotz, Terrence McDonough and Michael Reich eds. *Social Structures of Accumulation: The Political Economy of Growth and Crisis*. New York: Cambridge University Press.

McKelvey, Blake 1934. "A Half Century of Southern Penal Exploitation." *Social Forces* 13, 1: 112–23.

1935. "Penal Slavery and Southern Reconstruction." *The Journal of Negro History* 20, 2: 153–79.

1977. *American Prisons: A History of Good Intentions*. Montclair, NJ: Patterson Smith.

Michalowski, Raymond J. 1985. *Order, Law, and Crime*. New York: Random House.

Michalowski, Raymond J. and Susan M. Carlson 1999. "Unemployment, Imprisonment, and Social Structures of Accumulation: Historical Contingency in the Rusche-Kirchheimer Hypothesis." *Criminology* 37, 2: 217–49.

Moeller, H. G. 1969. "The Continuum of Corrections." *Annals of the American Academy of Political and Social Science* 381: 81–8.

O'Connor, James 1973. *The Fiscal Crisis of the State*. New York: St. Martin's Press.

Rusche, Georg 1978. "Labor Market and Penal Sanction: Thoughts on the Sociology of Criminal Justice." *Crime and Social Justice* Fall-Winter: 2–8.

Rusche, Georg and Otto Kirchheimer 1967. *Punishment and Social Structure*. New York: Russell and Russell.

Scott-Hayward, Christine S. 2009. *The Fiscal Crisis in Corrections: Rethinking Policies and Practices*. Vera Institute of Justice.

Sellin, Thorsten 1965. "Penal Servitude: Origin and Survival." *Proceedings of the American Philosophical Society* 109, 5: 277–81.

Taylor, Carl S. 1990. *Dangerous Society*. East Lansing: Michigan State University Press.

Tibbitts, Clark 1933. "Penology and Crime." *The American Journal of Sociology* 38, 6: 896–904

Tinto, Eda Katharine 2001. "The Role of Gender and Relationship in Reforming the Rockefeller Drug Laws." *New York University Law Review* 76: 906–44.

Ubah, Charles A. 2004. "Abolition of Pell Grants for Higher Education of Prisoners: Examining Antecedents and Consequences." *Journal of Offender Rehabilitation* 39, 2: 73–85.

U.S. Bureau of Justice Statistics 2007a. "Selected Statistics: Trends in Justice Expenditure and Employment." U.S. Bureau of Justice Statistics.

2007b. "Selected Statistics: Justice Expenditure and Employment Extracts." U.S. Bureau of Justice Statistics.

West, Heather C. and William J. Sabol 2009. *Prison Inmates at Midyear 2008.* U.S. Bureau of Justice Statistics.

Western, Bruce and Katherine Beckett 1999. "How Unregulated is the U.S. Labor Market? The Penal System as a Labor Market Institution." *American Journal of Sociology* 104: 1030–60.

Weyand, L.D. 1926. "Wage Systems in Prisons." *Annals of the American Academy of Political and Social Science* 125: 251–60.

Wilhelm, Daniel F. and Nicholas R. Turner 2002. *Is the Budget Crisis Changing the Way We Look at Sentencing and Incarceration?* Vera Institute of Justice.

Wilson, William J. 1987. *The Truly Disadvantaged: The Inner City, the Underclass, and Public Policy*. Chicago: University of Chicago Press.

PART FOUR

SOCIAL STRUCTURE OF ACCUMULATION THEORY AND TRANSFORMATIONS OF THE CAPITALIST PERIPHERY

The Social Structure of Accumulation in South Africa

James Heintz

The social structure of accumulation (SSA) framework has been used to explain the dynamics of the South African economy under apartheid. Specifically, SSA analysis provides an explanation of why, after decades of rapid capital accumulation following the establishment of the apartheid state in 1948, the South African economy entered a period of economic crisis, beginning in the mid-1970s (e.g., Gelb 1987). The SSA approach offers an alternative to liberal explanations of the crisis years, which see apartheid and capitalism as antagonistic systems, and to traditional Marxist analysis, which argues that apartheid and capitalism were mutually reinforcing. However, the SSA approach, as it has been applied to South Africa, has been criticized for a lack of empirical rigor and a tendency toward functionalist arguments (Nattrass 1994). This chapter reexamines this critique and offers an empirical foundation for the SSA framework as it has been applied to apartheid South Africa.

If SSA analysis is relevant for understanding apartheid capitalism, can the same approach be applied to the economic transition in post-apartheid South Africa? Electoral democracy helped restore social stability after years of unrest, but, at the time of transition, the widespread deprivation that was the legacy of apartheid remained. This created a conundrum for capital: political stability needed to be restored, but doing so could unleash redistributive pressures unfavorable to business interests. In the second half of this chapter, we explore how, in post-apartheid South Africa, the new democratic state has attempted to solve this problem through a strategy of economic liberalization, thereby allowing the market to adjudicate major distributive conflicts. We examine whether this set of post-apartheid policies and institutions

267

constitutes a new SSA that would lay the foundation for future growth and accumulation.

The Social Structure of Accumulation
and Apartheid South Africa

As was noted above, the SSA approach has been used to explain the decline of the apartheid economy beginning in the 1970s, which intensified into a full-blown crisis by the mid-1980s (Gelb 1987). The economic crisis contributed to the political pressures that eventually led to the collapse of apartheid and the establishment of a liberal democratic state in 1994. Prior to the decline, South Africa, under the apartheid regime, had enjoyed rapid, and relatively stable, rates of capital accumulation. Figure 11.1 charts the rate of accumulation, as measured by the growth rate of the fixed capital stock, from 1950 to 2006. Figure 11.1 also shows an estimate of the long-run trend in the rate of accumulation, obtained by smoothing the annual series.[1] From this graph we see the relatively rapid rates of accumulation throughout the first two and a half decades of apartheid, the swift decline from the high rates of accumulation reached in the early to mid-1970s, the collapse in the 1980s, and in the post-apartheid era, a modest recovery.[2]

Theories of apartheid's relationship to capitalist development have traditionally been categorized into two broad schools of thought: the liberal interpretation and the Marxist-revisionist approach. The liberal school, while not uniform, generally emphasizes the incompatibility between the apartheid system and capitalist development, often stressing that apartheid would eventually collapse under the weight of these contradictions (see, for example, Horwitz 1967; Lipton 1985). Apartheid is portrayed as having racist ideological and political origins, independent of economic interests. Therefore, apartheid institutions, such as job reservation policies or control over geographical mobility, become a set of regulations exogenously imposed on a liberal market economy. Apartheid policies impose efficiency costs that constrain capitalist development. This conflict means that capitalist development would necessarily erode apartheid

---

[1] The long-run trend was estimated by applying a Hodrick-Prescott filter to the original data series.

[2] A few aberrations from this general pattern are apparent in Figure 11.1, including a down-turn following the Sharpeville Massacre in 1961 and a short-lived up-turn in the early 1980s associated with a sharp, speculative increase in the price of gold.

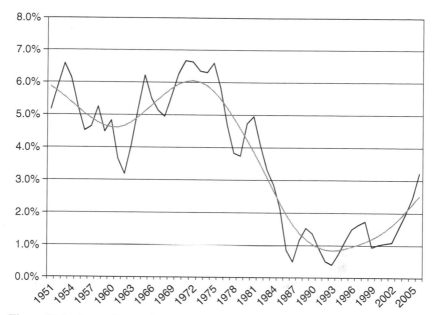

Figure 11.1. Annual rate of net accumulation of fixed capital stock, South Africa, 1951–2006.

Note: Calculated as the rate of change of the real fixed capital stock, as reported by the South Africa Reserve Bank (expressed in constant 2000 prices).

Source: South African Reserve Bank (2007).

institutions or that the maintenance of apartheid would eventually prevent further economic expansion. According to the liberal school, during the 1980s the inherent contradictions between progressive capitalist development and backward apartheid institutions reached a critical point, when the costs of apartheid distortions became overwhelming.

The liberal school faces one significant challenge: it does not adequately explain why in the 1950s and 1960s – decades in which apartheid institutions were relatively stable, the rate of fixed capital accumulation was much higher than in subsequent years. In contrast, the Marxist-revisionist school provides an explanation for the strong performance of the economy in the first decades of apartheid. The radical approach argues that the apartheid system was functional to capitalist development, supporting dominant class interests and the imperatives of accumulation (see, e.g., Wolpe 1972). The primary means of supporting accumulation was through the creation and reproduction of a low-paid, well-disciplined, black labor force that helped maintain high levels of profitability.

The crisis of apartheid-era capitalism posed a challenge to radical thinkers who argued that the apartheid system was structured to support rapid capital accumulation. The SSA framework offers an explanation for the crisis. The apartheid regime, which came to power following the 1948 elections, established a set of institutions that supported growth and accumulation of the South African capitalist economy. The apartheid era-SSA worked well until the 1970s, at which time contradictions emerged that undermined the effectiveness of this particular set of institutions (Gelb 1987). The crisis of the apartheid economy was therefore a structural crisis, arising from the collapse of the institutions comprising the SSA.

Building on the work of the Marxist-revisionist scholars, we can identify four pillars of the apartheid SSA:

(1) *Apartheid labor market policies and labor relations.* These institutions kept wages low and labor discipline high for the black working class. The color bar (the race-based job reservation system) and the pass laws (which governed residential rights) limited labor market opportunities for black workers. Displacement to the homelands drastically reduced the fallback opportunities available to blacks (Seekings and Nattrass 2006). The combination of limited labor market opportunities and a weak fallback position kept wages below the level that would have prevailed in the absence of these institutions (Wintrobe 1998; Wood 2000). At the same time, a capital-labor accord was established between relatively skilled white workers and South African capital in which white workers enjoyed near full-employment and social protections tied to their employment status (Seekings and Nattrass 2006).

(2) *Public provision of infrastructure and economic services.* The apartheid state pursued a high level of public investment that complemented the productive activities of the private capitalist sector. In many cases, this public investment was undertaken by various parastatals, or public corporations. Public enterprises dominated transportation services, communication services, and, perhaps most significantly, the provision of electricity and other forms of energy. These economic services were complementary inputs into private sector production, particularly the critical mining and minerals sector (Fine and Rustomjee 1996).

(3) *Finance-industry linkages.* The apartheid regime nurtured new financial institutions, often linked to nationalist Afrikaner interests, which mobilized the savings of the white population and

channeled financial resources to industry, thereby supporting more rapid accumulation of physical capital (O'Meara 1983, Fine and Rustomjee 1996). In some cases, these relationships were explicitly modeled after finance-industry linkages established in continental Europe (Verhoef 1992a, 1992b). These financial institutions included banks (e.g., Volkskas, Nedbank, and Trust Bank) and insurance companies (e.g., Sanlam). These institutions extended medium- to long-term credit for industrial development. This marked a break with the past. Prior to the establishment of the apartheid regime, the financial sector was dominated by short-term credit provided by two British banks (Standard Bank and, at the time, Barclays).

(4) *Macroeconomic stability.* Macroeconomic stability characterized the 1950s and 1960s, the period of rapid accumulation. The economic governance institutions that maintained this stability therefore constitute an important part of the apartheid SSA. Fiscal policy was generally well-managed, inflation was never excessive, monetary policy involved direct controls that kept real interest rates low (yet positive), and exchange rates were maintained at a stable level. Because of a system of capital controls, unexpected capital flows did not contribute significantly to volatility. South Africa was able to manage its external balance, despite its dependence on imports, because of the country's high export earnings from the mining sector (Gelb 1987). This favorable macroeconomic environment helped sustain the other institutions of the apartheid era SSA.

These four sets of institutions, taken together, can be used to explain South Africa's strong economic performance during the early decades of apartheid. During the crisis years, these institutions were no longer able to play the role that they once did. The reemergence of black trade unions led to widespread labor unrest and rising black wages. Public investment plummeted, possibly as a result of the growing uncertainty about the long-run prospects for maintaining control of the state and its assets. The financial sector reduced its role in financing domestic capital accumulation. Finally, macroeconomic stability became increasingly difficult to maintain in the face of low growth and international sanctions.[3]

---

[3] These developments have been discussed extensively, and space limitations prevent us from going into the details here. The rise of labor militancy and the resurgence of black trade unions have been extensively documented (e.g., for a quantitative analysis of strike activity as a component of political instability, see Heintz, 2002, 2001a). Official estimates of the Reserve Bank of South Africa show a dramatic decline in the level of

However, simply identifying a set of institutions that could theoretically constitute an apartheid SSA does not, in itself, show that such an SSA existed in South Africa. As Nattrass (1994) convincingly argues, the empirical record cannot be conveniently pushed aside when advancing a particular theoretical argument without being in danger of adopting a purely functionalist position. Simply showing that a set of institutions existed when the rate of capital accumulation was high does not necessarily imply that this set of institutions explains the rapid growth of the economy.

Nattrass (1994) presents a critique of the SSA approach based on the behavior of profit rates over the apartheid era. She argues that rates of profitability represent a key indicator of the validity of the SSA theory. Nattrass presents calculations that show that the rate of change of profitability of the manufacturing sector was generally negative in the 1950s, 1960s, and early 1970s, the period of rapid capital accumulation. Although she acknowledges that South African profit rates were extraordinarily high at the beginning of the period, she argues that falling rates of profit indicate that apartheid institutions could not sustain a viable SSA.

Efforts to apply an institutional analysis of capital accumulation to South Africa must take into account Nattrass' insights. Notwithstanding, there are problems with the critique. First, it relies on profitability trends in manufacturing. When both mining and manufacturing are considered, growth rates of the profit share were negative on average for only one business cycle, 1964–1970, during the entire period examined, 1948–1989. According to Nattrass' calculations, changes in the profit rate were more consistently negative across sectors, but the largest declines corresponded with the crisis years. Second, no attempt is made to estimate the relationship between the rate of accumulation and key variables, such as the profit rate, the cost of capital, and the growth of expenditures on output. Third, the critique is too narrow. By focusing only on profitability, other dynamics are ignored.

Aggregate measures of the profit rate – not confined to mining and manufacturing – show a different trend. Figure 11.2 presents an estimate

public investment during this period, including investment by South African parastatal enterprises (illustrated later in Figure 11.3). Fine and Rustomjee (1996) argue that financial institutions channeled their resources toward speculative activities and engaged in capital flight, instead of supporting domestic investment, and that state-led development finance institutions, such as the Industrial Development Corporation (IDC), played a vastly reduced role. Finally, a growing debt burden and a reduced ability to borrow internationally due to sanctions placed added constraints on macroeconomic management over this period.

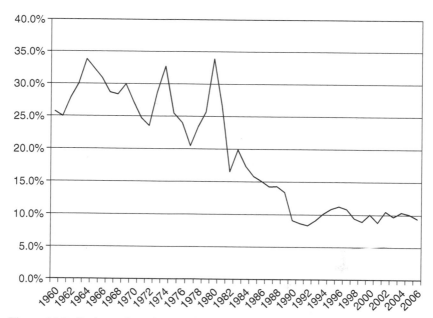

Figure 11.2. Estimated profit rate, South Africa, 1960–2006.
Note: After-tax rate of profit for nonfinancial corporate business. See note 4 in the main text for the full definition of the profit rate used here.
Source: South African Reserve Bank (2007).

of the profit rate for the nonfinancial corporate sector from 1960 to 2006, based on data from the South African Reserve Bank.[4] This profit rate estimate more closely follows the pattern observed with respect to the rate of capital accumulation. That is, the profit rate was generally high on average through the 1960s and 1970s. The profit rate declined sharply during much of the 1980s before stabilizing at a significantly lower level in the 1990s. Research has shown a positive relationship between profit rates and net investment in a multivariate, sectoral investment function for South Africa (Heintz 2001a, 2002). Trends in profitability and its relationship to capital accumulation therefore depend on how profitability

---

[4] Total income of nonfinancial incorporated businesses was estimated to be equal to the operating surplus generated by this sector plus net income from property. Direct tax payments were then subtracted to yield after-tax income. Total capital stock less the capital stock of financial enterprises and general government was used to derive an estimate of the relative size of the capital stock. The profit rate contained in Figure 11.2 represents the estimated after-tax income of nonfinancial corporations divided by an estimate of their total capital stock.

is measured, which sectors are included, and how the link between profitability and capital accumulation is analyzed.

More importantly, the focus on profitability misses a critical element
of the institutional environment of the early apartheid economy: the
maintenance of political, economic, and social stability. Distributive
outcomes, particularly the determinants of profitability, should directly
influence the process of accumulation. However, conflict over the process whereby distributive outcomes are determined can impact the rate
of investment independent of the actual level of profitability. The SSA
framework emphasizes the stability of institutions and social relations,
not simply distributive outcomes, in understanding the dynamics of capital accumulation (Kotz 1990). Disruptions that damage the integrity of a
set of social relations can undermine the regime of accumulation.

If a particular distribution of economic resources violates norms of
fairness, social tensions could arise as a way of contesting the way the
pie is divided. In this way, entrenched inequalities can produce political
instability that leads to reduced profit expectations and greater insecurity over property rights. Cross-country empirical evidence supports this
relationship between inequalities and political conflict (Schock 1996).
Inequalities need not be limited to the distribution of income, assets, or
wealth in order to contribute to social and political unrest. An unequal
distribution of political rights, access to basic services (e.g., health or
education), or social opportunities could also contribute to pressures
that engender conflict.

Michal Kalecki makes this type of distinction in his discussion of the
politics of full-employment. As an economy approaches full-employment, the bargaining power of labor rises, as do wages. However, it is
the conflict between capital and labor, not just a profit squeeze, which
Kalecki considers important. Expectations of institutional change that
threaten the economic position of the owners of capital can contribute
to lowering investment. As Kalecki writes, " 'discipline in factories' and
'political stability' are more appreciated by the business leaders than
profits" (Kalecki 1971: 141). Expectations concerning the sustainability
of a particular regime of distribution may be more important than the
distributive outcomes themselves. When the social position of the economic elites is threatened (be it a class position, a racial hierarchy, or
both), capital accumulation becomes compromised.

In South Africa, political repression of black social movements and
trade unions kept tensions over the distribution of resources in check.
A race-based welfare state extended high-quality public services,

maintained near full-employment, and provided good jobs to whites in order to maintain political support. In addition, the white-minority regimes in Rhodesia, Namibia, Mozambique, and Angola helped to justify the political "legitimacy" of the race-based distributive systems of southern Africa. However, beginning in the mid-1970s, mass mobilization against apartheid increased uncertainty throughout South Africa. This resurgence of resistance is perhaps most closely associate with the Soweto uprisings in 1976. Political instability grew to such a level that President P.W. Botha declared a state of emergency in 1985. Furthermore, the organizational strength of black trade unions grew, as did their influence over wage distributions. Rising black wages destabilized the racial income distribution of previous decades, but social unrest, rather than the changing income distribution, appears to have had a larger impact on capital accumulation.

Studies of investment in South Africa have shown that indicators of social unrest and political instability have an independent impact on capital accumulation, holding other, more purely "economic," determinants constant (Heintz 2001a, 2002; Fedderke, de Kadt, and Luiz 2001). Furthermore, changes in an index of political unrest explain more of the decline in the average rate of accumulation during the crisis years than do changes in the profit rate, although the contribution of the profit rate is not negligible (Heintz 2001b).

In short, there is empirical evidence supporting the argument that capital accumulation in South Africa was governed by an apartheid SSA. A full-scale empirical defense of the SSA framework in South Africa is beyond the scope of this chapter. However, Nattrass' empirical critique of the SSA approach – that profitability trends are inconsistent with the arguments of SSA theorists – is not borne out. Profitability has been shown to be a determinant of investment in South Africa, controlling for other explanatory variables. Moreover, changes in profit rates are sensitive to which sectors are included and how profitability is measured. Perhaps most significantly, researchers who have tried to assess institutional stability by measuring social and political unrest have shown that instability had a measurable, negative impact on capital accumulation during the last two decades of apartheid.

The above discussion raises an obvious question: if an apartheid SSA existed and if the collapse of that SSA caused the economic crisis of the 1980s, thereby contributing to the eventual collapse of the apartheid regime, then how do we characterized the post-apartheid era? According to SSA theory, the collapse of one set of institutions supporting capitalist accumulation will be followed by the establishment of a new set of institutions that will reinvigorate the capitalist economy, that is, a new SSA will eventually follow the old. Has a new SSA been established in South Africa and, if so, how would it be characterized?

A Post-Apartheid Social Structure of Accumulation

In resolving the crisis of accumulation of the final decades of apartheid, South Africa faced the twin challenges of restoring political stability and adopting economic policies to revitalize investment. The transition to true electoral democracy would help restore political stability and improve South Africa's international reputation. However, as the discussion of the determinants of investment in the previous section showed, accumulation in South Africa depends on profitability as well as social stability. This created a dilemma for South African capitalists: political stability needed to be restored but doing so could create pressures for redistribution unfavorable to capital. The mechanism for redistribution could easily extend beyond a tax-and-spend fiscal strategy. For example, the African National Congress (ANC), which came to power in the 1994 elections, had formed a political alliance with the Congress of South African Trade Unions (COSATU), raising the possibility that labor-government cooperation could shift the future policy environment in the favor of workers.

One solution to this tension – and the one that was eventually adopted in South Africa – is to allow relatively liberalized markets to adjudicate distributive conflicts. In effect, the strategy would extend liberal democratic rights to all people in the political sphere while relying on market-determined outcomes in the economic sphere. Economic liberalization would limit the extent to which competing claims on South Africa's economic resources would affect incentives for capital accumulation. Take the example of real wages. By liberalizing labor markets and maintaining a high degree of "flexibility," wage demands and efforts to improve standards could be kept in check by the specter of growing unemployment. Likewise, by drastically reducing restrictions on trade and capital flows, redistributive policies would be more difficult to pursue without compromising the country's competitiveness or risking capital flight.

The idea that macroeconomic policy is endogenous to efforts by states to curb redistributive pressures has been applied to other contexts (e.g., Boddy and Crotty 1975). In South Africa, this approach to economic policy was first presented in an integrated form in the macroeconomic framework – *Growth, Employment, and Redistribution (GEAR)* – released in June 1996 by the Department of Finance (now the National Treasury). The strategy proposed a set of medium-term policies aimed at liberalizing the South African economy. These policies included a relaxation of exchange controls, trade liberalization, "regulated" flexibility in labor markets, deficit reduction targets, and monetary policies aimed at stabilizing the rand through market interest rates. Another component of the strategy, the privatization of state assets, was to be negotiated through an agreement between government and labor, called the National Framework Agreement (NFA).

The argument behind this approach to macroeconomic management was that these policies would stabilize the economic environment in South Africa and create a favorable climate for investment. The framework adopted a profit-led growth argument, stressing that productivity increases must exceed real wage gains in order to promote investment (i.e., a shift in distribution away from the labor share was implicit).

The free-market approach introduced by the macroeconomic strategy should be seen in historical context. GEAR did not represent a shift in policy as much as it represented a continuation of changes already underway. Democratic reforms to apartheid often coincided with liberal, more market-oriented economic policies. For example, in the late 1970s and the 1980s, the then President P.W. Botha pursued a number of reforms, such as the legalization of black trade unions, the establishment of parliamentary structures for the Indian and Colored populations, the removal of prohibitions on mixed marriages, and the de-racialization of some aspects of public social life (Morris and Padayachee 1988). These reforms can be seen as a limited adoption of more democratic practices, although still within the larger system of apartheid. These changes were accompanied by more market-oriented economic policies – a reform of monetary policy to embrace market-determined interest rates, a brief removal of exchange controls (1983–85), and a liberalization of labor markets with the elimination of influx controls and job reservations. Furthermore, during the negotiated transition to democracy under President de Klerk (1989–94), additional policies of economic liberalization were pursued.

Also, the GEAR document does not encompass all the macroeconomic reforms adopted during the post-apartheid period. Perhaps most significantly, the introduction of a formal inflation-targeting monetary policy regime by the South Africa Reserve Bank was not fully anticipated in the GEAR strategy. Nevertheless, the GEAR document does represent an important, and reasonably coherent, articulation of this approach to revitalize accumulation in the South African capitalist economy.

Within this context, it is important to recognize the negotiated nature of the transition from apartheid, particularly as it involved the country's business interests. In the late 1980s, business in South Africa increasingly supported negotiations to end the apartheid system. The ascendancy of big business in South Africa affected the balance of power during the transition period and meant that redistributive policies would be incremental, market-focused, and non-threatening to established property rights (Gelb 2004). Ironically, some of the conglomerates supporting the end of apartheid had grown out of the corporations that primarily benefited from the apartheid government's policies to support the accumulation of industrial capital, particularly Afrikaner capital. This change in business interests grew out of a fundamental shift in the balance of power from the state to capital.

The international condemnation of apartheid meant that the global reach of South African capital was constrained until an acceptable political solution was reached. Business had to forego profitable opportunities because of this lack of international openness (Gelb 2004). This constraint was compounded by the low profitability of domestic investments in the last years of apartheid. Global re-integration was therefore a crucial business objective for the transition from apartheid. Since the democratic transition, South African business has rapidly internationalized, including making significant investment in other African countries, shifting to non-South African capital markets (e.g., Anglo-American's listing on the London Stock Exchange), and acquiring foreign companies (e.g., South African Breweries purchase of foreign firms including the U.S. Miller Brewing Company).

The ANC-led government pursued redistributive policies within the general framework of economic liberalization. Perhaps the most significant of these policies are the cash transfer programs: the Old Age Pension, the Child Maintenance Grants, and the Disability Grants. The system of cash transfers was extended in the post-apartheid period and, when necessary, de-racialized. These cash transfers have had a significant impact on the living standards of low-income families (Case and Deaton 1998; Barrientos and DeJong 2006). Again, it is important to place these grant programs in a historical context. The system of cash transfers does not represent a wholly new approach to redistribution adopted as part of the democratic transition, but instead reflects an extension and modification of policies that had been developed and implemented by the apartheid regime (Seekings and Nattrass 2006).

Other redistributive policies have been pursued since 1994. A policy of land restitution has returned property seized by the apartheid government. The housing program has provided grants to assist with the purchase of new homes. Infrastructure investments in communities – such as the installation of water taps – have improved people's lives. Nevertheless, in many cases, significant components of these redistributive efforts remain market-focused and involve public–private partnerships. Therefore, many of the redistributive policies that have been adopted tend to be mediated, at some level, by market forces, which is consistent with the market-based approach to determining distributive outcomes in the larger economy.

Has the Strategy Worked?

Have the institutional and policy changes adopted in the post-apartheid era laid the groundwork for a new SSA in democratic South Africa? A short answer to this question is that it is too early to tell. As shown in Figure 11.1, the rate of accumulation has improved since the 1994 elections, at least compared to the extremely poor economic performance of the last years of apartheid. Nevertheless, the improvements appear modest in a long-run historical perspective – that is, compared to the rapid rates of accumulation of the 1950s and 1960s. Growth rates of GDP have also improved in recent years, reaching 5 percent per year in 2005–07, but this improvement may not represent a long-run trend. By 2008, the annual growth rate had fallen to 3.1 percent. Relatively rapid and stable rates of growth and investment would indicate the establishment of a new SSA in South Africa. Wolfson and Kotz (Chapter 3) argue that an SSA can also be characterized by an institutional setting that stabilizes class conflicts, even if economic growth is not particularly rapid. Although economic performance has been improving on average, and distributive conflicts have been managed to a large extent, the long-run political and economic sustainability of the post-apartheid institutional structure is difficult to assess at this stage.

South Africa faces a number of challenges in reconstituting a vibrant regime of accumulation in the post-apartheid period. We highlight three of these challenges here: the decline in public investment, the global interests of South African capital, and heightened economic volatility.

The establishment of a post-apartheid SSA does not hinge on the need to address any one of these challenges. However, these problems may impede the process of capital accumulation and growth within the new institutional setting.

Public Investment. As discussed previously, one of the pillars of the apartheid SSA was public investment in infrastructure and state-led provision of key economic services. These public investments were complementary to the activities of the private sector and were important in sustaining profitability and industrial development. During the crisis years, the rate of public investment fell to historically low levels and has not recovered. Figure 11.3 shows total public investment, by both the government and public corporations, as a share of GDP from 1970 to 2006. Given the public goods nature of these investments and the existence of economies of scale, markets are unlikely to provide close substitutes or, when substitutes exist, markets will undersupply these complementary goods and services. Unless public investment is revived or an alternative institutional arrangement for coordinating such investment is developed, capitalist accumulation in the post-apartheid era will likely be compromised in the long-run.

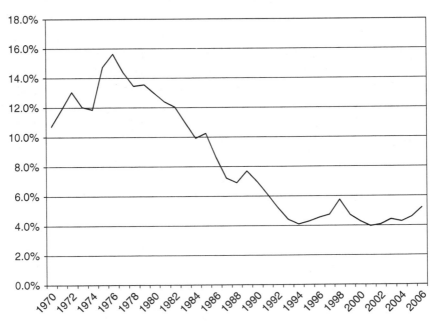

Figure 11.3. Total public investment (gross) as a percentage of GDP, South Africa, 1970–2006.
Source: South African Reserve Bank.

Global Interests of South African Capital. As noted above, business interests in South Africa had an interest in a negotiated end to apartheid to gain access to international markets and investment opportunities. Since 1994, South African capital has extended its global reach in numerous ways. This raises the possibility that the economic interests of capital may become increasingly independent of the domestic regime of accumulation. In other words, the institutional setting that encourages the growth and expansion of capital with origins in South Africa may diverge over time from the institutional setting that encourages the growth and expansion of the South African economy.

As long as business interests have a stable and acceptable set of institutions regarding property rights, legal protections, and taxation policy in their base of operations, the importance of other supporting policies that would generate more rapid domestic accumulation in South Africa itself may diminish over time. For example, foreign direct investment allows capital to seek out profitable investments elsewhere if domestic institutions do not maintain sufficient profitability at home. Similarly, domestic capital markets are of secondary importance to conglomerates that have access to much deeper financial markets abroad. Political pressures from big business may therefore support institutions that secure their own global interests, but would not, by themselves, revitalize capital accumulation in the South African economy.

Economic Volatility. Liberalization of the South African economy has increased volatility in ways that may undermine long-run investment and the stability of a post-apartheid SSA. During the post-apartheid years, heightened volatility has been most apparent with regard to short-term capital flows and exchange rates. The country has experienced an increase in short-term capital inflows since the first democratic elections in 1994. However, these inflows have been subject to sharp reversals. In 2001–02, the rand experienced a rapid, nominal depreciation due to a reversal of inflows of short-term portfolio investments. This reversal occurred despite the continued existence of exchange controls. Exchange controls have been relaxed as part of the liberalization strategy, and their enforcement has frequently been uneven. The rand has since stabilized, but the build-up of short-term capital flows has also resumed. In 2006, net inflows of portfolio investments in securities totaled $U.S. 20 billion, by far the highest level recorded since the end of apartheid, but these net inflows were not sustained in 2007 and 2008.[5]

---

[5] Estimates of net portfolio inflows are from the IMF, 2009.

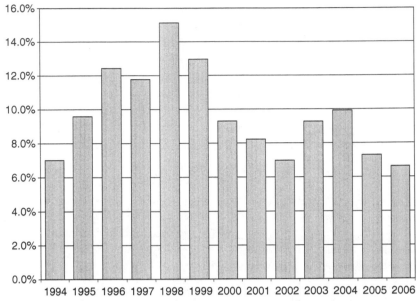

Figure 11.4. Real prime lending rates, South Africa, 1994–2006.
Note: The real prime lending rate was calculated by subtracting the rate of change of the consumer price index from the nominal prime lending rate.
Source: IMF (2007).

Given low inflation rate targets and the adoption in 2000 of a formal inflation-targeting monetary policy, real interest rates have remained high since 1994 (Figure 11.4). High real interest rates attract the type of short-term portfolio investment that can lead to the type of destabilizing reversals that happened in 2001–02. Ironically, policies aimed at short-term price stability at very low rates of inflation may actually destabilize other dimensions of the economy. Moreover, the high interest rates needed to maintain macroeconomic stability, defined largely in terms of maintaining low inflation, will themselves have a negative impact on growth and investment. According to Figure 11.4, real interest rates have declined somewhat in recent years, but they remain high compared to real interest rates in many other countries. High interest rates, unstable capital inflows, and exchange rate volatility may all undermine the establishment of a stable SSA in the future.

Finally, the end of apartheid and the advent of electoral democracy have provided South Africa with a relatively stable social and political environment. Nevertheless, large social pressures persist, despite the positive contributions of the redistributive policies that have been pursued.

Open unemployment remains extremely high. The unemployment rate stood at 21 percent in 2007 using a relatively conservative estimate of unemployment (Statistics South Africa 2009). The HIV/AIDS pandemic has killed thousands of people in their prime. These realities, along with other factors, create enormous social tensions. When the ANC-led government came to power in 1994, it did so in alliance with two major partners from the anti-apartheid struggle: the Congress of South African Trade Unions (COSATU) and the South African Communist Party (SACP). This political alliance, together with broad-based support for the ANC-led government, has helped maintain stability despite the enormous social problems South Africa must confront. However, the potential remains for social unrest to undermine economic growth in the new South Africa, just as it led to the collapse of the apartheid SSA.

Conclusion

This chapter has argued that the social structures of accumulation approach can contribute to our understanding of the dynamics of the South African economy during the apartheid years. Contrary to critics of the SSA approach as it has been applied to South Africa, there is significant empirical evidence supporting the existence of an apartheid-era SSA. Moreover, the SSA framework provides valuable insights into the relationship between apartheid and capitalism and an explanation of the economic crisis that contributed to the end of apartheid and the democratic transition in 1994. Traditional liberal and Marxist analyses have failed to either explain the rapid growth of the economy in the 1950s and 1960s or the emergence of the crisis beginning in the 1970s. In this respect, the SSA approach makes a significant contribution.

It is too early to say whether the SSA framework can provide the same sort of valuable insights when applied to the post-apartheid period. Although there are signs of significant improvements in growth performance and capital accumulation in recent years, the long-run stability of these improvements cannot be determined at this time. During the post-apartheid transition, the government has attempted to reinvigorate the South African economy by a policy of economic liberalization and consolidation of liberal democracy. Economic performance has certainly improved since the crisis years of apartheid. However, future research will be needed to establish whether the right set of institutions have been created to establish a foundation for long-run growth and manage distributive conflicts in the new South Africa.

References

Barrientos, Armando and Jocelyn DeJong 2006. "Reducing Child Poverty with Cash Transfers: A Sure Thing?" *Development Policy Review* 24, 5: 537–52.

Boddy, Richard and Crotty, James 1975. "Class Conflict and Macro-policy: The Political Business Cycle." *Review of Radical Political Economics* 7, 1: 1–19.

Case, Anne and Angus Deaton 1998. "Large Cash Transfers to the Elderly in South Africa." *Economic Journal* 108, 450: 1330–61.

Fedderke, J. W, R. H. J. de Kadt, and J. M. Luiz 2001. "Growth and Institutions: A Study of the lInk between Political Institutions and Economic Growth in South Africa: A time series study: 1935–97." *Journal for Studies in Economics and Econometrics* 25, 1: 1–26.

Fine, Ben and Zavareh Rustomjee 1996. *The Political Economy of South Africa: From Minerals-Energy Complex to Industrialization*. Boulder, CO: Westview.

Gelb, Stephen 1987. "Making Sense of the Crisis." *Transformation*, 5: 33–50.

    2004. "The South African Economy: An Overview, 1994–2004." Pp. 367–400 in J. Daniel, J. Lutchman and R. Southall eds. The *State of the Nation: South Africa 2004–05*, East Lansing, MI: Michigan State University Press.

Heintz, James 2001a. *Investment, Labor Demand, and Political Conflict in South Africa*. Ph.D. Dissertation, Department of Economics, University of Massachusetts.

    2001b. "Political Conflict and the Social Structures of Accumulation: The Case of South African Apartheid," *Review of Radical Political Economics* 34, 3: 319–26.

    2002. "Capital Accumulation and Macro Policy in South Africa: Political Instability, Distributive Conflict, and Economic Institutions," Working Paper 29, Political Economy Research Institute, Amherst, MA.

Horwitz, Ralph 1967. *The Political Economy of South Africa*. London: Weidenfeld & Nicolson.

IMF 2009. International Financial Statistics CD Database.

Kalecki, Michal 1971. *Selected Essays on the Dynamics of the Capitalist Economy 1933–1970*. Cambridge, UK: Cambridge University Press.

Kotz, David M. 1990. "A Comparative Analysis of the Theory of Regulation and the Social Structure of Accumulation Theory." *Science and Society* 54, 1: 5–28.

Lipton, Merle 1985. *Capitalism and Apartheid*. Totowa, NJ: Rowman and Allanheld.

Morris, M. and V. Padayachee 1988. "State Reform Policy in South Africa." *Transformation* 7: 1–26.

Nattrass, Nicoli 1994. "Apartheid and Capitalism: Social Structure of Accumulation or Contradiction?" Pp. 253–73 In David Kotz, Terrence McDonough and Michael Reich eds. *Social Structures of Accumulation: The Political Economy of Growth and Crisis*. New York: Cambridge University Press.

O'Meara, Dan 1983. *Volkskapitalisme: Class, Capital, and Ideology in the Development of Afrikaner Nationalism, 1934–1948*. Cambridge, UK: Cambridge University Press.

Schock, Kurt 1996. "A Conjunctural Model of Political Conflict." *Journal of Conflict Resolution* 40, 1. 98–133.

Seekings, Jeremy and Nicoli Nattrass 2006. *"Class, Race, and Inequality in South Africa."* Durban: University of KwaZulu Natal Press.

South African Reserve Bank 2007. Data from website http://www.reservebank.co.za.

Statistics South Africa 2009. *Labour Force Survey*, Historical Revision September Series 2000 to 2007, March.

Verhoef, Grietjie 1992a. "Nedbank, 1945–89: The Continental Approach to Banking in South Africa." Pp. 80–114 in S. Jones ed. *Financial Enterprise in South Africa Since 1950*. London: MacMillan Press.

1992b. "Afrikaner Nationalism in South African Banking: The Case of Volkskas and Trust Bank." Pp. 115–53 in S. Jones ed. *Financial Enterprise in South Africa since 1950*. London: MacMillan Press.

Wintrobe, Ronald 1998. *The Political Economy of Dictatorship*. Cambridge, UK: Cambridge University Press.

Wolpe, Harold 1972. "Capitalism and Cheap Labour-Power in South Africa: From Segregation to Apartheid." *Economy and Society* 1, 4: 425–456.

Wood, Elisabeth 2000. *Forging Democracy from Below*. Cambridge, UK: Cambridge University Press.

TWELVE

Social Structures of Accumulation and the Condition of the Working Class in Mexico

Carlos Salas

Introduction

Since 1982, Mexico has been facing a new model of accumulation. The new model replaces one that stood for fifty years. To situate the current stage of Mexico's capitalist development in a broader context, we use as a guide the idea of a social structure of accumulation (SSA): an articulated, historically specific set of institutions that organizes the process of capital accumulation in different ways in different locations and historical periods.[1] Every historically situated model of accumulation is, in fact, an SSA. Almost every account of the twentieth century economic history of Mexico leaves aside the role of institutions in the accumulation process (see, e.g., Solís 1981; Lustig 1998). Even the most progressive accounts, such as (Moreno-Brid and Ros 2009), tend to downplay the relevance of several institutions and institutional arrangements that foster economic growth and capital accumulation.

And none examines how the resulting accumulation affects the growth of occupations and the evolution of wages. It is our contention that, by leaving aside these aspects of economic life, standard analyses of the Mexican economy are unable to explain the impact of the economic structure on the working class.

In this chapter we will show how the notion of an SSA is a useful tool to understand the evolution of the Mexican economy. We will also show that such a notion needs to take into account the institutional evolution of employment and income during most of the twentieth century, in order to better depict the living condition of the majority. With the goal of

[1] A recent review of the SSA literature can be found in McDonough 2008.

contrasting the two SSA – two accumulation processes with the accompanying social and political institutions – we will also examine in a very general way the principal characteristics of the former SSA, whose economic base was centered in the internal market. As was said above, in particular, we will stress labor issues throughout our analysis.

The initial steps toward the former social structure of accumulation began during the Mexican Revolution (1910–21), in particular with the promulgation in 1917 of the current Constitution, which included several progressive measures in labor relations, communal property of land, and social safety institutions, that started to be put in practice toward the end of the 1930s.

It entered its phase of exhaustion first on the terrain of agricultural activities in the mid-1960s, and in a more generalized manner during the 1970s. Nevertheless, it was not until the 1980s that it fully expressed the structural crisis that characterizes the deepest part of the declining phase. In particular, the last twenty years can be seen as a kind of bridge between the exhaustion of the old model and the rapid consolidation of the new one.

The current state of Mexican development is characterized by the redefinition of the activities that act as the axis of the new continuous process of accumulation. Until now the result has been the creation of a two-level economy: one level is linked to exports and the international financial system, while the other is made up of economic units oriented to the internal market and outside of financial circuits, especially without access to credit. This transition period also implies changes in the manner in which many distinct activities are articulated among themselves.

Mexican capitalism was restructured in a stage during which the global economy experienced a great increase in productive capacity, accompanied by a decline in the ability of national economies to generate large numbers of stable, decent-paying jobs. Economic restructuring also translated into an accelerated process of the installation of production sites outside the areas that traditionally had been the geographical centers of the old model of accumulation. This movement has its most palpable expression in the *maquiladora*[2] activities along the country's northern border. However, the geographical relocation process cannot be reduced to the *maquiladoras*. It has also involved the growth of

---

[2] These are firms that operate in Mexico, using U.S. tariff code provisions (HTS 9802), which allows U.S. firms to send U.S.-made inputs abroad for assembly and then return those semifinished or finished products to the United States, paying a tariff only on value added abroad. Most of these *maquiladoras* are owned by U.S. firms.

several mid-size cities located away from the central area of the country where traditionally most of the economic activities were concentrated.

Despite these regional expansions, the working population has experienced a long crisis at the national level, expressed in a growing concentration of income and a systematic deterioration of living standards. This deterioration can be explained, fundamentally, by the decline in income derived from work. In fact, there are two parallel processes at work here, creating a clear expression of the polarization of the present-day Mexican economy. On the one hand there is an insufficient creation of stable, well-paying jobs in large and mid-size establishments; on the other hand, there is a growing generation of jobs in microenterprises, where the level of remuneration is notoriously low.

In the present phase of the current long wave of development, the social role of the state has been redefined and transformed. The state has centered its activity on the creation of the best global conditions for the economic performance of capital and has dismantled key parts of its social activity. In this scenario, the small units, operating as a mechanism by which a large number of people can earn some income, have functioned as an "obstacle" to high levels of open unemployment over the past two decades. The presence of these small firms is limited to areas where a potential market exists for the goods and services they offer. The growth of these activities is thus limited by overall urban income and it is, therefore, in the large and mid-size cities that we see the greatest proliferation of microenterprises.

Today, small-scale activities represent a mechanism by which capitalism can reproduce itself and minimize the conflicts derived from its diminished ability to absorb its labor force. Small enterprises play a role analogous to the role traditionally played by the peasantry in underdeveloped countries. They do not participate directly in the process of accumulation, but they help the process through the reproduction of a large part of the labor force.

Long-Term Trends and Breakpoints in the Mexican Economy: 1921–2007

The evolution of the Mexican economy during the long period that spans 1921 to 2007 can be summarized in the following figures. Figure 12.1 shows the evolution of GDP at constant 1993 prices along with a trend line (rates of growth smoothed with a Hodrick-Prescott filter). It is visible that the economy regained growth after the Great Depression and

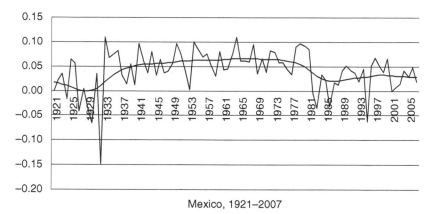

Figure 12.1. GDP rate of growth and trend, Mexico 1921–2007.
Source: GDP data from Mariña (2007) and trend from author's calculations.

begin an upswing wave that stopped in the early 1980s. Through the mid-1930s up to the end of the World War II, a renewed industrialization process started to build (Moreno-Brid and Ros 2004). During the 1950s, manufacturing became the main engine behind GDP growth (Banco de México 1960; Moreno-Brid and Ros 2004).

After that came a period of instability, with an average rate of growth half of that experienced during the previous long wave. A transition period ensued, which led to a new SSA, one that can be called the neoliberal SSA (Houston 1992; Kotz and McDonough 2009). Its main components are an implicit capital-labor accord that emphasizes labor flexibility and job permanence in exchange for lower wages (De la Garza 2001); a new capital-citizen accord that expressed itself in the replacement of PRI (Partido Revolucionario Institucional) as the ruling party in 2000, as it reflects general support for pro-free market policies; the emergence of powerful new business groups and a redefinition of the market competition rules; and an integration into the global economy that emphasizes economic and social links with the United States.

Figure 12.2 shows the evolution of GDP per capita for the same period discussed above. It shows a behavior that parallels that of GDP, but with lower rates of growth. In the absence of wage data for the entire economy during the 1930–80 period (Aguila and Bortz 2006), these data suggest a steady rise in well being for the Mexican population that ended in 1981 (a year before the debt crisis). These trends can be examined more closely only for the last two decades (see below).

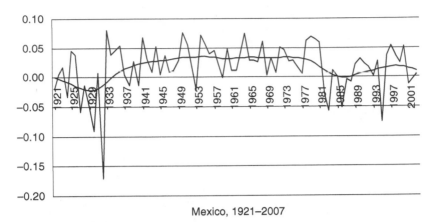

Figure 12.2. Per capita GDP rate of growth and trend, Mexico 1921–2007.
Source: GDP data from Mariña (2007) and trend from author's calculations.

Figure 12.3. Profit rate and trend, Mexico 1939–2004.
Source: GDP data from Mariña (2007) and trend from author's calculations.

Figure 12.3 exhibits the evolution of the rate of profit from 1939 to 2004. Import substitution policies partially isolated Mexico from the world economy, allowing for profit rates well above international averages[3] (Mariña 2003). The slowdown in the rate of growth of GDP, as well as a decline in the profit rate after the mid-1960s, signals the end of the long upward swing that started in the early 1940s. The figure also shows

---

[3] For a discussion of the methodology used to estimate the rate of profit in México (measured by capitalist profit as a percentage of the total stock of capital investment), see Mariña and Moseley 2000.

that the trend is downward, despite a recovery during the late 1980s and early 1990s.

Social Structures of Accumulation and the Long Wave of Development During 1930–1980

As we have pointed out above, the 1930–1980 period can be studied as a long wave of capitalist development that begins with the aftermath of the 1910 Revolution, a violent transition from a process of accumulation based on the export of primary goods to a process based on industrial production for the internal market (Rendón and Salas 1987; Rodríguez 1994). The revolutionary war ends around 1920, but instability and economic crisis continue until the early 1930s. The initial stage of a new accumulation cycle takes place between 1930 and 1950, and its consolidation takes place between 1950 and 1970 (Villarreal 2000).

By the 1970–80 decade we begin to see evidence of a brake on the process of inward-looking development. All these periods are marked by a distinctive evolution of employment, as can be seen in Table 12.1, which includes total employment, both waged and nonwaged. In particular, the feminization of employment can be seen clearly after 1970, as well as a rapid growth in services and commerce, sectors characterized by their precarious labor conditions.

As was shown in (Rendón and Salas 1987) in their study of almost a hundred years of population census data, during the course of the 1930s, the massive displacement of craft production by manufacturing was concluded. Once the Mexican Revolution was consolidated, a period of relative stability prevailed that permitted the recovery of the economic activity that had been so weakened during the period of revolutionary fighting. During the 1930s, employment grew at a faster rate than during the previous decade. Female employment, in particular, recovered its growth rate after a systematic decline between 1900 and 1930. Of all new jobs created during the 1930s, only 15 percent were in the manufacturing sector. This poor showing was the result of the combined effect of strong economic growth during the Cárdenas period (1934–40), following the fall of employment created by the onset of the depression in 1932. Mexico's economic depression was, in great measure, a reflection of the Great Depression that had befallen the United States. From 1934 to 1939 real wages increased a little more than 20 percent (Rendón and Salas 1989). But a decline in real wages began in the last years of the Cardenista period – a decline that would continue until the early 1950s (Rendón and Salas 1989).

Table 12.1. *Employment by Industry and Share of Men in Sectoral Employment, 1895–2000*

	1895		1930		1970	
	Total	Percent Male	Total	Percent Male	Total	Percent Male
Total	4,606,009	85	5,352,226	93	10,488,800	81
Agriculture	2,979,140	100	3,626,278	99	5,103,519	95
Mining	85,771	99	56,906	100	104,612	94
Oil and Gas	0	0	7,693	99	93,714	90
Manufacture	793,463	49	672,127	83	2,393,935	79
Construction	50,341	100	70,644	100	627,966	97
Electricity, Gas and Water	0	0	16,580	100	58,669	91
Services	420,831	40	467,843	61	2,806,890	55
Transportation and Communication	63,293	100	123,440	99	442,856	93
Commerce	213,170	80	310,715	85	1,322,898	72

	1980–81	2000	
		Total	Percent Male
Total	17,296,325	33,730,210	68
Agriculture	5,056,430	5,338,299	91
Mining	147,981	144,421	91
Oil and Gas	121,658	na	Na
Manufacture	3,044,082	6,418,391	69
Construction	1,191,028	2,669,751	97
Electricity, Gas and Water	97,059	151,546	84
Services	5,116,292	11,361,852	56
Transportation and Communication	712,354	1,410,193	94
Commerce	1,809,441	5,597,992	58

Source: Data from 1895 through 1980, see Rendón and Salas 1988. Data for 2000, Population Census, INEGI.
Due to adjustments made on the original data, there are no figures available by sex. (Rendón and Salas 1988.)

Until 1940, the agrarian sector accounted for nearly all rural employment.[4] The significant weight of the agrarian sector is still an important phenomenon today. In fact, if one considers the entire economy, the largest portion of unwaged work remains concentrated in that sector. At the beginning of the 1940s, two-thirds of manufacturing workers received wages (Bortz 1988). Nonetheless, the percentage of wage workers in tertiary activities was still a little less than 50 percent. Owing to the economic changes in the cities as much as in the countryside, the following years were characterized by a constant growth of wage work, with a consequent broadening of the labor market.

Between 1950 and 1970, the development of Mexico's internal market was consolidated, and at the same time there was an increase in paid agrarian employment. The counterpart of this growth was a strong process of de-ruralization, as is shown by Schejtman (1981). During these twenty years, paid jobs in the nonagrarian sectors grew more rapidly than the unwaged jobs; the exception to this tendency was the service sector, within which self-employment experienced an extraordinary growth. This can be explained by the rapid growth of a number of service activities (repairs, food preparation, house cleaning, etc.) that are characterized by the prevalence of small firms run by their owners and family members, with no wage labor (Rendón and Salas 1987).

Since the 1930s, unwaged labor within commercial and service activities grew as a response to the general dynamism of the economy and to the general level of the country's development. For example, small-scale buying and selling of products was for many years the "natural" manner of distribution. This responded to two facts, first the geographical dispersion of the national market, and second, the prevailing levels of income throughout the country. Stated in another manner, these activities did not grow as residual activities, but parallel to general economic dynamism (Rendón and Salas 1987, 1989).

In this sense, the most outstanding phenomenon of the 1970s was the brake on the growth of wage work. This fact is observed and discussed by García (1988). This tendency within overall employment was fundamentally rooted in the experience of the agricultural sector, since it is there that we saw the systematic reduction in the number of wage workers over the period 1970–79. In contrast, wage work in the nonagricultural

---

[4] Between 1940 and the middle of the 1960s, this sector played an important role in the process of the accumulation and reproduction of capital by financing industrial development and providing hard currency for the purchase of foreign raw materials for industry.

sectors grew more rapidly than nonwage work. And beyond that, the relative importance of wage work in the net growth of nonagricultural employment was greater in the 1970s than in the years 1950–70. The intensity of this process is reflected by the fact that during this same period, waged jobs registered a bigger growth than nonwaged jobs in the commercial sector (García 1988).

During the 1970s, we also observe a relative reduction in the ability of manufacturers to create jobs, which lent a slower pace to the growth of agricultural employment. Both phenomena, together with the systematic growth of commerce and services, explain the accelerated tertiarization of employment (Rendón and Salas 1987).

In sum, until the 1970s, wage work grew in a significant, though decelerating, manner. The deceleration was the result of the growing obstacles to sustained economic growth. By the 1980s, it was expressed most powerfully when the economy, fully and totally, entered into crisis.

Beginning in 1939, the long wave that covered the period 1930–80 exhibited cyclical behavior in regard to the compensation of labor. The information available does not permit even a general sketch of the behavior of wages and salaries during the 1930s. Nonetheless, beginning in 1939 it becomes possible to reconstruct the movement of industrial wages, from which it becomes possible to construct some solid hypotheses regarding the general behavior of wages during the period.

According to Bortz (1988), between 1938 and 1979 the economy experienced a complete wage cycle; industrial wages began to suffer a systematic decline in 1939, which was halted in 1952. Between that date and 1976, real industrial wages climbed uninterruptedly. Over the following years we observe a new decline, which slowed down only in the final years of Carlos Salinas' administration, but afterward continued its steady fall (Aguila and Bortz 2006). It has been shown (Bortz 1990) that a strong correlation exists between the behavior of industrial wages and average wages in the nonagricultural sectors of the rest of the economy. This correlation is so strong that the movement of average industrial wages reflects the behavior of average wages in other sectors.[5]

The absence of general data relative to the form of income received by Mexican families over the years running from the 1930s through the 1950s impedes a precise investigation of this topic. There is indirect evidence

---

[5] For the years following the 1960s, this can be conclusively demonstrated with data from the National Accounts System, which, for more recent years, can be confirmed with data from the National Survey of Employment (ENE).

(Rendón and Salas 1989) that supports the existence of an improvement in income distribution during the Cárdenas years. Nevertheless, the manner in which the distribution of income evolved can only be reconstructed beginning in the 1950s when the first national income surveys were conducted (Altimir 1983; Hernández Laos 1999).

Despite a series of problems involving the comparison of sources, Hernández Laos (1999) shows that between the end of the 1950s and the end of the 1970s, income clearly became concentrated in the highest deciles at the cost of those in the lowest deciles. The behavior of income distribution over the entire period does not show a clear tendency; distribution becomes more equal between 1950 and 1963, only to become more unequal in 1968, with a Gini coefficient greater than the corresponding one in 1950 (Altimir 1983; Hernández Laos 1999). There is a noticeable difference in the concentration of income in urban and rural areas; in cities there is a greater concentration of income than in the countryside. Nevertheless, we should point out that average income in urban areas is between two and three times greater than in rural areas (Hernández Laos 1999).

We should stress that, in spite of the way income distribution evolved over the period 1950–68, real wages increased in a sustained manner. Furthermore, we must remember that employment opportunities also grew systematically. Both of these factors produced an improvement in living conditions among broad sectors of the population. Between 1968 and 1984, the concentration of income diminished significantly, as the Gini coefficient fell from 0.498 to 0.461, a phenomenon accompanied by a decline in the level of absolute poverty, both in urban and rural areas (Hernández Laos 1992; Altimir 1996).

The long wave of 1930–80 consolidated and sustained itself on the basis of a diverse series of institutions, which we will briefly discuss below. This set of institutions constitute an SSA, as that concept is understood in the relevant literature, that is, a coherent set of institutions that promoted and structured capital accumulation.

In the first place, the ejido – communal land property as a social institution – guaranteed the right to the land for hitherto landless peasants (campesinos) and represented a form of social organization for their control and permanence on their territories of origin (Córdova 1973, 1974; Rendón 1976). Even today the ejido functions as an important reserve of unwaged labor. The ejido played both an economic and social role, as it allowed for a steady flow of agricultural products to the urban sector; it provided a source of foreign currency to sustain the initial stages of twentieth century industrialization; and it ameliorated the living conditions of campesinos (Shejtman 1981).

Second, corporatism, understood as the coalition of trade unions, campesino (peasant) organizations, middle-class professionals and office workers within the ruling party, which later became the Institutional Revolutionary Party (PRI), represented a form of organization and political control of workers, as well as a form of relation between the state and the entrepreneurial sector (Córdova 1972, 1974). With the exception of trade unions, the above mentioned organizations were created by the political apparatus that was consolidated after the 1910 Revolution. The chipping away of the corporatist apparatus as a medium of control of the workforce represents an important component of the exhaustion of the SSA that was dominant up to the early 1980s.

Third, a series of key institutions came out of the triumphant project of the Mexican Revolution. These included social security – the Mexican Institute of Social Security (IMSSS) as well as the Social Security Institute for Workers in State Service (ISSSTE) – the Secretariat of Public Education,[6] and the Secretariat of Health and Assistance (Bustamante et al. 1982).

Fourth, the creation and consolidation of the Bank of Mexico (Córdova 1973; Brothers and Solís 1967) permitted the subsequent development of the country's banking system, a necessary condition to guarantee the process of sustained accumulation.

The whole group of institutions worked together to promote capital accumulation during the long wave of growth that started during the World War II. As can be seen in figure 12.1, the whole period from 1921 to 1934 was one of unstable growth (the "exploration" stage of any SSA).

Both the ejido and the corporatist arrangements represented a new form – in the 1930s – of institutional setup that involved the state, capital, and labor. This was complemented by the set of institutions listed under the third group above.

As a whole, the first three sets of institutions, together with the dissemination of the so-called "ideology of the Mexican Revolution," expressed new relations among the state, capital, and citizens. The relations among the several fractions of capital were always mediated by the state (Córdova 1972), although it is important to emphasize that the presence of the state in economic activities was of great importance in

---

[6] Pérez Rocha (1983) closely examines the role of the Secretariat of Public Education in the political and social project that emerged from the Mexican Revolution.

the period 1930–80. In fact, the most important economic element of this SSA was an economic policy that occupied the core of the national development of the internal market (Barkin 1990; Soria 1997). The policy implied a strong economic role for the state, establishing the state's collaboration in the formation of several nuclei of economic power that benefited from the development of the internal market and that gradually acquired autonomy with respect to the state project. State-capital relationships started with a re-creation of the capitalist class that now included nuclei of former revolutionaries and their heirs (Cordova 1973).

These nuclei, the disputes among them, and their internal contradictions, created, in the 1980s, a new profile of the entrepreneurial class in Mexico (Thacker 1999), characterized by a preeminence of the financial sectors and of businessmen that have no family links to the descendants of the PRI groups that held power until 1982.

The Unstable Growth Cycle During 1980–2007 and the Transition to a New SSA

A major economic transition began with the foreign debt crisis in 1982. Prior to the debt crash, the previous growth model – one that relied on the domestic market, as conceived since the late 1930s when the Mexican state reached stability under President Cardenas's administration[7] – underwent a crisis in the agricultural sector. During the previous SSA, the economy had remained closed to the foreign sector and had established high import tariffs and prohibited the entrance of a wide range of commodities. This, however, was not accompanied by an efficient program that would replace the imported inputs on which the national industry depended as it leaped to higher industrial levels. Ultimately, production depended on the availability of foreign exchange with which to purchase the necessary inputs in foreign markets.

Foreign exchange was obtained mainly through trading agricultural goods and outputs from the mining industry (i.e., oil). As agricultural production fell into crisis around the mid sixties (Solís 1981), the oil boom of the mid seventies temporarily forestalled the crisis but also facilitated an acceleration of the foreign debt. When international oil prices dropped,

---

[7] See Boltvinik and Hernández Laos (1981) for a discussion of the exhaustion of the model of development oriented toward the domestic market, commonly known as the *import substitution model.*

the country no longer had access to foreign exchange, triggering the 1982 crisis.

This domestic market-oriented model was gradually dismantled by a group of young neoclassical economists and politicians that supported "pro-market" policies[8] under the De la Madrid administration (1982–1988). Their new growth strategy asked for a different kind of state, which would certainly not play the leading role in the economy that it had played for almost fifty years. Hence, the wave of privatizations and reprivatizations, legal reenactments, and the abandonment of income redistribution mechanisms that followed (Moreno- Brid and Ros 2009; Salas and Gallahan 2004). In addition, the economy opened up to foreign competition, a process marked by Mexico's joining the GATT in 1986 (Lustig 1998; Calva 2000).

The lower direct participation of the state in economic activities, lower social expenditure *per capita* (Chávez 2002), and the sudden opening up to international trade directly accentuated the natural tendency toward polarization typical of developing countries such as Mexico (Dussel 1997). Ever since its inauguration, the Salinas administration (1988–94) pushed forward the new foreign-oriented model at full throttle. The new strategy was advertised as a mechanism that was to allow Mexico to join the select group of privileged First World countries (Aspe 1993). It was expected that the signing of the North American Free Trade Agreement (NAFTA) in 1993 would certainly crown all such enthusiasm. But an unexpected chain of events help to bring a downturn by the end of 1994: the Zapatista rebellion, the assassinations of notable politicians, and a new peso crisis (Blecker 1996). The impact of this crisis showed how unstable the Mexican economy really was (a fact that resurfaced in the current crisis).

We now turn our attention to an apparent paradox in the operation of Mexican labor markets.[9] When compared with nations whose economies reach a similar size and state of development, Mexico reports surprisingly low indices of urban unemployment. It would nevertheless be a great mistake to think that this fact points to any efficiency in the Mexican labor market. On the contrary, a detailed analysis of unemployment using the National Employment Surveys (see, e.g., Salas 2003) reveals a list of certain important facts. First of all, most of the unemployed are

---

[8] A sociological analysis of the social and intellectual origin of these pro "free market" economists and politicians can be found in Baab 2001.

[9] For comprehensive discussions of Mexican employment and labor income trends, see Salas and Zepeda 2003a,b.

young men or women with a schooling level above the national mean. Second, the unemployment rates are systematically lower for men than for women. Third, only 20 percent of the unemployed are household heads. Finally, the average span of unemployment is less than a month.

When workers' savings are practically nonexistent, and when the government does not provide any kind of unemployment assistance, only a limited number of workers can afford the luxury of remaining unemployed for long. The workers – either those who have recently joined the labor market or those who have just lost their previous job – are forced to accept any available job whatever the payment, working conditions, or compatibility with their training, education, and skills. In fact, only 12 percent of those who remained unemployed for over three months decided to withdraw from the economically active population (Salas 2003).

This is the hidden reality beyond the official pleasantly low unemployment rates in Mexico: unprotected employment with a low income and inadequate conditions of work. Within the Mexican labor market, nonwaged labor activities are significant. Employment in small economic units or microunits (businesses with five workers or less), including single-person establishments, prevails among such activities. It has been shown elsewhere that these establishments have very low levels of investment and productivity, and their average incomes tend to be low (Salas 2003).

Another element that helps explain the low levels of unemployment is migration to the United States, which is mostly illegal and estimated to be around 400,000 people annually. After 1994 there was a marked increase in the rate of migration (Passel 2005; Pew Hispanic Center 2009). Thus, migration and the remittances that come with it have become another factor reducing the pressure exerted by new entrants to the labor market.

Figures for the structure of employment by sector highlight the relative importance of the farming sector. This sector, which accounts for 14.3 percent of total employment, is shrinking as a result of the agricultural pressure brought about by NAFTA (Polaski 2003). On the other hand, the overall share of manufacturing jobs in the total grew significantly during the 1990s. It was particularly notable that the growth occurred in less urbanized areas and even in rural areas (Salas and Zepeda 2003b).

Table 12.2 illustrates the evolution of labor income since 1991. Real income fell substantially for both self-employed workers and wage workers from 1991 to 1997, while after 1997 the trend was upward for both groups. However, by 2008 neither group had attained its peak income

Table 12.2. *Average Monthly Income (Constant 2002 Pesos), 1991 = 100*

Year	Self-employed Workers	Wage Workers
1991	100.0	100.0
1993	66.5	110.2
1995	44.3	94.1
1996	41.8	79.8
1997	37.0	79.4
1998	38.4	81.2
1999	38.1	81.1
2000	46.3	91.2
2001	44.3	96.5
2002	45.3	98.1
2003	46.4	100.3
2004	45.5	100.8
2005	50.1	100.7
2006	51.8	103.3
2007	52.1	106.0
2008	51.2	104.6

Source: For 1995–2004, calculations from Encuesta nacional de empleo, For 2005–2008, calculations from Encuesta nacional de ocupación y empleo. 2008 data covers the first half year.

level in the early 1990s, and for the self-employed real income fell about in half over the whole period.

Special mention should be made of the performance of the minimum real wage. This wage is determined by a tripartite commission, which includes representatives from the federal government, business owners, and the official labor unions. By constitutional mandate, the minimum wage should be "sufficient for a family." But data (Coneval 2007) on the cost of the basic food basket for an average family show that, in 2006, the minimum wage allowed the buying of only 1/8th of a basic food basket. Nevertheless, the minimum wage is important due to the fact that it serves as a reference point for collective negotiations and for calculating various kinds of worker benefits.

Regarding income distribution, we face a paradoxical situation. In spite of the poor performance of the economy in terms of GDP and

Table 12.3. *Gini Coefficient for Monetary Income, 1996–2006*

1996	1998	2000	2002	2004	2005	2006
0.489	0.509	0.480	0.453	0.455	0.458	0.473

Source: INEGI, National Income Expenditure Survey, several years.

the types of jobs created, poverty diminished. Although there was an improvement in the distribution of personal incomes between 1998 and 2002, from 2004 on, income distribution worsened (see Table 12.3). These findings are influenced by the relative growth in real salaries and by increased transfers to poorer groups. The figures we have examined demonstrate that recent years have brought about increasing labor precariousness.

In addition to the importance of the number of jobs generated in the microenterprise sector, the analysis of labor trajectories in the short term (a year and a half) prove the importance of small-scale activities in absorbing workers in open unemployment, as well as that part of the working population that has been economically inactive (Salas 2003). Those results, along with the analysis of the National Survey of Micro businesses (INEGI 2003), also show that a high proportion of workers remain in small-scale activities for long periods of time for voluntary reasons. In other words, the microenterprise sector is not a simple sponge that retains workers who want to return to waged work, losing them when there is a growth in paying jobs. The fact that many workers remain in the sector shows that, in the case of Mexico, the hypothesis that microenterprises are simply a buffer between unemployment and salaried activity completely lacks empirical validity.

This sector is an alternative site of work, production, distribution, and services for a broad swath of the low-income population. In the discussion of microenterprises in Mexico, it has been shown that small-scale activity is not a homogeneous whole. A majority portion represents a homeostatic mechanism by which capitalism reproduces itself, minimizing the conflicts that flow from capital's reduced ability to absorb the labor force and the retreat in the redistributive activity of the state. Thus, a significant set of small businesses (those that are owned and operated by self-employed workers) plays a role analogous to the role traditionally played by the peasant sector in countries such as ours. That is to say, they are businesses that, most of the time, do not directly participate in the accumulation process, but that take charge of the reproduction of a large group of the urban work force. From a Marxist point of view, microunits are formally subsumed under capital.

In sum, the apparent paradox of an economy in which the rhythm of GDP growth is unstable, in which we see an accelerated process of work precariousness, in which employment does not grow at an adequate rhythm and wages grow slowly, and yet which has a very low rate of open unemployment, is explained by the presence of the employment alternatives offered by microenterprises and international migration.

Conclusions

Regulation theory and the theory of the SSA offer us, in principle, a conceptual framework in which structural forces as well as class conflicts play an important role. But regulation theory does not pay enough attention to the independent effects of class conflict (and conflict between class sectors). We took as our theoretical point of departure the idea of the SSA, since it allows for the analysis of the impact of social and political processes in the accumulation process from a broad perspective. SSA theory prompts us to go beyond the binary perspective of capital-labor (almost ubiquitous in mechanistic Marxism), and as Albelda and Tilly (1994) point out, moves us to take questions of gender, race, and migration into account. (Unfortunately, lack of space prevents us from undertaking this task here.) It also requires us to analyze the residual structures of previous modes of production, which is especially convenient in the case of Latin America, where we can verify the coexistence of these residual structures alongside specifically capitalist forms and institutions.

The idea of the SSA, within the historical context of the study of long waves, allows us to emphasize two fundamentally important phenomena. First, capitalist development does not proceed in a linear manner, and second, such development is characterized by alternating stages. This suggests a cyclical movement in a process of broadened accumulation during which accumulation is strengthened and sectors of the economy expand in a more-or-less harmonious way, taking into account one or several activities that function as basic driving forces or axes of the accumulation process.

The SSA that can currently be seen in Mexico demanded that the open economy model be consolidated. At this point we have seen the transformation or even elimination of a great many institutions and institutional arrangements that once gave shape to the old SSA. In its discourse, the new pattern of growth privileges the activity of the free forces of the market and Mexico's integration into the global economy. In fact, not everything has been left to the free forces of the market, as we saw in the state-organized rescue of the banking sector. On the terrain of links to the global economy, the trade relation with the United States has been given priority over all others, with the consequences that this type of relationship brings: the Mexican economy is every day more dependent on U.S. economic cycles.

On the other hand, a smaller economic role for the state allows certain privileged entrepreneurial groups to claim spaces left behind by the state. And even more, the entrepreneurial group that benefits from the model oriented toward the external market has succeeded in consolidating its power in a manner that assures the continuity of the model. A proof of this is the persistence of economic policies despite the change of the party in power.

In examining how employment, income, and its distribution among households have evolved, it is clear that the institutions inherited from the old model of development have brought with them a deepening of the levels of social exclusion. In Mexico, employment has tended to polarize. On the one hand, employment is affected by the concentration of capital in activities linked to exports or financial activities, which has led to a situation in which less investment is directed to the satisfaction of the demands of the internal market. On the other hand, the weakened creation of employment opportunities, accompanied by a fall in purchasing power, has meant that large groups of the population are looking for alternative ways of obtaining an income. The result is that a few jobs with adequate wages and working conditions are available for an army of workers who are trying to survive in activities of low productivity and low monetary compensation.

From the evidence presented here we can affirm that the current social structure of accumulation has not been capable, in practice, of generating stable and well-paying jobs that would allow for a reasonably dignified retirement for a large number of workers. Beyond that, and despite the declarations of its apologists, neither has it improved the living conditions of the majority of Mexicans. In fact, in the past two decades we have seen an increase in the polarization of society. The search for greater benefits for the wealthiest sectors of society has been expressed in tangible form by the many millions of dollars deposited by Mexicans in U.S. banks and the opening of new options of investment for private capital. This has led to the squandering of funds and a transfer, from the public to the private sector, at low prices, of the efforts of many generations of Mexicans. This implies that the costs of adjustment have been borne by the workers. The absence of state redistributive policies only adds to this.

Facing this exclusionary model, the relative importance of micro-businesses continues to grow. The rest of the economy is unable to create good quality jobs, and the purchasing power of wages remains stagnant or in many cases is diminishing. In other words, microenterprises are not simply transitory elements within the model, entities condemned to disappear with economic growth. In reality, they are circumstantial mechanisms within a social structure of accumulation that produces more poverty among the majority and a greater spatial concentration of economic growth. In general, the past years have been accompanied by changes in labor relations, changes frequently characterized as "labor flexibility," but which imply, for example, the mutilating of labor contracts and, in general, a greater precariousness of new jobs. In contrast to what neoclassical economics affirms, these processes have not created a greater demand for labor power.

With the metamorphosis of the social role of the state, its activity is oriented to the creation of global conditions that would allow for the greater economic freedom of capital. It has therefore given up large parts of its social and redistributive activity. In this context, small businesses, operating as mechanisms of obtaining income for a large number of people over the past two decades, have, as indicated above, acted as "obstacles" to massive levels of open unemployment. Thus, microenterprises attenuate possible social conflicts that would flow from the absence of income, both for individuals and for families. On the other hand, the goods and services generated and distributed via the small-scale enterprises represent an alternative means of consumption for groups at the lowest income levels.

Seen from the vantage point of a new SSA, the present stage of capitalist development in Mexico is the initial part of a consolidated model of an open economy, in its neoliberal version. As we argue here, diverse institutions and institutional arrangements that took shape during the previous model of accumulation have been eliminated or transformed. Such transformations in institutions inherited from the past model of development have implied a worsening of the levels of social exclusion. Examples include the abandonment of many programs of assistance to the poorest rural sectors, the gradual destruction of the ejido, and the trade opening, all of which have implied a higher level of poverty in the Mexican countryside. It is a poverty that is reinforced by problems of access to the land, by absence of credits for poor campesinos, and by the growing necessity of migration (even temporarily) in order to obtain some monetary income.

In urban areas, social exclusion manifests itself in the growing importance of small-scale activities in the context of a constant reduction of stable, well-paying jobs. Facing growing poverty, we see a greater concentration of wealth and the squandering of public funds, which are now used to support the adventures of the owners of big businesses, principally those with ties to the financial sector. The privilege of some sectors to the detriment of the majority also leads to the deepening of differences of the levels of regional development, which expresses the social polarization of the country in a geographical context.

The current SSA is more exclusionary than the previous one, and microenterprises play an important role in expressing the realization that the social reproduction of a sector of workers who, excluded from employment in capitalist firms, have to look for other means of subsistence. Therefore, more than being an element that has to disappear with the passage of time and with economic development, micro-enterprises form an intrinsic part of the model that has been called "neoliberal."

For all the above reasons, it is evident that the neoliberal promise that the global benefits of the export sector of the economy will be eventually distributed throughout the economy cannot be kept. The current social structure of accumulation has not generated enough stable, well-paying jobs that would allow for a reasonably dignified retirement. Neither have the living conditions of the majority of Mexico's population improved.

References

Albelda, Randy and Chris, Tilly 1994. "Towards a broader vision: Race, gender and labor market segmentation in the social structure of accumulation." Pp. 212–30 in David Kotz et al. eds. *Social Structures of Accumulation: The Political Economy of Growth and Crisis*. New York: Cambridge University Press.

Altimir, Oscar 1983. "La distribución del ingreso en México, 1950–1977." Distribución del ingreso en México. Ensayos, Serie de Análisis Estructural. Banco de México, Cuaderno 2, tomo 1, México.

Aspe Armella, Pedro 1983. *El camino Mexicano de la Transformación Económica*. México: Fondo de Cultura Económica.

Babb, Sarah 2001. *Managing Mexico: Economists from Nationalism to Neoliberalism*. Princeton, NJ: Princeton University Press.

Banco de México 1960. *Informe Anual 1960*. México: Banco de México.

Blecker A. Robert 1996. *NAFTA, the Peso Crisis, and the Contradictions of the Mexican Economic Growth Strategy.* Working Paper No. 3. Center for Economic Policy Analysis. New School for Social Research.

Boltvinik, Julio and Enrique Hernández Laos 1981. "Origen de la crisis industrial: El agotamiento del modelo de sustitución de importaciones. Un análisis preliminar" in Cordera, Rolando (comp.) *Desarrollo y crisis de la economía mexicana*, Colección Lecturas del Trimestre Económico. No. 39. Fondo de Cultura Económica, Mexico.

Bortz, Jeffrey 1988. *Los salarios industriales en la Ciudad de México 1939–1975.* México: Fondo de Cultura Económica.

1990. "Política salarial en México. In James W. Wilkie and Jesús Reyes Heroles (cord.) *Industria y Trabajo en México.* Universidad Autónoma Metropolitana Azcapotzalco, México.

Bortz, Jeffrey and Marcos Aguila 2006. "Earning a Living: A History of Real Wage Studies in Twentieth-Century Mexico." *Latin American Research Review* 41, 2: 112–38.

Brothers, S. Dwight and Leopoldo Solís 1967. *Evolución financiera de México.* México: CEMLA.

Bustamante, Miguel Angel, Carlos Viesca, Federico Villaseñor, Alfredo Vargas, Roberto Castañon and Xochitl Mártinez 1982. *La salud pública en México. 1959–1982.* México: Secretaría de Salubridad y Asistencia.

Calva, José Luis 2000. *México más allá del neoliberalismo.* Mexico: Plaza y Janés.

Chávez, Marcos 2002. "El fracaso de las políticas de estabilización en México. Retos y opciones de política económica." In José Luis Calva ed. *Política Económica Para El Desarrollo Sostenido Con Equidad.* Casa Juan Pablos, Instituto de Investigaciones Económicas, UNAM: Mexico.

Coneval 2007. "Aplicación de la metodología para la medición de la pobreza y pruebas de hipótesis 2006." Nota Técnica 001/2007, Consejo Nacional de Evaluación del desarrollo de la Política Social, México.

Córdoba Montoya, José 1992. "La reforma económica de México." *Lecturas del Trimestre Económico* 73. México: Fondo de Cultura Económica.

Córdova, Arnaldo 1972. *La Formación Del Poder Político En México.* México: Ediciones Era.

1973. *La ideología de la Revolución Mexicana.* México: Ediciones Era.

1974. *La política de masas del Cardenismo.* México: Ediciones Era.

De la Garza, Enrique 2001. *La Formación Socioeconómica Neoliberal.* México: UAMI-Plaza and Valdés.

Dussel Peters, Enrique 1997. *La economía de la polarización.* Mexico: Jus-UNAM.

García, Brígida 1988. *Desarrollo Económico y Absorción de Fuerza de Trabajo en México, 1950–1980.* México: El Colegio de México.

García Cruz, Miguel, 1972. *La Seguridad Social en México, Tomo 1.* México: Costa Amic.

Hernández Laos, Enrique 1999. "Evolución de la distribución del ingreso de los hogares (1963–1989)." Pp. 154–90 In Boltvinik, J. and E. Hernández Laos. *Pobreza y distribución del ingreso en México.* México: Siglo XXI.

Houston, David 1992. "Is There a New Social Structure of Accumulation?" *Review of Radical Political Economics* 24, 2: 60–67.

INEGI 2003. *"Encuesta Nacional de Mirconegocios 2002."* Instituto Nacional de Estadística, Geografía e Informática (INEGI): México.

Kotz, David M. and Terrence McDonough 2009. "Global Neoliberalism and the Contemporary Social Structure of Accumulation." Chapter 3 in Terrence McDonough, Michael Reich and David M. Kotz eds. *Contemporary Capitalism and its Crises: Social Structure of Accumulation Theory for the 21st Century*. New York: Cambridge University Press.

Lustig, Nora 1998. *Mexico, the Remaking of an Economy*. Washington DC: Brookings Institution.

Mariña, Abelardo 2003. "Crisis estructural capitalista y globalización neoliberal: Una perspectiva desde México." Pp.139–56 in Ernesto Soto, Jaime Aboites and Etelberto Ortiz eds. *Estado versus mercado: Ruptura o nueva forma de regulación*. México: UAM-X/Porrúa.

——— 2007. *"Estimaciones de formación de capital y tasa de ganancia en México, 1921–2000."* Reporte de Investigación. Departamento de Economía, UAM Azcapotzalco, México.

Mariña, Abelardo and Fred Moseley 2000. "The Rate of Profit in the Postwar Mexican Economy, 1950–1993." Pp.134–92 in Ron Baiman, Heather Boushey and Dawn Saunders eds. *Political Economy and Contemporary Capitalism*. Armonk, NY: M.E. Sharpe.

McDonough, Terrence 2008. "Social Structures of Accumulation Theory: The State of the Art" *Review of Radical Political Economics* 40: 153–171.

Moreno-Brid, Carlos and Jaime Ros 2004. "México: Las reformas del estado desde una perspectiva histórica." Revista de la CEPAL 84, December: 35–57.

——— 2009. *Development and Growth in the Mexican Economy: A Historical Perspective*. New York: Oxford University Press.

Passel, Jeffrey 2005. *Estimates of the Size and Characteristics of the Undocumented Population*. Pew Hispanic Center. Washington D.C. March 21.

Pérez Rocha, Manuel 1983. *Educación y desarrollo: La ideología del estado mexicano*. México: Editorial Línea.

Pew Hispanic Center 2009. *Mexican Inmigrants in the United States, 2008.* Fact Sheet, Pew Resarch Center, Washington D.C. April 15.

Polaski, S. 2003. "Jobs, Wages, and Household Income." Pp.11–38 in J.J. Audley et al. eds. *NAFTA's Promise and Reality: Lessons from Mexico for the Hemisphere.* Washington, DC: Carnegie Endowment for International Peace.

Rendón, Teresa 1976. "Utilización de mano de obra en la agricultura mexicana, 1940–1973", *Demografía y Economía* 10, 3 El Colegio de México.

Rendón, Teresa and Carlos Salas 1987. "La evolución del empleo en México: 1895–1980. *Estudios Demográficos y Urbanos*, Vol II, no. 2; 189–230. Centro de Estudios Demográficos y Urbanos de El Colegio de México.

——— 1989. "La distribución del ingreso." Pp.219–24 in Agustín Herrera and Lorena San Martín (comps). *México a cincuenta años de la expropiación petrolera*. Mexico: Coordinación de Humanidades UNAM.

Rodríguez, Mauro 1994. "Los ciclos Kondratiev en la economía mexicana (1895–1992)." *Investigación Económica* 207, enero-marzo: 175–97.

Salas, Carlos 2003. "Trayectorias laborales entre el empleo, el desempleo y las microunidades en México." *Papeles de Población* 9, 38:159–94.

Salas, Carlos and Eduardo Zepeda 2003a. "Empleo y salarios en el México contemporáneo." In De la Garza, Enrique and Carlos Salas eds. *La situación del trabajo en México*. Plaza y Valdéz: México.

2003b. "Employment and Wages: Enduring the Cost of Liberalization and Economic Reform." Pp.522–60 in Kevin J. Middlebrook and Eduardo Zepeda eds. *Confronting Development: Assessing Mexico's Economic and Social Policy Challenges*. Stanford: Stanford University Press and UCSD Center for U.S.-Mexican Studies.

Salas, Carlos and George Callaghan 2004. "Labor and free trade: Mexico within Nafta." Pp.217–52 in Bromley, Simon, Maureen Mackintosh, William Brown and Marc Wuyts eds. *Making the International: Economic Interdependence and Political Order*. London: Pluto Press and Open University.

Schejtman, Alejandro 1981. *Economía campesina y agricultura empresarial, Tipología de productores del agro mexicano*. México: Siglo XXI.

Solís, Leopoldo 1981. *La realidad económica de México. Retrovisión y perspectivas*. Siglo XXI: Mexico.

Villarreal, René 2000. *Industrialización, deuda y desequilibrio interno en México, Un enfoque macroindustrial y financiero (1929–2000)*. México: Fondo de Cultura Económica.

THIRTEEN

Social Structure of Accumulation Theory for the Arab World: The Economies of Egypt, Jordan, and Kuwait in the Regional System

Karen Pfeifer

Applying SSA Analysis to the Arab World

The theory of social structures of accumulation (SSA) was developed to explain long swings of alternating expansion and stagnation in Western capitalist economies. The post-World War II SSA led by the United States entailed the projection of U.S. military power overseas, the allocation of U.S. foreign aid to allies and protégés, and the investment of U.S. surplus capital abroad. U.S. hegemony provided assurance of energy and raw material supplies and new arenas for the global spread of capitalist production, as well as the growth of markets for the United States and, increasingly, Western European and Japanese exports. Because many areas of the Arab region were rich in easily extractable sources of energy and conveniently located near Europe, controlling the region became an integral part of the U.S. economic and political strategy as it replaced shrinking British and French imperial power.

The importance of SSA analysis is double-barreled for understanding economies of the Arab World. First, the establishment and evolution of this "post-World War II SSA" led by the United States, and its evolving contradictions, constituted the international context within which the Arab territories attained political independence as new "nations" and undertook "modern" economic development. Second, the SSA conceptual apparatus can be used to examine the economic achievements and internal contradictions of the Arab countries and the institutions facilitating or impeding accumulation in each period of their postwar history.

The cases of Egypt, Jordan, and Kuwait illustrate the spectrum of variation within the regional SSA in both internal economic features and external relations.[1] Egypt represents the subgroup of more populated countries that have bigger agricultural sectors, a greater degree of industrialization, larger domestic markets, and more internal economic articulation than the other groups. Jordan represents a second subgroup with smaller populations, small agricultural sectors, small but significant industrialization, and greater dependence on the export of labor to generate national income. Kuwait represents a third subgroup, "rentier" economies defined by the export of oil and natural gas and very small agricultural and manufacturing sectors, which, with small populations of citizens and relatively high per capita incomes, are dependent on the import of goods, labor, and other services to be economically viable.

While the SSA approach was developed with an economy like that of the United States in mind, an industrialized capitalist country with a long history of internal articulation, a full analysis requires consideration of the United States' place in the international system. In parallel, both the internal and the external aspects are also important for analysis of the Arab economies, but the balance between the two is reversed. The Arab region has its own internal dynamics, but it does not have a long history of capitalist development in which internal articulation could have occurred. Furthermore, the region's proximity to and continuous interaction with Europe, and the conflicted place of the Arab countries in the U.S.-dominated international system, have pressed much more urgently on their internal economic policy and institutional structure than vice versa (Lockman 2004: chap.4).

There is an overarching regional SSA for the Arab World, with local national variations on its central institutions and with significant interaction among the countries that make up the region. Arabic language and culture, including music, food, cinema, and now media (e.g., Al Jazeera television network), continue to provide a strong identity to the native Arabic speakers of the region. They shared a pervasive sense of common history, of a civilization without national borders until the early twentieth century. "Arab nationalism" as an ideology of cultural and political unity arose in the late nineteenth century in the context of the decay of the Ottoman Empire and the spread of European economic power and direct political intervention. In the second half of the twentieth century, while Arabs came to be identified as citizens of distinct nation-states, many still viewed the borders as having been drawn either arbitrarily or

---

[1] See Pfeifer and Posusney (2003) and Richards and Waterbury (2008: chapter 2) for explanations of this method of categorization and dimensions of variation.

with deliberately divisive intent by the European powers and a handful of self-interested elites. The contradictory promises of the British and French mandatory powers regarding Arab self-rule, on the one hand, and a Zionist homeland in Palestine, on the other, culminating in the founding of an exclusionary Jewish state in 1948, were considered the final betrayal by those powers and their successor, the United States. Subsequent constant friction with Israel, the failure of the Western powers to provide justice or restitution to Palestinians, and regular Western political and military intervention in the region keep these polities continually off balance, and ironically reinforce the sense of cross-national Arab identity.

The economic dimensions embedded within this cultural-political framework are based on a set of common social assumptions and structures. Although it seemed in the 1950s that there were important differences between the Arab republics (e.g., Egypt after the abdication of King Farouk) and the monarchies such as Jordan and Kuwait, all three adopted formal constitutions that established parliamentary systems with elected representation and that defined the mutual obligations between state and citizen. Even the World Bank has come to realize, after many frustrated rounds of structural adjustment, that the distinctive features of the region cannot be so easily undone and replaced with neoliberal institutions. As one recent work puts it, the differences between the republics' "commitment to radical populism" and the monarchies' "paternalistic rationale for statism" tended over the decades since independence toward "a measure of convergence around an interventionist-redistributive form of social contract" (World Bank 2004: 23). This contract entails preferences for "redistribution and equity," for planning and for "states over markets in managing national economies," and visions for a large "role of the state in the provision of welfare and social services" and "of the political arena as an expression of the organic unity of the nation, rather than as a site of political contestation" (World Bank 2004: 25). The World Bank calls for a "new social contract" that respects regional culture and sensibilities, but uses this notion to promote the familiar neoliberal reform agenda, such as flexible labor markets and precisely targeted social welfare (World Bank 2004: chapter 7).[2]

---

[2] The author gave a lecture entitled, "Rethinking the Social Contract in the Middle East," at a symposium sponsored by The Middle East Institute in 1992 (National Press Club, Washington DC, Oct 16–17, 1992). The counter lecture was delivered by a representative of the World Bank, Caio Koch-Weiser, then director of the Middle East Division, who hewed to the narrow neoliberal line at the time and spoke vociferously against the idea of the "social contract."

In addition to these core features, intraregional economic relations are circumscribed by the proximity to Europe in trade, investment, and institutional structure, and by the global energy market as driver of economic cycles for both the energy-exporters and those countries that export labor to them. Economic integration comes, most importantly, from labor migration and other personnel transfer (tourism, family links, vacation residence), remittances from émigré labor, cross-national investment and aid and, to a lesser extent, intraregional trade. There is repeated and persistent interest by regional economists in *region-focused* development that resonates with citizens across national boundaries (e.g., Galal and Hoekman 2003). An important example is that the Arab League's proposal to Israel in 2002 for full recognition and a complete peace settlement with all Arab countries, in exchange for a two-state solution to the Israel/Palestine conflict along the lines of United Nations resolutions like 242, met with broad popular approval across the Arab World, for it would have meant not only a final resolution of the exhausting Palestine question, but also peace and prosperity for a more integrated region overall. Even the World Bank has come to recognize this powerful motivation and has taken it up as another tool for promoting *global* integration (World Bank 2003: chapters 1 and 7, 2008a).

Viewed in this light, our representative cases of Egypt, Jordan, and Kuwait entered their postwar SSA when British domination ended, and meaningful political independence was attained (Egypt 1952, Jordan 1948, Kuwait 1961). The economic exigencies of nation building propelled these countries toward some variant of "state-led development," entailing institutional changes like nationalization of natural resources, economic planning and infrastructure investment, import-substitution industrialization, agrarian transformation, and changes in enterprise and labor law. While the state occupied the commanding heights in investment, private capital played the role of a junior partner, participating in but not dominating the direction of economic growth and social change. This mode of development also required the cultivation of an educated middle class and skilled and unskilled working classes to fill the new occupations of an expanding "modern" economy, necessitating their incorporation into the political system in ways that would minimize class conflict.

The state-led pattern of growth contained two deep contradictions, internal and external, that grew more pressing and obvious as this SSA reached its limits in the 1980s. First, each regime in our sample was formally committed to representative government, but the concentration of economic power in the hands of the state and the myth that there are no class antagonisms fed into authoritarian political tendencies. Alongside "state-led development" and in exchange for their citizens' acquiescence in limitations on political freedom, there blossomed a social contract. The state promised public guarantees on the debt incurred by public and private enterprises, guarantees of employment for all high school and, later, college graduates, and universal welfare programs such as education, healthcare, housing, and subsidies for consumer necessities. While much progress was made in human development, fulfilling this social contract in terms of continuous growth of employment and income would become increasingly difficult by the late 1980s, leading to erosion of political quiescence.

Second, the growth that took place during the boom years was less internally generated than anticipated. Instead, it was more dependent on a number of external circumstances, such as high oil and phosphate prices in the world market, intercountry labor migration, and the concurrent availability of intraregional or international aid and credit. Most of these conditions would turn out to be unsustainable in the changing international economic climate of the 1980s.

Even as the Arab economies grew and developed in the 1960s and 1970s, a major structural crisis was brewing in the West that would undermine the regional boom. By the early 1980s, recessionary conditions in the west led to the decline of raw material prices on world markets, while the monetarist attack on inflation in Britain and the United States caused international credit to become increasingly scarce and much more expensive. By the late 1980s, the Arab countries' efforts to sustain economic growth and meet social contract obligations in these straitened international circumstances translated into rising government deficits, more international borrowing at higher cost, and the inevitable foreign exchange crises, as earnings from exports failed to keep pace with the cost of imports and debt service. Investment and productivity growth faltered, and aggregate economic growth slowed or even turned negative in some years.

Dependence on hydrocarbon-export revenues made this region more vulnerable to fluctuations in the global economy, not more independent as their leaders had promised, and the more dependent the country was on oil export revenues, the worse was the crisis (see Figure 13.1 for real GDP per capita growth 1975–2005). The costs of Dutch Disease[3] in the

---

[3] "Dutch Disease" was first recognized when The Netherlands experienced the cycle of rise and fall of oil prices and accompanying fluctuations of foreign exchange revenue from

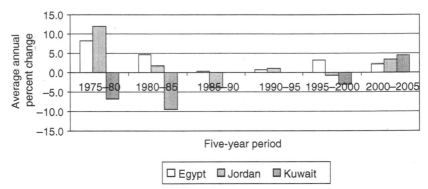

Figure 13.1. Growth of real GDP per capita: Egypt, Jordan, Kuwait, 1975–2005.
Source: Askari, 2006: 97, Table 6.7; World Bank 2008a: 143, Table A4.

region were generally high, as relatively cheap imports had discouraged productive domestic investment during the growth years. Subsequent stagnation in the standard of living for ordinary people and the slow growth of job opportunities, even as demographic, education, and health-care outcomes continued to improve through the 1980s, would feed into a deep political and social malaise and create particular alienation among a growing educated workforce queuing for a limited number of jobs in the public sector.

Disgruntlement with the inadequacies of state-led development grew, as did popular disgust with the intrusion of western culture along with western products into the region. But political expression of dissent became increasingly difficult as authoritarian governments repressed secular nationalist and socialist opposition movements. Led mainly by well-educated professionals, political opposition adopted the form of "Islamism," the legitimacy of which was harder for states to challenge.[4] This movement does not have much to do with the religion of Islam or

North Sea oil exports. International oil transactions are denominated in dollars. When oil prices are relatively high, the infusion of oil revenues tends to drive up the value of the local currency. This makes imports relatively cheap and undermines the competitiveness of nonoil exports, favoring a shift of investment out of agriculture and nonoil industry into other sectors. When oil prices fall and the infusion of foreign currency abates, a less-diversified economy then faces rising relative prices for imports and reduced capacity for domestic production and export of nonoil products.

[4] The Islamist movement's main significance as an economic ideology or program is through "Islamic banking," a form of "socially responsible" investment using noninterest bearing instruments. The instruments can be translated into traditional profit-making formulae, as demonstrated by the "Islamic banking" departments of international institutions such as Citicorp and HSBC.

Islamic civilization, which have been highly variable from place to place and time to time over their fourteen-century-long history. Islamism's contemporary importance is as a broad, variegated, and clearly modern political movement, most elements of which try peacefully and persistently to push their governments to become more inclusive and responsive to citizens' demands. In our cases as elsewhere in the region, the backing of the United States and European Union has facilitated the ruling regimes' ability to curb serious challenges to their authority by this and other forms of opposition. Such repression further fuels popular anger and, as with repressed opposition movements in other places and times in history, has led the more extreme groups to take up violence.

The Arab region's "developmental" experience over the post-World War II period not only reflects but also is dialectically interwoven with the long wave of growth and stagnation in the world economy and the subsequent turn to neoliberalism in the west. Whereas the U.S.-led postwar expansion of international trade initially stimulated growth throughout the periphery, with a time lag of about ten years, the subsequent stagflation of the OECD economies, particularly the United States, was then transmitted to the region through the mechanics of international commercial and official lending, again with a time lag of about ten years. Efforts to transplant the purported solution to stagflation, neoliberal ideology, and "supply-side" policy as embodied in Thatcher's and Reagan's programs in Britain and the United States, were conveyed to the region by the intervention of international financial institutions (IFIs). By the early 1990s, the International Monetary Fund's stabilization agreements and the World Bank's structural adjustment programs were being administered to poorer debtor countries, such as Egypt and Jordan, and to crisis-stricken oil exporters such as Kuwait. The enforced openings to foreign capital, promotion of nontraditional manufactured exports, and contraction of the government's role in the economy exacerbated internal contradictions and further undermined the social contract that was key to social peace in the Arab World.

Given this overarching scheme, this chapter examines the specific forms of institutional structure adopted in each of the three cases in the postwar SSA, including growth and accumulation, state/capital relations, capital/labor relations, and regional integration. It then considers the erosion of those structures in the 1980s, the cases' experience in adapting to, and resisting, the influence of neoliberalism after 1990, and the nature of the struggle to conceive a viable and sustainable SSA for this region in the context of the worldwide crisis of neoliberalism.

POSTINDEPENDENCE SSA: STATE-LED DEVELOPMENT

Egypt, Jordan, and Kuwait were defined as "nations" only in the twentieth century under the tutelage of the British, who supported a monarchy in each area as it was wrested from local and, more distantly, Ottoman control. Their self-identification as modern nation-states did not solidify until the post-World War II era of national liberation in the territories controlled by the British and other European empires.

The British-backed Egyptian monarchy was overthrown in a bloodless coup d'état in 1952, and between 1952 and 1954, when Gamal Abdul Nasser became president, a new form of republican Arab nationalism came to the fore. British military forces continued to occupy the crucial Canal Zone until 1956; when Nasser nationalized the Suez Canal to great popular acclaim in Egypt and across the Arab World, the British were compelled to withdraw entirely, and the "Arab socialist" movement was born.[5]

The seeds of Jordan's emergence as a nation were planted after World War I, when the British extended their mandate over Palestine, east of the Jordan River, to encompass what they called Transjordan, created a kingdom in a territory the size of Indiana, and appointed a monarch.[6] Nomadic pastoralists inhabited the eastern desert region, while settled agricultural villages and animal herding predominated in the rainfed northwest hill country. Commercial activity and other urban services were provided mainly by Palestinians, thanks to monopoly licenses meted out by the mandatory authority. Jordan changed dramatically after its military occupied the territory of eastern Jerusalem and the West Bank of Palestine in the war of 1948. Overnight, Jordan's population was tripled by its newfound control over one million Palestinians, half of whom were refugees from the new state of Israel, and its economy was quickly expanded and enlivened by the incorporation of the agricultural, small-industrial, and commercial life of that region of Palestine (Piro 1998: chapter 2).

Before the turn of the twentieth century, Kuwait had been a city-state with a distinct role in the regional economy as a hub for fishing, pearling

---

[5] With their allies France and Israel, Britain went to war with Egypt over this matter (the Suez War of 1956), but the military campaign was halted by the refusal of the United States to condone it, as the latter asserted its rising hegemony in the region.

[6] To give the monarchy legitimacy, the British agent chose the king from the Hashemite clan of Arabia, the presumed descendents of the Prophet, and appointed a brother from the same family to the monarchy it created in Iraq under its mandate there.

and trading, organized through its natural harbor in the northwestern cul-de-sac of the Arab/Persian Gulf.[7] But in the late nineteenth century, trade shifted to suit the needs of the expanding British empire. In 1898, the emirate (princedom) of Kuwait was created when a member of the leading shaikhly family, the Al-Sabahs, usurped power and secured his rule as Emir by signing a secret treaty with Britain giving Kuwait "protectorate" status in exchange for Britain's assuming control of its foreign affairs, "defending" its "national" borders vis-à-vis the Ottomans, and later taking first dibs on oil exploration (Pfeifer 2003).

Growth and Accumulation under the PostIndependence SSA

Egypt provides a clear and early example of the state-led development model, shaped by a series of efforts dating back to the mid-nineteenth century, when the ruling elite first initiated industrial development to contend with European incursions. But it was under Gamal Abdel Nasser in the 1950s and 1960s that a more thorough and planned program of infrastructure investment, agricultural transformation, and import-substitution industrialization was undertaken, including basic industries such as iron and steel as well as consumer goods such as processed foods, textiles, and automobile assembly. Complementary to this economic program, the government delivered increased access by ordinary people to education, health care, and other social services, as well as what were then considered revolutionary steps toward greater equality through land reform in the countryside and the growth of industrial jobs and organized labor in the cities (Pfeifer and Posusney 2003).

The economic centrality of the state grew and, as indicated in Figure 13.2, government expenditures rose to almost half of GDP while public capital expenditures rose to 20 percent of government spending (Askari 2006: 124). The construction of the Aswan High Dam was the lynchpin of the program, generating enough electricity to serve the entire country's consumption and production needs. The overall plan was to facilitate intensification of agriculture and raise productivity in cash crops, increasing rural income and saving, and thus, in the virtuous circle of agriculture-led development, enhancing resources for investment,

---

[7] This fascinating story is told well by Ismael 1993: chapters 1–4, and Crystal 1995: chapters 1–4.

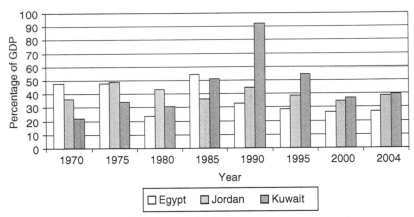

Figure 13.2. Central government expenditure as a percentage of GDP: Egypt, Jordan, Kuwait, 1970–2004.
Source: Askari 2006: 121, Table 7.2.

freeing labor to shift from agriculture to industry, and building the domestic market for growing domestic production.[8]

However, the vision of autonomy from the world market was a chimera. The new industries required the increased importation of capital equipment, technology, and other inputs in order to catch up quickly with modern production systems. In the early years, these imports were paid for mainly by Suez Canal dues and by the export of cotton and other agricultural products. In order to have the cotton to export and to have sufficient wheat and rice to feed the population, the bulk of these cash crops was requisitioned by a government agency at prices below those on the world market. The resale of the domestic portion helped to keep urban wages low, facilitating industrial growth, and the resale of the exported portions at world prices helped to bring in the foreign exchange needed to pay for essential imports. The closure of the Suez Canal between 1967 and 1975 put the agricultural sector under more pressure to supply the surplus for export earnings (Pfeifer and Posusney 2003).

Investment exceeded saving by a large margin every year from 1969 to 1989, just as imports exceeded exports (World Bank 1991: 229), but the economy thrived due to Egypt's key place in the region's economy and polity. The domestic "resource gap" was closed by inflows of hard currency from several sources, including oil exports, Arab aid and investment, U.S. aid linked to the 1979 peace treaty with Israel (half of

---

[8] A synopsis of this vision of bottom-up development is provided in Richards and Waterbury (2008: 28–29).

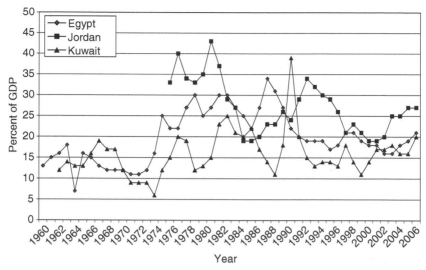

Figure 13.3. Gross fixed capital formation as a Percentage of GDP: Egypt, Jordan, Kuwait, 1960–2007.
Source: World Bank 2008c: World Development Indicators Online.

which was military aid), tolls from the reopened Suez Canal, renewed international tourism, and remittances from migrant workers, as well as the build-up of debt to foreign lenders. With the infusion of these resources, Egypt achieved record macroeconomic growth averaging 8.4 percent per year for 1974–85, while investment reached a historic high at 25 percent of GDP, as did total factor productivity growth, at 5 percent per year (Handy 1998: 5–8). Figure 13.3 indicates the surge in gross capital formation. Egypt also fared comparatively well in attracting foreign direct investment, ranking fourth among developing countries in total amount received during the 1981–90 period (World Bank 1991–92, v. 1: 25).

Jordan's defeat in the June War of 1967 enabled Israel to conquer and occupy the West Bank and all of Jerusalem. On one hand, this was a great loss to Jordan, and, at first, wildly disruptive. Another 300,000 Palestinian refugees from the occupied West Bank fled or were driven east to Jordan. Palestinians and their descendents, many of whom became citizens of Jordan, came to comprise more than 60 percent of the population, constituting both a burden and a boon to the Jordanian economy. The poorer and less educated among them wound up in refugee compounds (still extant in 2008) where education, healthcare, and social services were provided by a special United Nations agency (UNRWA). The

Jordanian system provided them with public goods such as transportation, the electricity grid, and higher education, and incorporated them into the economy (Piro 1998: chapter 2).

On the other hand, much of the Palestinian population was relatively well-educated and occupationally skilled, as compared to the eastern Jordanian population. Many were able to get work as skilled or professional labor, or to go into banking or government service, or to collect enough capital to restart their economic activity. Furthermore, Palestinians made up the bulk of the labor force that migrated to other Arab countries for work. This émigré labor became one of Jordan's main exports, and workers' remittances served as a mainstay of family income and a key source of foreign exchange as long as the economies of the Gulf grew (Pfeifer 2009).

Jordan's economy not only recovered but thrived as its economic fate became more tightly bound to that of its Arab neighbors. Real GDP per capita growth reached 15.8 percent per year from 1975 to 1980, and was still high at 5.2 percent per year from 1980 to 1985 before the regional crisis hit, while gross fixed investment rose to over one-third of GDP, as shown in Figure 13.3. Unemployment reached a record low of 1.6 percent in 1976. Foreign grants, mainly used for investment in public goods, were critical to long-term growth. Grants from the Arab oil states approximated 12 percent of GDP from 1975 to 1988, with debt finance running second at 10 percent of GDP (Maciejewski and Mansur 1996: 14, 16–17, 21).

As in Egypt, the Jordanian government poured public capital into physical infrastructure and the "heavy industry" involved in extraction, processing, and export of Jordan's only known natural resources, its phosphates, potash, and other minerals. It also channeled investment into small-scale manufacturing and commercial agriculture, the burgeoning system of universal public education, and near-universal access to health care. Commercial agriculture grew quickly with the use of greenhouse and drip irrigation technologies to cultivate nontraditional fruits, vegetables, and flowers, and with the development of dairy and poultry farming. An important part of the manufacturing sector was composed of factories processing these goods for export to the region as well as for the domestic market. Tourism became another developing "industry" built on natural, historical, and cultural resources (Piro 1998: chapter 3; Pfeifer 2000).

Kuwait's comparative advantage was transformed by the discovery of oil and the beginnings of its extraction by foreign oil companies during the 1930s, thrusting it into the global economy on entirely new terms.

The Kuwaiti economy then developed with the oil industry at its core and thrived under the U.S.-led post-World War II expansion. By the 1950s, it had become a rentier state, with the bulk of government revenues and more than half of GDP accounted for by royalties ("rents") paid by oil companies for the right to extract oil from Kuwaiti territory. In 1980, 71 percent of GDP originated in the oil sector, of which 68 percentage points were from crude oil (EFB 1983, 5: 6). In 1983, the GDP per capita of Kuwaiti citizens was $20,300 in current dollars, in the same league as the United States and West European countries. Even the per capita income of all residents of Kuwait (citizens and expatriates) was $12,646, in the middle-income range of the world's economies (EFB 1985, 8: 6; EIUc 1991–92: 10).

The oil wealth generated unprecedented funds for both domestic and international investment. Kuwait was the first Gulf country to take full control of its petroleum industry in the 1970s, paying £32 million to compensate Gulf Oil and the British Petroleum company (Day et al. 2007). In the 1970s, the savings rate rose to 50 percent of GDP, and investment and consumption, both public and private, soared. An index of gross fixed capital formation rose by a factor of 4.5 between 1970 and 1983, to more than 20 percent of GDP (Al-Yousuf 1990: 72, and see also Figure 13.3). As in Egypt and Jordan, the Kuwaiti government invested heavily in modern infrastructure, in equipping its own national companies with the technology to extract and refine oil, and in universal education, healthcare, and welfare systems. In the boom years, these were extended to the large populations of émigré workers and, in the case of the Palestinian community, to their families as well. In addition, the Kuwaiti government set up the Kuwait Fund for Arab Economic Development (KFAED), and cosponsored the Arab Fund for Economic and Social Development, both lending for development and giving foreign aid to poor countries in the Arab World, Africa, and southern Asia.

State-Capital Relations under the PostIndependence SSA

In the first two decades after Nasser came to power in Egypt, private capital was subordinated to the state and confined to the interstices among public sector enterprises. However, the two wars with Israel in 1967 and 1973 were a great strain on the economy, and the new regime of Anwar Sadat undertook to adjust to this reality with an opening to international capital. Just as Egypt had been a pioneer in state-led development in the

1950s and 1960s, so did the announcement of the new Egyptian "open door" economic policy (*infitah*) in 1974 mark the first acknowledgement of the state-led model's contradictions. But the effort to curry favor with foreign capital was made without giving up the core role of the state and without major structural change in the Egyptian economy. The state economic enterprises, social contract with labor, and other promises of the Nasser era were left intact, and queues began to form for public sector jobs even as the growth of the public sector slowed (Richards 1991).

While a private domestic capitalist class remained in the shadow of the state, the *infitah* helped to create a new wealthy comprador class, serving as the local agents for import/export companies and as representatives and junior partners of foreign capital. The United States became Egypt's largest trading partner, source of foreign investment, and aid donor. One indication of the growing wealth of the comprador class and of the magnitude of remittances from émigré labor was the sudden materialization of previously unrecorded savings that had apparently long been stashed away outside of the state-regulated banking system, in the form of deposits in the hot new "Islamic" investment companies that mushroomed in this era. On the basis of the surprisingly large quantity of these savings, an Egyptian economist constructed an estimate that actual gross national product might be up to twice its officially measured size (Oweiss 1990: chapter 1).

In Jordan, the state took the lead in the growing economy, but was less involved in direct production than in Egypt, leaving more space to patronize and cultivate the entrepreneurial class and to encourage its expansion into productive investment. Under the British Mandate, the small Transjordanian economy had been linked to that of Palestine through a merchant class that cooperated with the British and supported the king both financially and politically. After independence in 1948, most of this elite moved to Amman and served to integrate the economies of the East and West Banks more tightly. This class and the market it served were widened and deepened by the two waves of Palestinian refugees that entered Jordan, in 1948 and 1967, but retained its dependence on the monarchy for patronage (Moore 2000: 185).

The state organized investment in the core of the economy and let the private capitalist system grow up around it. In the first stage in the 1960s, the independent central bank was created, which served actively in its first two decades to direct capital flow in the economy, but otherwise left the banks alone to be "privately owned, prudently run, and profitable" (ERF and Femise Coordinators 2005: 49). The Social

Security Corporation was established and assigned the role of passive portfolio investor to maximize returns to the pension fund system for private employees. In the second stage in the 1970s, the financial system was deepened by the addition of two more institutions: the Amman Financial Market (AFM), which became one of the most sophisticated stock markets in the region, and the Jordan Investment Corporation (JIC), which was established to invest in growth assets to fund civil service pensions. The JIC created state economic enterprises (SEEs) to develop core industries in mining, electricity, water, transportation and communication, airlines, ports and railroads, and public sector companies (PSCs) to process commodities such as oil, phosphates, and potash. The PSCs then issued shares for private purchase on the AFM (Kanaan 2001: 190–92).

The private sector thrived during the expansion of the 1970s and Jordan's per capita income rose at 12 percent per year from 1975 to 1980 (Askari 2006: 97). Increased exports of goods and of labor to the booming Gulf States and Saudi Arabia brought in surges of revenue that fed domestic demand for housing, services, and locally made consumer goods, and Amman became more important as a regional commercial and banking center as Beirut went into eclipse during the Lebanese civil war of the 1970s and 1980s. Furthermore, the oil-rich countries undertook programs of generous aid to the "frontline states" such as Jordan for major infrastructure projects.

Prior to the advent of the oil era, Kuwait's ruling family, the Al-Sabahs, had been considered "a first among equals" by the other elite merchant families whose ancestors had settled in the area, such heritage being the defining feature of legal citizenship. Oil revenue, however, elevated the ruling family's political status by allowing it to become financially independent of its merchant-elite citizens. In exchange for political acquiescence, the rulers created a patronage system that guaranteed the privileged economic status of their clients, the merchants, by supporting them directly and preserving a residual vitality for the now-truncated private-sector economy. For example, the government essentially gave away the rights to undeveloped land that would become very valuable in the soon-to-be-built modern and expanded Kuwait City, and made generous subsidies available to start new types of small scale private business in the real estate, commercial, import/export, and even agricultural sectors (Pfeifer 2003).

Given Kuwait's relatively small absorptive capacity, the government used surplus oil revenues to fund overseas investment, foreign aid, and international loans. In 1953, the Kuwaiti finance ministry set up The General Reserve Fund (the original "sovereign wealth fund") to be administered by the Kuwait Investment Office in London to generate a second source of rentier income. Another mainly international portfolio was created in 1976, the unique Reserve Fund for Future Generations. These funds purchased shares in large Western companies. As of 1990, the two funds together were estimated to be worth $100 billion, yielding average annual returns of five percent (Day et al. 2007). From 1980 on, annual gross national income was between 15 and 20 percent greater than gross domestic product (Pfeifer 2003, Figure 1).

Capital/Labor Relations under the PostIndependence SSA

Virtually all countries in the Arab region underwent a profound transformation in the class structure as they developed in the postindependence era. In Egypt, Jordan, and Kuwait, part of the national economic project entailed creation of a parliamentary system with regular contested elections, and, in the case of Egypt, elections for the head of state. It also entailed recognizing the contributions of the working classes to the country's development and compensating workers, at least in the large productive organizations (50+ employees), with regular wage increases, pension and health benefits, and, in the case of Egypt, profit-sharing. These were supplemented with universal subsidies for basic necessities and low-cost housing and guarantees of employment in the public sector to those with high school or college diplomas. Formation of unions was legal, but they were closely supervised by the government, with "elected" leaders accountable more to the state than to the rank and file and, in Egypt, no right to strike (Posusney 1997).

Strikes took place in Egypt anyway, under the leadership of rank-and-file activists, in spite of the police repression that intensified during the 1980s crisis years under the Mubarak regime. These actions were sometimes quite militant and political in their challenge to management and to the government (Posusney 1997). Such movements, especially when allied with political parties or organizations, had some impact on government policy and put constraints on the freedom of capitalists and landlords to ignore workers' rights under the state-led import-substitution regime and the subsequent opening to foreign capital. The political left (in various forms) helped lead or joined these movements, but was either repressed (parties made illegal, newspapers closed) or co-opted by the state with its close control over formal leadership of the unions, effectively preventing the organization of an enduring structure of opposition (Beinin 2002).

Effective organizing of labor was also undermined by the structural fragmentation of the working classes. The combination of rural-urban migration, rising levels of unemployment and underemployment, the growth of the informal sector, and opportunities for labor migration fractured the potential unity of workers' organizations and "weakened the position of working people in the coalitions that supported authoritarian-populist regimes pursuing state-led ISI" (Beinin 2002: 117). About 3.5 million Egyptians, including professional, skilled, and unskilled workers and peasants, migrated for some period during the 1973–85 boom to the oil-exporting countries, especially Libya, Saudi Arabia, and Iraq. This relieved a potentially explosive unemployment crisis in the 1980s and raised the standard of consumption and saving. Figure 13.4 shows the magnitude of remittances. As Beinin put it,

In Egypt, transfers of migrant workers constituted the single largest source of foreign exchange, amounting to 12 percent of the gross domestic product in the mid-1980s. By 1988, at least 20 percent of the labor force [had] worked abroad [at some time], and annual official transfers of migrant workers reached about $3.2 billion; unofficial transfers were estimated at [an additional] $2 billion to $4 billion (Beinin 2002: 117).

Jordan has long been called a "liberal monarchy" because the regime usually allowed some diversity of representation in its elected parliament. However, the monarch could dismiss parliament at will, ignore the laws it passed and make policy by decree. Indeed the king banned all political parties from 1957 to 1992, preventing trade unions and other

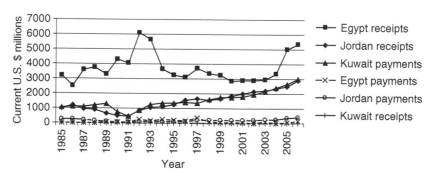

Figure 13.4. Remittances, Egypt, Jordan, Kuwait, 1985–2005.
Source: UNCTAD Online 2009, http://stats.unctad.org/Handbook/TableViewer/tableView.aspx

civil society groups from building explicit political affiliations or external support (Carroll 2003: 271–73).

In the context of state-led development, trade unions were legally recognized, and, as in Egypt, Jordan's workers were considered part of the nation-building coalition, and were granted legal protections against job loss. Temporary work contracts automatically became permanent when they were renewed. Workers could appeal arbitrary firing and delay it for a long time while the appeal was considered by a government-appointed labor board. Firms were required to give advance warning of possible mass layoffs, which the government could abnegate, no matter what the firm's profit or loss situation. However, the trade-off for these privileges in the formal sector was that unions were subject to government interference in their internal affairs, their top officers were tightly tied to the regime, and the right to strike was strictly constrained (Posusney 2007).

The definition of the working classes in Jordan became more complicated in the era of strong economic growth, as Jordan became both an exporter and an importer of labor. While educated Jordanians left to work in the Gulf, the lower tiers of the economy were filled by agricultural, manufacturing, and service workers from poorer Arab countries such as Egypt and, increasingly, poorer regions such as South Asia. This too made it difficult for labor to achieve long-term unified organizing and political coherence vis-à-vis the state and private employers.

Kuwait's history as a long-lived city-state prior to the advent of oil led to a unique postindependence political structure. A constitutional monarchy with a formal commitment to the separation of executive, legislative, and judicial powers, its legitimacy has no connection with religion, and there is little influence of *shariah* on contemporary law. Although the Emir can suspend the constitution and shut down the National Assembly, there is a lively political culture, with vigorous debates among elected members of a variety of political persuasions, such as Arab nationalists and Islamists of various stripes, in parliament and at the *diwaniyya*, evening gatherings at the homes of political notables where the issues of the day are freely discussed. The press too can be shut down by the Emir, but it is privately owned and competitive and has often been critical of the regime. For labor, this relative liberality meant that Kuwait was the only monarchy in the Gulf that allowed unions and that tolerated, and even supported, political organizing among Palestinians. For example, the Kuwaiti Teachers' Federation often backed the relatively militant (and mostly female) Palestinian Teachers' Federation (Pfeifer 2009).

While Kuwaiti/Palestinian solidarity was tolerated, there was little of the social and political integration among workers of various backgrounds that would have made long-term, coherent organizing possible. Kuwaiti society was strictly stratified into endogamous layers, both among Kuwaitis themselves and, separately, among the expatriate communities, layered each in turn by longevity of residence and their contributions to building the modern Kuwaiti economy, with Palestinians the best established, largest, and economically most significant community (Pfeifer 2003).[9]

The population of Kuwait more than doubled between 1975 and 1990, from 995,000 to 2,130,000. In the first decade, growth came disproportionately from the resident expatriates, whose share of total population rose from 52.5 percent in 1974 to a peak of 72.3 percent in 1985, up to 500,000 of whom were Palestinians. The non-Kuwaiti component of the labor force grew from 70 percent in 1975 to a peak of 85 percent in 1990. However, in the mid-1980s, a new nationalistic policy was adopted, promoting the "Kuwaitization" of employment at least at the professional and technical levels, and making it more difficult for expatriate workers to remain in Kuwait for long periods or for their families to accompany them.[10] By 1990, prior to any hint of invasion by Iraq, the balance had been shifted consciously so that the higher-paid, more politically nettlesome Arabs were reduced to less than 50 percent of the expatriate labor force, and the majority came to be made up instead of South Asians (Pfeifer 2003).

Human Development, Income Distribution, and Poverty

The three countries, like the Arab region in general, showed significant improvement in human development, including female development, over the whole period from independence to 2005 (see Figure 13.5 for the Human Development Index, 1975–2005). In education, for example, Egypt began from a very low base, with an illiteracy rate over 70 percent in 1966. Its Human Development Index rose 27 points from 1975 to 2005, one of the biggest increases in the world over that 30-year period, ending with an illiteracy rate of 29 percent. Jordan's HDI rose by about 12 points from 1980 to 2005, ending at a value of 77 (rank 86), leaving Jordan "more developed

---

[9] The story of the work and lives of Palestinians in Kuwait is documented in Ghabra 1987, especially pp. 39–52.

[10] The policy targeted the Arab community in general, and Palestinians in particular, who were the only group that lived in families in well-established communities.

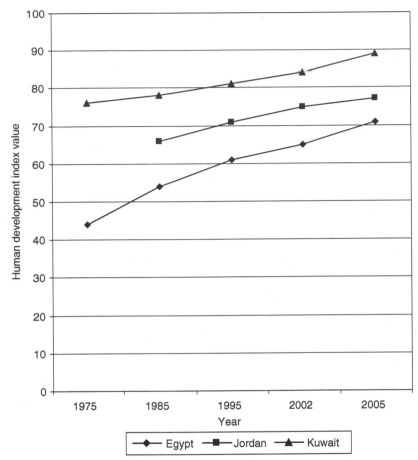

Figure 13.5. Human development index, Egypt, Jordan, Kuwait, 1975–2005.
Source: Askari 2006: 63, Table 5.6; United Nations Development Program 2007/2008.

than rich," in that its HDI rank exceeded its 2005 GDP rank by 11 points. Jordan's education system is one of the best in the region, yielding a literacy rate of 100 percent for women aged 15–24 in 2002. Kuwait's HDI rose 13 points from 1975 to 2005, ending at 89 (rank 33), but with the caveat that it was still "richer than developed," in so far as its GDP per capita rank in 2005 was higher than its HDI rank by 12 points. One of Kuwait's biggest achievements was to bring girls' school enrollment up to and beyond par with that of boys (United Nations Development Program 2007/08).

The Arab region had lower levels of inequality than most other regions of the developing world such as Latin America, South Asia, and

Africa, and lower rates of abject poverty than countries of comparable income levels. While state income tax systems were poorly developed or enforced, revenues from public-sector exports, taxes on services such as tourism, and tariffs on imports were important sources of public funding for common services. Relative equity in consumption was promoted by public sector subsidies on commodities and wage and benefit policies, as well as by well-resourced Islamic and other private charitable institutions that help to provide healthcare, education, and welfare services to the poorer parts of the population.[11]

The crisis years of the later 1980s and early 1990s were a period of rising income poverty for both Egypt and Jordan, and of falling average income for Kuwait as a whole, but the situation improved in the later 1990s as economic growth resumed (World Bank 2006: Table A1). As of 2000–02, Jordan's GINI index for consumption was 0.39 and Egypt's 0.34 (World Bank 2006: Table A2). In 2005, Egypt's and Jordan's Human Poverty Index (HPI-1) values of 20 and 6.9, respectively, and their ranks (61 and 11) were significantly better than their HDI and GDP per capita ranks (United Nations Development Program 2007/08).

Economic Relations within the Regional SSA

Economic relations among Arab countries entailed direct budgetary transfers, long-term low-interest development loans, private investment, trade, and the migration of labor.

Direct Aid. Outright budgetary support was provided by the Arab oil exporters to the "confrontation states" to sustain them and compensate them in the conflict with Israel. From 1963 to 1966, Egypt received $234.5 million in government-to-government transfers, including a grant from KFAED of $27.5 million to widen and deepen the Suez Canal. Between the 1967 war and the Camp David Accords in 1978 (after which Egypt made peace with Israel and was subjected to an Arab League boycott), Egypt received up to $17 billion in aid from Arab oil exporters, including $162 million from Kuwait alone between 1967 and 1970 (Feiler

---

[11] We have no data for Kuwait for either income distribution or poverty. It is well known, however, that there is dramatic inequality between Kuwaiti citizens and permanent residents, on the one hand, and the bulk of immigrant workers, on the other hand, in terms of *income* from work, investment, and government largesse. However, *consumption* is much more equitably distributed insofar as any resident may shop for a broad array of commodities in the "cooperative" grocery stores and buy gasoline and other petroleum-derived products at government-owned gas stations, all at subsidized prices.

2003: 40). From 1973 to 1988, Jordan received an average of 43 percent of government revenue from external aid and loans, with a high of 53.4 percent in 1980 at the peak of the oil boom (Brand 1994, Table 1: 44–45). As one of the most generous donors, Kuwait was motivated by more than altruism, in so far as "… the substantial Kuwaiti aid payments to Jordan were in large part aimed at reinforcing the security and military apparatus of a politically like-minded and supportive state" (Brand 1994: 123).

Development Aid, Loans, and Investment. Oil export revenues were used for development by both the oil exporters and poorer Arab nations, through the region-based recycling of petrodollars. Figure 13.3 shows similar trajectories for gross capital formation in Egypt and Jordan from 1960 to 1975, and in Egypt, Jordan, and Kuwait from 1975 to 1987.

Total Arab investment in Egypt through 1985 was $4.55 billion, $2 billion of which was deposited directly into the Central Bank for public sector investment, with the remainder designated for project-specific development aid and private for-profit enterprise (Feiler 2003: 93). From 1962 to 1989, the length of the postindependence SSA and its erosion, Jordan received $401 million in development loans from the Arab oil exporters and $2.154 billion in cash contributions for various projects (Brand 1994: 149). Kuwait's contributions to total loans to Jordan rose throughout the 1960s and 1970s to a peak of 6 percent in 1983. Most of these funds went into infrastructure projects, such as the phosphate, potash and fertilizer industries, thermal power, BirZeit University in Ramallah, West Bank municipal services, the port at Aqaba, the Amman water system, and the Jordan Valley Authority, including agricultural irrigation (Brand 1994, Tables 1 and 11: 44–45 and 130).

Private investment from Kuwait to Jordan mainly took the form of joint ventures but accounted for only a few percentage points of Kuwait's overseas investments (Brand 1994: 143, 147). These ventures focused on real estate, including both housing and agricultural land development, commerce, tourism, bus transportation services, and food production such as dairy, poultry, and fishing. Manufacturing investment was focused on processed foods, fodder, and fertilizer, mainly for export to the region.

Trade. Jordan's relations with Egypt were cool until the common experience of the 1967 war losses brought them closer. After 1970, Jordan sought to expand exports to Egypt's growing domestic market, in order "to overcome some of the diseconomies of scale that had hindered Jordanian attempts at domestic commercial and industrial expansion," and to enhance its regional political security through economic links (Brand 1994: 243). However, Jordan's imports from Egypt averaged only

2 percent of all imports in the 1970s, while exports to Egypt averaged about 3 percent of all exports, with Jordan running a consistent trade deficit with Egypt. While Jordan purchased less than 2 percent of total imports from Kuwait, for example, 1.7 percent in 1973, its exports to Kuwait were significant, for example, 11 percent of all exports in 1973, and Jordan maintained a trade surplus with Kuwait throughout the 1970s (Brand 1994, Tables 7 and 8: 78–79).

Jordan was the first Arab country overtly to break the embargo on Egypt in 1983, in order to facilitate Egypt's material support of Iraq in the Iran-Iraq war and to help Jordan's private sector replace shrinking Iraqi markets with Egyptian customers. Many joint ventures were discussed but only two significant projects were realized, the Aqaba-Nuwaybi line in 1975, for maritime shipping between the Suez Canal and Jordan's Red Sea port, and a joint development bank in 1984, with branches in both countries (Brand 1994: 243–44, 248–49, 255–56).

Émigré Labor and Remittances. At the zenith in 1982–83, about 23 percent of the Egyptian labor force, or 2.9 million workers, were employed abroad. Their remittances amounted to $3.98 billion in 1984, with a cumulative total for the 1974–84 period of $22 billion (Feiler 2003: 100, 111, 116), more than ten times the value of Kuwait's direct investment in Egypt around the same time. Egyptian labor played an important role in Kuwait, ranging from 150,000 workers in 1978 to 200,000 in 1982–83, and in Iraq during the eight-year-long Iran-Iraq war, involving a total of up to 1.25 million, mainly farm, laborers (Feiler 2003: 101, 244).

Jordan sent many professionals, teachers, and military advisers to Kuwait, and Kuwait sent its own students to Jordan to be trained as teachers and military officers. There were at least 350,000 Jordanian émigrés (mostly of Palestinian origin) in Kuwait in 1985 (Brand 1994: 134). During the same era, and despite the embargo on Egypt, Egyptian labor continued to work in Jordan, mainly in agriculture and construction. As of 1987, there were 250,000 Egyptian workers in Jordan, a number that then declined with the economic crisis of 1988–89 (Brand 1994: 264–65). As shown in Figure 13.4, at their first peak in 1986, Jordan's receipts of remittances reached almost $1.2 billion and Jordan's payments of remittances reached $247 million.

EROSION OF THE STATE-LED SSA AND THE ADVENT OF NEOLIBERALISM

By the mid-1980s, as oil prices and oil revenues declined, the internal contradictions of state-led development and the region's dependence on oil revenues and labor remittances came together to generate a crisis. The core symptom was the failure to sustain productivity growth. An exercise in growth accounting showed that "the MENA region as a whole has experienced the lowest contribution of total factor productivity to economic growth in comparison with the rest of the [world's] regions," and that TFP's contribution to growth was actually negative on average over the whole of the 1960–97 period (Makdisi et al. 2007: 48). Similarly, average per-worker real GDP growth rates for Egypt fell from 6.49 in the 1975–84 decade to 0.78 in the 1985–94 decade, and Jordan's fell from 8.24 percent to minus 3.13 percent, while Kuwait's were negative for the whole of the 1965–2004 period (Esfahani 2007: 63). The main difference in severity among these results seems to be due to the degree of dependence on capital-intensive oil extraction or employment in the Gulf as the basis of economic growth.

In Egypt's case, four core internal contradictions came to the surface. First, instead of following through on the promise of agricultural led ("bottom up") growth based on the land reform and Aswan High Dam that would have enabled peasants' income and saving to rise, the state turned to paying very low, controlled prices for requisitioned crops such as cotton, in order to sell them for higher prices on the world market. Peasants shifted to producing uncontrolled crops, the most famous being *berseem*, a kind of clover fed to cattle, in response to rising urban demand for meat. As Egypt became a net importer of food grains and import costs rose, this tactic for increasing foreign exchange was self-thwarting. Second, the state's industrialization strategy relied on importing western technology wholesale in large chunks of capital-intensive investment. This caused early growth to be based on additions to capital and labor, without much technological innovation or long-term expansion in the demand for industrial labor. The combination of the first and second factors led to rapid rural-urban migration and emergence of a growing informal sector.

Furthermore, in contrast to the East Asian model – Egypt is often compared unflatteringly to South Korea – ISI protection for domestic industry was allowed to go on for too long, with little expectation that these firms would "pay back" the support with innovation that would make their products more competitive in world markets and earn their own share of foreign exchange. And, finally, the promise of jobs in the public sector for all graduates, and the job protections that formal sector labor had won as part of the state-led social compact, led to overstaffing, wasted time and resources, and declines in real compensation as inflation overtook nominal wage growth.

Consequently, Egypt's GDP growth, national saving, and public spending all plummeted in the later 1980s. Real per capita GDP growth fell from 4.7 percent per year during the 1980–85 period to 0.3 percent per year from 1985 to 1990 (Askari 2006: 97). Domestic saving seemed to evaporate overnight with the collapse of several pseudo "Islamic" investment companies that ran Ponzi schemes with the investors' purchases of shares, undermining confidence in the private sector. At the same time shortages of foreign currency to finance imports of industrial inputs and food fueled the debt crisis that struck Egypt as elsewhere in the Third World. External debt rose to more than 100 percent of GDP in 1985. By 1990 the government had cut wages in the public sector, and real wages in manufacturing had fallen below their 1970s levels. Unemployment and poverty rose, even as the government cut subsidies on necessities such as bread and fuel (Beinin 2002: 129–30).

This combination of internal crisis and the new reality of declining oil revenues and remittances made the Egyptian state more vulnerable to pressure from the importers and financiers who had flourished under the *infitah* since 1974 and also more susceptible to pressure from the Bretton Woods institutions. Prior to 1990, the Washington Consensus had not been making headway in Egypt due to resistance from organized labor and the possibility of escape for émigré workers. However, "cancellation of nearly half of Egypt's $55 billion foreign debt in return for participating in the U.S.-led coalition against Iraq in the (1991) Gulf War opened the way to concluding a successful agreement with the IMF and gave the regime sufficient political capital to begin the long-delayed privatization of public-sector enterprises" (Beinin 2002: 116–17).

During the same time period, Jordan experienced two major shocks that left its economy in disarray. First, the oil price declines of 1983 and 1986–88 sent the oil-exporting economies into recession. That led them to reduce their demand for émigré labor, curb their imports of Jordanian products, and cut their foreign aid. Unemployment rose to 10 percent in 1988 and by 1990 manufacturing wages here, as in Egypt, had fallen to levels below that of the early 1970s (Beinin 2002: 129–30). In 1989, Jordan experienced its first massive bread riots as the government cut subsidies. Real GDP per capita fell by 3.9 percent per year from 1985 to 1990 and debt rose to more than 200 percent of GDP in 1990 (Askari 2006: 97, 166). As foreign exchange reserves fell precipitously, Jordan reached the limits of its ability to borrow on the international markets, and the dinar had to be devalued by 60 percent, severely curbing the country's ability to import the final and intermediate goods it did not produce itself.

The second major shock came with the Gulf crisis of 1990–91. Jordan's trade with Iraq, its major trading partner, fell by half as war and then economic sanctions took effect. Furthermore, the Gulf country allies halted their aid to and trade with Jordan in retaliation for its neutrality and expelled large numbers of expatriate workers, especially Palestinians, many of whom had nowhere to go but Jordan. Thus remittances plunged at the same time that the domestic labor force suddenly bulged with an additional 60,000 to 70,000 workers, half of whom were unemployed in 1991. The unemployment rate for 1991 is variously estimated to have risen to between 14.4 and 25 percent. Real GDP per capita grew by less than one percent per year from 1990 to 1995 (Askari 2006: 97) and, while the number of registered private enterprises had grown from 1,990 to 4,349 between 1987 and 1992 (Kanaan 2001: 192), the capitalist class was weak and demoralized and did not take up the chance to assert its interests more strongly vis-a-vis the state (Moore 2000: 185–91).

Like Jordan, Kuwait experienced several sharp reversals in the 1980s. The world-wide recessions of 1980–82, the shift toward alternative fuels and conservation in the oil-consuming countries, and the entry of more non-OPEC suppliers into the oil market all contributed to a fall in the demand for OPEC oil and falling prices. Kuwait's "real" oil revenues (nominal revenues deflated by an import price index) were 13 percent lower in 1982 than their 1974 value. Oil prices fell again in 1986 and in 1988, and Kuwait's oil revenues plunged once more, to 58 percent of their 1974 value (Al-Yousuf 1990: 6–8). Economic growth then plummeted, with real GDP per capita falling by 9.4 percent per year from 1985 to 1990. As Figure 13.3 shows, by 1990 gross capital formation had slipped to about 11 percent of GDP. Gross domestic saving was a tiny 4 percent of GDP, while, in contrast, gross national saving was 17 percent, indicating that capital was being held abroad rather than invested inside the country (Askari 2006: 97, 100, 110).

The sense of demoralization in Kuwait was underpinned by the failure of the nonoil commodity sectors to grow rapidly. Excluding petroleum refining and a few essentially European "model firms," real value added per worker fell from KD 2,836 in 1976 to KD 2,312 in 1984 (Al-Sabah 1988: 26). This poor performance was due partly to the Dutch Disease real-sector hangover from the oil boom years. It was also due to the financial-sector problems based on the Souk al-Manakh stock market crash of 1982 and subsequent liquidity crises, which undermined confidence in real private investment in the domestic economy, even though the government stepped in to buy up both stocks and bank shares at much-higher-than-market prices (Looney 1992).

Planners and consulting economists repeatedly proposed reform programs intended to tackle Kuwait's "structural problems" and reduce its dependence on both oil revenues and expatriate workers. The key idea was to shift resources to favor productivity-enhancing, "high value-added" ventures at home and abroad, such as financial service, industrial-design, and engineering, to be organized and managed by well-educated and highly skilled Kuwaitis (Al-Sabah 1988), to encourage private entrepreneurial activity and to move the economy toward a more East Asian model of development.[12] Instead, Kuwait intensified its pursuit of the old, familiar course that had brought it wealth and success in the 1960s and 1970s. In violation of its OPEC quota, and in competition with other OPEC members similarly seeking to cheat on their agreement, Kuwait stepped up oil production, from June of 1989 until the disastrous invasion by Iraq in August 1990 (EIUc 1991–92: 13), and replaced the expatriate labor force with a less expensive one after the restoration in 1991. See Figure 13.4 for the sharp dip in remittances received by Jordan and remittances paid out by Kuwait from 1988 to 1991.

Disintegration and Reconstruction of Regional Economic Relations, 1985–2000

The crisis years of the later 1980s and the Gulf War of 1991 entailed radical changes in the structure of intraregional economic links. When links were reconstructed in the 1990s, the process affected Egypt, Jordan, and Kuwait quite differently. With Egypt, Gulf Cooperation Council (GCC)[13] links were greatly reduced during the boycott years, but were restored in the later 1980s and strengthened in the 1990s. For Jordan, on the other hand, GCC links, with Kuwait in particular, weakened steadily in the later 1980s and were ruptured almost entirely in the 1990s. Figure 13.3 shows that the paths of gross capital formation diverged widely among Egypt,

---

[12] Two of the researchers involved in the project, Lance Taylor and Alice Amsden, are well known for their critique of the IMF/World Bank formula and their analyses of the success of the various East Asian development strategies.

[13] The Gulf Cooperation Council was founded in 1980, with the support of the United States, as a grouping of Arab Gulf countries opposing the Islamic Republic of Iran and supporting Iraq in the Iraq-Iran War (the "first Gulf War"). Comprised of six countries, Bahrain, Kuwait, Qatar, Saudi Arabia, the United Arab Emirates and, a bit later, Oman, it subsequently evolved to have economic dimensions as well, similar to the European Economic Community.

Jordan, and Kuwait during the years of crisis and stagnation, 1988–1997, in contrast to the synchronization that existed before and was to appear again after this depressed decade.

Aid. Arab aid to Egypt was negative from 1981 to 1985, due to the boycott, but resumed from 1986 to 1989 on a much smaller scale than in the 1960s and 1970s, with a total of about $210.5 million over those four years (Feiler 2003, Table 6.1: 233). Meanwhile, Egypt received aid of about $2 billion per year from the United States after the peace treaty with Israel in 1979.

In reward for its participation in the war to expel Iraqi forces from Kuwait, Egypt received a record amount of aid, $4.8 billion, in 1990–1991, of which $3 billion came from the Gulf oil exporters, and the cancellation of $13 billion of its international debt. Arab aid then declined again due to low oil revenues, to a grand total of just $8 billion over the 1995–2001 period, while U.S. aid continued at about $2 billion annually. Despite Kuwait's continued straitened circumstances, it was responsible for about 15 percent of that Arab aid and debt cancellation, and, in 1999, KFAED provided Egypt with a big boost, $50.8 million in development loans, for projects involving land improvement, power transmission, paper and printing, a drainage system, and the Social Development Fund (Feiler 2003: 232–42).

Jordan received a declining share of government revenues from external aid and loans in the 1980s, down from a peak of 53.4 percent in 1980 to 28.8 percent in 1988 while Kuwait's share of foreign loans to Jordan fell from a peak of 6 percent in 1983 to 1.3 percent in 1988 (Brand 1994, Table 1: 44–45). Furthermore, in response to Jordan's attempt to remain "neutral" after Iraqi forces occupied Kuwait in 1990, Kuwait withdrew its recognition and support, and the two countries did not reconcile until 1999.

Investment. Arab investment in Egypt increased in the later 1980s, rising to 23 percent of total Arab investment in 1990 and accounting for 12.5 percent of private FDI into Egypt in that year (Feiler 2003: 240). Private Arab capital continued to flow into Egypt in the later 1990s, with Kuwait responsible for about 20 percent per year, for example, $17.6 million out of a total inter-Arab FDI of $88.2 million in 1999. In 1999, there were 1,799 Arab companies in Egypt, with a registered capital stock of $16.28 billion, including the Kharafi Investment Group from Kuwait, accounting for $725 million. These companies were involved in a diversified range of activities including industry, agriculture, banks, transport services, investment companies, and free zone commerce (Feiler 2003: 241).

Private Egyptian capital also flowed out into other Arab countries in the later 1990s. Out of a total Egypt-Arab flow of $4 billion from 1985 to 2000, $1.1 billion went to Kuwait alone, reinforcing Egypt's special relationship with Kuwait (Feiler 2003: 243).

Trade. Jordan's trade with Egypt declined during the core boycott years from 1979 to 1983, with imports from Egypt falling to 0.4 percent of all imports and exports to Egypt falling to 1.2 percent of all exports. After Jordan abandoned the boycott, both imports and exports rose again (to 1 percent and 2.2 percent of total imports and exports, respectively, by 1988) and Jordan actually ran a trade surplus with Egypt in one year, 1987. Jordan's imports from Kuwait became somewhat more important in the 1980s, rising from 0.5 percent of all imports in 1984 to 2.2 percent in 1988, as it shifted away from dependence on Iraq for fuels. However, its exports to Kuwait declined in importance, falling from 11 percent of total exports in 1973 to 4 percent in 1984 and 3 percent in 1988. Jordan incurred a trade deficit with Kuwait for the first time in 1987 and 1988 (Brand 1994, Tables 7 and 8: 78–79).

Tourism. Tourism is an important intraregional phenomenon. World Bank indices show that Jordan and Egypt underperformed relative to their potential in 2000 on all measures of trade integration (the trade-to-GDP ratio, exports to GDP ratio, product diversification, intraregional trade, nonoil exports and FDI), but they performed higher than their potential in tourism (World Bank 2003: 43, 48, 49, 72–74, 76–78). Tourism receipts averaged 4 percent of GDP for Egypt in 1998–2000, 9.3 percent for Jordan (World Bank 2003, Appendix Table 4: 234). In 1998–99, Arabs from other countries constituted 56 percent of all overnight visitors, including tourists, to Jordan.[14]

Émigré Labor and Remittances. The crisis years of the late 1980s saw a sharp reduction in the demand for specifically Arab labor in the Gulf, as those countries tried to place their own citizens in higher-echelon occupations and to expand the proportion of non-Arabs in the lower echelons. As indicated in Figure 13.4, remittances received by Jordan fell by about half from 1985 to 1990, while Kuwaiti payments leveled off and then dropped precipitously in those years as well.

Although more than 700,000 Egyptians returned from the Gulf countries in 1990–91 in the wake of the Iraqi occupation, their numbers revived, with about 2 million Egyptians working in other Arab countries in the later 1990s. Of those, about 227,000 worked in Jordan in 1999

---

[14] www.dos.gov.jo/ari_dep/ari_dep_e/20.html

(Feiler 2003: 244–45). As can be seen in Figure 13.4, remittances leaped up in 1990–91, as Egyptians were recruited on a temporary basis to support the war effort against Iraq, and then settled into a normal range of between $3.2 and 3.6 billion per year from 1994 to 1999.

Up to one-third of the Jordanian labor force had been working abroad in 1990, but 60,000 to 70,000 workers were expelled from Kuwait and other Gulf countries, and their families, most of whom had fled the war zone, were not allowed to return. As a result, on the one hand, remittances did not grow from 1991 to 1995, hovering at about $1 billion per year (Figure 13.4), but, on the other hand, gross capital formation leaped up from 1993 to 1995, and remained above its 1990 level until 1998, as returnees established businesses and invested in real estate (Figure 13.3). Based on the increased size of the labor force, a growing number of Jordanians worked abroad (but not in Kuwait) in the later 1990s, and remittances to Jordan again grew from about $1 billion to 1.5 billion.

For both Jordan and Egypt, workers' remittances remained a crucial source of national income. Remittances per capita, at an annual average of $355 and $60, respectively, in 1998–2000, significantly exceeded FDI per capita, $72 and $18, and aid flows per capita, $98 and $26, in those same years (World Bank 2003, Appendix Table 5: 236).

Accommodation and Resistance to the Neoliberal Agenda

In the 1990s, Egypt, Jordan, and Kuwait were repeatedly urged to structurally adjust their institutions to match Washington Consensus requirements, that is to stabilize by reducing government spending, to privatize state economic enterprises, and to liberalize foreign trade, access for foreign investment and labor law. Failing to accommodate in full and yielding no coherent version of a neoliberal SSA, they generated sometimes bizarre results that contradicted Washington Consensus expectations. For example, Jordan's domestic capitalist class responded to almost full privatization by lobbying the regime to pursue a "developmental state" model (Carroll 2003: 268).

Rebalancing State/Capital Relations. Egypt reduced the ratio of government spending to GDP by half from 1985 to 2004, cutting public employment from 39 to 30 percent of the labor force. The government liquidated holdings in 189 of 314 state economic enterprises, halving employment in that sector from 1.08 million employees (about 6 percent of the labor force) to less than one-half million (Carana Corporation

2002: 8–11). Stock market capitalization rose from 35.6 to 105 percent of GDP, the official unemployment rate fell from 11.7 to 8.3 percent, and employment in the formal private sector rose 6 percentage points to 27 percent. Unexpectedly, however, the share of the formal private sector in GDP actually decreased between 2000 and 2007, from 70.7 to 62.3 percent, and private ownership became more concentrated as the number of companies listed and traded on the stock exchange fell by about 50% (American Chamber of Commerce in Egypt 2008). Furthermore, by 2006, the *informal* sector had expanded to absorb 75 percent of new labor force entrants, accounted for 61 percent of actual employment, and produced between one-third and one-half of officially measured GDP (Assaad 2007: 1, 12–13; Nassar 2008: 6).

Kuwait reduced its government-spending-to-GDP ratio from more than 50 percent during the 1985–95 decade to less than 40 percent by 2004. However, it resisted IFI urgings to curb its "wasteful" spending on universal subsidies for necessities and to reduce higher salaries and pensions and other benefits to public sector employees (Chalk et al. 1997: 1–2, 6–7, 14–15, 24; EIUb 2000 4: 16). Instead, the government restored subsidies and other current transfers to their level of 1980, 24 percent of total government spending, from a low of 20 percent in 1990, and expanded public employment benefits to cover Kuwaiti citizens working in the private sector (Askari 2006: 131).

Similarly, Kuwait's hydrocarbons remained firmly in the public domain, and even its small manufacturing sector, just 6.4 percent of GDP in 2005, remained dominated by state economic enterprises such as petrochemicals, building materials, and aluminum (World Bank 2006: 297). Private capital played an active role in finance, as banking alone accounted for one-third of stock market capitalization in 2005 (NBK 2006). Private investment dominated construction and real estate, but the government supplied the framework with subsidies for land and residential development and incentives to expand into new projects in tourism, hotels and resorts, and public housing (Day et al. 2007).

Openings to Foreign Trade and Foreign Investment. Egypt and Jordan liberalized foreign trade, but both had consistent trade deficits of about 20 percent of GDP over many years into the 2000s and émigré remittances remained key to filling the gap (ERF and Femise Coordinators 2005: 65–68; World Bank 2008b). The export of labor remained as important as the export of goods.

The World Bank ranked Kuwait as number 52 out of 181 countries in its "ease of doing business" index, much higher than Egypt or Jordan, based on the generous tax cuts offered to foreign business in 2008, and the room carved for foreign capital in the stock exchange, banking, air transport, and mobile phone service (EIUb 2008: 9–10), despite the closed hydrocarbon sector receiving big infusions of public capital (Day et al. 2007).

In contrast, Egypt and Jordan liberalized foreign access to almost all sectors, but with minimal impact on diversification. The stock of FDI in Egypt rose to just under 40 percent of GDP in 2007. However, the bulk resided in the hydrocarbon industry, with U.S.-based oil corporations accounting for three-fourths of that stock (EIUa 2007: 182; World Bank 2008b). Similarly, in Jordan, the tradables sector experienced a surge of FDI in free-enterprise zones (QIZs), where mainly Asian entrepreneurs employed mostly Asian labor, to produce duty-free exports of textiles and garments to the United States and Europe. While Jordan's exports to the United States grew to $1.5 billion in 2008, as compared to 25 million in 1997 (Abdelkrim 2009: 71–72), this created few jobs for Jordanian workers and few opportunities for Jordanian capital, with little technology transfer and only minor linkages into the domestic economy (ERF and Femise Coordinators 2005: 66, 69–70, 85).

Rebalancing Capital/Labor Relations. After years of protracted negotiations, both Egypt and Jordan passed liberalized labor laws in the 2000s that granted business more flexibility to hire and fire on economic grounds alone. In Egypt's case, the law eliminated the stronger job protections workers had had under the old social contract, with a "quid pro quo" granting labor more freedom to organize and strike (Posusney 2007). Labor responded with a huge wave of strike activity in 2006–07, including lockouts of management, demanding living wages and the right to elect their own leaders. This militancy spread into the general population in 2008, with more politicized demands, protesting rising food prices, and asserting the right to freely assemble, a movement that won the backing of many thousands more sympathizers via an internet solidarity campaign that seemed to awaken even the somnolent left (Agbarieh-Zahalka 2008: 6–8; Beinin 2008: 2–3).

In Jordan, unexpectedly, the new code retained more of the old job protections than in Egypt, but made it harder for workers to contest firings and kept restrictions on strike activity (Posusney 2007). Jordanian labor did not take up the challenge as in Egypt, perhaps because its strength was muted by rigid labor market segmentation between the Jordanian citizenry working at home or abroad in business or professional jobs and non-Jordanian immigrants concentrated in more lowly occupations.

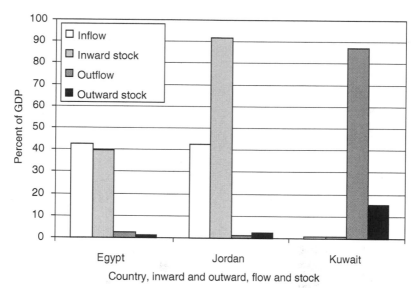

Figure 13.6. Foreign direct investment, Egypt, Jordan, Kuwait, 2007.
Source: UNCTAD 2008, Country Fact Sheets. www.unctad.org/fdistatistics

world, only part of it was for new investment, and many projects did little to create jobs in the long run (Henry 2008: 18, 22).

The GCC countries accounted for one-third of total FDI (in dollar terms) to the Mediterranean countries (MEDA),[22] in particular, from 2003 through 2007, with Egypt receiving 40 percent of these GCC flows and Jordan 11 percent. Energy, heavy chemical industry (such as fertilizers), cement, and metallurgy accounted for 13 percent of GCC FDI, while telecom and banking accounted for 15 percent. The remainder focused on transportation, high-end real estate development, tourism, and shopping malls, with only a small proportion allocated to the production of light industrial products and consumer goods for mass domestic consumption (Henry 2008: 14–16, 31–32).

Half of the FDI went for acquisitions of existing firms, including the purchase of privatized public sector enterprises, rather than for new facilities. In 2007, for example, a company from the UAE took over the Egyptian Fertilizers Company (Henry 2008: 23, 26–27, 30). Similarly,

[22] The thirteen "MEDA" countries include Morocco, Algeria, Tunisia, Libya, Egypt, Jordan, Israel, the Palestinian Territories, Lebanon, Syria, Turkey, and two island nations that were admitted to the EU in 2004, Cyprus and Malta.

Orascom Construction, an Egyptian corporation that was listed as one of the top 100 nonfinancial transnational corporations (TNCs) from developing countries in 2006 (UNCTAD 2008), was acquired in 2007 by LaFarge of France (Henry 2008: 22).

Of the GCC total FDI to MEDA from 2003 through 2007, Kuwait was responsible for 100 projects worth 11 billion Euros, 23 projects in Egypt, and 18 projects in Jordan (Henry 2008: 30–31). Kuwait's stock of investment in Egypt stood at $25 billion in early 2009, mostly in real estate. Aside from Kuwait's participation in a consortium to expand the international airport, its investments in Jordan in 2007 were mainly acquisitions, such as an increase in Noor Telecom's stake in Jordan Telecom to 22 percent and the purchase of a 20-percent stake in a public works and utilities contractor. (Henry 2008: 34, 67, 117–20).

Portfolio Investment. Region-based financial institutions were active in the 2000s pursuing local "financialization." Two of Kuwait's biggest investments in 2007 were the acquisition by the (private) National Bank of Kuwait of one of Egypt's most successful private banks, Al Watany Bank, and the purchase by the Global Investment House, a private equity firm, of a significant stake in the private brokerage firm, Capital Trust, of Egypt (Henry 2008: 35, 67).

Arab investors were prominent in securities trading on the Amman Financial Market. In the first quarter of 2007, while Arab traders were just 5.7 percent of "natural persons" whose buying and selling of stocks represented about 10.5 percent of market value, their investing companies were 14 percent of "judicial persons," whose buying accounted for one-third of the market value of shares traded and whose selling accounted for 22 percent.[23]

The Regional SSA Amid the Structural Boom and Crisis of Neoliberalism

The intraregional investment described earlier was part of a larger, global pattern of expanded sovereign wealth fund (SWF) activity in the 2000s.[24] The capital for SWFs is based on government accumulation of current account surpluses, which are then invested in a diverse portfolio to

---

[23] www.sdc.com.jo/english/images/stories/pdf/2007eng.pdf);www.ase.com.jo/pages. php?menu_id=2&local_type=0&local_details=0)

[24] Sovereign wealth funds (SWFs) are investment agencies owned by governments but usually run by professional managers as autonomous firms. They are distinct from the private holdings of wealthy individuals and families and distinct from private equity firms, which

generate a dependable stream of income to supplement or, in a situation of falling commodity prices, to replace the income from exports. Gulf countries that rely on hydrocarbon exports know well, after their experience of the 1980s and 1990s, that oil prices and revenues can fluctuate widely and that they must prepare for the day when the oil runs out or the world shifts to noncarbon-based or renewable energy. The appropriate strategy is to invest in nonhydrocarbon projects that contribute to the country's development, diversify its economy, and broaden sources of income.

Prior to the early 2000s, Gulf SWFs generally kept about half of their assets in lower-risk dollar, euro, or yen denominated forms, such as bonds or blue-chip stocks, that provided a relatively dependable income over the long run. The other half was held in portfolio or foreign direct investment involving more risky equity commitments, which surged in the 2000s in the form of domestic nonoil-based development. Including real estate and infrastructure, large-scale endeavors such as the building of whole cities to serve new industries and services, and complex projects in solar and wind power development, "the non-oil sectors in the 6 states of the GCC averaged around 7 percent annual growth in the past half decade [i.e., 2002–2007]" (Teslik 2008). This was paired with increased FDI in the Arab region and other "emerging markets" as described earlier.

The Boom. This investment program was too limited to accommodate the unprecedented gush of oil revenues after 2002. GCC SWFs, except for Saudi Arabia's SAMA fund, which remained conservative, then shifted their portfolios to favor more equity, more "alternatives" like derivatives, and faster-growing emerging markets over the traditional slower-growth U.S. and E.U. assets (Setser 2009: 23).[25] Total GCC

tend to be closely held partnerships of very wealthy individuals, and publicly traded mutual funds or investment companies. The top twenty SWFs as a group include funds – in some cases, more than one – from China, Hong Kong, Singapore, Russia, Norway, and several other non-Middle Eastern countries as well as GCC funds from the UAE, Saudia Arabia, Kuwait, Qatar, and Bahrain. As a group, these twenty had accumulated $2.5 trillion in assets as of January 1, 2008, and had grown impressively over the previous eight years (Knowledge@Wharton, 9/22/08). Useful research on sovereign wealth funds can be found in Aizenman and Glick 2008, Harris 2009, and at the websites of the Wharton School (knowledge.wharton.upenn.edu) and the Council on Foreign Relations (www.cfr.org). Information, news articles, and opinion about them can be found in a series of articles in *The Guardian* of London from June of 2007 to March of 2009 (www.guardian.co.uk/business).

[25] See also Raphaeli and Gersten 2008 on this shift, plus their opinion that the biggest impact of this shift in investment may be to stimulate the entrepreneurial spirit in the sluggish Arab region (Raphaeli and Gersten 2008: 6).

outflow from 2002 through 2006 approximated $560 billion, including up to 60 percent to the United States, 30 percent to the EU, 5 percent to Asia, and 5 percent to the MENA region (Setser 2007: 12). Part went for acquisition of U.S. properties, amounting to over $2.6 billion from 2000 to 2005, for diverse activities such as aircraft manufacture and a coffee distribution and retail chain, and purchase of Manhattan real estate, such as the Chrysler Building (Blustein 2006). The funds then expanded further to purchase shares in alternative risky assets such as hedge funds and private equity (Setser 2007).

GCC SWFs were swept up into the final throes of neoliberalism's financial fireworks, and ended 2007 holding more than $1 trillion in assets (Setser 2007:1). Following the Yale University endowment model, the Kuwait Investment Authority (KIA) reduced the dollar denominated share of fixed income assets and "traditional" U.S. equities to 40 percent, and increased purchases of both emerging market equities to 10 percent and more risky alternatives to 15 percent (Setser 2007: 7, 10, 12, 14; Setser 2009: 23). KIA's assets rose from $55 billion at the end of 1999 to $275 billion at the end of 2007 (Setser 2009: 1, 9), equivalent to about 250 percent of GDP (Aizenman 2008: 19, 37). When prices of alternative financial assets stopped rising in early 2007, and before the markets began their descent, Gulf investors increased purchases of shares in troubled western financial institutions, especially in the United States, that were threatened by the sub-prime mortgage crisis and the collapse of "alternatives" such as collateralized debt instruments, apparently to "tap into [Anglo-Saxon] banks' expertise in trade finance and financial systems" (Olson 2007).

The Crash. Once they had bought into the more risk-prone strategy, and the markets began to decline in 2007–08, Gulf SWFs and wealthy private investors bought shares in well-established western financial institutions such as Citigroup, Merrill Lynch, Morgan Stanley, Bear Stearns, UBS, Credit Suisse, Barclay's, Kaupthing, and the London Stock Exchange, among others, to help stabilize the markets for their own as well as the system's sake.[26] They then incurred steep losses as the crisis deepened in the latter half of 2008, sucked down by one of the core contradictions of neoliberalism's demise, the financialization of asset creation and trade without sufficient real investment to undergird the system. KIA's portfolio shrank from $262 billion to 228 billion from the end of 2007 to the end of 2008, a net loss of 36 percent. As a group, GCC SWF external

---

[26] See *The Guardian of London*, articles from June 2007 to March 2009 illustrating this role www.guardian.co.uk/business.

portfolios had a capital loss of 27 percent. The current account surpluses from increases in oil revenues in 2008 were essentially erased by these losses (Setser 2009: 102).

Impact on the Region. Output growth in the GCC remained positive in 2008 due to ongoing projects in their domestic economies. However, as credit became scarcer and more expensive and as the number of bond and equity issues to finance important projects was reduced, the value of other financial assets fell across the region. From their peaks in spring 2008 to November, GCC stock markets fell 50 percent, and Egypt's bourse index dropped 54 percent (World Bank 2009: 161). Profits at most firms traded on the Kuwait Stock Exchange dropped 94 percent in the first quarter of 2009 as compared to the first quarter of 2008, with the biggest impact on investment companies and banks, especially those that had been active in mergers and acquisitions in MEDA, such as the National Bank of Kuwait.[27] Even financial entities that were not involved in the machinations of western institutions were hit. For example, 25 Islamic funds were liquidated in 2008–09, only 89 were launched (as compared to 271 over the same period a year earlier), and average returns in 2008 were -39 percent as compared to 23 percent in 2007.[28]

GDP growth in the region overall was expected to remain positive in 2009, slowing from 5.8 percent in 2008 to 3.9 percent in 2009, as indicated in Figure 13.7. Investment growth was also expected to remain positive, but to fall from 18.9 percent in 2008 to 7 percent in 2009 (World Bank 2009: 163–65), sustained by public investment[29] and ongoing commitments to a number of large infrastructure projects, real

---

[27] www.kuwaittimes.net/read_news.php?newsid=MzkxODIyMTI

[28] For example, see www.business24-7.ae/Articles/2009/5/Pages/25052009/0526; corp. gulfinthemedia.com/gulf_media/view_article_en_print.php?action+print&id=472247

[29] News reports were full of efforts by governments to help cushion the blows. Kuwait bought up worthless shares on its stock exchange (www.kuwaittimes.net/read_news. php?newsid=MzkxODIyMTI). Saudi Arabia and Bahrain announced new Islamic bond issues to finance more diversified real estate such as home mortgages and mutual funds (www.business24-7.ae/Articles/2009/6/Pages/SaudieyesFannie…; corp.guildinthemedia.com/gulf_media/view_article_en_print.php?action=print&id=471595; corp. gulfinthemedia.com/gulf_media/view_article_en_print.php?action=print&id=471503). The Abu Dhabi Investment Authority (ADIA) announced 52 new projects in infrastructure, agriculture, and housing in Egypt for 2009 (www.business24-7.ae/Articles/2009/5/ Pages/30052009/0531). Kuwaiti businesses negotiated new manufacturing projects for the Asyut region, as Egyptian ministers traveled to Kuwait to recruit $10 billion more in real estate, energy, railways, roads and ports, "for investors to profit with a timetable" (corp. gulfinthemedia.com/gulf_media/view_article_en_print.php?action=print&id=472198; www.kuwaittimes.net/read_news.php?newsid=ODYwMzEONjA1).

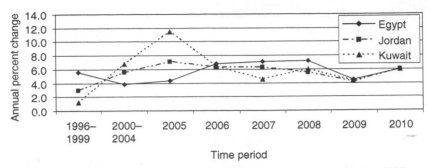

Figure 13.7. Growth projection for real GDP, Egypt, Jordan, Kuwait,* 2007.
Source: World Bank 2008: Table A.1; World Bank 2009: Tables A.7 and A.8.
Note: * "Kuwait" values for 2008, 2009, 2010 are for "the resource rich labor importing group," which also includes Bahrain, Oman, and Saudi Arabia.

estate, commerce, and industrial development, in Egypt and Jordan in particular.

The MEDA economies did not fare as badly as the region as a whole, with a drop of 35 percent in incoming FDI in 2008 and a decline of 6 percent in the number of projects funded by the GCC (Abdelkrim 2009: 7).[30] Egypt's GDP growth in 2009 was expected to be half of its 2008 rate, between 3.5 percent and 4 percent (Abdelkrim 2009: 66–67; and see Figure 13.7), sustained by 102 new investment projects from 2008, about of third of which were sponsored by the GCC. Jordan's growth was projected to slow somewhat to 4.2 percent in 2009, down from 5.5 percent in 2008, buttressed by 37 new FDI projects carried over from 2008, in energy, construction, transportation, communications, and manufacturing, including expanded commitments from Kuwait to the international airport, railway, and Aqaba industrial development projects, and because Jordan "appears as a haven of stability in the eyes of investors ... even if the infatuation of Gulf state investors [with real estate in Jordan] have [sic] been affected by the crises" (Abdelkrim 2009: 71–72).

PROGNOSIS FOR BUILDING A NEW SSA

As of 2009, the region remained profoundly affected by oil price fluctuations and global financial markets, the GCC exporters of oil and capital having been badly burned in both these arenas in 2008. Given their

---

[30] For example, see www.business24–7.ae/Articles/2009/5/Pages/27052009/0528

current economic structures, the price of oil has to be at least \$50 per barrel (in constant 2007 dollars) in order to cover essential imports without having to liquidate some capital assets (Setser 2007: 2, 2009: 1–4). If oil prices stabilized at \$65 to\$75 in 2009 (at least \$60 in 2007 constant dollars), the region would be able to sustain positive investment and growth out of surplus revenues (World Bank 2009: 166), and higher prices would enable the GCC SWFs to start growing again.[31]

Perhaps the more important lesson from the crises of 2008–09 is that the diversification of domestic investment and greater sophistication of intraregional FDI cushioned these economies, as well as the economies of FDI recipients such as Egypt and Jordan, and kept growth prospects positive for 2009 despite a financial crisis and global recession. It is not apparent, however, that a new SSA was engendered. There were many problems and limitations to the institutional framework that governed economic growth and capital accumulation in the Arab region in the 2000s. Intraregional FDI created wealth without much dispersion for raising incomes to industrial or agricultural workers. It was focused on polluting industries such as hydrocarbon energy and chemical fertilizers, and on real estate, telecom, and tourism projects that served an already wealthy clientele from Europe and the Gulf with little concern for ordinary consumers, working conditions, or human development. It was focused more on the superficial passing around of funds – banking, brokerage, and the local version of "financialization" – with insufficient concern for investment in production for mass consumption or for long-term job creation. It generated too few multiplier effects and linkages in local economies, leaving the poorer countries as dependent as ever on remittances to fill critical gaps.

If a new SSA is to bloom in this region, the institutions will have to involve more thorough regulation and organization of capital on an international level, deeper and broader real investment, a commitment to "more sustainable and more socially useful projects," (Abdelkrim 2009: 8) closer regard for the needs of consumers, and attention to the legitimate demands of both domestic and émigré labor. Whatever

---

[31] If the price of oil were \$75 in next 5 years, one analyst predicts that GCC SWFs would grow to \$1.7–1.8 trillion. At that point, the bulk of income would come from investments rather than oil, and the SWFs would be growing due to interest, dividends and capital gains being added back in to the principal. It is very likely, at \$75/bbl or above, that portfolios would be rebalanced to increase the more conservative portion, again about 50 % to bonds (Setser 2009: 16). If the price rose to \$100/bbl, the GCC SWFs would grow to \$2.1 or 2.2 trillion by 2012 (Setser 2009: 6, 15, 17–18).

the balance between government and private capital, this region requires a new social contract to frame a culturally appropriate and sustainable SSA.

References

Abdelkrim, Samir and Pierre Henry 2009. *Foreign Direct Investment in the Med Countries in 2008, Facing the Crisis.* Study No. 3, March 2009. NP: ANIMA Investment Network. http://www.animaweb.org/en/etudes.php?base=143

Agbarieh-Zahalka, Asma 2008. "Egyptian Workers Impose a New Agenda." *Challenge* (Tel Aviv, Israel) 19, 3, No. 109: 6–9.

Aizenman, Joshua and Reuven Glick 2008. "Sovereign Wealth Funds: Stylized Facts about their Determinants and Governance." Working Paper 2008–33. December 2008. San Francisco: Federal Reserve Bank of San Francisco.

Al-Sabah, Mohammad, Director 1988. *Study of the Kuwait Economy: Summary, Vol. 1.* Cambridge MA: CMT International, Inc., and Kuwait Institute of Scientific Research.

Al-Yousuf, Ala'a 1990. *Kuwait and Saudi Arabia: from Prosperity to Retrenchment.* Oxford, UK: Oxford Institute for Energy Studies.

American Chamber of Commerce in Egypt 2008. *Economic Indicators: Stock Market Indicators.* http://www.amcham.org.eg/BSAC/EconomicIndicators/EcIndicators.asp

Arouri, Fathi 2008. "Circular Migration in Jordan, 1995–2006." CARIM: Euro-Mediterranean Consortium for Applid Research on International Migration. Florence, Italy. www.carim.org/circularmigration

Askari, Hossein 2006. *Middle East Oil Exporters, What Happened to Economic Development?* Northampton MA: Edward Elgar.

Assaad, Ragui 2007. "Labor Supply, Employment and Unemployment in the Egyptian Economy, 1988–2006." Economic Research Forum (Cairo, Egypt), Working Paper Series N. 0701. www.erf.org

Beinin, Joel 2008. "Underbelly of Egypt's Neoliberal Agenda." *Middle East Report Online*, April 5, 2008, 5 pages. www.merip.org/mero/mero040508.html

          2002. "Late Capitalism and the Reformation of the Working Classes in the Middle East," Pp 113–33 in Israel Gershoni, Hakan Erdem, and Ursula Woköck, eds. *Histories of the Modern Middle East: New Directions.* Boulder: Lynne Rienner Publishers.

Blustein, Paul 2006. "Mideast Investment Up in U.S." *The Washington Post*, 7 March 2006: A01.

Brand, Laurie 1994. *Jordan's Inter-Arab Relations, the Political Economy of Alliance Making.* New York: Columbia University Press.

Carana Corporation 2002. "Special Study: the Results and Impacts of Egypt's Privatization Program." *Privatization in Egypt – Quarterly Review*, April–June 2002. PCSU – Privatization Coordination Support Unit (for USAID) www.carana.com/pcsu/monitor/Q2/Impacts%20and%20Results.pdf

Carroll, Katherine Blue 2003. *Business as Usual? Economic Reform in Jordan.* Lanham MD: Lexington Books.

Crystal, Jill 1995. *Oil and Politics in the Gulf, Rulers and Merchants in Kuwait and Qatar*. Cambridge UK: Cambridge University Press.

Chalk, Nigel Andrew, Mohamed A. El-Erian, Susan J. Fennell, Alexei P. Kireyev, and John F. Wilson 1997. *Kuwait: from Reconstruction to Accumulation for Future Generations*. Washington DC: International Monetary Fund.

Day, Alan J., P.T.H. Unwin, Richard German and Elizabeth Taylor 2007. "Economy (Kuwait)" in *Europa World Online*. London: Routledge. http://www.europaworld.com/entry/kw.ec

Economic and Financial Bulletin ["EFB"] Kuwait: National Bank of Kuwait, 1985 (8) May; 1983 (5) July.

Economist Intelligence Unit (EIUa) 2007. "Country Profiles: Egypt," *World Investment Prospects to 2100, Foreign Direct Investment and the Challenge of Political Risk*, London: the Economist Intelligence Unit: 182–183. www.eiu.com

(EIUb) *Country Report: Kuwait* 2008 (July); 2000 (4). London.

(EIUc) *Country Profile: Kuwait* (annual) 1991–92. London.

Economic Research Forum, and Femise Coordinators 2005. *Jordan Country Profile: the Road Ahead for Jordan*. Cairo: Economic Research Forum, and France: Institut de la Méditerranée.

Esfahani, Hadi Salehi 2007. "A Re-Examination of the Political Economy of Growth in the MENA Countries." Pp 61–102 in Jeffrey B. Nugent and M. Hashem Pesaran eds. *Explaining Growth in the Middle East*. Boston: Elsevier.

Feiler, Gil 2003. *Economic Relations between Egypt and the Gulf Oil States, 1967–2000*. Brighton, UK: Sussex Academic Press.

Galal, Ahmed and Bernard Hoekman eds. 2003. *Arab Economic Integration, Between Hope and Reality*. Egyptian Center for Economic Studies. Washington DC: Brookings Institution Press.

Ghabra, Shafeeq N. 1987. *Palestinians in Kuwait, the Family and the Politics of Survival*. Boulder CO: Westview Press.

Greenhouse, Steven and Michael Barbaro 2006. "An Ugly Side of Free Trade: Sweatshops in Jordan." *New York Times*, May 3. www.nytimes.com/2006/05/03/business/worldbusiness/03cloth

Handy, Howard and Staff Team 1998. *Egypt: Beyond Stabilization, Toward a Dynamic Market Economy*. Washington DC: International Monetary Fund.

Harris, Jerry 2009. "Statist Globalization in China, Russia and the Gulf States." *Science and Society* 73, 1: 6–33.

Henry, Pierre, Samir Abdelkrim and Bénédict de Saint-Laurent 2008. *Foreign Direct Investment into MEDA in 2007: the Switch*. Study No. 1, July 2008. NP: ANIMA Investment Network. http://www.animaweb.org/en/etudes.php?base=143

Ismael, Jacqueline S. 1993. *Kuwait: Dependency and Class in a Rentier State*. Gainesville FL: University Press of Florida.

Kanaan, Taher H. 2001. "State-Owned Enterprise in Jordan, Strategy for Reform," Pp. 189–202 in Merih Celasun, ed. *State-Owned Enterprises in the Middle East and North Africa: Privatization, Performance and Reform*. New York: Routledge.

Lockman, Zachary 2004. *Contending Visions of the Middle East*. New York: Cambridge University Press.

Looney, Robert E. 1992. "Employment Creation in an Oil-Based Economy: Kuwait" *Middle Eastern Studies* 28, 3: 565–76.

Maciejewski, Edouard and Ahsan Mansur eds. 1996. *Jordan: Strategy for Adjustment and Growth*. Occasional Paper 136. Washington DC: International Monetary Fund.

Makdisi, Samir, Zeki Fattah, and Imed Limam 2007. "Determinants of Economic Growth in the MENA Countries." Pp 31–60 in Jeffrey B. Nugent and M. Hashem Pesaran eds. *Explaining Growth in the Middle East*. North Holland: Elsevier.

Moore, Pete W. 2000. "Business-State Relations after Liberalization in Jordan." Pp 180–200 in Remonda Bensabat Kleinberg and Janine A. Clark eds. *Economic Liberalization, Democratization and Civil Society in the Developing World*. New York: St. Martin's Press.

Nanes, Stefanie 2007. "Jordan's Unwelcome 'Guests.'" *Middle East Report* 37, 3: 22–24.

Nassar, Heba 2008. "Temporary and Circular Migration: the Egyptian Case." *Analytic and Synthetic Notes – Circular Migration Series*, Florence Italy: European University Institute, Euro-Mediterranean Consortium for Applied Research on International Migration (CARIM). www.carim.org/circularmigration.

National Bank of Kuwait (NBK) 2006. *Economic Review*. www.nbk.com/NR/rdonlyres/E4233305-CA3A-4899–9B85-C03C4169FA95/0/NBK_Review_0610.pdf

Olson, Parmy 2007. "Sovereign Shift." *Forbes.com,* 19 December 2007. www.forbes.com/2007/12/19/saudi-arabia-uae-biz-wall-cx_p

Oweiss, Ibrahim ed. 1990. *The Political Economy of Contemporary Egypt*. Washington, DC: Center for Contemporary Arab Studies, Georgetown University.

Pfeifer, Karen 2000. "Does Structural Adjustment Spell Relief from Unemployment? A Comparison of four IMF 'Success Stories' in the Middle East and North Africa." Pp 111–51 in Wassim Shahin and Ghassan Dibeh eds. *Income Inequality, Poverty, and Unemployment in the Middle East and North Africa*. Westport CT: Greenwood.

    2003. "Defining Boundaries: Kuwait's Economic Reconstruction, 1991–2001." Pp 207–29 in Hassan Hakimian and Jeffrey B. Nugent eds. *Trade Policy and Economic Integration in the Middle East and North Africa: Economic Boundaries in Flux*. London: Routledge Curzon Press 2003.

    2009 forthcoming. "Kuwait and the Israeli-Palestinian Conflict." In Cheryl Rubenberg ed. *Encyclopedia of the Israeli-Palestinian Conflict*. Boulder CO: Lynne Rienner.

Pfeifer, Karen and Marsha Pripstein Posusney 2003. "Arab Economies and Globalization: An Overview," Pp.25–54 in Eleanor Abdella Doumato and Marsha Pripstein Posusney eds. *Women and Globalization in the Arab Middle East: Gender, Economy and Society*. Boulder CO: Lynne Rienner.

Piro, Timothy J. 1998. *The Political Economy of Market Reform in Jordan*. Lanham MD: Rowman and Littlefield Publishers.

Posusney, Marsha Pripstein 2007. "Free Trade and Freer Unions? Globalization and Labor Market Changes in the Arab World." Paper presented at Middle East Studies Association Meetings, Nov. 2007, Boston.

1997. *Labor and the State in Egypt: Workers, Unions, and Economic Restructuring.* New York: Columbia University Press.

Rapheli, Nimrod and Bianca Gersten 2008. "Sovereign Wealth Funds: Investment Vehicles for the Persian Gulf Countries," *Middle East Quarterly*, Spring: 45–53. www.meform.org/1863/soverign-wealth-funds-investment-vehicles-for …

Richards, Alan 1991. "The Political Economy of Dilatory Reform: Egypt in the 1980s." *World Development* 19, 12: 1721–30.

Richards, Alan and John Waterbury 2008. *A Political Economy of the Middle East.* Boulder CO: Westview Press.

Setser, Brad and Rachel Ziemba 2009. "GCC Sovereign Funds, Reversal of Fortune," Working Paper, January 2009. Center for Geoeconomic Studies, via Council on Foreign Relations. www.cfr.org

2007. "Understanding the New Financial Superpower – the Management of GCC Official Foreign Assets." Executive Summary, *RGE Monitor.* Via Council on Foreign Relations. www.cfr.org

Teslik, Lee Hudson 2008. "Growing Cities in the Arabian Desert," New York: Council on Foreign Relations. www.cfr.org/publication/16408

United Nations Commission on Trade and Development (UNCTAD) 2009. *UNCTAD Online 2009.* http://stats.unctad.org/Handbook/TableViewer/tableView.asp

Weisskopf, Thomas E. 1996. "Marxian Crisis Theory and the Contradictions of Late Twentieth Century Capitalism." Pp. 368–391 in Victor D. Lippit, ed. 1996. "Radical Political Economy: Explorations in Alternative Economic Analysis." NY: M.E. Sharpe.

2008. *World Investment Report*, Country Fact Sheets. www.unctad.org/fdistatistics

United Nations Development Program 2007/2008. *Human Development Report.* New York: United Nations.

World Bank 2009. "Appendix: Regional Economic Prospects," *Global Economic Prospects.* Washington DC: World Bank: 141–80.

2008a. *"Middle East and North Africa Region: Economic Developments and Prospects, Regional Integration for Global Competitiveness."* Washington DC: World Bank

2008b. "Egypt at a Glance." "Jordan at a Glance." www.worldbank.org

2008c. *World Development Indicators Online.*

2006. *World Development Report.* Washington DC: World Bank.

2004. *Unlocking the Employment Potential in the Middle East and North Africa, toward a New Social Contract.* Washington DC: World Bank.

2003. *Trade, Investment and Development in the Middle East and North Africa, Engaging with the World.* Washington DC: World Bank.

1991–92. *World Debt Tables.* Washington, DC: World Bank, 1 [accessible in 2009 via *World Development Indicators Online*]

1991. *World Tables*, Washington DC: World Bank [accessible in 2009 via *World Development Indicators Online*]

Index

accumulation
  and criminal justice expenditures,
    253–56
  and criminal justice system, 241–42
  and police expenditures, 256
  and rate of profit, 112
  and social stability, 274
  by dispossession, 160
  finance-led regime, 230–35
  flexible, 133, 135, 139
  model of, 24
  new centers of, 161
  pace, 76–80
  role of the state, 241
  South Africa, 283
African Economic Community (AEC),
  178
African Union (AU), 178
Aglietta, Michel, 4, 6
agrarian empoyment, 293
Aid to Families with Dependent
  Children, 201, 207
air traffic controllers strike, 202
Alderson, Arthur S., 124–125
Althusserian tradition, 56
Amman Financial Market, 323
Amsterdam school, 173
Anti-Drug Abuse Act of 1986, 249

Anti-Drug Abuse Act of 1988, 249
apartheid and capitalist development
  liberal interpretation, 268
  Marxist-revisionist school, 269
  SSA approach, 270
Arab region. *See also* Egpyt; Jordan,
  and Kuwait
  and world economy, 315
  cultural-political framework, 311
  economic relations, 329–31, 335–38
  foreign trade and investment, 339–40
  income distribution, 328
  nationalism, 310
  neoliberal boom and crisis, 344–48
  neoliberalism, 331–35
  political opposition, 314
  regional economic relations, 312,
    341–44
  social contract, 313
  state-led development, 312
Arena, John, 33
Asia Free Trade Agreement, 179
asset bubbles, 116, 211
automatic wage adjustments, 198

Barlow, David E., 27
Barlow, Melissa Hickman, 27
Bluestone, Barry, 124

Bowles, Samuel, 24, 35, 48–51, 150
Boyer, Robert, 5, 6, 16
Brady, David, 15, 27, 124–25
Bretton Woods, 52, 60
Bull, Hedley, 175
Burris, Beverly, 136
Bush (George W.) administration, 210

capital-citizen accord, 49–51, 59
capitalist class, transnational, 28, 34,
    174–75
capital-labor accord, 25, 49–50, 58, 62, 63
capital-labor relations, 9, 25, 68, 104,
    195–212, 324–27, 340–41
Caribbean economies, 28
CARICOM, 179
Carlson, Susan M., 16, 27, 32, 35,
    240–41
Carter administration, 96, 200, 202
Central America, 28
CEO compensation, 103, 219–28
China, 12, 115
class contradictions, 80–81, 83
Clinton administration, 206–07
Coase, Ronald, 94
collateralized loan obligation, 157
Comprehensive Crime Control Act of
    1984, 249
consumer debt, 211
contingent work, 205
co-respective competition, 83
corporate profitability, 218
corporate transformation, 29, 34
corporatism, 296
Cox, Robert, 173–74
creative accounting, 227
credit derivatives, 156
Crime Control Act of 1990, 249
criminal justice system, 27, 109, 239–59

debt crisis, Mexico, 297
de-equitization, 155
deindustrialization, 124, 133

Denniston, Ryan, 125
deregulation, 72, 76, 108, 150, 200–02
deunionization, 124, 134, 202–05
dialectic of states and markets, 172–73
downsizing, 134
drug laws, 247
Dutch Disease, 313

Earned Income Tax Credit, 206
economic crisis of late 2000s, 66–70,
    156–62, 234, 346, 349
  and the transnational state apparatus,
    187–89
  causes, 11
  responses, 11–14
economic expansion, 1990s, 207
Edwards, Richard, 1, 46, 47, 55, 74, 77,
    127, 132
Egypt, 309, 314, 316, 317–19, 321,
    324–25, 328, 331–33, 338, 343, 348
ejidos, 295
entitlements, 64, 106, 278
environmental movements, 65
European Free Trade Association
    (EFTA), 178
European Union (EU), 35, 178

Favereau, Oliver, 6
federal minimum wage, 201, 206
fictitious capital, 156
financial capital, 103
financial crisis of late 2000s.
    See economic crisis of late 2000s
financial deregulation, 68
financial reforms, 1930s, 51
financial re-regulation, 69
financial systems. *See* international
    financial system
financial systems, post WWII, 50–52, 60
financialization, 10, 72, 104, 145–65,
    227–35
Freeman, Richard, 161
Friedman, Milton, 94

Friedrichs, Jorg, 177
Full Employment Act of 1946, 50

G20, 182, 188–89
G8, 181
Gamble, Andrew, 146
GDP growth, 73, 113, 288–89, 314, 320, 347
General Motors, 197
global warming, 39
globalization, 9, 12, 34, 69, 95, 99, 122–26, 135, 149
Goldstein, Morris, 156
Gordon, David, 1, 23–26, 46, 47, 48–51, 55–56, 74, 77, 122, 150
Gramsci, 40, 173–74
Grant, Don Sherman, 27, 40
Great Depression, 50
Greece, 28
Gruneberg, Stephen, 29
Gulf Area Free Trade Agreement, 179
Gulf Cooperation Council (GCC), 335

Hall, Peter, 6
Hamilton, Rosalea, 28, 32
Harrison, Bennett, 124
Harris-White, Barbara, 28, 32
Harvey, David, 160
Hayek, Friedrich, 94
hedge funds, 154, 155–56
Heintz, James, 17, 28
Henry, David, 158
household debt, 68
housing bubble, 68, 117
Houston, David, 34
Human Development Index, 327
human rights, 185
Hutchinson, Richard, 27

income distribution, 288, 295, 300
income inequality, 13, 72, 79, 125, 205, 211
India, 28

inequalities and political conflict, 274
Institutional Revolutionary Party (PRI), 296
intercapitalist competition, 49, 51, 60, 83
internal labor market, 208
International Chamber of Commerce (ICC), 181
International Court of Justice, 185
International Criminal Court, 185
international financial system, 52, 180
International Monetary Fund (IMF), 35, 102, 177, 179, 315
Islamism, 314
Ive, Graham J., 29

Jamaica, 32
Japan, 52–54, 66
Jeong, Seongjin, 28
Jordan, 309, 314, 316, 318, 319–20, 322–23, 325–26, 328, 333–34, 343, 348
Jordan Investment Corporation, 323
June War of 1967, 319

Kalecki, Michal, 274
Kay, Tamara, 124
Keynesianism, 2, 61, 63, 149
Kirchheimer, Otto, 240
Kondratieff, N.D., 47
Kotz, David M., 5, 14–15, 37, 47, 54–56, 64, 160, 163, 164
Krippner, Greta, 149
Kurdelbusch, Antje, 125
Kuwait, 309, 314, 316, 318, 319, 320–21, 323, 325, 326–28, 334–35, 339, 343, 348
Kuwait Investment Authority, 346

labor control, systems of, 25, 27, 127–28
  bureaucratic control, 130–32
  homogenization, 130
  proletarianization, 130
  segmentation, 105, 130, 198

labor control, systems of (*cont.*)
  technical control, 130
  technocratic control, 132–38
labor flexibility, 133, 205
labor force participation rate, 207–208
labor market, Mexico, 291–95, 298–302
labor productivity, 207
Latin America, leftwing upsurge, 13, 117
Law Enforcement Assistance
    Administration, 246
leveraged buyouts, 154
Li, Minqi, 38–39
liberalism, 93
Lippit, Victor, 14, 31
Lobao, Linda, 33
long cycles, 46–47
long swings. *See also* long cycles
long waves, 62

macroeconomic models, 23–25
Magnani, Elisabetta, 124
Martinez, Ramiro, 40
Marxism, 2, 30, 40, 56.
    See also neoMarxian theory
McDonough, Terrence, 14, 15, 16,
    35–36, 47, 54–56, 62, 164
Mexico, 286–305
Michalowski, Raymond J., 27, 32, 35,
    240–41
micro-enterprise sector, 288, 301
Mihail, Dimitrios, 28
military interventionism, US, 12
Minsky, Hyman, 156
monetary policy, 72, 200

Naples, Michelle, 32
Nardone, Emily, 16
National Labor Relations Board, 202,
    210
Nattrass, Nicoli, 272
Nayyar, Deepak, 150
neoGramscian school, 173
neoliberalism, 9, 72, 79, 94–96, 146–47

and capital accumulation, 110
and domestic institutions, 104–09
and finance sector, 147–62
and international institutions, 98–104
and profit, 109
and the state, 165, 184
as basis of new SSA, 37, 72–73
class analysis of, 163
contradictions, 116–18
debt creation, 151
definition, 67
labor, 195–212
uneven spread, 116
neoMarxian theory, 46–47
New Deal, 50
New Medievalism, 175–77
NGOs, 181
Nielsen, Francois, 125
Nilsson, Eric, 25
North American Free Trade Agreement
    (NAFTA), 179, 298
North Atlantic Treaty Organization
    (NATO), 35

O'Connor, James, 241
O'Hara, Phil, 36, 38
offshoring, 151
oil industry, 321
oligopolistic market structure, 51,
    54, 60
Omnibus Crime Control and Safe Streets
    Act, 246
OPEC, 334, 335
Organisation for Economic Cooperation
    and Development (OECD), 181
overdetermination, 56–61, 66

Pax Americana. See United States
    hegemony
peak oil, 39
pension fund restructuring, 154
pension reform, 228
Perrucci, Robert, 33

Personal Responsibility and Work
Opportunity Act, 207
Pfeifer, Karen, 17
Polanyi, Karl, 85, 172, 184–85
Ponzi financing, 156
Prechel, Harland, 29
Prentice, David, 124
prison labor, 243
private equity funds, 153–55
productivity growth, 49
profit share, 79
profit-squeeze crises, 86

rate of profit, 290
Reagan Administration, 75, 96, 200–02
redistributive growth, 160
Regional Economic Communities
(RECs). *See* regional trading blocs
regional trading blocs, 178–79
regionalization, 184
regulation theory, 4–6, 30, 215
Reich, Michael, 1, 26, 30, 46, 47, 55,
74, 77
religious fundamentalism, 12
rentier state, 321
Resnick, Stephen A., 56
risk
concentration, 159
systemic, 156–59
Robinson, William, 28, 36, 175, 177,
182–83
Rosenberg, Samuel, 16, 133
Rusche, Georg, 240

Saillard, Yves, 6
Salas, Carlos, 17
Sanderland, John, 153
Saros, Daniel, 30
Scheve, Kenneth, 126
Schumpeter, Joseph, 47
securitization, 152
segmentation. *See* labor control,
systems of

Sklair, Leslie, 123, 125
Slaughter, Matthew J., 126
social structure of accumulation
and criminal justice system, 239–59
and economic crises, 85–87
and profitability, 75
collapse, 63, 66, 67
construction, 77–78, 80, 97
crisis tendencies, 36–39
dating of contemporary SSA, 34–39,
73
definition, 46, 74, 127
durability, 62
duration, 31, 61–64, 66, 67
environmental limits, 59
formation, 64–66
geographical scales, 35–36, 186
global scale, 33
ideology, 84
liberal SSA, 37, 81–88, 160, 251
nature of institutions, 30–31, 45
outside the US, 27–29, 33
profit and growth, 76–80
profitability, 88
rate of growth, 87–88
regulated SSA, 37, 81–88
role of class conflict in, 64–66
stability, 74
structural integrity, 57
systems of labor control, 126–38
varying timescales, 31–33
social structure of accumulation theory
and global neoliberalism, 96–98
and institutions, 2
and rate of growth, 98
and related theories, 4–8
and states, 172
definition, 1, 45–46
flexibility, 30
historical background, 1–2, 46–47
pace of accumulation, 76–80
regulation theory, comparison with,
5–6

social structure of accumulation
    theory (*cont.*)
role of, 48
role of growth in, 74–76, 87–88
social structure of accumulation,
    historical periods
apartheid South Africa, 276
contemporary (neoliberal), 10, 58,
    65–70, 72–73, 75, 79, 85,
    98–118, 145–65, 185–87,
    195–212, 215–36, 251–53
first SSA (1820s to 1890s), 130
post WWII, 45, 48–52, 54, 57–61,
    72, 75, 94, 130–32, 195,
    242–51
post WWII, Japan, 52–54
post-apartheid South Africa,
    276–83
post-independence SSA, Middle East,
    316–35
second SSA (1890s to 1930s), 38, 54,
    130
twentieth century, Mexico, 305
United States, 3–4
Soskice, David, 6
South Africa, 28, 267–84
South Korea, 28
sovereign wealth fund, 344
spatialization, 26, 33–34, 35, 132–40
special purpose entity, 152
stagnant wages and benefits, 203, 211
state role in the economy, 82–83,
    95, 296
state-capital relations, 324, 338–39
state-led development model. *See*
    Arab region, state-led
    development
stock market bubble, 68
stock options, 217, 223–27
Sweezy, Paul, 150

Tabb ,William, 15
taxes, 107, 229
technological change, 50
Thatcher, Margaret, 96
Thornton, Emily, 157
transnational capitalist class, *See*
    Capitalist class, transnational
transnational institutions, 101
transnational state apparatus, 189

UNASUL/UNASUR, 179
unemployment
    and crime rates, 240
    and imprisonment, 240
    rates, 106, 251, 252
    rates, Mexico, 298–99
unemployment insurance, 201, 206
unions, 197–200, 202, 208, 210. *See also*
    deunionization
United Auto Workers, 197
United States hegemony, 46, 49–50, 58

Varieties of Capitalism school, 8
Violent Crime Control and Law
    Enforcement Act, 251

wage inequality, 209
wage structure, 205, 206, 209
Wallace, Michael, 15, 27, 124
Weisskopf, Thomas, 24, 48–51, 150
welfare reform, 207
Went, Robert, 35–36
Western, Bruce, 124
Wolff, Richard D., 56
Wolfson, Martin, 14, 37, 50, 51, 163
working class, transnational, 34
World Bank, 35, 102, 179, 315
World Economic Forum, 178
World Trade Organization (WTO), 35,
    101, 177, 180